Understanding

AMERICAN GOVERNMENT and POLITICS

SAMUEL STEINBERG, Ph.D.

Chairman, Social Studies Department
Stuyvesant High School, New York City

History II   Civil War (1861-65) — Present time

History I Colonies to Civil War

KEYSTONE EDUCATION PRESS

NEW YORK

FOREWORD

Basic Premises

Few would deny an important place to the study of American government in the secondary school curriculum. But there is considerable disagreement as to what the nature and scope of the course in American government should be. Some believe—and probably the vast majority of teachers so practice—that structure and process properly form the essential subject matter of the study of government. Others are so oriented that they give more emphasis to the relevance of history, sociology, psychology, biography, and anthropology within the field of government. Thus, in a sense, a debate has taken shape between the "traditionalists" or "institutionalists" on the one hand and the "behavioralists" on the other.

Faced by this situation, what choice is the author of a secondary school textbook on government to make? In the opinion of the author of this text, he must be eclectic. He dare not assume that the student comes to the secondary level equipped with a basic understanding of the framework and functioning of government. If he does make this assumption, he may find that the students flounder hopelessly because they lack the basic information on which to erect a sound structure of ideas. On the other hand, if the teacher aims at a more sophisticated, three-dimensional picture of how our government operates, he must provide not only a description of formal institutions but also a wide variety of data drawn from the history of the past and from the many-faceted events and problems of our own day. All of this is essential to throw light on why public officials behave as they do, on the methods they use to achieve their purposes, and on the role played by political parties, pressure groups, and public opinion in the formulation and execution of governmental policy.

Considerable attention has been paid in this book to the unfinished business of government, an aspect of the subject that is treated in each chapter under the heading of "Proposed Reforms." The student is thus prompted to see government as a process, rather than as a condition or a structure. Furthermore, there is an implicit invitation to the young people to participate in this process of change. The dynamic quality of government in a democracy is well brought out by the observation of Rexford

Tugwell: "The Constitution has not been a document written
for once and all. It has been rewritten a little on every day of
American history—not, usually, by changing its words, but by
giving those words different meanings for different times."

The Main Body of the Text

This text is divided into ten chapters. The first introduces the
reader to the Constitution of the United States. The Preamble
and eleven basic principles are discussed in terms of their genesis
and modern application. While the enduring nature of the Constitution is accented, the variables of history, geography and
culture (the latter including national ideals) are introduced as
forces that help shape public policy today.

Chapters 2 to 7 describe the three major branches of our
government, both as they operate interdependently and as they
impinge on local government units. Attention is given to the
changing nature of the Presidential office and to the establishment by Congress of "independent" regulatory agencies with
their far-reaching executive, legislative, and judicial powers. The
widening influence of the Supreme Court is presented in seven
historic stages. The history of the Bill of Rights is traced from
its beginnings as a restraint on the national government to its
contemporary meaning as a protection for Americans in relation
to *all* governmental authority. The overall picture that emerges
from Chapters 2 to 7 is of the national government as an initiator
and director of social changes which, in the last analysis, are no
more than a response to the needs of a democratic society.

Chapter 8 portrays state governments and their increasing
burdens—burdens that have recently become so overwhelming as
to challenge both the states' key position in the American governmental structure and their traditional status as "laboratories
for social change."

Chapter 9 deals with local government, particularly with the
proliferating metropolitan areas that have become the home of
the great majority of Americans and the focal points of many of
our most urgent social problems.

The last chapter, "What's to Come Is Yours" delineates guidelines for responsible citizenship in the last third of the 20th
century. In this context, stress is placed not only on the citizen's
full use of his voting privileges and on active membership in
political parties and other aspects of associational life—the
Jacksonian ideal—but also on the continuous advancement of

knowledge and understanding as preparation for dealing with the ever-growing complexities of life—the Jeffersonian ideal—and on the need for creative participation in public affairs.

Each chapter is divided by headings and subheadings into a large number of relatively short sections. It is believed that this will be psychologically helpful to the student in following the development of the text and in checking his own mastery of the subject matter. Moreover, since many of the main sections approximate an average day's reading assignment, this arrangement should aid the teacher in planning the work of the course.

The sequence of chapters is one which the author has found both logically and psychologically sound. However, since each chapter can be read as a self-contained unit (with many relations, of course, to the other chapters), the teacher can readily change the chapter sequence as he finds most convenient.

Teaching Aids

Each chapter is followed by an abundance of teaching aids that will meet the needs of all types of classes.

Terms You Should Know will help the student sharpen his grasp of the vocabulary of political science. These lists can also serve as a basis for drill and review as each chapter is concluded.

Questions and Problems Based on the Text include both significant factual matters and problems for further analysis and discussion. Many of the items aim simply to afford students an opportunity to grapple with issues reflectively and in a spirit of give-and-take.

Ideas to Think About and Discuss have a threefold purpose: (1) to bring value judgments into focus, thus taking political science into the realm of social study; (2) to give students a sense of the complexity and difficulty of many social problems, without which they may lapse into the simplistic "either-or" pattern of response; and (3) to impress students with the ultimate potency of ideas.

The select bibliography (*Books About American Government and Its Problems*) is designed to make students aware of the existence of a vast reservoir of reading materials which can enhance their knowledge of government and its problems, while providing intellectual stimulation and enjoyment. All of the books listed are highly readable, and all will be found valuable for individual study, as well as for group analysis and reporting. Many titles are available in inexpensive paperback editions.

The *Final Examination*, consisting of 100 multiple-choice questions, can serve not only as a review of basic facts and ideas but also as a stimulus to thought and analysis. In most cases, the reasons for rejecting the foils are as revealing as the basis for selecting the correct answer. A wise pedagogue under whom the author trained many years ago had this to say: "What can a teacher do with the right answer? It is the *incorrect* answer that should do most to establish his rationale."

The *United States Constitution* is presented in the Appendix in convenient form, with helpful headings and footnotes.

The *illustrations* are varied and numerous. They have been planned not to prettify the printed page but to add interest, impact, and factual precision to the text.

Where Should the Book Be Used?

It is believed that this book can be used effectively in any eleventh-year or twelfth-year class involved with the study of American government. This includes courses in American government as such, American history, problems of democracy, great issues, and others. In spite of the simple, compact language, the level of ideas is mature enough to make the text fully suitable for use by junior or community college classes and by adult study groups of various types.

A Final Note

More than 50 years ago, Charles A. Beard wrote in the preface to his *American Government and Politics* that he hoped his work would be viewed "with charity by those who know how difficult a thing it is to describe a complex political organism which is swiftly changing under our very eyes." The author feels constrained to echo this plea for charity in a day when changes are even more rapid, complicated, and startling. It need hardly be said that it is impossible for any publication to keep up with the day-to-day march of events. It is now up to the teacher and the student to supplement this book with newspapers, magazines, radio-TV programs, recordings, public discussions, and the other communication media typical of the modern world. The sustained, disciplined effort to keep well informed on matters relevant to intelligent citizenship can be useful to the community and highly rewarding to the individual. It is hoped that this text will make some contribution toward developing such an attitude in the young people who read it.   S. S.

CONTENTS

To Michael, Bobby, Jane, and Laurie
and to Their Generation

Richard M. Nixon delivers his Inaugural Address, after taking the oath of office as the 37th President of the United States (January 20, 1969). An ever more complicated technology, the apparatus of the welfare state, the crisis of the cities, modern armaments, global diplomatic relations, and wars (hot and cold) have added enormously to the authority and the problems of the President.

CHAPTER 1

The Constitution of the United States

The Preamble to the Constitution

We, the people of the United States, in order to form a more perfect union, establish justice, insure domestic tranquillity, provide for the common defence, promote the general welfare, and secure the blessings of liberty to ourselves and our posterity, do ordain and establish this Constitution for the United States of America.

The paragraph above is the *Preamble* (introduction) to the United States Constitution. The Preamble tells us why the Founding Fathers met at Philadelphia in 1787 and also expresses the goals which they considered essential for effective government and a good society.

The reason the Constitutional Convention met, as stated in the Preamble, was simply "to form a more perfect union." It was generally agreed that the existing government under the Articles of Confederation (the first constitution of the thirteen American states, 1781-1789) had not worked out satisfactorily. The Founding Fathers at the Philadelphia Convention thought that the Confederation's constitution did not give enough power to the central government. Hence the emphasis on forming "a more perfect union."

Now let us consider each of the other specific goals mentioned in the Preamble.

To establish justice. The first goal stated specifically in the Preamble is to "establish justice." To do so, the Constitution provided for a Supreme Court and gave Congress the power to create lower courts as such courts became necessary. Thus, a national judiciary was added to the existing court system of each state. Justice was to be administered in these state and Federal courts.

To provide a guide for the administration of justice, the Founding Fathers quickly added in 1791 the first ten amendments, collectively called the *Bill of Rights*. The Bill of Rights aims to guarantee basic civil rights. (See page 9.)

To insure domestic tranquillity. The purpose stated in this phrase is essential to a civilized society. It recognizes the importance of solving any internal conflict by peaceable methods. Of course, there have been many instances in the history of the United States when "domestic tranquillity" was shattered. We may mention the rebellion of the Pennsylvania farmers against a Federal tax on whiskey (1794); the secession of eleven Southern states that resulted in the Civil War (1861-65); violent labor-management difficulties, such as the national railroad strike of 1877; the struggle over the enforcement of desegregation and civil rights laws in the 1950's and 1960's. In all these instances, the Federal government stepped in to restore order.

Nature, as well as man, can and often does disturb "domestic tranquillity." Such catastrophes as epidemics, floods, hurricanes, and tornadoes strike peaceful communities, and the stricken regions may be declared "disaster areas." Here, too, the Federal government often steps in with food, clothing, medical supplies, temporary shelter, and other forms of aid.

To provide for the common defence. The thirteen states had joined forces in their struggle against England in 1776. With the adoption of the Constitution, the people of the United States looked to the new government to protect them against any future threat to their security. The Constitution, consequently, gave Congress the power to raise and support armies; to provide and maintain a navy; and to arm and train a militia (National Guard). The President of the United States was made Commander-in-Chief of the armed forces. Thus, the Constitution placed the responsibility of providing for "the common defence" in the Legislative and Executive branches of the Federal government.

To promote the general welfare. The first power given to Congress by the Constitution is that of taxation, the purposes of which are "to pay the debts and provide for the common defence and general welfare of the United States." The concept of the *general welfare* is so broad that it has enabled the Federal government to engage in a tremendous range of activities, including many of which the Founding Fathers could not have dreamed.

Promoting the general welfare starts with an adequate defense against foreign enemies and the prevention of violence and disorder at home. It calls for such social services as the advancement of public education, the improvement of working conditions, and the protection of public health and safety. In recent years, it has involved the Federal government in vigorous efforts to insure civil rights, adequate education and suffrage for all—regardless of race, color, creed, or religion.

It would take volumes to list the laws that Congress has passed over the years to "promote the general welfare." Suffice it to say that the limits to Federal power are growing less restrictive as time goes on. The explanation for this was clearly expressed by the United States Supreme Court upholding the tax features of the Social Security Act in 1937. The Court declared: "Nor is the concept of the general welfare static. Needs that were narrow a century ago may be interwoven in our day with the well-being of the nation. What is critical or urgent changes with the times."

To secure the blessings of liberty to ourselves and our posterity. Note that this phrase speaks of the "*blessings* of liberty," rather than liberty by itself. We may assume that this detail of wording was not an accident. Liberty by itself means merely being free,

The Statue of Liberty, standing on an island in Upper New York Bay has served as a beacon of hope for millions of newcomers to America from all parts of the world.

in the sense of not being subjected to some outside constraint, such as confinement or forced labor. But of what value is such freedom to a man who cannot get a job and lacks the necessities of life? Or to one who is sick and cannot pay for adequate medical care? Or to one who has no chance to obtain an education and prepare himself for a satisfactory role in society?

In 18th-century rural America, where land was to be had for the asking, liberty from governmental tyranny may have been adequate. But to Americans living in a 20th-century industrialized society, liberty without a means of livelihood, without access to education, and without health services and other advantages would be a sham rather than a "blessing." Hence, the Federal government has expanded its powers so that they include subsidization of education on all levels, measures to insure a high level of employment at decent wages, and an elaborate program of social security, now comprising medical care for the aged. All of these, and many others, are steps designed "to secure the blessings of liberty."

The phrase in question goes even further. Government must secure the blessings of liberty, not only to ourselves, but also to "our posterity" (those who come after us). Hence, the program to conserve the nation's natural resources.

Basic Principles of Our Government

Popular sovereignty. The principle of popular sovereignty is clearly stated in the Preamble: "We, the people of the United States." Whatever powers the Federal government now possesses have been given to it by the people through the Constitution. And where the powers are limited, it is the people who have limited them. Nor can the government exercise any of the powers that it possesses in an arbitrary or unfair manner. In short, the United States Constitution, the supreme law of the land, rests upon a delegation of power by the people to their government.

The written and the unwritten Constitution. The written Constitution, in the narrow sense, includes only an outline of the machinery of government. It is the basic law which tells in advance what the rules of the game are. But there are many rules, and they are not always perfectly defined. What is more, these rules are interpreted and executed by men. It makes all the difference in the world whether a President is an idealist or one

THE WRITTEN AND UNWRITTEN CONSTITUTION

Preamble

Article I — Legislative Branch

Article II — Executive Branch

Article III — Judicial Branch

Article IV — Relations of states to states and of states to the Federal government

Article V — The amendment process

Article VI — General provisions: Constitution and Federal laws supreme law of land; Federal and state officials bound by oath to support the Constitution

Article VII — How the Constitution is to be ratified

AMENDMENTS TO THE CONSTITUTION

UNWRITTEN

UNWRITTEN

1-10 The Bill of Rights (1791)

11 States may not be sued in Federal courts (1795)

12 Separate ballots for President and Vice President (1804)

13 Slavery prohibited (1865)

14 Civil rights for Negroes (1868)

15 Negro suffrage (1870)

16 Federal income tax (1913)

17 Direct election of Senators (1913)

18 National prohibition (1919)

19 Woman suffrage (1920)

20 Lame Duck Amendment (1933)

21 Repeal of prohibition (1933)

22 Presidency limited to two terms (1952)

23 Suffrage in Presidential elections for District of Columbia residents (1961)

24 Abolition of poll taxes in Federal elections (1964)

25 Power of succession to Presidency by Vice President clarified; provision for appointment of Vice President when that office is vacated (1967)

SUPREME COURT PASSES ON CONSTITUTIONALITY OF LAWS

RISE OF POLITICAL PARTIES

ELECTORAL COLLEGE VOTE PLEDGED ON BASIS OF POPULAR VOTE

PRESIDENT SERVES AS LEADER OF HIS PARTY

PRESIDENT AND ADVISERS RESPONSIBLE FOR ECONOMIC STABILITY AND GROWTH OF NATION

PRESIDENTIAL SYSTEM OF GOVERNMENT EMERGES

CIVIL RIGHTS EXPANDED TO INCLUDE HUMAN RIGHTS

"SEPARATION OF POWERS" BECOMES SHARING OF POWERS

GROWTH OF PRESIDENTIAL POWERS IN TIME OF CRISIS: WAR, DEPRESSION, REBELLION

EXPANDED PRESIDENTIAL RESPONSIBILITY FOR FOREIGN POLICY DECISIONS

CENTRAL GOVERNMENT BECOMES A SOURCE OF INCOME FOR LOCAL GOVERNMENT whose horizon is limited by purely "practical" considerations; whether a Supreme Court Justice is a liberal or a conservative; whether or not a Congressman believes in dynamic use of the powers of government. Nevertheless, the written Constitution contains guarantees which inform those who govern, as well as those who are governed, what their position is in regard to law. Means are available, if the people are intelligent and willing enough to use them, by which officials who do not "play the game" fairly can be held in check and even punished.

But the United States Constitution, as written in 1787, and amended since then twenty-five times, does not by itself give one a true picture of the national government as it operates today. Were a person to memorize with full understanding the 7000 words of the written document, his knowledge of our government would still be far from complete. He would not know, to cite just two examples, how many members there are in the Cabinet, or who has the power to regulate radio and television broadcasting. The Constitution does not say a word about budgets, lobbying, the functioning of committees in Congress, and the role of political parties in the affairs of government. All of these and many other vitally important phases of our government are the result of a series of customs, traditions, precedents, and practices which have come to be regarded as the *unwritten Constitution.*

Our federal system of government. The United States is a vast and highly diversified country. There are many different regions, with distinctive historical traditions, natural conditions, and economic interests. Because there are such significant differences, each of the 50 states has a considerable measure of self-government. But the American people learned long ago that there are also great advantages in *unity.* Unity is indispensable if the entire nation is to enjoy security, social progress, and a high level of economic development. To meet the special needs of the 50 states, and at the same time make it possible for all the people of the United States to act in concert, a *federal system of government* has been developed. Under this system, political powers are divided between the central (Federal) government and the states.

The Federal government has only those powers specifically delegated to it by the Constitution (chiefly in Article I, Section 8) or implied by these powers. These powers are referred to as *delegated, expressed, enumerated, or implied.*

Under the 10th Amendment, the "powers not delegated to the United States by the Constitution, nor prohibited by it to the States, are reserved to the States respectively, or to the people." These so-called *residual* (or *retained*) powers give the state governments a broad range of authority in regard to many of the activities, relationships, and problems of everyday life. They involve such matters as education, marriage, divorce, traffic control, professional standards, inheritance of property, judicial procedure, and the right of suffrage. Moreover, under their *police powers*—that is, their authority to protect the health, safety, and morals of the people—the states have been empowered by the courts to legislate in regard to wages, working conditions, the operations of public utilities and other businesses, housing, gambling, health standards, and many other matters which Supreme Court Justice Holmes characterized as "greatly or immediately necessary to the public welfare."

It is the federal system which explains the great diversity which we observe in certain areas of American life—for example, the relatively high educational standards in such states as New York

Different states have set the pace for the nation in different areas of social progress. California. for example, is particularly proud of her pioneering efforts in public higher education. The state has developed a three-level system, composed of the University of California, with nine campuses; the state colleges, serving various regions of the state; and the locally controlled junior colleges. The system has multiplied opportunities for post-high school education for young people in California. The problems that have arisen are largely those of rapid growth. This photograph shows a scene on the campus of the University of California, San Diego.

and California; the "easy" divorce laws of Nevada; the advanced social legislation of several states compared with the rather low standards in others; the fact that not all states have a minimum voting age of 21. (This last was rectified by the Voting Act of 1970—page 221.)

All such diversity, however, exists within the context of an overall national unity, made possible by the powers delegated to the national government.

Implied powers. The last of the enumerated powers granted to Congress (Article I, Section 8, Clause 18) reads: "To make all laws which shall be necessary and proper for carrying into execution the foregoing powers. . . ." This is known as the *implied-powers clause* of the Constitution. Sometimes it is called the *elastic clause*.

The effect of this clause has been to lend far greater scope to the relatively few powers specifically granted to Congress, and to enable the government to adapt its functioning to changing conditions. For example, one specific power of Congress is the regulation of interstate commerce. In its efforts to "make all laws which shall be necessary and proper" for regulating interstate commerce, Congress has undertaken the regulation of interstate telephone, telegraph, radio-television, air transport, and other means of communication and transportation which did not exist when the Constitution was written.

Concurrent powers. Powers exercised by both the Federal government and the state governments are said to be *concurrent*. The Federal government and the states may act jointly or independently in the exercise of such powers. The power to tax, for example, is a concurrent power.

Separation of powers by checks and balances. Fear of tyranny prompted the framers of the Constitution to separate the powers of government among three separate branches: Legislative, Executive, and Judicial. Thus, in broadest outline, Congress *enacts* laws, the President *enforces* them, and the Federal courts *interpret* them. Our national laws are the product of cooperative action among the three branches of government.

Each of the state constitutions follows the same scheme of separating powers among three branches. In each state, powers are divided among the state legislature, the governor, and the state courts. Only in local government does the principle of separation of powers sometimes fail to apply. For example, in the commission form of city government, a group of elected officials, called commissioners, exercise both legislative and executive powers. (See Chapter 9.)

The framers of the Constitution feared hasty and radical legislation as much as they did tyranny. To prevent such legislation, they armed each branch of government with powers to check operations of the others. For example, Congress passes bills but the President may veto them. Even when a bill is passed by Congress and signed by the President, it may still be subject to review by the courts. The Supreme Court has invalidated laws which it judged unconstitutional. The principle of *checks and balances*, as this system is called, is seen in many other ways. For example, the President appoints officials, but the Senate may refuse to confirm the appointments. The President draws up treaties, but the Senate may refuse to ratify them. The House of Representatives passes a bill, but the Senate may refuse to do so (or vice versa). This system of checks and balances is used in state governments as well.

One might suppose that this system of checks and balances is so restrictive that very little is actually accomplished. In practice, the system acts merely as a brake. Particularly in times of war or depression, or when for some other reason a strong sense of urgency is felt, the President and Congress are likely to work together closely, and even the courts may be prevailed on to "go along." Under such circumstances, the ship of state can move ahead at terrific speed.

Protection of individual liberty. The Constitution imposes restrictions on the Federal government in defense of the individual. These restrictions are found mainly in the first ten amendments to the Constitution, known as the *Bill of Rights*. These amendments provide for freedom of speech, of the press, and of religion; freedom from unreasonable search and seizure; the right of the accused to a speedy and public trial; and the right of protection of the individual's life, liberty, and property.

The Bill of Rights, as noted, is a check on the Federal government only. There are, however, also bills of rights in the state constitutions. These are designed to guard against infringement by the states. The individual is further protected against state invasions of his liberties by the 14th Amendment to the Federal Constitution, which provides: "Nor shall any state deprive any

person of life, liberty, or property, without due process of law."*
The 14th Amendment places another prohibition on the states:
"nor (shall any state) deny to any person within its jurisdiction
the equal protection of the laws." This provision has been invoked by the Supreme Court in its decisions forbidding segregation in public schools on racial grounds and other forms of racial
segregation.

There are other provisions in the Constitution which protect
the rights of the individual. For example, in Article I, Section 9,
we find that Congress is forbidden to suspend the right of *habeas
corpus,* or to pass *bills of attainder* or *ex-post-facto laws.* (See the
list of "Terms You Should Know" on page 13-15.) In Article I,
Section 10, similar restrictions are placed on the states.

Interstate relations. Article IV, Section 1 of the Constitution
states: "Full faith and credit shall be given in each state to the
public acts, records, and judicial proceedings of every other
state." The purpose of this provision is to make certain that the
states will work as a team, so that we have a truly national society.
For example, a marriage contracted in any state is valid in all
other states; a driver's license issued by any state is valid in all
other states; a person who commits a crime in one state and
escapes to another will in most instances be surrendered to the
police of the state in which the crime was committed.

Division of powers between nation and states. In the early
days of the Republic, and up to the Civil War, patriotism in this
country frequently meant devotion to the state, rather than to
the nation. Most people were far more interested in local affairs
than they were in those of the national government. There was
generally lacking what we might call a *national consciousness.*
This is evidenced in the rather grudging way in which the states
gave up some of their powers in 1787, and in the numerous restrictions they imposed on the newly created central government
immediately thereafter. In the 9th Amendment, for example, the
states intended to make clear that the Federal government could

---

* *Due process of law* refers to the established legal procedures (based
upon both written laws and unwritten principles) by which the rights of an
individual are protected. In criminal procedures "due process" means a fair
and impartial trial, providing all recognized safeguards for the accused. "Due
process" may also refer to other (non-criminal) procedures, such as drafting
men for military service or taking over property for public use.

exercise only those rights and powers granted to it in the Constitution. Also, the 10th Amendment reinforces this by providing: "The powers not delegated to the United States by the Constitution, nor prohibited by it to the States, are reserved to the States respectively, or to the people." The Federal government, in other words, originally was limited to the powers that were expressly or implicitly granted by the Constitution. The states, on the other hand, retained all the powers not granted by the Constitution to Congress or forbidden by it to the states. The division of powers between the state governments and the Federal government leads to the following categories of powers:

1. Powers exercised by the Federal government alone.
2. Powers exercised by the state governments alone.
3. Powers exercised by both the Federal and state governments.
4. Powers denied to the Federal government.
5. Powers denied to the state governments.
6. Powers denied to both Federal and state governments.

Subordination of the military establishment to the civilian government. The system of checks and balances, the separation of powers among the three branches of government, and the division of powers between the Federal government and the states all aim to insure *civilian* control of governmental authority in the United States. The President and Congress (the first by virtue of his authority as Commander-in-Chief, and the second by control of the purse strings) are in full control of the armed forces. The law even requires that the Secretary of Defense must *not* have served in the armed forces for at least ten years before his appointment to the Cabinet. Nor have we ever had a President who took active command of the armed forces—even though the Constitution vests in him the powers of Commander-in-Chief in time of war and peace. As a final precaution, Article I, Section 8, Clause 12 of the Constitution stipulates that "no appropriation of money to that use [that is, military use] shall be for a longer term than two years."

A flexible scheme of government. The men who wrote the Constitution in 1787 realized that unless the basic law was made flexible, it would not be able to meet changing conditions and might have to be replaced at frequent intervals. Accordingly, they made provision for change without altering the basic principles. One of these provisions is the process of amendment* described so clearly in Article V. Twenty-five amendments have been added to the Constitution since 1789.

There are critics, however, who feel that the amending process is now so slow and difficult that it should be subjected to amendment. They point to European constitutions, most of which are amendable by legislative action alone. The proposals which have been made along these lines include the following: (1) that Congress be empowered to propose amendments (submit them to the states) by a mere majority vote of both houses, and that a mere majority of the states be made adequate for ratification; (2) that amendments be proposed by a mere majority in two successive Congresses, with ratification by a majority of the states; (3) that amendments be proposed by petition of a certain number of state legislatures, to be ratified by a popular vote in the several states or in the nation as a whole.

It would appear, however, that the weight of opinion is in favor of continuing the present amendment process. Admittedly, it may be slow and cumbersome, on occasion, but this is considered a safeguard against hasty action. Moreover, recent experience has shown that an amendment may be proposed and ratified with surprising speed when it is strongly supported by public opinion. The 26th Amendment, which was approved by Congress in March, 1971, and was ratified by the 38th state in June of the same year, is an outstanding example of this. Even more important is the fact that the Constitution has been expanded by processes other than amendment—by use of the implied powers of the "elastic clause," by Congressional and Presidential action (especially during periods of emergency), by custom and usage, and by court decisions and interpretations. It may be assumed that these processes will continue to operate.

* Article V provides that an amendment may be *proposed* in either of two ways: by a two-thirds vote of both houses of Congress, *or* by a national convention called by Congress at the request of two-thirds of the states.

An amendment, however, does not become effective until it is *ratified* by three-fourths of the states (today 38 states). Such ratification may be by the state legislatures, *or* by special conventions called by the states.

No amendment has ever been proposed by a national convention. Moreover, of the 25 amendments adopted, all but one (the 21st, repealing Prohibition) have been ratified by state legislatures.

Terms You Should Know

Amendment. Revision of a bill or law; specifically, revision of a basic law, such as the Constitution.

Articles of Confederation. The first constitution of the thirteen American states (1781-1789). It set up a weak central government, which was supplanted by the present form of government under the United States Constitution.

Bill of attainder. A law passed by a legislative body which imposes punishment on an individual or group of individuals without a regular judicial trial. (Forbidden by Article I, Sections 9-10 of the Constitution.)

Bill of Rights. Statement of the basic rights of the people, thus guaranteeing them against governmental tyranny. Found in the first ten amendments of the United States Constitution and in various state constitutions.

Checks and balances. Principle by which the powers of government are divided among different branches so that none can exercise excessive power.

Civil rights. The personal liberties and privileges of the individual. Under the United States Constitution, they are guaranteed mainly in the first ten amendments and in the 14th Amendment.

Concurrent powers. Powers which are exercised independently in the same field of legislation by both the Federal and the state governments—*e.g.*, the power to tax.

Constitution. The basic laws or principles that govern a nation. May be written, unwritten, or both.

Due process of law. The established legal procedures which provide protection against arbitrary or unreasonable infringement of private rights. In criminal procedures, this means a fair trial according to law.

Equal protection of the laws. A phrase of the 14th Amendment which means in essence that all persons are equal before the law and are entitled to receive the benefits and protection of the law without discrimination. The "equal protection of the laws" clause of the 14th Amendment has been used by the Supreme Court to outlaw racial segregation in education and other fields.

Ex-post-facto law. A law which imposes criminal penalties on a person for having performed an act which was not illegal at the time it was performed. (Forbidden by Article I, Sections 9-10 of the Constitution.)

Federal system of government. A system of government under which powers are divided between the central government and political subdivisions or regions—for example, the United States government and the governments of the 50 states. The opposite of a unitary or centralized government, as in France.

"Founding Fathers." The statesmen present at the Constitutional Convention in 1787 who framed this nation's basic law.

General welfare clause. The clause of the Constitution (I, 8, 1) which authorizes Congress to raise and spend tax revenues "to provide for the . . . general welfare of the United States." Today, this clause is broadly interpreted to justify expenditures for education, housing, social security, health, and many other purposes.

Habeas corpus, writ of. A legal paper which directs police officers to bring before the court a person being held in custody so that the judge may decide whether or not his detention is justified under the law. This is considered a basic safeguard against unjust imprisonment. Under the Constitution (Article I, Sections 9-10), the writ of *habeas corpus* may not be suspended except "when in cases of rebellion or invasion the public safety may require it."

Implied powers. The powers which Congress exercises on the basis of the "elastic clause" of the Constitution (I, 8, 18). These powers are not expressed in so many words, but they are "implied" as "necessary and proper for carrying into execution" the powers which are expressed.

Judicial review. The power of courts to nullify or invalidate statutes which, in the opinion of the judges, violate the United States Constitution or a state constitution.

Militia. The body of able-bodied male citizens subject to military service when called out by the government. Organized state militias constitute the *National Guard.*

Police powers. The authority of state governments to place reasonable limitations on private rights and privileges in order to protect the health, safety, and morals of the community. The Federal government indirectly applies police powers when it regulates private enterprise under the taxation and commerce clauses of the Constitution.

Popular sovereignty. The doctrine or principle under which final political power is vested in the people. A basic principle of democratic government.

Residual powers. The powers which are reserved to the states or to the people under the 10th Amendment. (Also called *reserved* or *retained powers.*)

Separation of powers. Independence of each of the three branches of government—legislative, executive, and judicial—in relation to the other two. (See "Checks and balances.")

Suffrage. Right to vote.

Unwritten Constitution. The body of customs, precedents, and accepted practices that have acquired the force of law in the operation of our government.

Questions and Problems Based on the Text

1. How does the Preamble to the United States Constitution throw light on the weaknesses of our government under the Articles of Confederation?

2. Define: *domestic tranquillity; general welfare; blessings of liberty.*

3. Distinguish between the "written" and the "unwritten" Constitution. *written > recorded laws   unwritten - customs, etiquette*

4. What are the advantages of a federal system of government in a country such as the United States? Can you think of any disadvantages?

5. (a) Define the following terms and give a specific example for each: *residual powers, implied powers, concurrent powers, elastic clause, police powers.* (b) Give a synonym for each of the following: *retained powers, enumerated powers, expressed powers, reserved powers.*

6. Explain how Article IV, Section 1 of the Federal Constitution serves to carry out the motto of the United States—*E Pluribus Unum* ("One Out of Many").

7. What is meant by *judicial review?* *power to void anything that is unconstitutional*

8. What is meant by *civil rights?* In what ways has this concept been broadened to justify the new term "human rights"? *all people.*

9. Explain how the American system of government embodies the principle of *separation of powers.*

10. What is meant by the system of *checks and balances?* What are the advantages of this? What criticisms have been made of it?

11. What criticisms have been leveled against the amending process provided in the United States Constitution? Why do many students of government feel that no change is needed?

12. Under the American system of government, the military is clearly subordinated to the civilian authority. (a) How is this provided for in the Constitution? (b) Why has this principle become particularly important in recent years?

Ideas to Think About and Discuss

1. "What has gone wrong is the (political) process. Left and right, in their zealotry, have abandoned the ordinary decency, the spirit of skeptical toleration, that alone can make a non-totalitarian political system work." —ANTHONY LEWIS

2. "Where federalism has been established during the last hundred years, there has been indebtedness to the American experiment." —R. L. SCHUYLER

3. "I would not amend the Constitution. I would amend men's social and economic ideas." LOUIS D. BRANDEIS

4. "The United States Constitution is the most wonderful work ever struck off at a given time by the brain and purpose of man." —WILLIAM E. GLADSTONE

5. "The Constitution is an expression of the clear and deliberate will of the whole people." —JOHN MARSHALL

6. "There are but three directions in which a people can go governmentally. A people can ground its government on a centralization of power, a decentralization of power, or an organized balance of powers. There are these three ways and none other." —GLENN FRANK

7. "These words (the Preamble to the Declaration of Independence) are more revolutionary than anything written by Robespierre, Marx, or Lenin, more explosive than the atom, a continual challenge to ourselves, as well as an inspiration to the oppressed of all the world." —SAMUEL E. MORISON

8. "The people's government, made for the people, made by the people, and answerable to the people." —DANIEL WEBSTER

9. "Those who make peaceful revolution impossible make violent revolution inevitable." —JOHN F. KENNEDY

10. "Are we becoming aware that systems of government other than ours may be feasible for other nations, and that our concern should be not about communism but about imperialism, not about the form of a government but about the acts of a government?" —LESTER MARKEL

11. "I believe that in 99 cases out of a hundred the American people will make the right decision—if and when they are in possession of the essential facts about any given issue." —ADLAI E. STEVENSON

CHAPTER 2

Lawmakers and Lawmaking in the National Government

I. HOW CONGRESS IS ORGANIZED

Why Two Houses?

The historic basis. The lawmaking branch of the United States government consists of two bodies: the *Senate* and the *House of Representatives.* This twofold (or *bicameral*) composition of the national legislature grew out of conditions which existed at the time of the writing of the Constitution. The Senate was intended to preserve the equality of the states, or the *federal* principle in government. It was also expected to safeguard the interests of the sparsely populated agricultural states. The House of Representatives (commonly referred to as "The House") was a concession to the idea of representation according to population, or the *national* principle in government. It was created, therefore, to protect the interests of the larger, commercial states.

The situation today. The question has frequently been raised as to whether a bicameral Congress is still needed. The states ratified the Constitution only because they felt that their economic interests would be effectively served by a Congress of two houses. It was believed in 1787 — indeed, the belief exists today — that each house acts as a check on the other in preventing the passage of hasty, ill-considered, sectional or class legislation. But despite the movement for a one-house legislature in some states of the Union, there is little likelihood of a change in the present bicameral organization of Congress.

The Senate

The basis of representation in the Senate. Each state, large or small, is entitled to two Senators. The Constitution provides that "no state, without its consent, shall be deprived of its equal suffrage in the Senate." The Senate, therefore, consists of 100 members. The justice of this constitutional provision for equality of representation has frequently been challenged. Should Alaska, the least populous state, have as much representation in the Senate as California, the most populous state? The answer lies in recognition of the principle which guided the makers of the Constitution. This principle was that the equality of the states in the Union could be assured only by equality of representation in the Senate.

Qualifications of Senators. Under the Constitution, a Senator must be at least 30 years of age. He is required, at the time of his election, to have been a citizen of the United States for nine years and "an inhabitant of that state for which he shall be chosen." In addition, the Constitution declares that the Senate, like the House, "shall be the judge of the elections, returns, and qualifications of its own members." The Senate may expel a member by a two-thirds vote.

The election of Senators. Since the ratification of the 17th Amendment in 1913, Senators have been elected directly by the people of each state. Nomination for the office is secured either

The floor of the chamber of the United States Senate.

through direct primaries (that is, choice by the enrolled voters of the party), or through statewide party conventions. The primary method of selection is more common. Vesting the power of nomination and election of United States Senators in the people, instead of the former method of choice by state legislatures, has had the effect of producing Senators of greater independence, broader vision and more responsiveness to public opinion.

When a vacancy occurs in the Senate during the regular term of office, the governor of that state, or whoever is the "executive authority," calls for a special election to fill the vacancy. However, the legislators of the state may give the governor power to make a temporary appointment until provision is made for an election by the people.

Tenure of office. Senators serve for a term of six years. Very often they are re-elected, and it is not unusual for them to serve three or more terms consecutively. In accordance with the provision in the original Constitution, one-third of the membership of the Senate stands for election every two years. The Senate is thus a continuing body. Length of tenure has assured it an experienced membership at any time. For this reason, among others, it has gained much prestige.

The House of Representatives

The basis of representation. Representation in the House is based upon the population of the states. Every state, however, is entitled to at least one Representative. Lacking a reliable census, the original Constitution fixed the basis more or less arbitrarily as one Representative for every 10,000 people and provided for a total membership of 65 in the House. As a result of the first census (1790), the House increased its size to 106. Then, from census to census (taken every ten years) the number of members of the House was increased, as new states were added and as the population of the nation grew. After the census of 1910, the membership stood at 435, a size considered favorable for efficient legislative action. This has continued to be the size of the House ever since, except for a brief period after the admission of Alaska and Hawaii, when membership was raised temporarily to 437. In 1929, Congress passed a law providing for a reapportionment of its seats following the 1930 census. A distribution made in 1930

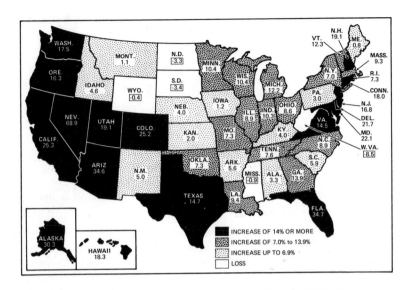

Changes in the population of the states, 1960 to 1970. (Based on preliminary data of the Bureau of the Census, 1970.)

determined the basis of representation as one Representative for every 280,000 people. By a measure enacted in 1940, the President submits to Congress after each census a report showing the population of each state and the number of Representatives to which the state is entitled. Today, the average population of a Congressional district is about 470,000.

Preliminary figures for the 1970 Census showed that the nation had a population of more than 204 million—a gain of 14.2% over 1960. The reapportionment of the House of Representatives based on the 1970 Census points to a shift of 12 seats. *California* is expected to gain five seats; *Florida*, three; and *Arizona, Colorado, Connecticut* and *Texas* one each. The losers are likely to be *New York* and *Pennsylvania* (two seats each), and *Alabama, Iowa, North Dakota, Ohio, Oklahoma, Tennessee, West Virginia,* and *Wisconsin* (one seat each).

Practices in distributing Representatives. The question of how Representatives are to be distributed in each state was left at first by Congress to the state legislatures. The result was that in some states Representatives were chosen by individual districts.

In others, they were elected "at large." Obviously, the latter plan was unfair; the dominant political party in any state might, by controlling no more than a small majority of the total vote, elect *all* the Representatives of that state.

Through a series of measures enacted at various times, the following principles of apportioning Representatives have been established. Each state having more than one Representative is divided into Congressional districts. Each Representative is elected for a separate district. Such districts are to be contiguous and compact. They are to contain approximately the same number of inhabitants. Provision exists, also, for the election by the entire state of one or more Representatives-at-large. This may occur when the reapportionment after a new census increases the representation from a given state. The state, in such a case, may find it convenient temporarily to retain the existing pattern of Congressional districts and to elect the new Representative or Representatives on an at-large basis.

So much for principles or theory. In actual practice, Congressional districts have often been decidedly unequal in population. For example, in 1962, one Congressional district in Connecticut represented 318,000 people while another contained 690,000 people. They have often been far from contiguous and compact. Political parties have, almost since the beginning of our government, resorted to *gerrymandering*. They have so shaped districts in their state—sometimes in grotesque forms—as to give the dominant party complete control. Both the Republicans and the Democrats resorted to such practices.

Challenge to unfair apportionment and gerrymandering. From time to time, political parties have blocked legislative redistricting in various states purely for political reasons. Failure to carry out necessary reapportionments seemed to justify the charge that our legislative bodies (both Federal and state) had fallen far short of the ideal of fair representation. And nothing was done to compel the states to provide equality of population in Congressional districts, in spite of the 1872 law of Congress which stated that districts should have "as nearly as practicable, an equal number of inhabitants."

But in 1962, the Supreme Court ruled (in the case of *Baker v. Carr*) that courts may examine legislative apportionments and may compel states to provide equal representation. Two years later, in 1964, the Supreme Court ruled (*Wesberry v. Sanders*) that "as nearly as is practicable, one man's vote in a congressional district is to be worth as much as another's." Also in 1964 (*Reynolds v. Sims*), the Court stated: "As a basic constitutional standard, the equal-protection clause requires that the seats in both houses of a bicameral (state) legislature must be apportioned on a population basis." In 1965, Congress passed an act designed to end gerrymandering and equalize populations in Congressional districts. The act sets two standards: Congressional districts must be as compact as practical; and their population must be within 15% of that of the state's average district.

The qualifications of Representatives. A member of the House of Representatives must be at least 25 years old, and must have been a citizen of the United States for seven years at the time of election. He must reside in the state from which he is elected. Custom (or what might be called the "Unwritten Constitution") and legal requirements in some states make it necessary for members of the House to live in the district from which they are

The family trip to Washington, marked by a brief visit to the Representative from the "home" district, has become a familiar feature of American life.

Ewing Galloway

chosen, although there is no such provision in the Constitution itself.

The latter requirement has been the subject of much discussion among students of government. There is, perhaps, as much to be said on one side as on the other. Residence in the district may insure closer attention to the wishes of constituents and to local needs. On the other hand, candidates of higher talent and broader national outlook may often be found outside a particular district. The fact is that much of the "pork-barrel" politics in Congress — that is, politics aimed at securing appropriations for purely local, and often unnecessary, purposes — is traceable to the emphasis on choosing "home-town boys" as Representatives.

The House, like the Senate, has the power to judge the qualifications of its own members, and may exclude a person by majority vote. Also, the House, like the Senate, may expel a member by a two-thirds vote.

The election of Representatives. The qualifications of citizens who vote for members of the House may be determined by the states in accordance with constitutional provisions. This specifies that "electors (voters) in each state shall have the qualifications requisite for electors of the most numerous branch (the lower house) of the state legislature." When a vacancy occurs in the representation of a state, the governor is authorized to call for a special election to fill the vacancy. If, for any reason, the state authorities fail to take action, Congress may itself provide the machinery for holding such an election.

The method of nominating candidates for the House is left to each state. In most states, the choice is by direct primaries in the various Congressional districts. In others, it is by district party conventions. Nominees for Representative-at-large are chosen either by statewide primaries or by statewide conventions.

The term of office. The term of a member of the House of Representatives is two years. This might appear, on the face of it, to be unduly short. A new member necessarily consumes much time in acquainting himself with the duties of his office and in learning "what makes the wheels go round." Moreover, several months may be needed in campaigning for re-election every two years. The fact is, however, that many Representatives are usually elected time and again, so that the "fragmenting" effect of the short term is minimized.

Regulations Applying to Both Houses of Congress

Time, place, and manner of electing Congressmen. The power to determine the time, place, and manner of choosing Representatives and Senators is given by the Constitution to the states. Congress may, however, make changes in these regulations. Since 1872, by act of Congress, elections have been held on the same day throughout the United States, the Tuesday following the first Monday in November. Maine is a notable exception; since the 1870's it has been allowed to conduct its Congressional elections in September.

Sessions of Congress. It is customary to refer to each Congress by a number, counted consecutively from the first Congress, which met in 1789. The 91st Congress was elected in November, 1968 and opened in January, 1969. The length of a given Congress is considered to be two years.

Before the adoption of the 20th Amendment in 1933, every Congress had two types of sessions.* The "short" session began in December of the even-numbered year (following the election) and lasted until the following March 4. The "long" session began in December of the odd-numbered year and lasted until mid-summer of the next year. The newly elected Congressmen (comprising the entire House and one-third of the Senate) did not take office until March 4 following the election. But the "short" session, as noted, *ended* on March 4. Thus, except in the unlikely eventuality of a special session called by the President, a newly elected Congress would not meet until the following December, 13 months after election. Moreover, the "short" session of Congress usually included many "lame ducks"—Representatives and Senators who had failed of re-election but who nevertheless continued in office. These "short" sessions were often periods of inactivity, or even worse, of bad legislation.

This illogical, and even ludicrous, situation was ended by the 20th ("Lame Duck") Amendment, which was added to the Constitution in 1933 after a fight of many years spearheaded by Senator George Norris of Nebraska. Each Congress now holds two "regular" sessions. The first begins on January 3 following the election. The second begins on January 3 of the following

---

* For the effect of the 20th Amendment on the President's term of office, see page 87.

CONGRESS AT A GLANCE

HOUSE OF REPRESENTATIVES

Membership: 435 members, elected every 2 years in the even-numbered years; may not hold any other office in U. S. government.

Qualifications: 25 years of age; citizen of the U. S. for at least 7 years; resident of state represented; may not hold any other office in U. S. government.

Compensation: $42,500 per year.

Allowances:

1. Three round trips a year between home and Washington.

2. Suite of offices in Washington; an office in the home district; office staff, number depending on size of district.

3. "Franking privilege" and with some limitations, free long-distance telephone calls and telegrams; paid expenses on official inspection trips in United States and abroad.

4. $3000 tax reduction for members who maintain homes in Washington and in home district.

5. Pension, to which member contributes.

SENATE

Membership: 100 members, 2 from each state; 6-year term, with ⅓ elected every 2 years; may not hold any other office in U. S. government.

Qualifications: 30 years of age; citizen of the U. S. for at least 9 years; resident of state represented; may not hold any other office in U. S. government.

Compensation: $42,500 per year.

Allowances:

1. Three round trips a year between home and Washington.

2. Suite of offices in Washington; an office in the home state; office staff, number depending on population of state.

3. "Franking privilege" and with some limitations, free long-distance telephone calls and telegrams; paid expenses on official inspection trips in United States and abroad.

4. $3000 tax reduction for members who maintain homes in Washington and in home state.

5. Pension, to which member contributes.

year. Each session lasts as long as is necessary. Under the 20th Amendment, Congress has the power to change the dates of the meetings. Under the Constitution, special sessions of Congress, or of either House, may be held at the call of the President.

Privileges and immunities of Congressmen. The salaries of members of Congress are fixed by that body itself. Congressmen now receive $30,000 a year. After a stated period of service, they may contribute to a pension fund. In addition, they receive certain allowances, such as expenses for traveling, for secretarial and clerical assistance, and for postage (the "franking privilege"). If a Congressman maintains a home both in Washington and in his home district, he may make a tax deduction up to $3000. It has been pointed out repeatedly that this generosity on the part of Uncle Sam helps explain why Congressmen so often hesitate to displease their constituents.

THE MOST IMPORTANT BUSINESS BEFORE CONGRESS

Green in the *Providence Journal*

It implies no disrespect for Congress or for the democratic process to suggest that one of the main considerations on the minds of the great majority of Congressmen as they go about their duties in Washington is to make a favorable impression on the voters at home and to win re-election.

Two privileges are granted to Congressmen to prevent interference with their official duties. One exempts them from arrest
during their attendance at the session of their chamber and in
going to, or returning from, the same. Exceptions may be made
for acts of treason, felonies (crimes of major character) or
"breaches of the peace." The other privilege guarantees freedom
of discussion, in the sense that no Congressman may be legally
prosecuted for remarks made on the floor of either house.

II. THE WORKING METHODS OF CONGRESS

The Senate and the House—A Study in Contrasts

The Senate at work. The "upper house" of Congress was
originally conceived of as a small, conservative, tempering body.
It was to carry on more or less in the tradition of the Senate in
ancient Rome, of the House of Lords in England, and of the
various governor's councils in colonial days.

In large measure, these expectations have not been realized.
The Senate has developed into a legislative body very different
from the rather austere models that evidently guided the 18th-
century founders. But in one respect at least the original plan has
been fulfilled: the Senate has become one of the most powerful
and prestigious of all our institutions of government. This is so
for a number of reasons.

The Senate consists of only 100 members. Most of them are
lawyers or professional men of other callings. Most of them are
past the age of 50. They enjoy long terms in office. Very likely,
they have had extensive political experience. Not a few have been
governors of states or Representatives before they entered the
Senate. In both state and national politics, they are powers to be
reckoned with. They jealously guard the right to freedom of discussion, hesitating at all times to apply rules which may limit
debate. They share with the President of the United States the
important power to make appointments and treaties. They initiate
much legislation, practically as much in recent years as does the
lower house. They dare in many cases to be independent and
even boldly outspoken. Surely, an indelible impress has been left
upon American history by such Senators as Calhoun, Webster,
Douglas, Seward, and Davis, titans of the era of Western expansion and sectional conflict; by Sherman, Beveridge, Lodge, and
La Follette, great figures in a world of technological revolution

and struggling internationalism; by Borah, Glass, Norris, Vandenberg, and Fulbright, statesmen of the crisis of democracy and world peace. These are only a few typical figures. We might name many others from earlier eras and the contemporary scene.

CLAY   WEBSTER   CALHOUN

LA FOLLETTE   TAFT

Some years ago, a special committee of Senators (including the late John F. Kennedy) was formed to choose "the five greatest Senators," whose portraits were to be hung in the anteroom of the Senate Chamber. The committee named the five Senators above. Can you suggest why each of them was considered an epoch-making figure in the history of the Senate?

The House of Representatives at work. An experienced observer * of the work of Congress has the following comments to make about the House of Representatives:

> One is impressed by the dignity of the Senate, despite a few of its members, but the House confuses and astonishes when it is in action. Nearly every type of human being is found there; the cold, incisive man who knows exactly what he is doing and why he is doing it; the bawling, ranting demagogue; the dramatic and emotional pleader; the deft parliamentarian; the bewildered and ineffectual little man; and the silent and supine person who sits through session after session merely answering to his name. There

* George B. Galloway, *Congress at the Crossroads.*

are those inspired by an ideal of real service to their country as well as their district, and others who represent special interests and care only for their own group.

The "confusion" and the "astonishment" presented by the House rest on those elements which make it a distinct contrast to the Senate. The House is large. The membership, drawn from many walks of life, consists of somewhat younger, less experienced men and women who serve comparatively short terms. The opportunities for prominence and leadership come slowly and grudgingly. Pressure from the "folks back home," particularly from special-interest groups, as well as from the "whips" in the House itself, is less likely to be ignored than it is in the Senate. Debate is severely restricted. The votes of individual members are often subject to strict party controls.

The Constitution gives the House certain special powers, the most important being the power to initiate bills for raising revenues. Yet, in actual practice, revenue bills may originate in both houses.

Strategy in Congress

The curtain rises on a new Congress. The opening of a new Congress is marked by a number of formalities, simply and quickly executed at times, or performed in an atmosphere of bitter conflict at others.

The House of Representatives is called to order by the clerk of the previous House, who administers the oath of office. The House then selects its officers (notably the presiding officer, the *Speaker*), and adopts the rules of procedure of the last House, possibly with some changes. It votes on the designation of committees and notifies the other house of Congress and the President of the United States that it is ready for business.

Much of the same procedure is followed in the Senate. Here, however, there is no struggle over the choice of a presiding officer, as is often the case in the House, since the Vice President of the United States presides over the Senate. But this body does choose from its membership a president *pro tempore*, who is to take the chair in the absence of the Vice President. When formalities of organization have been disposed of, the houses meet jointly to receive the Presidential message.

And so a great drama is enacted on the national stage, a drama filled with plots and counter-plots, with heroes and villains, with

The *Congressional Record* is a daily publication that records all debates, all votes, and all other important activities as they occur on the floor of both houses of Congress.

successes and failures, with comedy and tragedy. Backstage there are countless shrewd and subtle maneuvers, invisible to the beholder of the spectacle "out front." Yet that is how the spectacle is made possible. An audience of nationwide and even worldwide dimensions watches this drama for several months. Moreover (to end our analogy here), the drama is a highly meaningful one for all of us. What Congress does or fails to do will inevitably have far-reaching effects on our lives—perhaps in ways of which we are not even dimly aware at the moment.

Throughout each session, Congress is extremely busy. In 1965 alone, for example, more than 14,000 measures or resolutions were introduced, not counting the appointments voted on by the Senate. Almost hopelessly, Congress tries to satisfy the thousand-and-one forces that try to influence it, demanding, threatening, or pleading for action of one kind or another.

Control of the House: The Speaker. For the reasons that we have already considered in this chapter, the process of legislation in the House, far more than in the Senate, resembles the workings of a vast machine. It is a machine operated and controlled, for the most part, by small contributing groups, or even by individual leaders, in whom great powers are vested.

Foremost is the *Speaker*, himself a member of the House, who exercises a strong influence on legislation. He is elected to his position by the members of the House itself, the actual power of choice being vested in the majority party. He is more than just a presiding officer. He casts a vote, as does every other Representative. He has much to say about appointments to committees. Moreover, by a law passed in 1947, the Speaker became the third individual in the Presidential succession. In other words, he succeeds to the Presidency in the event that the offices of both the President and the Vice President become vacant.

"Invisible government" in the House. The Speaker of the House is a person of great influence. He not only has the power to recognize or ignore Representatives who wish to address the House but also steers the course of legislation. He does this primarily by choosing the committee to which each bill will be referred. In many cases, he may be able to choose between a committee which is known to be hostile to a bill and one which is considered more favorable. This is not to say that the Speaker single-handedly determines the course of action. Actually, he is assisted by a small group of leaders of his party and their aides.

First, there is the *Rules Committee*. This group decides what matters shall be debated on the floor of the House—when; for how long; and when a vote is to be taken.* Second, there are the "floor leaders" of each party, including both majority and minority leaders. Each assumes general direction over the solidarity and the discipline in his party ranks. Each is aided by prominent members of the party—known traditionally as "whips" but now more politely as "assistant majority (or minority) leaders." In the case of the majority party, there is also a "steering committee" in charge of the party program, which may have the backing of the White House. Finally, back of the entire scene is the party caucus, or the private and secret conference of the party members, for the purpose of uniting in common action. It is the caucus which decides on policies to be followed regarding rules, choice of committees, treatment of refractory

* In 1965, the House adopted a rule under which a majority of its members can prevent the Rules Committee from "strangling" legislation. Under the rule, a majority (218) can bring any bill to the floor for a vote after 21 days regardless of the attitude of the Rules Committee. Another method for preventing a committee from bottling up a bill is to get a majority of the House (218) to back a "discharge petition." Such action takes the bill away from the committee and brings it to the House for a vote. The Speaker of the House usually does not sign discharge petitions.

members, and the fate of pending legislation. Such action is usually binding on the participants. The caucus itself is, not infrequently, subject to the domination of powerful leaders of the party in the House and in the administration.

Leadership in the Senate. The character of individual and group leadership in the Senate is quite similar to that in the House, but with some exceptions. The Vice President of the United States, who presides over the Senate, is hardly comparable to the Speaker of the House. His role is more like that of an ordinary chairman. He exercises little influence on the politics of the Senate, especially when his own political affiliation is different from that of the majority. It is, rather, the chairmen of the more important committees who wield decisive power. In the Senate, too, the caucus is a less binding force than in the House. This is further evidence of the relatively greater freedom of the individual Senator.

Self-discipline in both Houses. The Constitution gives both houses much latitude in the matter of their day-to-day procedures. For example, the sessions are generally open to the public, but each house may determine when a session is to be secret. In this respect, the rules of the Senate are of particular interest. That body often meets in "closed," "secret," or "executive" session to consider treaties or appointments. The Senate recently adopted a rule specifying the circumstances under which matters are to be considered in a "closed" session.

The Constitution provides that a "majority of each House shall constitute a quorum to do business," and that "at the desire of one-fifth of those present" the vote of each member on any question must be recorded. Yet, the determination of what constitutes being "present" is left to each house. Similarly, each house adopts for itself a large number of other rules regarding the introduction of bills, their consideration, and the method of voting upon them.

The Constitution declares that each house may "punish its members for disorderly behavior, and with the concurrence of two-thirds, expel a member." In the interpretation of this rule, much is obviously left to the discretion of each house. On occasion, the House of Representatives has disciplined members for various infractions of its rules, such as absenteeism or engaging in a brawl. It has expelled some members, or refused to seat them, for acts considered treasonable or grossly improper. The

Senate, in contrast, has been more restrained in exercising this privilege. Any extremes in discipline would hardly be acceptable in what many still regard as a "gentlemen's club." Nevertheless, in 1955, Senator Joseph McCarthy of Wisconsin, who had been chairman of an investigating committee, was "condemned" for his abuse of fellow-Senators by a vote of 67 to 22.

In 1967, the House of Representatives voted to *exclude* representative Adam Clayton Powell of New York City from the 90th Congress because of charges of misconduct. He filed suit, arguing that a Congressman who met the constitutional requirements (see Art. I, Sec. 2, Cl. 2) could not be kept from taking his seat. (In the meantime, Powell was re-elected to the 91st Congress.) In 1969, the Supreme Court agreed with Powell, ruling that the exclusion was unconstitutional. In other words, Congress is limited to judging whether an elected representative meets the qualifications of age, citizenship, and residence. Any other interpretation would be incompatible with representative government because it would give Congress, not the people, the ultimate electoral power. Of course, Congress still has the power to *expel* a member, but such action requires a two-thirds vote (See Art. I, Sec. 5, Cl. 2).

The lone dissenter to this decision, Justice Stewart, argued that, since the 90th Congress had already passed into history, the Court would be wise to refrain from deciding on so difficult a case. But the Warren Court thought it was important to draw a distinction between the exclusion of a duly elected member and his expulsion.

The Committee System

The composition and the selection of committees. So vast, detailed, and specialized is the work of Congress that the membership of each house is divided into a number of permanent *standing committees* and many temporary ones. These are occupied with special fields of activity and constitute, in effect, small legislative groups. As of 1971, there were twenty-one standing committees in the House and sixteen in the Senate. They are listed on page 34.

Each standing committee contains members of both the majority and the minority parties, roughly in proportion to the division of party membership in the entire house. Membership is

COMMITTEES IN THE HOUSE	COMMITTEES IN THE SENATE
Rules	Rules and Administration
Ways and Means	Finance
Appropriations	Appropriations
Foreign Affairs	Foreign Relations
Banking and Currency	Banking and Currency
Armed Services	Armed Services
District of Columbia	District of Columbia
Post Office and Civil Service	Post Office and Civil Service
Judiciary	Judiciary
Public Works	Public Works
Agriculture	Agriculture and Forestry
Government Operations	Government Operations
Interior and Insular Affairs	Interior and Insular Affairs
Science and Astronautics	Aeronautical and Space Sciences
Interstate and Foreign Commerce	Commerce
Education and Labor	Labor and Public Welfare
Merchant Marine and Fisheries	
House Administration	
Veterans Affairs	

Internal Security (*formerly* "Un-American Activities")
Standards of Official Conduct

selected, as far as possible, on the basis of seniority and special aptitudes or interests. Seniority also plays a determining role in the choice of committee chairmen, although many observers of Congress feel that the choice ought to be determined more on the basis of ability and willingness to work. In theory, the selection of committees is a function of the entire chamber. In reality, as we have seen, the choice is made by a caucus of each party, or more specifically, by a few dominant individuals in the caucus.

The prestigious committees. In most cases, the sphere of a committee's work and authority is indicated fairly well by its name—*e.g.*, Agriculture, Armed Services, Banking and Currency, etc. But this does not apply to several important committees.

The House *Rules Committee*, for example, has vast powers. So many bills are introduced in the House each year that some sort of screening is essential before they can be considered by the full chamber. Not only has the Rules Committee the power of life and death over most bills introduced in the House, but it also determines the length of debate on a given bill and which sections of a bill may be amended during the debate. Another key group in the House is the *Ways and Means Committee*, which is in charge of all revenue-raising measures. It corresponds to the Finance Committee of the Senate.

In the Senate, the *Foreign Relations Committee* is of prime importance because of the Senate's authority in foreign affairs, specifically in regard to the ratification of treaties. This power is not matched by the House Foreign Affairs Committee.

The work of committees. A committee decides the fate of almost every bill that is introduced within its sphere of activity. The committee may approve the bill, thus practically assuring its passage by the house. The committee may alter the bill. It may fail to report on it, or reject it outright, in either case "burying" the bill. The committee may even write a new bill. Each house has the machinery for "calling out of committee" bills that have been "pigeonholed" or "buried," or for rejecting the recommendations of a committee. This is especially true of the Senate. But in most instances the committee's decision stands.

Special investigative functions. There is another aspect of the work of Congressional committees which forms an integral part of the lawmaking process. This is the power to conduct hearings or investigations. Such inquiries are held by a standing committee or by a specially selected committee of either house, or by a specially selected committee of both houses. A hearing may grow out of a desire to get facts or viewpoints on pending bills, or to remedy possible shortcomings in such bills. Also, an investigation of some disturbing conditions may lay the groundwork for remedial legislation.

Investigating committees are granted special appropriations and are equipped with facilities for collecting data. They have the advice of experts and of witnesses who have a particular interest or some specialized information about the area being investigated. A Congressional committee can serve subpoenas and force an individual to appear before it and testify. This power has often been upheld by the courts. (Of course, witnesses may take refuge in the 5th Amendment guarantee against self-incrimination.)

One of the investigative duties of Congressional committees is the so-called "watchdog" function by means of which Congress determines whether the administrative agencies are carrying out their duties as prescribed by law. The need for this probing into the operations of the Federal bureaucracy is easy to understand when one bears in mind the vast powers which have been entrusted to these Executive bodies. (See Chapters 5 and 6.) In recent years, Congress has steadily increased the number of probes conducted per session. Conspicuous among the investigations that have attracted much attention and caused widespread debate are those dealing with activities that threaten internal security.

The pros and cons of the committee system. Much criticism has been leveled against our committee system of lawmaking. Some observers maintain that the committee system concentrates enormous power in the hands of a few legislators. It tends to cause a reduction of interest in the work of the house as a whole. It reduces opportunities for open, vigorous debate. It encourages the secret activities of pressure groups or lobbyists, and promotes "logrolling" or the "swapping" of favors among Congressmen. It has been widely charged that due process (see Chapter 1) was denied to witnesses or "defendants" who appeared before such groups as the House Un-American Activities Committee (now the Internal Security Committee) and the Senate Government Operations Committee. Critics have alleged that the reputation of many witnesses was irreparably damaged, even when there was no solid evidence against them.

Frequent criticism has also been directed against the seniority rule observed by committees. Under this rule, as we have already noted, a member of a committee holds his post until he dies or leaves the House or Senate, unless he quits the committee to become a member of a more important group. The resulting vacancy, should one of these things happen, gives a new member a chance to take his place at the bottom. The newcomer must then begin to accumulate his own seniority, and it may be a long time before he can hope to exercise much influence.

The member of the majority party who has the greatest seniority becomes the chairman of the committee. Seniority is not just one factor determining the chairmanship; it is the *only* factor. The chairman of a committee may be, and often is, a conscientious and knowledgeable legislator. The fact is, however, that if he belongs to the majority party and has the seniority, he will become chairman without regard to his qualifications.

The importance of this seniority rule is magnified by the fact that a committee chairman is in a position of great influence. True, he has only one vote in committee proceedings, like all his fellow-members, but he also exercises a number of special powers.

(1) He calls the meetings of his committee and generally manages the schedule of legislation to be considered. (2) He names members to subcommittees and apportions bills among them. (3) He decides whether committee sessions are to be open or closed. (4) He often casts proxy votes which absent committee members have left to his discretion. (5) In conducting hearings on proposed bills, he decides which witnesses will have a chance to express their views and for how long. (6) He may choose whether or not to recognize a committee member seeking to get the floor at a committee session.

From time to time, there has been criticism of the "autocratic" manner in which some committee chairmen exercise their extensive powers. Committee members in both houses have been known to "revolt" against what they considered excessive domination by a strong chairman. A well-publicized example of this occurred in 1966, involving Representative Adam Clayton Powell of New York, Chairman of the House Education and Labor Committee. By a 27-1 vote, the members of that committee stripped Mr. Powell of many of his powers. The chairman was forbidden to act alone on any matters of substance, including the delay of bills and the hiring of staff members. Mr. Powell was re-elected to the 90th Congress (convening in January, 1967), but the status of his chairmanship was never settled because the House voted to exclude him before he took his seat. (See page 33.)

These criticisms of the committee system, as it actually operates, have been emphasized by many students of government, and there have been repeated demands for remedial action. On the other hand, it can scarcely be denied that the committee system, for all its questionable aspects, greatly facilitates the operation of our national government. If not for the use of committees, Congress would be hopelessly "swamped"; many bills, including highly constructive ones, would necessarily receive little or no attention. With all the weaknesses of the seniority rule, many committee members do develop invaluable experience and special qualifications in the field with which they are dealing. Thus, they are in a position to provide expert leadership in expediting a sound legislative program. The workings of a Congressional committee are usually brisk and businesslike, with emphasis on getting things done and with a notable absence of the "talking to the gallery" that sometimes characterizes Congressional sessions.

How Bills Become Laws

The machinery for passing bills. A draft of a proposed law is known as a *bill*. Such a measure may be introduced by any Representative or Senator. The bill, in all probability, has been drawn up by some appropriate committee, or by a government official or department, or by an interested group outside Congress. It may have been urged by the administration and recommended by it as necessary or "must" legislation. Very likely it has been closely examined by experts before being introduced.

Some of these experts serve on the staff of the *Legislative Counsel*. They render technical aid to Congressmen drafting bills. Another body called the *Legislative Reference Service* conducts research on questions pertinent to current legislation. All information accumulated in this way is available to Congressmen.

Once presented in either house, the bill is assigned by the presiding officer to the proper committee. The committee disposes of it in one of several ways outlined above. A bill which is finally "reported out" by the committee is placed on the calendar for consideration by the entire house. But bills of exceptional importance are likely to be given priority on the calendar. The extent of discussion on a measure depends on its importance, on the amount of opposition to it, and on the rules of each house. Frequently the recommendation of a committee is acceptable to both houses.

When a bill has been approved by a majority in each house of Congress, it is sent to the President. He may make the bill law by signing it. Or he may veto it and return it with a statement of his objections to the house in which it originated. The bill can then be passed over the veto by a two-thirds vote of each house. Or the President may take no action at all. In that case, if, at the end of ten days (Sundays excepted) Congress is still in session, the bill becomes a law without the President's signature. If, however, Congress has adjourned within the ten-day interval, the bill is "dead." The latter course is known as a *"pocket veto."* Bills which have failed of passage by the time Congress adjourns must be introduced afresh in the subsequent Congress if they are to receive consideration again.

Resolving conflicts in conference. Before a bill may be sent to the President for his action, it must be passed by each house in

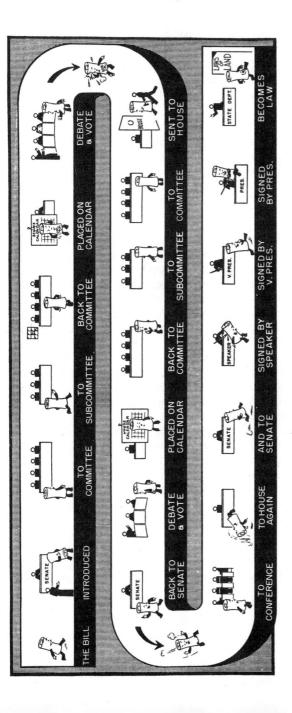

This chart summarizes the "life history" of a bill that is introduced in the Senate.

Weekly News Review

identical form. But when the two houses pass somewhat different versions of the same bill, a *conference committee* is created—unless the house which first passed the bill accepts all of the amendments added by the second, or the second retreats from its position.

The task of a conference committee is to prepare a single measure acceptable to both houses. Such a committee is composed of Senators and Representatives appointed by the President of the Senate and the Speaker of the House of Representatives. The Senators and Representatives are not necessarily equal in numbers but they have an equal voice in arriving at decisions.

Debate and filibustering. Whatever truth resides in the phrase "our billion-dollar debating society," by which a recent book described Congress, it can hardly apply with equal force to both houses. The general rules of procedure in the House of Representatives are far more stringent and inflexible than are those of the Senate. A former Speaker recognized the difference when he said, "The only rule observed by the Senate is to do what it wants when it wants to." The most conspicuous difference between the two houses lies in the attitude toward debating.

Chiefly because of the size of the House, opportunities for debate are severely limited. No member may speak on any question for more than an hour. An exception is made if a member has received unanimous consent to speak longer, or if he is the sponsor of the bill, or is a committeeman reporting on a bill. The Speaker need not recognize members in the order in which they rise to speak. Even when the House resolves itself for more informal and more extensive discussion into a "Committee of the Whole," the length of debate is restricted. A motion to take up the "previous question," if carried, ends debate, and the House proceeds at once to a vote.

The Senate, on the other hand, presents a paradox. It is, at the same time, "the greatest deliberative body in the world" and, according to President Wilson, "the only legislative body in the world which could not act when its majority was ready for action." By this Wilson meant that in the United States Senate, as in few other legislative bodies, a small minority may have the power to prevent the majority from exercising its will, or even from bringing a matter to a vote. Senate rules provide for the right of unlimited debate, which means that there is no limit set as to the amount of time a Senator who has the floor can continue to speak. Senate rules also require the presiding officer to grant the floor to members in the order in which they rise.

The results of these practices have been both good and bad. They have been good because they have promoted free speech, which is essential to democratic government, and have encouraged careful deliberation. They have helped to bring out the talents of strong personalities, to block objectionable legislation, to give hope to minorities, and to stimulate an interest in the processes of government. They have been bad because they have encouraged *filibustering*. This is a practice of delaying or blocking a vote by speeches (often long and extraneous), motions, amendments, and roll calls. In effect, the aim of a filibuster is to "talk a bill to death." Filibustering was at one time particularly effective in obstructing legislation during the closing days of the "short session" of Congress (page 24). But at all times, it can be a potent weapon in the hands (or rather, the mouths) of well-organized minorities or of unyielding individuals. Whoever they are, they have cultivated and perfected the art of "killing time" by such devices as reading endlessly from the Bible or from the Washington telephone directory, or even reciting the multiplication table.

PUTTING THE JACK IN THE BOX

This cartoon was published in 1917, shortly after the passage of the original cloture rule. The cartoonist confidently predicted that this rule would bring filibustering under effective control. Like many other political prophecies, this one was not too well borne out by events

Portland Oregonian

There is, to be sure, a *closure* (or *cloture*) rule, adopted in 1917, when a "little group of willful men," as President Wilson characterized them, blocked his proposal for arming merchant vessels. This closure rule provides that a petition to close debate on a bill becomes operative when signed by sixteen Senators. On the second day after such a petition is filed with the President of the Senate, the Senate must vote on whether or not to limit debate. A full two-thirds of the membership (67 Senators) is necessary to approve closure. If closure is voted, each Senator has only one hour in which to discuss the bill, and when discussion is finished, a final vote on it must be taken. In 1963, an attempt was made to change the closure rule so that only a three-fifths vote would be required to limit debate, but this proposal was itself filibustered to death. As of 1966, the closure rule had been invoked only seven times since its adoption in 1917. In 1964, closure was invoked by a vote of 70 to 30 after 24 days of debate on a bill aimed at protecting the voting rights of Negroes (*Civil Rights Act of 1964*).

"The Third House of Congress"

The influence of lobbies. Edmund Burke, a great British parliamentarian of the 18th century, once said to his constituents: "Your representative owes you not only his industry but his judgment." To that statement Burke might have added "and his independence." Senator Carter Glass of Virginia observed: "I prefer to think of a United States Senator as the representative of the sovereignty of his state and subject every moment to the promptings of his own conscience and the preservation of his intellectual integrity." Nevertheless, it is a characteristic of both Congress and our state legislatures that complete independence of judgment has become next to impossible. For the average legislator is hemmed in on all sides. Pre-election promises, memorials, letters, and petitions always haunt him. He cannot ignore the dictates of his party leaders, or the presence of powerfully organized groups and minorities outside Congress, or the thundering of the potent mass-communications media.

The Bill of Rights in the Federal Constitution and in the constitution of every state protects the right of the people "to petition the Government for a redress of grievances." And petition they do, grievances or no grievances. Our concern here,

Lobbyists and pressure groups have often played a constructive role in bringing about reforms in our social and political institutions. In this photograph, taken in New York City in 1913, we see a group of women about to leave on a "pilgrimage" to Washington to plead the cause of woman suffrage.

however, is not with the right of petition as such. The danger lies in the domination of our lawmaking bodies by "pressure groups" and their agents in the legislative capitals. Originally, the tactic used was to approach the lawmakers in the lobbies or ante-chambers of the legislative halls (hence the expression "lobbying"). The methods, today, are far more comprehensive and subtle.

There is hardly an economic or social interest of any consequence in the United States today which, in one way or another, does not resort to lobbying in an effort to influence and control legislation. In the national capital, these attempts are wide and varied as to purpose and method. They may represent agitation for appropriations to please a local constituency—for example, for construction of a new post office. They may strive to satisfy some widespread popular demand, as for tax relief. Much of this sort of agitation is undoubtedly "pork-barrel" politics. Its aim is, frankly, to make a raid on the "pork-barrel"—meaning, the national treasury. The work of lobbyists may be to secure legislation favorable to such interests as farmers, organized labor, the public utilities, businessmen, teachers, and religious and reform organizations and movements.

Many lobbies are temporary. They come and go. They succeed or fail. Either they disappear altogether, or they rise with new vigor, as the occasion warrants. Other groups, like the U.S. Chamber of Commerce, the National Association of Manufacturers, the American Medical Association, the National Education Association, the AFL-CIO, the American Legion, and the various farmers' associations have a permanent organization. It is said that the organizations engaged in lobbying fill a few closely printed pages in the Washington telephone directory. In 1965, there were 4000 lobbyists in Washington (more than seven for each Senator and Congressman) courting the nation's lawmakers with one paramount objective: to influence legislation.

How lobbies work. In the nature of things, effective lobbying is no longer the province of amateurs. It is, rather, that of highly trained "go-getters." In the ranks are so-called "public-relations counselors," journalists, lawyers, politicians, ex-Congressmen, ex-military figures, and other former government officials. They are masters of their craft. They know how to "cut through red tape," how to "see the right people," and how to raise large sums of money for their purposes. They also know how to whip up public opinion, and how to organize letter-writing or telegram-sending campaigns directed at Congressmen or at the President. The lobbies are effective, and there is evidence that they are becoming more effective. Indeed, we now hear of "super-lobbies."

Can lobbies be controlled? It has been charged that lobbies tend to make government a "mere recording machine" for the demands of special groups and localities. "Our representatives," said one newspaper editorial, "have become political robots merely to be worked by telegrams and radio speeches." To remedy these alarming and possibly dangerous conditions, it has become necessary to exercise much more rigid control over lobbyists and their activities. Under the Legislative Reorganization Act of 1946, lobbyists are required to register with the Justice Department, to supply detailed data about themselves and their methods of operation, to file periodic reports as to their sources of contributions and expenditures, and to make annual reports to Congress.

Lobbies, an inevitable feature of democratic government. In a democratic country as large and as diverse as the United States, lobbies are a natural, and indeed inevitable, feature of government. Admittedly, the motives of the lobbyists are often based on self-interest, but it is only fair to add that they have many constructive achievements to their credit. Consider, for example, the lobby of the National Education Association for Federal aid to education, the lobby spearheaded by Negro organizations for civil rights legislation, the labor lobby working (among other things) for protective legislation for migratory workers, the anti-billboard lobby, and the Medicare lobby. Such lobbies have represented, in the main, a sort of informal alliance among labor, consumer, and "uplift" groups. Then, too, lobbyists are often experts in their field (for example, control of narcotic drugs) and are in a position to give specialized information to Congressmen at public hearings and in other ways. Such information may be slanted, but it may also be valid and valuable. It is well known that a substantial proportion of the bills presented in Congress are actually written (at least in their original form) by lobbyists.

In short, lobbying represents a sort of see-saw of achievement and frustration within the context of the democratic process. For the achievements to outweigh the frustrations, we need not only responsible lobbyists but also an alert citizenry and intelligent, public-spirited legislators.

NOTE: For proposed reforms of Congress, see Chapter 3, pages 77-81.

Terms You Should Know

At large. Chosen by and representing a large political unit, rather than a specific subdivision of that unit. For example, a Congressman-at-large is elected by the voters of an entire state; a Councilman-at-large by the voters of an entire city.

Bicameral. Composed of two houses, as the U. S. Congress.

Calendar. A list of bills up for consideration by a legislature, or a list of cases pending in court.

Caucus. A meeting of party leaders (usually within a legislative body) to name candidates or determine policy.

Census. Official counting of the population. Since 1790 the national census has been taken every ten years.

Cloture (Closure). Method of ending legislative debate by forcing the question to an immediate vote.

Conflict of interest. A conflict between a legislator's private financial interests and his public role as a representative of the people.

Filibustering, The practice of delaying a vote by speeches (often long and extraneous) and by other time-wasting tactics, such as motions, amendments, and roll calls.

Gerrymandering. The practice of drawing the boundaries of legislative districts in such a way as to give advantage to one party.

Immunity. Exemption from a duty or penalty.

Lobbying, Methods employed by special-interest groups to influence members of legislatures.

Logrolling. Mutual help or vote-trading among legislators in order to gain passage of a bill—often "pork-barrel" legislation.

Majority. More than half. In an election, more than half the total number of votes cast.

"One man, one vote." Principle enunciated by the Supreme Court according to which legislative representation (for state legislatures and for Congress) is to be apportioned in such a way that, as nearly as practicable, one man's vote will be worth as much as another's in electing legislators.

Pairing. An agreement between two members of a legislative body, such as Congress, not to vote on a forthcoming bill. The two members in question are usually of different parties, or are aligned on opposite sides in relation to the bill. Thus, the two votes "cancel out," and neither party gains or loses as a result of the paired abstention. A member of Congress may seek to pair his vote when he finds it difficult or impossible to be present on the day when a bill is scheduled to come up for a vote. Also, a legislator may try to arrange a pair when he prefers, for political reasons, not to be recorded as casting a vote either for or against a controversial measure.

Patronage. Power to make appointments to public office.

Pigeonholing. The process of laying something aside indefinitely, ostensibly for future consideration but actually as a means of getting rid of it. In Congress, for example, bills may be "buried" in committee.

Plurality. Largest vote in an election; not necessarily a majority.

Pocket veto. Process by which a President may prevent a bill from becoming law by failing to act on it. This applies if Congress adjourns within less than ten days after submitting the bill to him. Some governors also have the pocket-veto power.

"Pork-barrel." The term applied to legislation or other governmental action to secure appropriations for projects of doubtful utility which are favored by local political interests.

Private bill. A legislative act which applies to an individual, rather than to the population as a whole.

Reapportionment. Redrawing the boundary lines of election districts so that legislative representation (for example, within a state) is redistributed.

Redistricting. Essentially the same as reapportionment.

Resolution. A formal expression of opinion by a legislative body. In Congress, a resolution passed by one house is said to be *simple;* a resolution passed by both houses is said to be *joint.* A joint resolution has the force of law when signed by the President.

Seniority rule. Assignment of committee members and committee chairmen on the basis of length of service. This rule is followed both in Congress and in state legislatures.

Session. Period during which a court or legislature is sitting.

Speaker. Presiding officer of the House of Representatives.

Term. Period fixed by law for which a person is elected or appointed to public office.

Veto. Power of an executive to reject bills passed by the legislature which require his signature in order to become law.

Questions and Problems Based on the Text

1. Explain the historical origin of the *bicameral legislature* of the Federal government.

2. What are the constitutional qualifications for members of the House of Representatives? For United States Senators?

3. How do you account for the recent increase of Congressmen from the South and the Pacific Coast states? Which states have *lost* Congressmen? Why?

4. How have recent court decisions checked gerrymandering? Why have rural areas, in general, been opposed to these decisions?

5. What control exists in each house of Congress over the admission and the expulsion of its members? Give examples to show how each house has exercised this control.

6. When vacancies occur in the House of Representatives and the Senate, how are they filled?

7. How did the 20th ("Lame Duck") Amendment come to be passed? What reforms did it introduce?

8. What special privileges are granted by the Constitution to members of Congress? Do you agree that these privileges are justified?

9. It is generally agreed that members of the United States Senate have greater power and prestige than Representatives. How do you explain this?

10. Compare the Speaker and the Vice President in their roles as presiding officers of their respective houses of Congress.

11. What is mean by "invisible government" in Congress?

12. What functions do the committees in Congress perform? What are the reasons for their power and influence? What benefits and what evils result from our committee system of legislation?

13. How does a bill become a law in the Federal government?

14. Why is filibustering resorted to much more readily in the Senate than in the House? What reforms have been suggested for limiting the filibuster? With what results?

15. What is the reason for lobbying? What methods do lobbyists use? Is lobbying good or bad? Give reasons.

16. The following reforms have been proposed by United States Senator Joseph C. Clark of Pennsylvania. What do you think of each? Give your reasons.

   (*a*) To change the rules and procedures of both houses of Congress so that a majority can act when it is ready to act.

   (*b*) To prohibit participation in party conferences to a member of Congress who refuses to support his party's Presidential candidate.

   (*c*) To develop party discipline to the extent that no Congressman unwilling to support the national platform plank of his party in the area of jurisdiction of a particular committee be allowed to serve on that committee, much less be permitted to become its chairman.

   (*d*) To overhaul the policy committees of both parties so that the committees of the majority party in each house may meet with their opposite numbers in the other house and develop ways of enacting their party platform into law. This might be supplemented by periodic conferences with the President for the purpose of carrying out his legislative program.

   (*e*) To prohibit a Senator from holding the floor for more than two hours unless he is floor-managing a bill or has the unanimous consent of the Senate.

   (*f*) To fill committee vacancies without regard to seniority.

   (*g*) To amend the Constitution so that representation in the Senate will be based more or less on state population.

Ideas to Think About and Discuss

1. *"The people never give up their liberties but under some delusion."*
   —EDMUND BURKE

2. *"Act as if the whole election depended on your single vote, and as if the whole Parliament on that single person whom you now choose to be a member of it."* —JOHN WESLEY

3. *"I believe the Senate is constantly legislating in the shadow of both the House Rules Committee and the filibuster."*
   —U. S. SENATOR JOSEPH S. CLARK

4. *"Tyranny does not reveal itself all at once; it matures slowly, in the course of a series of arbitrary acts on the dictator's part and a series of concessions and abdications on the part of the people."*
   —IGNAZIO SILONE

5. *"A spirit of national masochism prevails, encouraged by an effete corps of impudent snobs who characterize themselves as intellectiuals."*
   —VICE PRESIDENT SPIRO T. AGNEW

6. *"A weak President means a strong Congress. But a strong Congress does not mean a Congress united in determination of its direction. It means a Congress led in many directions by men whose particular purposes have never been fused into one strong and central purpose."*
   —HAROLD J. LASKI

7. *"Senators under the Constitution have the duty, not merely the right to render advice, not on the day-to-day conduct of foreign policy, but on its direction and philosophy as these are shaped by major decisions."*
   —U. S. SENATOR J. WILLIAM FULBRIGHT

8. *"If truth were self-evident, eloquence would not be necessary."*
   —CICERO

CHAPTER 3

How Congress Uses Its Powers

The Powers of Congress and the "Shadow of the Constitution"

The powers delegated to Congress by the Constitution. If you were to search our Constitution for detailed statements of how Congress is legislating for a nation of close to 200 million people, confronted by numerous complex domestic and world problems, your task would be a disappointing one. No one can get an adequate idea of the vast powers which our national government possesses, which it has exercised, and which it could exercise, merely by examining the Constitution. In a number of places in the Constitution, particularly in Article I, Section 8, you will find a listing of the powers which have been delegated to Congress. But these powers in themselves hardly serve to explain how we have evolved from the horse-and-buggy era to an era of jet aircraft, radio-TV, atomic energy, automation, and space travel.

The framers of the Constitution, for all their wisdom, could not foresee this astonishing transformation. It is perhaps the greatest possible testimonial to their foresight that they expressed the powers of the national government in broad and general terms. They crowned this delegation of authority with the "elastic clause." This has made possible the expansion of powers otherwise definitely enumerated and, therefore, limited.

The everlasting question of constitutionality. The area of our government which has been instrumental in giving direction to our national growth has been the United States Supreme Court. Bear in mind that ours is a government which exercises authority limited by a written Constitution. We can then understand more readily the ultimate significance of what the Supreme Court says the national government may or may not do. The great battles over constitutional authority, from the beginnings of the Republic to the present day, have, sooner or later, been contested and decided in the Supreme Court. Hamilton, the exponent of a "loose" or "liberal" interpretation of the Constitution, might challenge Jefferson, the defender of "strict" or "literal" construction, on the constitutionality of the United States Bank. Calhoun and Webster might differ over the constitutional right of the national government to control slavery in the territories. McKinley and Bryan might be at odds over the constitutional power to annex and control territories beyond the seas. Conservative Republicans might see in New Deal legislation a threat to the liberties guaranteed by the Constitution; and liberal Democrats might as staunchly appeal to the same Constitution to justify a far-ranging program of economic and social legislation.

Sooner or later, the issue of constitutionality has been decided by the Supreme Court. It is always in the "shadow of the Constitution" (to borrow a phrase from Charles Beard) that these decisions have been made. The eminent English jurist, William Blackstone, said, "True it is, that what Parliament doth, no authority upon earth can undo." That, in view of the ever-recurring question of constitutionality, cannot be said of our Congress. The United States Congress, unlike the British Parliament, is checked by the Federal judiciary.

The Supreme Court as the arbiter of the powers of Congress. Are we to infer, then, that our Constitution is so inflexible, and the Supreme Court so unresponsive to changing conditions, that progress is always arrested? To draw such a conclusion would be to disregard the marvelous advances which the nation has made. To concede this would be to forget that the Constitution, through amendment, custom, legislative acts, and judicial interpretation, has been made to conform to changing needs. Chief Justice John Marshall said about 150 years ago: "The Constitution must be adapted to the various crises in human affairs." The Constitution has been adapted to various crises ever since, by Congress, with the approval of the President and the judiciary.

Today, a century and a half after Marshall, the principle of necessary conformity to the "letter and spirit of the Constitution" is still the guide in determining how far the national government may go in exercising its powers. There is no better proof of this contention than can be found in a large number of the decisions of the Supreme Court. For example, in the epoch-making opinion which nullified the National Recovery Act in 1935, a unanimous Court decided that "extraordinary conditions may call for extraordinary remedies. But the argument necessarily stops short of an attempt to justify action which lies outside the sphere of constitutional authority." In other words, the Constitution is still the supreme law of the land, and must not be "adapted" too freely.

The powers of Congress in the light of economic changes. The powers exercised by the government have had to be within the framework of the Constitution. But the swift and tremendous economic changes since 1865 have repeatedly raised the question of whether or not the adjustments to these changes have been consistent with the "letter and spirit of the Constitution." Since the Civil War, the Federal government has steadily extended its power, often at the expense of the states. The war itself set a precedent for centralization and expansion of Federal authority. "Big business," in the era that followed the Civil War, crossed state lines and extended overseas, requiring greater control by the national government. Many corporations, notably in the field of public utilities, sought redress in the Federal courts against state and local regulation. They claimed that this sort of regulation deprived them of property rights in violation of the 14th Amendment. More recently, World War I, the economic crisis following 1929, World War II, and the social changes following it have called forth an unprecedented enlargement and concentration of power. This recent development has affected both Congress and the Executive branch.

Small wonder, then, that citizens have asked: Is all this within the "sphere of the Constitution"? Shall the national government continue to interfere with private business and play the role of "economic policeman"? Is Washington encroaching unduly upon the powers of the states? How are we to regard the existence of a vast, intricate system of public authorities? Has this veritable army of officials and employees become a bureaucracy seeking to promote its own interests and those of its masters, rather than to serve the people? Or is it rather an establishment necessary to carry out the economic and humanitarian programs of modern society? Shall we admit that state lines are gradually disappearing and that the older distinctions between *interstate* and *intrastate* can no longer apply to effective control? Are we to view the assumption of authority by the President as something that resembles a dictatorship? Or is this necessary to deal effectively with urgent problems? Shall we say that the prime business of government is to promote economic well-being? If this is true, it follows that in a conflict between human rights and property rights, the former must prevail. All of these are pressing questions that face American citizens today.

How the powers of Congress are treated in this chapter. The powers of Congress are, for the most part, economic in character. They deal with control over commerce (that is, with transportation and communication, as well as trade), and over finance. It is the purpose of this chapter to discuss, at some length, the expansion of Federal control over "commerce," a field in which the Federal government is virtually paramount.

The development of the powers pertaining to finance will be treated later in this chapter and in subsequent chapters. Then we shall consider a number of miscellaneous powers concerning the administration of the Executive and Judicial branches, military matters, and Federal property. Finally, special powers of each house of Congress are covered in this chapter.

The Powers of Congress over Commerce and Business

The meaning of the word "commerce." The Constitution bestows upon Congress the power "to regulate commerce with foreign nations and among the several states and with the Indian tribes." Out of this general grant of power, and a few others no broader or more specific, have grown a vast number and variety of governmental activities. They have developed as a result of constant rapid changes from small colonial beginnings to highly organized business and world markets. To end the confusion which resulted from individual state control during the Confederation (1781-1789), the new Constitution lodged the power of regulating interstate and foreign commerce in the hands of the Federal government. It left the control of commerce within each state to the state itself.

At first, the Federal government was limited in application of the "commerce clause" to commodities which might be bought, sold, or exchanged. The powers were increased, however, by virtue of two noted Supreme Court decisions. In *Gibbons v. Ogden* (1824), the Court widened the scope of the world "regulate" and came close to saying that the power of Congress over interstate commerce is absolute. This decision "did more to knit the American people into an indivisible union than any other force in our history excepting war."* The other decision was the case of *Wabash Railroad v. Illinois* (1886), in which the Court gave Congress authority over the actual means of transportation.

Control over transportation: The railroads. Federal regulation of transportation took on greatly increased significance in 1887, with the passage of the Interstate Commerce Act. Prior to that year, the railroads had been under the control of the states. As a result of the decision in *Wabash Railroad v. Illinois,* control passed to Congress.

The *Interstate Commerce Commission,* created by Congress in 1887, is today one of the most important agencies for economic control in this country. During the early stage of its existence, however, the Commission was unable to accomplish much. It was overwhelmed by the aggressive and obstructive tactics of the railroads. But later Congressional legislation endowed it with immense regulatory powers over the railroads and their co-ordinated marine services, as well as over sleeping and dining cars, express companies and pipelines transporting oil and gas. Later, the ICC was given power to regulate motor buses and trucks engaged in interstate commerce.

Today, the ICC has the right to prescribe such matters as rates, schedules, hours of labor, safety devices, division of traffic, and mergers for the railroads and other transportation facilities under its jurisdiction. It also has the right to check on state regulations. For example, it may oppose state measures which appear likely to hinder the normal operation of commerce between the states.

The railroads are still an important artery of transportation, but they have experienced serious difficulties. They have often been operated uneconomically and wastefully. They have faced stiff competition from motor vehicles and airlines. Labor troubles have occurred again and again. Numerous attempts have, therefore, been made to modernize the railroads and to bring the competing forms of transportation under Federal control. Recent legislation has provided for new bases of rate-fixing designed to secure better income for the railroads. The consolidation of lines has been permitted by suspension of antitrust laws. Huge loans have been made by various Federal agencies, and special facilities have been provided to settle labor disputes.

However, many railroads continued to be in deep trouble, largely because their passenger operations, suffering from com-

* A. J. Beveridge, *The Life of John Marshall.*

petition of airlines, buses, and private cars, had become highly unprofitable. To deal with this situation, Congress set up in 1970 a quasi-governmental corporation called the *National Railroad Passenger Corporation*. This agency (as of May, 1971) took over all of the intercity passenger operations of American railroads. It began by leasing engines and passenger cars from the railroads but will eventually buy new equipment. It also rents from the roads use of their tracks and buys the services of operating crews. (Freight service remains entirely in the private ownership of the railroad companies.) The NRPC will run its service "for profit," and it is *not* subject to the restrictions of the ICC regarding such matters as fares and abandoning or increasing rail service. Indications are that the new national rail passenger system, known as *Amtrak*, will seek to upgrade passenger service in many ways, while getting rid of unprofitable runs already adequately served by other facilities.

Even with this major adjustment, the American railroad industry faces many serious problems: Will the government continue to help with large infusions of credit? Will management and labor cooperate in the public interest? Will the railroads work effectively with metropolitan transit authorities to help solve the headaches of mass transportation in urban-suburban areas?

The air transport industry is closely regulated under legislation enacted by Congress. This picture shows the interior of a giant "747" airliner capable of carrying 362 passengers.

Pan American World Airways, Inc.

Control over transportation; The airlines. The growth of transportation by air has been phenomenal. The airlines in 1940 accounted for about 12½% of all non-local commercial transportation (computed by passenger miles). By 1948, this figure had risen to 34½%, and to 46% in 1950. In 1969, the airlines flew about 96 billion passenger miles, representing roughly half of all commercial passenger transportation.

The rapid growth of civil aviation so overwhelmed existing regulatory agencies that Congress was prompted, in 1958, to create another agency—the *Federal Aviation Agency (FAA)*. The chief functions of the FAA are to control the air space over the United States, to promote air safety, to license planes and pilots, and to direct air and landing traffic. The *Civil Aeronautics Board (CAB)* retains jurisdiction over airline rates, routes, and schedules. Together, FAA (now in the Department of Transportation) and CAB (still an independent agency) exercise comprehensive powers to control and guide the civil aviation industry.

Control over transportation: The merchant marine. Transportation by water has likewise been subject to control by Congress. This control has been applied to navigation on inland waterways, to coastwise transportation, and to commerce on the high seas. The scope has included such matters as the inspection of goods and persons carried by vessels; the supervision of ships and their crews; the regulation of rate schedules; the construction and maintenance of harbors, lighthouses and bridges; the protection of our merchant shipping against foreign competition.

During the period between the two world wars, the Federal government spent some 900 million dollars to provide for an adequate merchant marine which could serve our mercantile, industrial, and agricultural interests, as well as possible wartime needs. In 1936, the Merchant Marine Act was passed to put into effect a long-range merchant shipbuilding program under a *Maritime Commission* of five members. Direct aid was provided for American steamship companies and shipyards. As the war emergency grew, the ship construction program was accelerated.

In the postwar years, the country was faced with the problem of what to do with its enormously expanded merchant marine. By the late 1960's, we still had one of the largest merchant fleets in the world (although somewhat smaller than that of such countries as Britain and Japan). But our ships were experiencing great trouble in meeting foreign competition. The

Merchant Marine Act of 1970 attempted to deal with this situation by granting subsidies to cover the extra costs of building ships in American yards, and also the extra costs of operating American ships, primarily because of higher wages.

Control over mass communication. Supervision over the communication of information and ideas represents not only an aspect of the application of the power to regulate commerce but also of the power "to establish post offices and post roads." Under these grants of power, Congress has regulated the mails and communication by telegraph, cable, telephone and radio-television broadcasting. It has exercised control over those agencies which are regarded as "post roads," that is, railroads, steamships, buses, and airplanes. It has given them franchises for transporting mail. Through the postal organization, Congress has provided for such familiar conveniences as systems of delivery even in remote sections of the country, money orders, parcel post, and postal savings banks. It has prescribed penalties for attempts at interfering with the mails. The importation and circulation within the country of various types of objectionable matter are considered criminal offenses.

In 1934, Congress centralized control over the telegraph, telephone and radio industries in a *Federal Communications Com-*

Television has had a far-reaching impact on every major phase of American political life. Here we see TV being used to bring a Presidential message to every corner of the land.

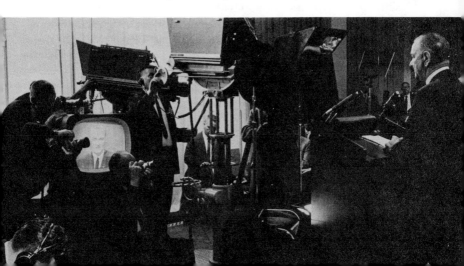

mission (*FCC*). Congress gave this body jurisdiction over the rates charged and the services furnished by the private organizations operating in the field. Radio broadcasting and, starting in the late 1940's, television became the subject of extensive government regulation. The FCC has the authority to license stations, to assign wave lengths, and to check harmful competition. It may require modification of programs that threaten to become prejudicial to the public interest.

Used to the fullest, the power to control the communication of ideas is tremendous. It can become a factor for good or evil. It can mold and mobilize public opinion. It can be transformed into a great educational and inspirational reserve. In time of peace and war, it has been used by countries ruled by dictatorial regimes to censor and to suppress information.

Commerce and the growth of our international prestige. The preceding discussion is sufficient to indicate that the control and the promotion of commerce constitute one of the most important activities of the Federal government. The Constitution itself gives little more than a hint of the vast powers and undertakings with which the government is concerned in the field of "commerce." This concern is both domestic and foreign, and its scope extends to areas hardly foreseen even a generation ago. With the ever-expanding international rule of the United States, the regulation, control, promotion, and protection of commerce may be said to have entered the most important phase of national economic activity. Our politics, our statesmanship, our decisions as to war and peace, and our relations with distant peoples, weak or powerful, depend, to a large extent, upon the wisdom of our actions in the field of commerce.

The protection of commerce. Congress has, in numerous ways, imposed prohibitions against undesirable tendencies which may arise in interstate and foreign commerce. For example, Congress has forbidden the passage from state to state, and the importation from abroad, of adulterated, misbranded, or falsely advertised foods, drugs, and cosmetics; of diseased plants and animals; of objectionable literature and "get-rich-quick" schemes such as lotteries. It has extended the application of the term "commerce" to restrict the movements of persons from state to state. This is illustrated by the "Lindbergh Law," which was designed to curb kidnapping.

To protect American agriculture and industry against foreign competition, Congress has, through its tariff-making powers, placed complete or partial curbs on imports. Tariff duties are the device most commonly used for this purpose. Congress has also restricted the character or the quantity of goods that may be imported. On the one hand, Congress has sought to protect commerce against excessive interference by the states. On the other hand, it has aimed to respect the regulatory activities of each state, in so far as these are concerned with the safety, health and comfort of its people—that is, with the exercise of the state's "police powers" (page 7). Congress has likewise exercised control over exports.

Control over "big business" combinations. American economic life is increasingly dominated by a relatively small number of giant corporations. These have expanded into practically every field of our economic life. Their tendency toward concentration, sometimes toward monopolistic or semi-monopolistic status, has led increasingly to governmental regulation. The operations of these corporations have been, for the most part, interstate in character. Effective control could hardly remain in the hands of each state. Control by Congress, therefore, became essential.

In the earlier period, the policy of the Federal government was basically to encourage competition and to proceed against combinations which interefered with the free movement of trade and commerce. Thus, the *Sherman Antitrust Act* of 1890 declared "every contract, combination in the form of trust or otherwise, or conspiracy in restraint of trade or commerce among the several states, or with foreign nations" to be illegal. Under this law, a number of corporations (such as Standard Oil and the American Tobacco Company) were prosecuted as being monopolies "in restraint of trade" and were ordered to dissolve.

Yet, the Sherman Act was vague in its wording. It failed to distinguish for instance, between "reasonable" and "unreasonable" restraint of trade. For this reason, among others, it was often difficult to enforce. Moreover, its application to non-profit labor unions and farmers' organizations was strongly resented. To meet this situation, the *Clayton Antitrust Act* was passed in 1914. This law defined more clearly those practices which constituted unfair competition. It exempted from its operation labor and agricultural organizations which were not conducted for profit, in the usual sense of the term. At the same time, the *Federal Trade Com-*

Courtesy, Dorman H. Smith (*Collier's Magazine*)

This cartoon, published some years ago, expresses one point of view with regard to the antitrust laws. How would you characterize this point of view? What arguments might be offered in opposition?

mission was set up to investigate business corporations and to aid in the enforcement of fair trade practices.

After World War I, there was a noticeable change in the Federal government's policy toward "big business." The government began to take the attitude that, under certain circumstances, business combinations are unavoidable or even desirable. In line with this policy, the government has sanctioned, if not actually encouraged, the formation of some combinations. Thus, the government extended partial exemption from the application of the antitrust laws to organizations engaged solely in the export trade and to meatpackers' and farmers' associations. It has repeatedly fostered, as we have seen, a movement for consolidation among the railroads.

On the other hand, the Federal government has instituted rigorous controls over the institutions and facilities for financing large corporations, chiefly to protect investors in stocks and bonds. It vested the regulation of stock exchanges in a *Securities and Exchange Commission* (1934). It has been grappling with the problems of controlling the field of public utilities—a field regulated hitherto almost exclusively by the several states, yet rarely recognizing state boundaries. One major aim has been to release the grip which giant financial combinations have held on many operating companies.

Immigration and naturalization. Implied in the power to regulate commerce is the power to control immigration. Prior to World War I, the nation's immigration policy was predominantly liberal. It is true that Congress, by a series of measures dating from 1882, excluded Chinese immigrants and also various types of "undesirables," such as contract laborers, polygamists and anarchists. Provisions were made for medical inspection of immigrants, so that persons with infectious diseases could be turned back. Congress also imposed head taxes and, in 1917, required new arrivals to pass a literacy test. Nevertheless, immigration was relatively unrestricted and for many years continued on a large scale. In 1914, for example, nearly 1¼ million aliens entered the United States.

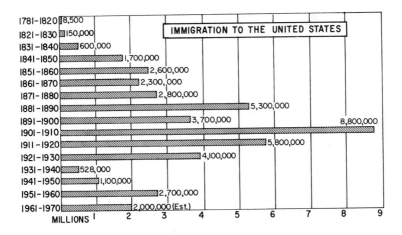

The period of World War I, naturally, witnessed a sharp decrease in immigration. After the close of the war, Congress adopted a new system of restrictions based on quotas assigned to the various nations of Europe, while immigration from the Orient was suspended entirely. Thus, immigration was held to a low level. In 1938, only 68,000 immigrants entered this country; in 1948, only 28,550.

Since the close of World War II, our immigration policies have been modified several times. On a number of occasions, Congress relaxed the quota system to allow the entry of refugees—persons who had been the victims of political oppression. The ban on Oriental immigration was ended. In 1965, a new immigration law was adopted which repealed the quota system based on national origins. Although the total number of immigrants to be admitted annually is still sharply restricted, the new law has had a significant liberalizing effect. In 1966, the United States admitted more than 50,000 immigrants who, under the quota system, would not have been eligible for entry.

Control over the admission of immigrants carries with it control over *deportation*—that is, the expulsion of aliens regarded as a menace to the public welfare. In the years immediately following World War I, there was frequent resort to the deportation of allegedly dangerous enemy aliens. During World War II, our government set up special internment camps for the "relocation" of persons who had come here from enemy countries and had not been naturalized. This applied particularly to Japanese living on the West Coast who were not eligible for citizenship. Indeed, many native-born persons of Japanese ancestry were also "relocated." Since World War II, the power to deport aliens has been applied mainly to Communists and to persons with criminal records.

Related to the control over immigration is the process of *naturalization*, by which a foreigner becomes a United States citizen. Congress has specified who is and who is not eligible for naturalization. It has, on occasions, modified its policies regarding the naturalization of women and children, of the American Indians, of Orientals, and of the people resident in our overseas possessions. It has, likewise, determined the circumstances under which Americans who have lived abroad for a certain period or who have assumed citizenship in another country, may become expatriates, that is, lose their citizenship. An outgrowth of World War II was the *denaturalization* (revocation of citizenship), by court action, of those who had obtained their citizenship by fraud or who were convicted of disloyal or subversive activities.

Other measures to protect and promote orderly economic activity. The government has authority over a number of other matters which are essential to the orderly functioning of the nation's economic life. These powers are implied from the power to regulate commerce, or they rest on specific constitutional provisions.

1. The Constitution gives Congress the power to establish "uniform laws on the subject of bankruptcies throughout the United States." The first enduring bankruptcy law was not enacted until 1898 (amended in 1938). Congress designated what treatment shall be accorded to those unable to pay their debts, especially in the event of fraud. It now specifies who may be legally adjudged as a voluntary or as an involuntary bankrupt. Congress also determines what redress is given to creditors and what procedures shall be followed by the courts. Provision now exists, also, for treaties with other nations to apprehend fugitives who have been charged with fraudulent bankruptcy.

2. The establishment of uniform standards of weights and measures is likewise within the scope of Congressional power. The *Bureau of Standards* at Washington has general supervision over the standardization and the accuracy of many types of measuring devices. It has given invaluable assistance to industry, agriculture, and science, as well as to educational institutions, in setting reliable and recognized criteria. The functions of the Bureau ("the house of accuracy," as it has been called) are, therefore, of immense importance.

3. Congress has the power "to promote the progress of science and useful arts by securing for limited times to authors and inventors the exclusive right to their respective writings and discoveries." Under this general grant of power, Congress has enacted *copyright* laws, which establish the exclusive right to publish, sell, reproduce, or represent publicly, works of a literary, musical, or artistic character. Congress has recently considered a sweeping revision of the copyright laws to adapt them to the new conditions created by such technological advances as copying and recording devices. Foreign countries which extend to Americans the benefits of their copyright laws have similar rights accorded to them by our government.

Under the constitutional provision cited, Congress has also enacted *patent laws*. These secure the exclusive right to the manufacture, use, or sale of an invention which is really new and useful. Patents are now granted for 17 years, and they may be renewed by act of Congress. After this, the inventions in question become public property. To identify the manufacturer or seller of goods and to prevent "commercial piracy," Congress has enacted laws protecting trademarks or distinguishing words, symbols, or emblems for commercial products.

The administration of copyrights is vested in the *Copyright Office* in the Library of Congress. The jurisdiction over patents and trademarks lies with the *Patent Office*, a division of the Department of Commerce. The tremendous growth of these governmental agencies has been due in part to the creative energies of Americans, and in part to the rapid pace of technological development characteristic of our culture. It is interesting to note that the first million patents were granted in a period from 1791 to 1911, and the second million in the span from 1911 to 1935. Half a million patents were issued between 1935 and 1950. The individualistic and competitive character of our society requires us to guard jealously the product of a man's talents and to insure that he will receive the financial rewards which such achievements make possible. This is why we have copyright, patent, and trademark laws. There are now many attorneys in practice who specialize in copyright and patent laws. They may, for example, defend before a special tribunal a client's claim to have developed a genuinely new invention; or they may prosecute a suit for infringement of patent or copyright. Our government has made international agreements to protect authors, composers, artists, inventors, and manufacturers and merchants against "piracy" by foreigners who may ignore copyright or patent rights. We have not yet been able, however, to make such agreements with the Soviet Union and other nations of the Communist world.

The power to tax. The Constitution authorizes Congress to "lay and collect taxes, duties, imposts and excises, to pay the debts and provide for the common defence and general welfare of the United States." These provisions were written into the Constitution after it had been found that under the Articles of Confederation the lack of such a grant of power weakened the nation to the point of threatening its future existence. Under its taxing power, the government has been able to raise vast sums of money and to carry out innumerable programs of tremendous scope, from building small-town post offices to exploring outer space. Taxes have also been used as an instrument to regulate, promote, and in some cases confine, prohibit, or even destroy private business enterprise.

Under this power, Congress has laid a variety of taxes on business within the United States, on imports, and on the income of individuals and corporations. During the two great wars of the 20th century, in the critical interlude between them, and in the recent postwar years, the national government has stretched its taxing power to the utmost. Under the guise of the taxing power, it has created banks. It has controlled the destinies of business organizations within the United States. It has protected American industry and agriculture against foreign competition. It has attempted to achieve a more nearly equal distribution of wealth through levies on income, gifts, and estates. Thus, in a multitude of ways, the national taxing power has helped to shape our economy and to guide the evolution of our society.

Limitations upon the taxing power. Yet, wide as are these powers, they are not unlimited. The Constitution indicates limits on the taxing powers of Congress. For example, it suggests the purposes for which taxes may be laid. It specifically forbids duties on exports. It makes uniform duties and excises mandatory throughout the nation.

The courts have an additional checking influence. Thus, the Supreme Court decided in 1819 that Congress did not have the power to tax either the public agencies necessary to the conduct of state and local governments, or income received from these governments. Under this limitation, for example, Congress was not able to tax the income from state bonds, or the profits of a county-operated recreation center, or salaries paid by a local government. It was not until 1939 that this limitation was partly withdrawn. In that year, the Court ruled that a state can tax the income of an employee of a Federal agency, and that the Federal government can tax the income of a state employee.

In 1941, Congress went a step further and passed a law which eliminated the tax exemption which had applied to income derived from interest payments on most Federal bonds.

The power of Congress to expend public funds is subject to the following provisions of the Constitution. Public funds must be used to "pay the debts and provide for the common defence and general welfare of the United States." All appropriations must be made by law. Statements regarding the revenues and expenditures of the Federal government must be issued regularly.

The power to borrow. Congress may "borrow money on the credit of the United States" when it considers this necessary. The total amount of money which the government owes at any time as a result of such borrowing is called the *national debt.*

The Constitution places no limit on the power of the government to borrow money or to assume indebtedness. On occasions, however, Congress has by statute adopted a "debt ceiling"—a limit beyond which the debt may not legally go. This "ceiling" has been raised repeatedly since the close of World War II and now stands at 329 billion dollars. Many experts question seriously whether this self-imposed but elastic limitation serves any effective purpose in preventing deficits or controlling the national debt.

In the early years of the Republic, the government was careful not to spend beyond its income and thus avoided incurring a national debt. More recently, as the accompanying graph indicates, the national debt has risen steadily, to levels which only a generation ago would have seemed all but inconceivable.

There has been sharp disagreement as to the impact of this development on the United States. On the one hand, opponents

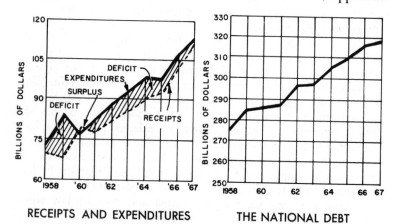

RECEIPTS AND EXPENDITURES   THE NATIONAL DEBT

Federal financing in recent years has been characterized by sizable deficits and by a rise in the national debt.

of "deficit financing" argue that it inevitably causes inflation; that it will saddle future generations with a crushing burden of debt; and that ultimately it may lead to economic disaster by undermining the credit of the United States. On the other hand, there are those who maintain that the national debt is *not* rising in proportion to the national income or the gross national product, and that the government can safely continue to borrow to meet urgent national needs and to insure adequate economic growth.

Control over currency. The Constitution authorizes Congress to "coin money" and to "regulate the value thereof." The states, on the other hand, are specifically forbidden to coin money and to "emit bills of credit." By thus giving the national government exclusive control over the medium of exchange, the Constitution wisely sought to rescue the nation from the confusing and demoralizing monetary policies of the several states during the period of the Confederation.

It is Congress which determines the nature of the currency in circulation and decides which forms are "legal tender" for the payment of public and private debts. Also, Congress has the right to punish counterfeiting. Although the power to issue paper money is not specifically granted to Congress by the Constitution, its exercise has been sustained by the Supreme Court.

Banking: The growth of an extra-constitutional power. Implied in the right to borrow, tax, and regulate the currency is the power to establish banks. This is an exercise of power which was hotly contested in the early years of the Republic. The constitutionality of the first and second United States Banks was finally sustained in 1819 by the Supreme Court. Under the related powers noted above, Congress has chartered and supervised thousands of privately owned "national banks." It has taxed out of existence notes issued by the state banks. It has established the Federal Reserve System. It has set up special banks designed to extend agricultural credits. It has established huge government "corporations" to extend financial aid to state and local governments, to private organizations, and to foreign nations.* It is a far cry,

---

* A few notable examples of such government agencies include the Reconstruction Finance Corporation, the Small Business Administration, the Federal Housing Administration, the Commodity Credit Corporation, the National Foundation for the Arts and Humanities, the Export-Import Bank, the Agency for International Development, and a host of others designed to cope with specific problems both here and abroad.

indeed, from Jefferson's alarm over the power of the first United States Bank to the scope of these activities, which are now virtually taken for granted by the vast majority of Americans.

What is a budget? Another matter that must be clearly understood before one can pass judgment upon Federal taxation and finances in general is the Federal budget. This is the government's way of accounting for all funds that are spent. The main questions involved in planning the budget are: How much money shall the Federal government spend during a particular twelve-month period? How shall this money be appropriated? Also, where is the money to meet these expenses to come from? In brief, a budget, as one observer put it, is a method of worrying *before* you spend, rather than afterward.

In earlier years, these matters were decided in a hit-or-miss fashion. Hundreds of bills were presented by Congressmen for the spending of Federal funds in their own localities. (It should be noted that such attempts to advance local interests by dipping into the "pork-barrel" are by no means a thing of the past today.) The heads of the various Executive departments and other agencies would make their several requests for appropriations without regard to the overall needs and resources of the government. A clear picture of what was to be spent during the fiscal year did not emerge until after all bills had been passed by Congress.

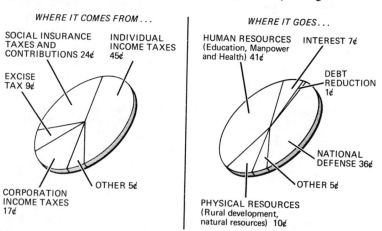

The "Federal government dollar." Main sources of the income of the Federal government and main fields of expenditures (1970-71).

This lack of a general financial plan was somewhat less important when the expenses of the Federal government were relatively small. But as expenditures increased sharply, the need for rational controls could not be ignored. (The expenditures of the Federal government were less than 9 billion dollars in 1940; about 40 billion dollars in 1950; and almost 122 billion dollars in 1966.)

The budget procedure. To meet this problem of controlling ever larger and more complicated financial operations, Congress passed a Budget and Accounting Act in 1921. This law (amended in 1950) set the general procedure still followed today. The authority and responsibility for formulating the budget (*fiscal policy*) are centered in the President, although he delegates much of the detailed work to the Bureau of the Budget and other subordinates.

Under the law, all heads of departments and other agencies must present annual estimates of their financial needs to the Director who heads the Bureau of the Budget. These appropriation requests will normally reach the Bureau of the Budget by about September 15. During the next few months, the requests are reviewed and analyzed. Hearings may be held at which the agency spokesmen explain and defend their proposed expenditures. On the basis of this information, the Director of the Budget sends a set of recommendations to the President, usually by the end of November. The President, in consultation with the Secretary of the Treasury and other advisers, then decides specifically how the government's money is to be spent and where it is to come from.

The following January, when Congress has reconvened, the President presents his Executive Budget to it, together with an accompanying message. It is to be noted that this is the budget for the government's *next* fiscal year, which will begin on July 1 and end on June 30 of the following year. Thus, the budget-making procedure begins almost a full year ahead of the fiscal year for which the budget is intended.

The budget in Congress. The Constitution directs that all revenue bills shall originate in the House of Representatives. Bills embodying the President's suggestions are introduced in the House, and the details of those bills are threshed out in the Ways and Means Committee. Often, the bills finally passed are quite different from those suggested by the President. Still more changes are made when these bills come to the Senate. This body examines the money bills through its Finance Committee, and the changes which it makes may result in the drafting of an almost entirely new set of bills.

Public opinion helps make the budget. While Congress is debating, the various mass communication media are spreading information about the budget and are helping to form public opinion. The budget may be the subject of newspaper editorials and columns, of magazine articles, and of discussions on radio and television. Citizens whose opinions are influenced by these media frequently write to their representatives in Congress, urging that they support or oppose various proposed expenditures or forms of taxation.

Another force influencing the final budget is the great number of lobbyists—representatives of various special interests—already described on page 42. They try to convince the legislators that the expenditures should be expanded or contracted along certain desired lines.

The final budget agreed upon by both houses is sent to the President, just as any other bill is. It is then the task of the Treasury Department, assisted by the Bureau of the Budget, to see that the various provisions of the bill are carried out.

'THERE ARE TWO SIDES TO THE SPENDING STORY'

Carmack in the *Christian Science Monitor*

Public opinion may sometimes wear many faces. The same citizens who criticize Congress for extravagance and who favor "governmental economy" in the abstract may demand large expenditures that serve local or personal interests.

The Police Powers of Congress

Definition. "Police powers" refer to the "reasonable" restrictions that government puts on individuals and property rights to protect public health, morals, safety, and welfare. Originally, only the states (including local governments) had the right to exercise police powers. (These were considered *reserved powers*, assigned to the states by the 10th Amendment.) Under their police powers, the states passed numerous public health laws, anti-gambling laws, laws regulating highway traffic and even rent-control laws—to mention only a few of a vast number of subjects. (See Chapter 8.)

Congress assumes police powers. But as the nation grew in size, population, and complexity, there developed a need for Federal regulation. Congress soon began to exercise police powers, which were derived from its delegated powers in Article I, Section 8 of the Constitution. A host of laws relating to taxes, to post offices and post roads, and especially to interstate commerce sprang from this section of the Constitution. The use of the "commerce clause" yielded much important legislation relating to such areas as pure foods and drugs, regulation of wages and hours (the Fair Labor Standards Act), control of crime (*e.g.*, laws against kidnapping), and control of child labor. A recent extension of the Federal police powers has been in the tightening of control over pollution of waters and over thermal pollution from atomic power plants.

Miscellaneous Powers of Congress

Control over the Executive and Judicial branches. The Constitution gives Congress the power to create Executive departments and to provide for their conduct. There are now twelve such departments, the oldest being the *State Department* (1789) and the most recent, the *Department of Transportation* (1966). As the business of government has increased, and more particularly as government has come to regulate diverse economic activities of both a public and a private character, Congress has created numerous independent administrative bodies. Examples of these are the Federal Reserve System, the United States Tariff Commission, the Tennessee Valley Authority, the Veterans Administration, the Agency for International Development, and the Atomic Energy Commission. (See Chapter 6.)

With the exception of the Supreme Court, for whose existence the Constitution, itself, makes provision, Congress may establish lower Federal courts and determine the types of cases which are to come before them and the modes of procedure. Even the Supreme Court is subject to the will of Congress in some areas. (See Chapter 7.)

Punishment of crimes. The definition and the punishment of crime are, under our system of government, left largely to the states. Nevertheless, certain offenses come within the jurisdiction of the Federal government. The Constitution makes specific references to such offenses as counterfeiting, treason, and crimes committed on the high seas or against international law. Moreover, any act committed in violation of a power exercised by Congress, or any offense perpetrated on territory over which the Federal government alone has authority (such as a military reservation), also comes under Congressional legislation.

The "war powers" of Congress. Matters relating to national defense and to the conduct of war are covered in several brief constitutional provisions. Congress has the power to declare war and to make rules concerning captures on land and water, although it should be pointed out that the "cold war" has given the President the initiative in taking active military measures without Congress (for example, in Korea, Vietnam, and the Dominican Republic). Congress may organize and support the national military and naval forces, as well as the militia of the several states (the National Guard).

The bare statement of the provisions gives hardly an inkling of the vast powers which Congress exercises. In time of war, there is very little which escapes governmental control. Men are drafted for compulsory military service; heavy taxes are voted; enormous loans are floated; and private property is taken for public use. The means of production, transportation, and communication are operated in the interests of the national war effort. Controls over labor and wages, management and profits, food prices, housing and civilian defense suggest only a few of the measures authorized by Congress in an "all-out" conflict.

When war comes to an end, Congress has to deal with new problems that are a direct outcome of the great military effort—for example, special services and benefits extended to veterans, disposal of surplus war property, and the reconversion of the economy to a peacetime level.

The National Park System maintained by the United States government comprises 188 different areas in all parts of the country, covering about 41,000 square miles. Here we see a scene in Bryce Canyon National Park in Utah.

Control over Federal territory. Under the Constitution, "territory or other property of the United States" comes under the jurisdiction of Congress. In accordance with this, Congress has control of the District of Columbia,* the National Forests, the National Parks, and other areas vital to conservation of natural resources. Indeed, a considerable part of the entire land area of

* Prior to 1871, the District was self-governing. From 1871 to 1967, it was under the direct control of the Federal government, administered by a three-man Board of Commissioners appointed by the President and the Senate. The Reorganization Plan of 1967 substituted a single commissioner (called Mayor), an assistant to the Mayor and a 9-member City Council—all appointed by the President. Budgetary funds are all appropriated by Congress. Residents have no vote in local matters.

Washington, D.C., is our ninth largest city, and there is considerable sentiment in favor of giving it local self-government on the same basis as any other large city. Walter E. Washington became the first Negro Mayor of any major American city in 1967 when President Johnson appointed him to head Washington's reorganized government. President Nixon reappointed him in 1969. A 1970 law gave the District a non-voting delegate in the House of Representatives.

the United States is owned by the Federal government and therefore subject to control by Congress. Property connected with the national defense, such as forts and arsenals, are also under Federal control. The same is true of many thousands of buildings, including post offices, customs houses, and the headquarters of governmental agencies, not only in Washington but in all parts of the country.

Under this same power, Congress has governed "territories," such as those ceded by the states to the national government after the War of Independence or secured from other countries through conquest or peaceful negotiation.* Admission of new states into the Union is granted by Congress. This is a power which Congress has exercised repeatedly throughout our history.

Special Powers of the House of Representatives

In this chapter, we have thus far considered the powers which are exercised by Congress as a whole. The Constitution also delegates special powers to each house of Congress. We shall consider first the House of Representatives.

Initiation of revenue bills. Bills for raising revenue, such as measures affecting internal taxation or duties on imports, must originate in the House of Representatives. It is from the people that the money must be obtained; it is the "people's branch of the legislature" which should have the first say. Thus reasoned the framers of the Constitution. In practice, however, the Senate may by proposing amendments to a revenue bill, change it markedly, or even frame an entirely different bill. As a result, this "special power" of the House has become a matter of form, rather than a difference of real significance.

Choice of the President under certain conditions. Upon the House devolves the choice of the President of the United States whenever the electoral system specified by the Constitution

---

* Puerto Rico, originally a territory through conquest, has been a "commonwealth" since 1952, a status unique in American history. Puerto Ricans are United States citizens and serve in the armed forces; they use United States money and postal systems. On the other hand, they are not subject to the Federal income tax, and they do not vote in Presidential elections. Although Puerto Rico is represented by a popularly elected "Resident Commissioner" in the House of Representatives, he has no vote in that body.

fails to give any candidate a majority of the electoral votes. This power has been exercised on two occasions: in 1801, when the House chose Jefferson; and in 1825, when it selected John Quincy Adams. Such a vote is taken by states, with the delegation from each state having a single vote.

Impeachment. The House has the sole power of impeachment —that is, the power to bring charges of misconduct against Federal officials. Subject to impeachment are the President, the Vice President and other civil officers of the United States whose functions are executive or judicial. Officers in the military service and members of Congress do not come within the scope of this provision. The Constitution specifies also the grounds for impeachment. They are treason (which is defined as levying war against the United States or giving aid and comfort to its enemies), bribery, and "other high crimes and misdemeanors."

Special Powers of the Senate

Treaty-making. The Senate shares with the President the power to make treaties. It considers proposed treaties in secret or "executive" session. This power over treaty-making goes well beyond the technical constitutional requirements that a treaty does not go into effect unless it is approved by two-thirds of the Senators present. Through its Foreign Relations Committee, the Senate may have an important advisory role in negotiating treaties. It may propose amendments and express reservations prior to its acceptance of a treaty. Also, it may undo the results of painstaking diplomatic activity by rejecting a treaty altogether. Our failure to ratify the Treaty of Versailles and to adhere to the League of Nations after World War I is a prominent example of how effectively the Senate can wield this "veto power."

Because it is often so difficult to obtain a two-thirds majority in the Senate, our government has developed various ways of making international agreements without negotiating a treaty.

One of these is the *joint resolution,* which requires a simple majority in each house of Congress. Although this brings the House of Representatives into the picture, it may present less of a problem than controlling two-thirds of the Senate. The joint agreement has played an important role in American history. It was used, for example, to annex Texas in 1845 and Hawaii in 1898, to declare a formal ending of the war with Germany in

1921, and to approve our adherence to the International Labor Office (a League of Nations Agency) in 1934.

Various Presidents have also skirted the treaty-making barrier by concluding "agreements" with foreign nations. This has sometimes been done with the specific approval of Congress, but more often without such authorization. For example, in 1934 Congress permitted President Roosevelt to negotiate a reciprocal trade pact with Canada without final Senatorial approval. Again, in 1940, the President acting "on his own" transferred 50 over-age destroyers to Great Britain in exchange for certain bases in the Western Hemisphere.

The House of Representatives has, as a rule, approved any legislation or financial appropriations necessary to carry out treaties. On rare occasions, however, it has balked. Such was the case, for example, when the House refused for a long time to vote funds needed to purchase Alaska from Russia in 1867.

Few countries experience the obstacles to treaty-making which are a common occurrence in the United States. For this reason, it has been frequently suggested that this machinery should be simplified so as to make possible the approval of treaties either by a majority vote in both houses of Congress or by a simple majority in the Senate.

Confirmation of appointments. The Senate also shares with the President the power of making appointments to a large number of public offices. Examples of these are Federal judges, ambassadors, ministers, and consuls, and a host of other officials whose appointment, by act of Congress, requires the consent of the Senate. The procedure in these cases is that the President presents his nomination for the office, and the Senate either confirms or rejects it. In most instances, the Senate has approved Presidential appointments as a matter of course. At times, however, it has shown stubborn resistance and has rejected the President's appointments.

Choice of the Vice President under certain conditions. When no candidate for the Vice Presidency has received a majority of electoral votes, the choice falls to the Senate. The Senators vote individually (not by states), and a simple majority is needed for election.

Trial of impeachments. Public officials who have been impeached by the House are tried by the Senate. A committee of the House prepares and prosecutes the case. The Senate acts as the court. Ordinarily the Vice President presides. However, if it is the Vice President or the President of the United States who is on trial, the Chief Justice of the United States presides. A vote of two-thirds of the Senators present is necessary for conviction. The penalty is removal from office and, if the Senate so desires, disqualification from holding any other office under the Federal government. Throughout our history, only thirteen men have been impeached. Among them have been an Associate Justice of the Supreme Court (1804) and a President of the United States (Andrew Johnson, 1868). Both were acquitted by the Senate. Most of the others were Federal judges. Of the thirteen men who were impeached, only four were convicted.

Proposals for Reform of Congress

The House of Representatives and the Senate, in the face of the expanding power of the Executive branch (see Chapter 5), are today on the horns of a dilemma. They have virtual control over the government's "purse" (revenue and appropriations) and over the "sword" (the power to declare war). But at the same time that they are exercising these life-and-death powers, the Executive branch (the President, the Federal bureaucracy, and the armed forces) has the actual power to make day-to-day decisions relating to great events, both at home and abroad. To help solve some of the perplexing problems involved in making laws for a swiftly changing modern society, experts in political science have made various recommendations to improve Congress. In fact, Congress itself, through the National Committee for an Effective Congress, has expressed an interest in reform in these words: "We must make a study of contemporary problems—technological change, organization, the revolution of rising expectations—in order to bolster our belief that we are now crossing the historical equivalent of a sound barrier unaware, and we are entering a new life unprepared."

Among the specific suggestions for Congressional reform emanating from various sources are the following:

◆ *Provide by constitutional amendment for the simultaneous election every four years of the President, the House of Representatives, and half of the Senate.* Under this arrangement, Representatives would serve four-year terms; Senators, eight-year terms. This, it is argued, would lessen the time which legislators must devote to campaigning. It would strengthen cooperation between the President and Congress, since the President and a majority of the lawmakers are more likely to be of the same party if they are elected at the same time. Finally, the change would give Congressmen (particularly Representatives) more time to master the duties of their office before facing a new election and possible defeat. A more limited proposal, backed by President Lyndon B. Johnson, is simply to increase the term of Representatives to four years.

♦ *Expand the two-party competition into all Congressional Districts.* The emergence of Republican Party strength in the once "Solid South," as reflected in recent national elections, may be one significant step toward such a goal.

♦ *Eliminate the present seniority system as the basis for appointment of committee chairmen.* Such a change, it is claimed, would counteract the unwarranted influence of Congressmen who become committee chairmen only because they are elected term after term, usually from a section of the country which is dominated by one party. These committee chairmen have often been associated with efforts to block progressive legislation, such as civil rights.

♦ *Do away with the filibuster in the Senate.* The filibuster, in effect, makes possible minority rule because it enables a small, determined group to prevent the Senate from even voting on measures which may be favored by a majority. The present *cloture rule* (to end a filibuster by limiting debate) is usually difficult to apply because it requires the approval of two-thirds of the Senate. One suggestion is that the cloture rule be changed so that it can be invoked by a simple majority.

♦ *Take action to abolish gerrymandering in the various states.* Under this practice, the dominant party in a state lays out Congressional districts (as well as districts for the state legislature) in such a way as to minimize the strength of the opposition party or parties. This has had the effect of weakening the two-party system in some states. Some experts have suggested that each state's allotment of Representatives be divided among the various parties in proportion to their relative voting strength, as shown in a statewide election (*proportional representation*). The recent rulings of the Supreme Court establishing the principle of "one man, one vote" may have the effect of curbing gerrymandering abuses.

♦ *Develop a fair and workable set of rules for committee investigations and hearings.* As we have already pointed out, the recent growth of Congressional investigations has brought a widespread demand for a code to guide Congressmen in conducting such probes.

A DAY OF A CONGRESSMAN

VISITED BY DISTILLER, COLLEGE TRUSTEE, FARM REPRESENTATIVE,

IN BEHALF OF FOOD COMPANY CONFERS WITH GOVERNMENT AGENCY

·BANKER

URGES SEC. OF AGRICULTURE TO SPEAK IN HIS DISTRICT

RUSHES TO COMMITTEE MEETING

RETURNS TO HIS OFFICE TO READ MAIL

BACK TO HIS OFFICE TO LEGISLATIVE WORK

Public Affairs Committee

One common criticism of Congress is expressed in this pictorial summary of "A Day of a Congressman." The charge is made that most Congressmen spend too much time tending to purely local matters and "running political errands," and correspondingly too little time studying national problems and working on legislative matters that involve the national interest.

♦ *Have each member of the House of Representatives serve the entire state, as does each Senator.* This would be achieved by abolishing Congressional districts and by changing residence requirements so that each House member would be elected by the people of the entire state.

♦ *Schedule regular appearances of Cabinet members and heads of Federal agencies before each house of Congress, to explain their programs and to answer questions.* This proposal would make for a closer cooperation between the Executive and Legislative branches. For example, it is argued, if the Secretary of State were to work more intimately with the Foreign Relations Committee of the Senate in planning and drawing up treaties, the chances for getting the necessary two-thirds ratifying vote would be enhanced. Aside from treaties, such closer cooperation would make for greater overall effectiveness in conducting foreign affairs.

♦ *Discontinue the practice of attaching riders to bills.* A rider is an irrelevant addition made to an important bill (often an appropriations bill) for the purpose of forcing passage of provisions that would have little chance of being passed on their own merits. Such a change would do much to eliminate "pork-barrel" legislation. An alternative to this suggested reform is to amend the Constitution so as to give the President the right to *veto specific items in bills.* He could then remove provisions which he considered undesirable without vetoing an entire piece of legislation.

♦ *Provide for stricter control of lobbies.* The Legislative Reorganization Act of 1946 (page 44) was a start in this direction, but there is a widespread feeling that it has not gone far enough. There are loopholes in the present law of which the "influence peddlers" readily take advantage. For example, in 1963, a Senate Foreign Relations Committee hearing headed by Senator Fulbright proved that one skilled lobbyist, who had previously dispensed campaign contributions to more than 20 Congressmen, had been successful in promoting a Philippine war claims measure. In 1965, Senator Wayne Morse revealed the activities of other lobbyists, some of them unregistered, on behalf of the dictator of Nicaragua, Ecuadorian sugar interests, and military aid to Indonesia. Working for these and other clients, the lobbyists were seeking grants and loans under the foreign-aid program, the sugar quotas, and other programs.

♦ *Reduce the power of the Rules Committee of the House by authorizing the Speaker to call a bill to the floor after it has been held without action by the Rules Committee for 21 days.*

♦ *Reduce the authority of all committee chairmen in the House by enabling the Speaker with the support of 175 House members, to discharge a bill from any committee.*

♦ *Provide for disclosure and limitation of all contributions for political campaigns by Congressional candidates.* In 1966, President Johnson proposed to Congress measures that would require more accurate accounting of political contributions, by both the donor and the recipient; would place ceilings on the amount of contributions; and would encourage more widespread participation in the financing of political campaigns by means of tax deduction allowances. Under the President's proposal, reports of such political expenditures would have to be filed with the Clerk of the House and with the Secretary of the Senate. Critics have argued that since these two officials are servants of Congress, and since they have no staff, there would be little prospect of a searching and adequate auditing of the reports.

Terms You Should Know

Budget. An estimate of governmental income and expenditures for the coming fiscal period.

Bureaucracy. The entire body of government personnel. (In a derogatory sense, "bureaucracy" is used to suggest an overly large amount of red tape and unnecessary officials.)

Commerce clause. Article I, Section 8, Clause 3 of the Constitution which gives Congress power to "regulate commerce with foreign nations and among the several States. . . ." An important legal basis for extension of the powers of the national government.

Denaturalization. Revocation of citizenship.

Deportation. The expulsion of aliens to their country of origin.

Expatriation. The banishment of a person from his own country.

Impeachment. The indictment of a civil official for a wrong-doing. High Federal officials (including the President) may be impeached by the House of Representatives, after which they are tried by the Senate.

Internment. Confinement; usually of enemy aliens or prisoners of war.

Laissez-faire. The theory or doctrine which holds that government should interfere as little as possible in the affairs of the people—particularly in economic affairs.

Naturalization. The process by which an alien becomes a citizen.

Police powers. The authority by which the states, as well as the Federal government, enact legislation to protect the health, morals, safety, and general well-being of the people.

Public debt. The total indebtedness of a government; usually applied to the indebtedness of the Federal government.

Rider. An irrelevant addition made to an essential bill (often an appropriations bill) for the purpose of forcing passage of provisions that would have little chance of being passed on their own merits.

Treason. The offense of attempting to overthrow a government to which the offender owes allegiance. (Defined in Article III, Section 3 of the Constitution.)

Treaty. Formal agreement with a foreign power concerning mutual rights and reciprocal obligations. A treaty is negotiated by the President, and when ratified by the Senate it has the force of a national law. (There may also be treaties between and among the 50 states.)

Vested interests. Persons and groups sharing common interests who seek to use their political and economic power to influence legislation and governmental administration. (Also called *interest groups* and *pressure groups*.)

Questions and Problems Based on the Text

1. What part has the Supreme Court played in expanding or limiting the powers of Congress under the Constitution?

2. (*a*) What effect have technological and scientific advances had upon the powers of Congress? (*b*) What has been the effect of the people's growing demands for a better life upon the powers of Congress?

3. (*a*) Show how the "regulation of interstate and foreign commerce" has grown in meaning throughout our history. (*b*) Show how this growth has been applied to transportation, to communication, to the protection of articles and persons engaged in commerce, and to the control of corporations.

4. (*a*) Explain the nature of the changes in our immigration policy, and account for these changes. (*b*) Define: naturalization, deportation, expatriation.

5. Explain how Congress has used its powers to (*a*) control bankruptcy; (*b*) establish uniform standards of weights and measures; (*c*) provide for copyrights and patents.

6. Give examples of how Congress has used its powers to provide for (*a*) the enforcement of laws; (*b*) judicial administration; (*c*) the management of Federal territory.

7. In what sense may the powers of Congress over military and naval matters be said to be dangerously vague?

8. What special powers does the House of Representatives have? The Senate? Illustrate each answer by reference to current events.

9. If it is socially desirable for the government to order monopolistic corporations to dissolve, why has the government in recent years been permitting railroads to merge?

10. (*a*) Do you believe that the granting of monopolies through copyright and patent laws is socially desirable? (*b*) Can you suggest other ways in which the government might guide and reward inventors, artists, writers, or other persons engaged professionally in cultural or intellectual pursuits? (*c*) Or do you think the government should keep its hands off in regard to such matters? Give reasons for your opinion.

11. "Seniority rule in the committee system causes Congress to use the procedure of smothering and strangling Presidential proposals, rather than of debating and voting, a principle which violates the basic principles of representative government."—WALTER LIPPMANN

Do you think Mr. Lippmann's charge is valid? Why or why not?

12. (a) Prepare a brief biographical sketch of the Representative from your district and of your two Senators. (b) What committee appointments have they had in Congress? (c) How have they voted on important measures? (d) Do they often communicate with their constituents? In what way? (e) Are you proud of their record? (f) Do any women represent your state in Congress? Has their record been commendable?

13. "The great central clauses of the Constitution are: (a) commerce among states; (b) due process of law; (c) equal protection of the laws. They are marked by a grand vagueness that facilitates the task of adaptation." Discuss this statement.

14. "Some Congressional investigations have given the nation invaluable information. Among these are: The younger Senator La Follette's investigation of anti-labor practices by employers, and Senator Wheeler's investigation of the monopolistic practices of utility holding companies — both during the 1930's; Senator Truman's investigation of defense contracts during World War II; and Senator McClellan's investigation of abuses in labor-management relations in 1957. Conspicuous among the probes that have aroused much debate have been those of the Senate dealing with un-American activities. Many people felt that these probes had done a useful job in ferreting out Communists and their sympathizers and in awakening complacent Americans to the danger of subversive activities. Others condemned what they described as 'inquisitorial methods' used particularly by the committees of which Senator McCarthy was a member. It was charged that due process was denied to witnesses or 'defendants' and had the effect of damaging the reputation of many witnesses even when there was no real evidence against them."

It would appear from this that some Congressional investigating committees have been good, while others have been bad. What can we do to protect and enhance the effectiveness of the "good" committees, while holding abuses in check?

15. "Our analysis of the Presidency and of Congress should give the reader a clue as to why Congress finds itself today in a dilemma. It is the dilemma of a legislature that still has virtual control of the purse (revenue and appropriations) and the sword (power to declare war)—two life-and-death powers—at a time when the Executive branch (the President, the Federal bureaucracy, the armed forces) has the *actual* power to make day-to-day decisions over great events, here and abroad." What policies would you advise to resolve this "dilemma"?

16. What do you think of each of the following suggested changes in our Congress?

(a) Make each Representative serve the entire state. This would be achieved by abolishing Congressional districts and changing residence requirements.

(b) Discontinue the practice of attaching riders to bills. This could be done by amending the Constitution to give the President the power to veto specific items in bills (a power held by the governors in many states). The President could then disapprove of sections without vetoing an entire bill. (The House of Representatives has already banned riders.)

(c) Grant the Speaker of the House discretionary power to bring to the House floor for a vote any bill approved by a House committee that has been bottled up in the Rules Committee for more than 21 days.

(d) Grant the Speaker authority to enable the House to send *immediately* to a Senate-House conference committee any bill passed in different forms. by the House and Senate. (Under the present rule, such a bill must go to the Rules Committee if any House member objects to sending it to conference.)

(e) Select each committee chairman from among the three top-ranking members (on the basis of seniority) of the committee's majority members. Select the ranking minority member by a similar minority caucus.

(f) Establish a Senate committee to deal with the problem of ethical standards and conflict of interest for its members. Such a committee would provide detailed guide lines for proper conduct. (The House has already moved in this direction by setting up the *Committee on Standards of Official Conduct* as one of its standing committees.)

17. In 1966, Congress passed a law that gave the government authority to take action against food processors guilty of such abuses as partly filled containers, deceptive "cents off" advertising promotion, and designation of package size by meaningless terms such as "giant economy size." (a) Under what constitutional power did Congress take this action? (b) Determine what Federal agency or agencies are administering this law.

Ideas to Think About and Discuss

1. *"Congress is the stepchild of the British Parliament, but has had a unique life of its own."* —JAMES RESTON

2. *"Necessity is the plea for every infringement of human freedom. It is the argument of tyrants."* —WILLIAM PITT

3. *"Frequent amending would destroy the citizen's faith in his traditional government and lead to instability. Legislate fearlessly but maintain the symbolic code (the Constitution). Thus this code will, through laws, be made to serve the nation's ideals."*

—JUSTICE LOUIS D. BRANDEIS

4. (a) *"The national government is a government of limited authority and definite structure, whose functions are defined and enumerated in a written Constitution."* —WENDELL WILLKIE
(arguing against the TVA)

(b) *"Must we let this power go to waste, depriving the people of comfort and happiness, because when our forefathers framed the Constitution, electric power was unknown?"*

—U.S. SENATOR GEORGE W. NORRIS

5. *"Only in nations in which the power of the people is supreme has liberty any abode."* —CICERO

6. *"I fear that it has a corroding effect on government generally when a member of the President's Cabinet can be ordered to jettison his corporate portfolio by Senators, who themselves may be dabbling in oil, cotton futures, television, hotel chains or uranium."* —U.S. SENATOR RICHARD NEUBERGER

7. *"Let us tend to our own business, which is great enough as it is. It's very great. We have neglected our own affairs. Our education is inadequate, our cities are badly built, our social arrangements are unsatisfactory. We can't wait another generation. Unless we can surmount this crisis, and work and get going onto the path of a settlement in Asia, and a settlement in Europe, all of these plans of the Great Society here at home, all the plans for the rebuilding of backward countries in other continents will be put on the shelf, because war interrupts everything like that."*

—WALTER LIPPMANN

8. *"The proper forum for adjudicating criminal guilt (whether it be of Communists or members of the KKK) is the courtroom and not the committee room; the rights of those whose views we abhor cannot be abridged without undermining the rights of all Americans."* —NORMAN REDLICH

9. *"The primary reason for my not running for a second term in the United States Senate is the high cost of political campaigning. It would cost well over $250,000 to run for re-election this year (1966) in my home state of Oregon."*

—U. S. SENATOR MAURINE B. NEUBERGER

CHAPTER **4**

The President—Qualifications, Nomination, and Election

The Nature of the Presidential Office

The Presidency, yesterday and today. What is there about the Presidential office that makes its holder the center of such a cyclone of activity? What makes the President's slightest utterance important news? Why is the office the traditional dream of "every American boy"?

The answers to these questions are not to be found in the Constitution, for it was the intention of the founders to create a Chief Executive whose primary function would be to carry out faithfully the laws enacted by Congress. Nor was the office designed to lend great prestige to the occupant. The minutes of the Constitutional Convention reveal much wrangling as to whether the term of office should be short or long; whether there should be a plural executive or a single one; whether the President should be addressed as "Your Excellency" or as "Mr. President." In the end, the framers fashioned an office with powers that were distinctly limited. But, as we shall see, the historical evolution of the Presidency has made the Chief Executive not only the key figure in our national government but quite possibly the most important and influential official in the world.

Constitutional qualifications. Under the Constitution, the President must be a native-born citizen, at least 35 years of age at the time he takes office, and 14 years a resident of the United States. The residence requirement does not mean that a person must have actually lived within the United States for 14 years, nor does it require that this period of time immediately precede his election. A "legal residence" for 14 years is sufficient.

Compensation of the President. The salary of the President is fixed by Congress, but it may not be either increased or reduced during the term for which he was elected. At present, the salary is $200,000 annually (fully taxable), plus use of the Executive Mansion, commonly called the White House, as well as entertainment, travel, and clerical expenses.

The Presidential term. The Constitution provides for a four-year term and says nothing in regard to eligibility for re-election. Until well into the 20th century, custom limited a President to two terms, and any departure from this tradition was regarded as dangerous and undemocratic. The tradition was broken, however, when Franklin D. Roosevelt was elected to a third term in 1940 and to a fourth in 1944. The President's term originally began on March 4th of the year after the election. Under the 20th Amendment (page 24), it commences at noon on January 20th.

The 22nd Amendment (1951) limits any President to two terms in office. Many citizens disapproved of this change in our basic law. It was charged that Congress and the state legislatures had acted more out of fear of Executive power than out of a full understanding of the spirit of the Constitution or of the history of our government under it. The threat to our democracy, it was argued, lies not in allowing the same man to be Chief Executive as often as the people may want him, but rather in failure to meet the insistent challenges of a revolutionary age, both at home and abroad. The supporters of the amendment, however, answered that it offered a valuable safeguard against possibly dangerous concentration of power in the hands of one successful and popular political leader. This argument, apparently, was sufficient to impress Congress and the state legislatures, which made the proposal part of the Constitution.

The inauguration. A President takes office! The pent-up emotions of the people, which have been stimulated by radio-television reports, newspapers and motion pictures dealing with the nomination and election of the President, reach their climax on the day the President is sworn in. Inauguration Day is made the occasion of a great pageant. The oath of office, prescribed in the Constitution, is usually administered by the Chief Justice of the United States in the presence of thousands of visitors from all over the country and from many foreign countries, and before millions watching on television. Following the custom set by George Washington, the President delivers a speech in which he

Inauguration of a President—a major event for the nation and for the world.

foreshadows the lines of policy which he expects to follow. The suspense is over; the people have received their President-elect, and go back to their daily routine. The ex-President passes out of the limelight, and the new President, watched by the entire nation, begins his great task of governing the country.

The Vice President "backs up" the President. The office of Vice President was created primarily to meet emergencies occasioned by some circumstances which prevent the President from carrying on his duties. In the event of the removal of the President from office, or of his death, resignation, or "inability to discharge the powers and duties of the said office," the Vice President is on hand to take over. Since 1789, eight Vice Presidents have succeeded to the Presidency because of the death of the incumbent, four of them in the 20th century. No President has ever resigned, nor has one ever been removed by impeachment and conviction.

Since the Vice President must always be available to serve as President, the constitutional requirements for the "number-two" office are the same as those for the Presidency.

If the President becomes disabled. The question of Presidential disability has come up several times in our history. President Garfield, the victim of an assassin's bullet, was completely incapacitated for more than two months before his death in 1881. President Wilson, during the latter part of his second term, was unable to perform his duties normally because of illness. In spite of the fact that on both these occasions the Executive branch of the government was, in effect, without a functioning head, nothing was done. President Eisenhower's three serious illnesses in the 1950's again focused national attention on the question of Presidential disability.

Over the years many different proposals have been advanced to deal with this situation. Finally, in 1965, the House of Representatives and the Senate approved a constitutional amendment providing for a smooth transition of power whenever the President becomes disabled, and also making sure that the nation will always have a Vice President in office. This proposal was soon ratified by the necessary 38 states and became the 25th Amendment in 1967. (See pages 135 and 350-351.)

Presidential succession after the Vice President. Who succeeds the President if there is no Vice President, or if the Vice President is unable for any reason to become Chief Executive? The *Presidential Succession Act*, passed by Congress in 1947, provided for the following order of succession: the Speaker of the House, the President *pro tempore* of the Senate, and then the Cabinet officers (Secretary of State, Treasury, Defense, etc.). In providing for the succession beyond the Vice Presidency, Congress was not dealing with a remote or theoretical contingency. In the course of our history, the Vice Presidency has been vacant sixteen times for a total of 38 years. Seven Vice Presidents died in office; eight vacated the Vice Presidency upon the deaths of Presidents; and, one, John C. Calhoun, resigned to become a United States Senator.

Thus far, the succession has never passed the Vice President. But the significant point to bear in mind about our system of transferring power when the President dies is this: In other countries, under other systems, the death of the head of state has often led to the overthrow of government, the quick seizure of power by unauthorized elements, the paralysis of a nation. Such a disruption is extremely unlikely in the United States, as was shown again by the smooth transition of power after the assassination of President Kennedy in 1963.

The Nominating Conventions and the Campaigns

The process of nomination is not in the Constitution. Neither the Constitution nor the laws give one an adequate picture of how the President is actually chosen. The Constitution provides for the choice of electors, the voting of electors and the counting of the votes (see page 99). Not a word is said about the nomination of a President—the process by which the political parties, meeting in convention, choose the rival candidates every four years. The choice of a candidate for President is a matter of custom—a custom which has grown up with the practices of political parties (fundamentally, since 1832). Let us consider the main steps in the nomination process.

The party "machine": A pyramid of influence. Each party has a structure much like a pyramid. At the base of this structure is the precinct organization; at the apex is the National Committee; in between are the ward, city, county, and state organizations of each party, under their respective leaders.

The business of the National Committee is threefold: It makes preparations for the party's National Convention. It directs the strategy of the Presidential campaign. It carries on the basic party organization between campaigns. In a sense, the Democratic National Committee and the Republican National Committee can be compared to the boards of directors of two giant competing corporations. The parties they represent sell not goods but rather a unique "service"; each is trying to offer the American voters a better Presidential candidate and a more attractive program ("platform").

In both major parties, the National Committee is made up of one man and one woman delegate from each state, from the District of Columbia, and from each of the principal dependencies. These members are nominated by party conventions, or by direct primaries, or by the state delegations in the National Convention. The final choice is made by the convention itself.

The chairman of the National Committee is designated by the Presidential candidate—quite naturally, because he is to be the candidate's campaign manager. For the time being, he is the party leader or "boss" in national affairs. Should the party elect its candidate, the chairman may be rewarded with a place in the Cabinet, possibly with the office of Postmaster General. This office has control over a great deal of patronage. The Chairman normally remains during the President's term in office a powerful influence in both national and state politics.

The campaign as a political adventure. Every four years, party machinery concentrates upon the Presidential campaign. Years of preparation have gone into this elaborate pageantry. The campaign is hardly over before the stage is being set for the next election. The party in power strives to keep itself in power. For the party out of power, there is hope that out of lessons of the past and by concentration upon new issues and new personalities, victory will emerge. All of this is not anything that the framers of the Constitution contemplated. In fact, the procedure for the election of President and Vice President set forth in the Constitution indicates that this was planned as a quiet, dignified affair, rather than as a stirring experience in which all the people of the United States might take part.

It was the rise of parties and party politics that brought about such a transformation. At first, the candidates were named by party caucuses in each state legislature, and later, by congressional caucuses. In time the suffrage became democratized. Caucuses of the state legislatures gave way to popular conventions. These chose delegates to the National Convention. Since the 1830's, the quadrennial National Convention has been a feature of all parties.

The composition of the National Convention. Delegates to the National Convention are chosen by conventions of party members in about half of the states. They are selected by primaries* in the other half. In certain states, the voters also have the privilege of expressing their preference for Presidential nominations. They may even advocate the inclusion of certain "planks" in the party platform. Delegates are apportioned among the states in accordance with party regulations. In the Democratic convention the delegation of each state is twice the size of that state's representation in both houses of Congress. The Republicans, on the other hand, make their distribution approximately in proportion to the vote polled by the party in each state. Each party permits the District of Columbia and certain of the dependencies to send delegates, even though the inhabitants of the latter do not vote for President. Each party also makes provision for alternates.

---

* *Primary elections* are elections *within* a party to determine the choice of party candidates or of certain party officials, such as delegates and committee members. Primaries are discussed in detail in Chapter 10.

A carnival? . . . Or a grassroots expression of American democracy? . . . Or perhaps a bit of both? Scene on the floor during the national convention of a major political party.

National Archives

Preliminaries of the convention. The call for the convention is sounded by the National Committee during the winter preceding the election. Even before this, a contest has already begun among the prospective candidates. They aim to win over state delegations, especially where these are chosen by primaries. Cities vie with one another for the privilege of playing host to the convention. They are ready to pay large sums to the National Committee for that coveted privilege.

Convention pageantry. The National Convention has been variously described as a synthetic product of public relations experts, a carnival belonging more to "show business" than to government, a grassroots expression of American democracy, a much-needed stimulus for the American electorate. Whichever characterization one may prefer, there is no denying that such a convention is an interesting and often impressive occasion. To the convention scene flock delegates, alternates, political hangers-on, spectators, curiosity seekers, and representatives of the press, radio, and television. The convention hall has been decorated with large flags, bunting, and portraits of the great men in the party's history. Delegations are grouped around their respective state standards. From time to time, each state chairman booms out the delegation's vote. Individual members mill about the vast hall, perhaps seeking to arrange political bargains and compromises. They join in demonstrations, parades, and stampedes. But somewhere behind the scenes, very likely closeted in hotel rooms, the bigwigs of the party are probably busy doing the real work. Perhaps this is as it should be. Can a noisy, confused throng be expected to consider the available choices and make sound decisions?

The procedure of the convention is along the following lines. After the customary prayer, temporary officers are selected. A "keynote speech" is delivered by one of the party's top orators. Committees are organized; each state is represented on them. Permanent officers are chosen. Two of these committees are of special importance. One of them is the *Committee on Credentials*, which passes on rival claims regarding the seating of delegates. The other is the *Committee on Platforms and Resolutions*. Its job is to report the party platform—a task which has given rise to many a bitter struggle on the floor of the convention. The reports of the committees are disposed of. The platform is adopted. The convention then proceeds to the all-important business of nominating the party candidates.

Sounding the tocsin: The platform. The party platform has been defined as a "declaration of political principles and a promise of political performance." The party in power at the time of the convention uses the platform to "point with pride" to its achievements and to "view with alarm" any change of administration. The party out of power "points with pride" to its achievements in the past and "views with alarm" what the current administration has done or what it may do if it is returned to power. In any event, most platforms have emphasized vote-catching, noncommittal generalities.

Many intelligent citizens have asked for reforms in party platforms. They have urged that these statements be short, understandable, and to the point. It has been suggested that the platform be worked out by regional conferences or by committees of the party, far in advance of the convention itself. Moreover, the voters in general have become more insistent that the pledges made in the platform be kept. Successful candidates are fully aware of the gibes and torments that will be visited upon them by the opposition if their pledges are violated.

Naming and choosing the standard-bearers. Each state delegation at the convention is called upon in alphabetical order to make nominations for the Presidential standard-bearer. Most of the fifty delegations, of course, will simply "pass." Quite often, a state which is early in the alphabetical sequence will "yield" to another state, so that a nominating speech for a major candidate may be made promptly. It should be noted that a candidate is not necessarily nominated by a delegate from his own state. It may be, and frequently is, advantageous, to assign this task to an accomplished orator, a well-known personality, or a political ally from another state.

On the other hand, as the roll of the states is called, some states may present the names of "favorite sons." These men are not serious candidates for the Presidency. They are rather popular political leaders in their own states, and the nominating speech is a sort of personal tribute or reward for outstanding service. The state delegation may vote for its "favorite son" on the first ballot or two, and then switch to one of the other candidates who has a real chance of nomination.

In any event a number of candidates are presented to the convention, including probably only two or three who are genuine aspirants to the Presidency. Each nominating speech is followed by several seconding speeches. The flood of oratory with which the convention becomes saturated must truly stir the ghosts of Demosthenes, Cicero, Burke, Webster, and William J. Bryan. There follow noisy demonstrations, often spontaneous, more often contrived.

What determines the choice? In the choice of the Presidential nominee, a number of considerations are usually of key importance. The candidate must not have made too many enemies. His views must not be too pronounced or too narrow in their appeal. He cannot be too strongly identified with local or factional politics. His religious connections are subject to scrutiny. Whenever possible, he is selected with a view to "carrying" a doubtful state or section or a "pivotal" state that casts a large electoral vote. All these considerations help to explain why in so many cases strong party leaders have not been nominated, and why conventions have resorted to the choice of "dark horses." The choice of the candidate for Vice President represents even more typically the politics of compromise. The deciding factor here is often to satisfy a state, section, or faction which is not too happy over the candidate for President.

The situation is likely to be markedly different, however, when an incumbent President is seeking re-election. A party will rarely, if ever, fail to renominate its own man in the White House, if he is both eligible and willing to serve again. Thus, Franklin D. Roosevelt easily won renomination by the Democrats in 1936, 1940, and 1944, although his New Deal program and his foreign policies were unpopular with important sectors of the party, and although (in 1940 and 1944) he was bucking the two-term tradition. Moreover, an incumbent President running for another term can usually choose his own Vice-Presidential running mate, although in doing so, he may be influenced by the need to placate some element within the party or some important sector of the population.

The convention ballots. Presently, the tumult and the shouting die down, and the balloting begins. Among the Republicans each delegate votes as an individual. Until recently, the Democrats adhered to the "unit rule," meaning that the entire vote of any state delegation was determined by the vote of the majority of the delegates from that state. Under this rule, it was impossible to shift any part of the votes of a state delegation, and the inflexibility resulting was likely to cause a stalemate whenever there were several strong would-be candidates. More than 100 ballots, for example, were needed to nominate a candidate at the 1924 Democratic Convention. The "unit rule" is now observed by the Democrats only when the party rules of a particular state so require.

Both parties now require a simple majority of the delegates to choose the Presidential and Vice Presidential candidates. The Democrats for almost a century had a "two-thirds rule," but this was ended in 1936.

In the course of the balloting, deadlocks often occur. Strong partisanship must occasionally yield to compromise upon a "dark horse," a personality who emerges from a relatively obscure background. Finally, a choice is grudgingly agreed upon. This need not occur, however. It is not likely to occur when one candidate, for whatever reason, strongly overshadows his rivals at the convention. It almost certainly will not occur when the candidate is already a President seeking a second term. His choice, as we have noted, is a foregone conclusion, and the convention nominates him by "acclamation."

When the hectic business of nominating the Presidential candidate is over, the convention reminds itself that a candidate for Vice President must be chosen. After that is done, the convention adjourns. A committee is chosen to "notify" the candidates and to receive their "acceptance speeches."

Campaign methods, past and present. The direction of the campaign is in the hands of the Chairman of the National Committee and his aids. These have been selected by the National Committee and by the party's nominee for President. National, state and local campaign headquarters are established. From these centers there pours forth a barrage of campaign "literature." Speakers assault the ears of the voters at indoor rallies, on street corners, over the air. Of special importance is the campaign treasurer. He must have valuable financial contacts and must exercise considerable foresight and shrewdness in expending his funds where they

Campaigning as it was—Grover Cleveland "whistle stops" during the 1888 Presidential race.

Campaigning as it is—Nixon and Kennedy in the famous "television debates" of 1960.

will "do the most good." He must concentrate his fire on the doubtful and strategic states.*

To the candidates, themselves, the campaign is a series of nerve-racking experiences. Radio and television have saved time and energy, but personal "whirlwind tours" are still desirable. It is good psychology to have the candidate make a series of personal

* Many laws have been passed to limit and regulate campaign expenditures. These apply not only to the Presidential campaigns but also the Congressional races. Moreover, state laws set similar standards for state and local elections.

Laws applying to Presidential and Congressional campaigns include the following: (1) Each party must file with the clerk of the House of Representatives a statement of campaign contributions and expenditures. (2) A series of *Corrupt Practices Acts* have placed limits on the amounts that may be spent by candidates for the House and the Senate. (3) Under the *Hatch Act*, solicitation of contributions (and other campaign activities) by most employees of the Federal government are forbidden or severely restricted. (4) Corporations, trade unions, and national banks are forbidden to contribute to national political campaigns. This, of course, does not apply to individuals affiliated with such organizations. (See also the proposed reform of Congressional elections on page 80.)

appearances. In the campaign of 1960, a new wrinkle was added to the campaign techniques: the nominees of both major parties, Richard M. Nixon and John F. Kennedy, faced each other and the nation in four debates on television.

Indeed, the performance of the candidates on television appearances has emerged as one of the most important single factors in the campaign. This has certainly helped to stimulate public interest and to bring the candidates closer to many millions of viewers—and voters. On the other hand, fears have been expressed that the TV screen tends to lend too much influence to such assets as youth, good looks, bearing, and mere glibness. Thus, the "image" which a candidate projects may become more important than such solid but unspectacular qualities as experience, integrity, and understanding of public affairs. It is undeniable that this danger exists, but it is equally clear that the best safeguard against such a danger is the same as for so many other potential evils—that is, an informed, alert, and intelligent electorate.

In the course of the Presidential campaign, slogans are coined and quickly gain widespread currency. Recall the magic of "Tippecanoe and Tyler Too," "54-40 or Fight," Bryan's "Cross of Gold" speech, Wilson's "He kept us out of war," Harding's "Back to Normalcy," Roosevelt's "New Deal" and "Forgotten Man," and Johnson's "Great Society." The candidate's own campaigning is, as a rule, one of dignity and honesty. The tactics of his followers and supporters often leave much to be desired. Rare, indeed, has been the Presidential campaign without its "whispers," its false issues, its unfounded charges and implications, its prying into the private lives of the candidates.

One final observation must be made: A pre-election campaign creates a lull in some fields of business, for there is uncertainty over the future. Once it is ended, there is a sigh of relief in all quarters. What is left is the memory of a rousing experience. For all the evils and abuses, that experience is, nevertheless, the groaning and the creaking of a great democratic machine. For all the machinations and limitations of politics, great and good men *have* reached the White House.

How the President Is Chosen

Original method of choosing the President. It was not easy for the Convention of 1787 to agree upon a scheme for electing the President. Most of the delegates wanted the President to be chosen by Congress. This plan was abandoned when objections were raised on the ground that it would undermine the whole system of checks and balances. It was finally decided to leave the choice of the President to a body of men called "electors," to be chosen in each state in such a manner as the legislature of the state might designate. Each state was to have as many electors as it had Senators and Representatives in Congress. A state having, for example, two Senators and ten Representatives would choose twelve electors. The electors, in due course, were to meet in their respective state capitals and vote for two persons. The ballots were then to be sealed and sent to the President of the Senate, whose function it was to count them in the presence of Congress and to announce the results. The candidate receiving the highest number of votes was to be declared President, and the one obtaining the next highest number was to be Vice President.

Changes in the election of the President. Experience, which revealed operational flaws in the original provisions of the Constitution, and the development of democracy in the 19th century produced far-reaching changes in the method of selecting the President. They may be summarized as follows:

1. In the early elections, the electors were chosen by the state legislatures. With the growth of democracy, the choice of electors was transferred from the state legislatures to the voters of the respective states. Today, each party places the candidates for electors on the party ticket. The voter marks his ballot for a certain group of electors on the first Tuesday after the first Monday in November every fourth year.

2. The framers had hoped that electors would use their independent judgment in voting for a President. However, with the development of political parties, it became the practice for the electors to pledge their votes to their party candidates. For example, in the election of 1800, every elector, with a single exception, voted either for Jefferson and Burr, or for Adams and Pinckney; that is, they voted strictly along party lines. Since then, the

electors have, by and large, become mere rubber stamps, who vote unfailingly for the candidates of their respective political parties. In many states, today, the names of the candidates for Presidential electors have even been removed from the ballot or the voting machine. This is true, for example, in New York, although a voter has the right to request the list of electors and may vote for them as individuals. At present, the voters continue to vote for electors whom, in many instances, they do not know; but they do so with the assurance that these electors will vote for the candidates whom the voters know and support.

3. Another change in the election of the President came out of the controversy over the election of 1800. The Constitution in its original form provided that each elector was to vote for two persons, without making any distinction between President and Vice President. The candidate who received the largest number of votes (provided this was a majority) was to be President, and the person who received the second largest number was to be Vice President.

In the election of 1800, Thomas Jefferson and Aaron Burr were the candidates of the Democratic-Republican Party, with the understanding that Jefferson was to be President and Burr, Vice President. The Democratic-Republicans won the election, and every one of their electors voted for both Jefferson and Burr, thus producing a tie. Fortunately, the Constitution provided that in case of a tie, the House of Representatives was to make a choice among the tied candidates who had a majority of the electoral votes. The House did so, choosing Jefferson as President.

To avoid a recurrence of such a snarl, the 12th Amendment was added to the Constitution in 1804. This requires the electors to *cast separate votes for President and Vice President*. The amendment also provides that if no candidate for President has a majority of the electoral vote, the House of Representatives is to make a choice among the *three* persons having the highest number of votes. Each state delegation votes as a unit. If no candidate for Vice President has a majority of the electoral vote, the Senate is to make a choice between the *two* persons with the highest number of votes. Each Senator votes individually.

4. The Reconstruction Period following the Civil War was productive of another troublesome election which led to a change in the election process. In 1876, two different sets of electoral

votes were received from several states. The Constitution had not anticipated such a situation. One set of returns would have insured election of the Republican candidate, Rutherford B. Hayes; the other set would have resulted in the election of the Democratic candidate, Samuel J. Tilden. After a bitter wrangle, in which each party accused the other of dishonesty, a special Electoral Commission, appointed by Congress, decided which sets of votes should be counted. The election went to Hayes. In order to prevent such a problem from coming up again, Congress, in 1887, passed a law dealing with the subject of disputed votes. This law, still in operation, provides that each state must determine, *in accordance with its own laws*, any disputed questions concerning the choice of Presidential electors. Congress reserves the right to reject the returns from any state when, in its opinion, there have been irregularities.

Counting the electoral votes. Although the system of "rubber stamp" electors* enables the nation to know the results of a Presidential election only hours after the polls have closed, the process of recording and counting the votes is still a complicated and cumbersome operation. First, the various local election boards throughout each state send the returns to the state election board. If the state board finds that the Democratic Party, let us say, has received a majority or a plurality of the votes cast in the state, the Democratic nominees are declared to have "carried" the state. In other words, all the electoral votes go to the Democratic candidates. The Democratic electors, now part of the nationwide Electoral College, meet in the state capital in December to cast their ballots for President and Vice President. These votes are signed by each elector, sealed and then sent by registered mail to the President of the United States Senate. Every state follows the same procedure.

* It should be noted that electors do not *always* act as a mere "rubber stamp." In 1948, a Tennessee elector running on both the Democratic and the States Rights tickets voted for the States Rights candidate, even though the Democratic candidate (Harry S. Truman) had a substantial plurality in the state. In 1956, a Democratic elector from Alabama refused to support the Democratic candidate, Adlai E. Stevenson, and voted instead for Walter B. Jones. In 1960, eight unpledged Democratic electors from Mississippi and six from Alabama voted for Senator Harry F. Byrd in place of the regular Democratic candidate, John F. Kennedy. Senator Byrd was not even a Presidential candidate. In the same election a Republican elector from Oklahoma also voted for Byrd, in place of Richard M. Nixon. (See pages 106-107.)

During the month of January following, the President of the Senate counts all the electoral votes before both houses of Congress. The candidate who receives a majority (today, 270) of all the electoral votes cast (538) is declared President-elect.*

If no candidate receives a majority of all the electoral votes, the House of Representatives chooses one of the three leading candidates. Each of the 50 states casts one vote, determined by a majority of the Representatives. If no candidate receives a majority of these votes (26) by January 20, the Vice President-elect becomes President. Only twice in our history (in 1800 and in 1824) was the election of a President thrown into the House of Representatives. In the 1824 election, Jackson had 99 electoral votes, Adams 84, Crawford 41, and Clay 37. The House chose Adams from among the first three candidates, although Jackson was probably the choice of the voters.

Too many "stay-at-home" voters. In the heated Presidential campaign of 1964, more than 70 million Americans went to the polls. This seems like a tremendous number, until we realize that the potential voting population that year was about 114 million. In other words, 44 million Americans, representing about 38% of the electorate, did *not* vote in that year. This represented a slight fall-off from the 1960 election, when 64.3% of the eligibles voted, and a marked decline from the Hayes-Tilden election of 1876, when it is estimated that 86 of every 100 eligibles voted. (However, there were only about 8,300,000 voters in 1876.)

In the 1968 Presidential election, a record total of 73,186,819 votes were cast compared with 70,913,673 in 1964. But it represented only 60.2 per cent of the estimated total of 121.5 million Americans of voting age. The remarkable thing about the 1968 election was that despite the distorting effects of a third candidate in the race, the popular vote of the two major party nominees divided almost evenly across the country: Richard M. Nixon received 31,770,238 votes (43.40 per cent); Hubert H. Humphrey, 31, 270, 533 votes (42.72); and George C. Wallace, 9,906,141 votes (13.53). An assortment of other candidates received 239,908 votes.

* The Electoral College had 531 members from 1912 to 1956. In 1960, after Alaska and Hawaii became states, membership rose to 537. For the 1964 election and thereafter, the size was set at 538. This figure was the result of two changes: passage of the 23rd Amendment, which gives three electoral votes to the District of Columbia (page 349) ; and a return of the House of Representatives to 435 members (page 19).

One reason for the indifference, it is believed, is the Electoral College system, which gives *all* the electoral votes of the state to the party which captures a majority of the popular vote. In states where one party (or perhaps one candidate) is clearly dominant, there is little or no doubt as to who will carry the state. Under such conditions, many voters seem to feel that their votes are meaningless because they cannot possibly affect the ultimate distribution of electoral votes. There is considerable evidence that many voters are encouraged to turn out at the polls by the prospect of a *close* election, in which a relatively small number of votes may actually determine the outcome.

Moreover, when one state is considered safely in the column of either of the major parties, it usually receives little attention in the Presidential campaign. Both parties prefer to concentrate on the large "doubtful" states which will probably decide the election. Thus, the campaign in the "safe" states may become little more than a half-hearted routine.

Other criticisms of the Electoral College system. This tendency of the Electoral College system to lessen the importance of individual votes and to weaken voter interest is perhaps the most telling criticism of the present method of electing the President. But there are other criticisms which have often been expressed.

1. The Electoral College system may result in the election of a President who has fewer popular votes than his opponent. The one case in which this definitely occurred was the election of 1888, in which Harrison was elected over Cleveland, even though the latter received about 100,000 more popular votes. This was made possible by the fact that Harrison carried several of the larger states, notably New York, by very narrow margins, while Cleveland won a number of the less populous states by large margins. There were several other elections in which victory may have gone to a candidate with a smaller number of popular votes—the Jackson-John Quincy Adams election of 1824, and the Hayes-Tilden election of 1876—although in both these instances the exact facts are somewhat blurred.

2. If no candidate receives a majority of the electoral vote, the election is thrown into the House of Representatives, where each state delegation has a single vote. This happened, as we have noted, in 1800 and 1824. There is no guarantee whatever that the vote in the House will reflect the popular will.

3. The Electoral College system may lead to great disparities between the popular and the electoral vote. In 1828, John Quincy Adams, running for re-election, gained heavy majorities in the Eastern states that brought his popular vote within 12% of Andrew Jackson's, but Jackson's support was so much more widely diffused that he won in the Electoral College by better than 2 to 1. In 1860, Lincoln received only about 40% of the popular vote, but he won a decisive victory in the Electoral College—180 votes to 123 for all his three opponents. In 1960, Kennedy defeated Nixon by 303 electoral votes to 219, although the difference in the popular vote was only one-tenth of 1%—perhaps the closest election in our history. Both Lincoln and Kennedy were "minority Presidents"—that is, they received less than half of all the popular votes cast. It may be said, however, that in such cases, if the election goes to the man who has gained more popular votes than his opponent (or opponents), the Electoral College system is not at fault.

4. The Electoral College system exaggerates the importance of the less populous states because their electoral vote reflects the allotment of two Senators, regardless of population. For example, Nevada with a population of 285,000, has three electoral votes (the minimum). This works out to ratio of 95,000 residents per electoral vote. New York, with a population of 16,700,000 has 43 electoral votes—a ratio of 388,000 residents per electoral vote.

This diagram shows graphically how it is that an individual vote in Nevada for Presidential electors has four times the weight of a similar individual vote in New York State.

Some observers, however, are of the opinion that this condition may not be altogether a bad thing. States like Nevada, Alaska, and Vermont, with their distinctive economic interests and needs, would be altogether insignificant in their influence on Presidential elections if their electoral vote were proportioned strictly according to population.

5. A final criticism, which can scarcely be refuted, is that the Electoral College represents a lot of cumbersome, outdated, expensive machinery.

Proportional representation proposed. To stimulate voting and to insure the election of "the people's choice," a constitutional amendment has been proposed to abolish the Electoral College and elect the President without changing the relative strength of the several states. Under the proposal, each state would keep its present quota of electoral votes, but would distribute them among the candidates, in proportion to their popular votes within the state. For example, Illinois in the election of 1948, gave President Truman 1,994,715 popular votes out of a total of 3,982,417. Because this was almost 50% of the popular vote of the state, under proportional representation, Mr. Truman would have been entitled to about 50% of the electoral votes—that is 14.2 out of the total of 28, instead of the entire 28. Thomas E. Dewey, who had about 49% of the popular vote, would have received 13.7 electoral votes, instead of none at all.

Suppose that a similar redistribution had been carried out in all the other states in the 1948 election. How would the election have shaped up? The following chart summarizes the actual results and the results under a system of proportional representation.

CANDIDATES	TOTAL POPULAR VOTES RECEIVED	TOTAL ELECTORAL VOTES RECEIVED	ELECTORAL VOTES UNDER PROPORTIONAL REPRESENTATION (approx.)
Truman (Dem.)	24,105,812 (49.5%)	303 (57.0%)	263 (49.5%)
Dewey (Rep.)	21,970,065 (45.1%)	189 (35.5%)	240 (45.1%)
Thurmond (States Rights)	1,169,021 (2.4%)	39 (8.5%)	13 (2.4%)
Wallace (Progressive)	1,157,152 (2.3%)	0	12 (2.3%)
All Others	434,500 (0.7%)	0	3 (0.7%)

Arguments for and against proportional representation. Leaders in Congress and elsewhere who have favored proportional division of electoral votes in the choice of the President point out that this method would give every voter the satisfaction of helping his favorite candidate for President, regardless of whether or not he votes with the majority in his state. This, it is claimed, would stimulate interest in elections and encourage voting. It would help to make the best qualified candidates politically available for nomination, regardless of their place of residence. Today candidates are often chosen in part because it is believed they can carry a large "doubtful" state. Thus, while most parts of the country have been represented by candidates for President and Vice President in the major parties, it is the populous states carrying large blocs of electoral votes (especially New York, Ohio, Illinois, and California) that have contributed the larger number of candidates in the 20th century. Finally proportional representation would make it virtually impossible for a Presidential candidate to win the election when a rival has gained a larger popular vote throughout the nation.

Those who oppose a change in the present electoral system argue that the present system preserves the unity of each state and makes it count more in the Presidential race. They maintain that proportional representation would tend to centralize our government still further, thus weakening state powers. Finally, it is pointed out that the present two major parties, one or the other of which has been in power since the Civil War, are extremely unlikely to support a plan that would inevitably strengthen minor parties and perhaps encourage the growth of a formidable third-party movement. A large number of parties competing for the Presidency would all too often produce deadlock, shifting and unstable party coalitions, and minority Presidents who had been forced to bargain and compromise their way into office.

A non-controversial reform proposal: Make electors function as "rubber stamps." We have already noted (see the footnote on page 101) that in a number of recent elections, individual electors or groups of electors have *not* voted for the Presidential candidates in whose names they were chosen. There can be no doubt that this is a dangerous abuse of nominal authority and a threat to our constitutional system. It is undemocratic and irresponsible in the extreme for individuals to depart from established custom and to exploit the theoretical constitutional independence of electors. By changing their votes arbitrarily, they may thwart the expressed desires of hundreds of thousands or even millions of citizens. While it is not likely that such a violation of pledges would swing an election, it is not impossible. It has been pointed out, for example, that in an election as close as the one of 1960, the single Republican elector in Oklahoma who refused to vote for Nixon might conceivably have decided the Presidency. If several state delegations refuse to honor their pledges, a close election may be thrown into the House of Representatives.

For this reason, it has been suggested that all electors be required by law to vote for the Presidential candidate in whose name they are elected.* Another way of accomplishing the same results would be to abolish the Electoral College and to assign each state's electoral vote automatically to the candidate who wins a plurality of the popular vote. Note that the relative electoral strength of the various states would be unchanged by such a reform. Speaking of this proposal in 1966, Attorney General Nicholas B. Katzenbach said: "The need for (such a) change is, I think, almost universally conceded, and it is the very minimum which is required to protect Presidential elections from the grave risks to which they are now exposed."

A number of states (seventeen according to a recent count) have laws which refer to the obligation of electors to vote for the candidates in whose names they are chosen. The laws, however, are of varying degrees of clarity and effectiveness, and the need for a Federal policy applying to all the states appears to be beyond question.

But somehow the system works. Perhaps the best defense that can be made of our present system of electing the President, cumbersome and outdated as it may be, is that in practice it has not worked badly. If one considers the Presidents who have been elected since the system settled into its present pattern, one finds four giants—Jackson, Lincoln, Wilson, Franklin D. Roosevelt— and at least four men of outstanding qualities—Polk, Cleveland, Theodore Roosevelt, Truman. (Only future historians can rank

---

* In 1968, a North Carolina elector who ran pledged to Richard M. Nixon switched his vote to George C. Wallace, candidate of the American Independent Party. But the Senate and the House of Representatives, voting separately on January 6, 1969, defeated a motion that would have wiped the controversial vote off the record.

the most recent Presidents—Eisenhower, Kennedy, Johnson, and Nixon.) Eight first-raters out of twenty-two Chief Executives (again excluding the four named above) is a good record by any reasonable standard. And it becomes even better when one realizes that fewer than half a dozen of the other Presidents could be ranked as mediocre or less than satisfactory. One admittedly ineffective President, Ulysses S. Grant, won two terms.

The 1968 election involved a three-way race which might have thrown the election into the House and thus produced a pointless and potentially dangerous delay of two months or more before the new President was chosen. Although the danger was averted, this revived the issue of electoral reform. An amendment was offered in Congress to abolish the Electoral College and substitute direct popular election of the President. The House approved this overwhelmingly in 1969, but the Senate in 1970 did not muster the necessary two-thirds support. Disappointed over their failure to rid the nation of "electoral roulette," supporters of reform had to await another day.

Proposals for Reform of the Presidency

Beyond reform of the Electoral College, various suggestions have been advanced over the years to make the Presidency a more effective institution. Some of these are set forth below. (In Chapter 5, we shall consider proposals which relate to the actual operation of the Presidential office.)

♦ *Danger in the long campaign.* Presidential campaigns have grown so long and arduous that they represent a threat to the health of the President-elect. It has been suggested that the campaign might be shortened by holding the nominating conventions later than they are now—perhaps in September. Such a change would have another value by reducing the time interval (the "interregnum") between the time of nomination and the date that the winner actually takes office. During this period, the authority of the President in office is usually diminished, unless he is a candidate for re-election.

♦ *The defeated candidate—a "forgotten man."* The United States is perhaps the only country in the world that raises a man to be the head of a major political party and then, if the party loses a national election, makes no special effort to keep him in public life. We are, indeed, the one country in which the losing party—the "loyal opposition"—ends up with no functioning head and with no clearly identifiable holder of public office about whom it can rally in defeat.

Proposals have, consequently, been made to add an amendment to the Constitution which would give a defeated Presidential candidate who received, say, at least 25% of the popular vote a seat in the House of Representatives for the next four years. This would provide the minority party with a recognized position for its leader. At the same time, the function of opposition, which is the responsibility of the minority party, would be better performed.

♦ A suggestion along the same lines has been made by Professor Clinton Rossiter, a well-known writer on the Presidency. He suggested an amendment to the Constitution which would offer unsuccessful candidates for the office of the President membership in the United States Senate for a term of four years.

Sidney Hyman, another authority on the Presidency, raised this objection to the above proposals: "The greatest objection of all remains a Constitutional one. Ours is a system of responsible power where every man is accountable to someone else for the consequences of his governmental acts. In such a system, a former President (or a defeated candidate), set down in the Congress, would be a disruptive force. He would have no fixed point of legal and political accountability. His sole source of responsibility would be to his own conscience and to his sense of patriotism . . ." The answer to this objection might well be "This is just the kind of public official we want."

♦ *The transition problem.* President Abraham Lincoln, anticipating defeat in the election of 1864, made careful plans to cooperate with his successor. President Wilson, equally concerned with the transition problems, and thinking that he might lose the election of 1916, was ready to suggest that he appoint Charles E. Hughes (his opponent) to the office of Secretary of State, after which he (the President), the Vice President, and the old Secretary of State would resign. Under the Presidential Succession Act in effect at that time Mr. Hughes would have immediately succeeded to the Presidency. Both Lincoln and Wilson, obviously, had the foresight and the sense of responsibility to want to provide for a smooth and rapid transition of government in critical times.

While recent Presidents have not contemplated such drastic measures, some of them have taken pains to do something about the transition. President-elect Kennedy, for example, immediately after the election designated Clark M. Clifford, an experienced Washington attorney, to serve as his liaison representative with the retiring administration of President Eisenhower. Soon after, meetings were held between the representatives of the incoming and outgoing administrations as well as between the President and the President-elect. It was thought that a degree of continuity could be effected by appointing some members of the old administration to continue in office—especially in the fields of foreign policy and defense. But no real, permanent machinery for the transition has yet been worked out by anyone.

♦ *Earlier inauguration.* "Time is of the essence"—an old adage which has never been truer than it is today. Recurrent national and world crises, coupled with machine voting and rapid means of communication, make earlier inaugurations advisable and feasible. The general election is held early in November. Why cannot the Electoral College meet early in December, with the inauguration taking place before Christmas? This would cut down the barren "interregnum" by one month and insure an earlier as well as a smoother transition. Of course, such a change would require an amendment to the Constitution.

♦ *Revision of national political conventions.* As long ago as 1913, President Woodrow Wilson was of the opinion that "there ought never to be another Presidential nominating convention." He proposed a nation-wide system of Presidential preference primaries. Under this form of primary, the voter would not nominate the Presidential candidates directly, but rather select delegates to the national conventions "pledged" or "instructed" to vote for a given candidate. It is interesting to note that Oregon extended the direct primary to Presidential nominations as far back as 1910. Today a Presidential preference primary is required by law in about one-fifth of the states, including California. In one-third of the states, voters elect delegates to the National Conventions. (See page 308 for treatment of the direct primary.)

In 1965, former President Eisenhower came out in favor of reforming National Conventions. He characterized them as "disorderly and undignified," a situation now dramatized for the nation by television. Another critic, John K. Galbraith, has been even more severe. "Now the airplane and the telephone have reduced the convention to a *ratification ceremony* . . . We should long ago have started to worry about it, were the convention not so repetitiously described by journalists as a great American spectacle; so stolidly defended by politicians who must justify the considerable expense and protect the small prestige of being chosen to attend; and so canonized by television commentators who, aware of the great costs to their employers, must persuade themselves and their audience that something is happening. I personally doubt the public can be persuaded much longer."

Terms You Should Know

Convention. A gathering of delegates or representatives, empowered to act on particular matters such as revision of a constitution, nomination of candidates, or preparation of a platform.

Dark horse. A relatively obscure figure who unexpectedly gains support for a party nomination and may actually receive that nomination. The term is used particularly in relation to candidates for the Presidency.

Electoral College. Body of electors chosen by the voters in the various states to select the President and Vice President of the United States. The Electoral College is supposed to act as a "rubber stamp" for the will of the people.

Favorite son. A candidate for the Presidency who is popular in his own state but has relatively little support outside that state. Usually not a serious aspirant to the Presidency.

Nomination. Selection by a political party of its candidate for an elective office. Also appointment to an executive post, subject to confirmation by some designated body, such as the Senate.

Party machine. A term (usually derogatory) used to describe a well-disciplined political party organization, often under the control of a "boss."

Plank. Any specific item or issue on which a political party declares itself in its platform.

Platform. Statement by a political party summarizing its policies and programs in regard to the main issues facing the nation (or state, or city, as the case may be). A party appeals to the voters on the basis of its platform, as well as its candidates.

Primary election. An election *within* a political party for the purpose of choosing that party's candidates in a forthcoming election. Usually, all registered party members are eligible to vote in a primary.

Pro tempore. Temporary. This term is used most commonly to refer to the Senator who is chosen to preside over the U.S. Senate in the absence of the Vice President. He is called the "President pro tem" of the Senate.

Unit rule. A regulation under which all of a state's votes at a national convention are cast for the candidate who receives a majority of those votes. State delegations at the Democratic National Convention are authorized to adopt the unit rule.

Questions and Problems Based on the Text

1. What are the constitutional qualifications for President of the United States?

2. What salary and other allowances does the President receive? Do you regard this as excessive? Why?

3. How long is the Presidential term of office? How many terms may the President serve according to the Constitution? When and why was the 22nd Amendment proposed? What do you think of it?

4. What is meant by the *inauguration* of the President? Read the oath of office in the Constitution (Article II, Section 1).

5. (*a*) What tasks are ordinarily performed by the Vice President? (*b*) Under what circumstances may he take the place of the President? (*c*) State the provisions of the Presidential Succession Act of 1947. (*d*) State briefly the provisions of the 25th Amendment to the Constitution. Why was this considered necessary?

6. What does the Constitution say about the nomination of the President?

7. Cite the pros and cons of the present methods of nominating a President.

8. Define the following terms: *"dark horse," "favorite son,"* party *platform, plank, keynote speech, unit rule, party slogan.*

9. Explain how the Electoral College is chosen, and explain its functions. What is meant by the statement that the Electoral College "operates like a rubber stamp"? Why is it important that it *should* operate like a rubber stamp?

10. What proportion of the electoral votes must a candidate for President receive in order to be elected? If no nominee receives this required proportion of the votes, how is the election decided?

11. What difficulties developed in the election of 1876? How was the election settled? What provisions were made to avoid a recurrence of such difficulties?

12. A candidate for the Presidency may receive less than half of the total popular vote and still be elected. Explain how this may happen. Mention one election in which the winning candidate (*a*) received less than half of the popular vote but more votes than any other candidate; (*b*) received fewer votes than the losing candidate. Do you think that either or both of these situations represent an undemocratic feature of our government? Explain.

13. Among the many suggestions which have been made for reforming our method of electing the President are the following:

(a) A direct popular vote.

(b) Proportional division of the electoral vote of each state in accordance with the popular vote.

(c) A law which would require the members of the Electoral College in each state to vote in accordance with the popular vote in that state.

State the pros and cons for each of these reforms. Which, if any, would you support? Explain.

14. It has been suggested that the President serve a six-year term, without being eligible for re-election. Would you support such a change? Why or why not?

15. "The Vice President should be selected by the President himself. He should sit in the Cabinet as of constitutional right." This suggestion was made by Professor William Y. Elliot many years ago. Would you support either of these proposals. Has either of them been carried out, at least in part, by recent developments?

16. In 1966, the U. S. Supreme Court turned down a suit by Delaware and a dozen other small states which had charged that the present electoral system (giving all of a state's electoral votes to the candidate who carries the state) is unconstitutional.

(a) Bearing in mind the Supreme Court's "one man, one vote" doctrine (see Chapter 7), what do you suppose was the reasoning behind this suit by Delaware and the other states?

(b) Why do you think the Supreme Court rejected their contention?

17. In 1966, Congress passed a law which provides that a taxpayer may authorize in his Federal income tax returns an allotment of $1.00 to go to Presidential campaign financing. The estimated 60 million dollars would be divided equally between the Democratic and Republican Parties.

(a) Senator Russell B. Long of Louisiana, sponsor of the measure, maintained that the funds raised in this way would do much to prevent undue influence by large campaign contributors. Senator Albert Gore of Tennessee opposed the measure on the grounds that "it would commingle public funds with private campaign money." Which argument do you favor? Why?

(b) Research the following question: How will third parties fare under this law?

Ideas to Think About and Discuss

1. *"I felt as if I had lived five lifetimes in my first five days as President. I was beginning to realize how little the Founding Fathers had been able to anticipate the preparations necessary for a man to become President so suddenly. It is a mighty leap from the Vice Presidency to the Presidency when one is forced to make it without warning."*

    —HARRY S. TRUMAN

2. *"No man is good enough to govern another man without the other's consent."*

    —ABRAHAM LINCOLN

3. *"The historical process has put clothes on our backs, shoes on our feet and meat in the mouth in spite of our wonted apathy."*

    —SAUL BELLOW (Herzog)

4. *"What the President is depends in large part upon his personality. His power is limited. What he is, or can get away with, depends upon his capacity to judge the limits of his own powers. That involves insight, knowledge, and a sense of the possible."*

    —CHARLES A. BEARD

5. *"The President does perhaps overrepresent the urban, liberal, labor, ethnic minority groups in the nation, both because of their sheer number and because of the winner-take-all impact of the Electoral College."*

    —JAMES M. BURNS

6. *"The national nominating conventions of either party are really ratifying conventions, since the nominees had already been chosen in caucus . . . The importance of the nominating conventions is just so much hoopla drummed up by journalists and commentators."*

    —JOHN K. GALBRAITH

7. *"Eloquence may set fire to reason."*

    —OLIVER WENDELL HOLMES, JR.

CHAPTER **5**

does the president have too much or too little power.

The Powers of the President

The Presidency—Yesterday and Today

The rise of "Presidential government." About a half century ago, when the U. S. Senate repudiated President Wilson and his support of the League of Nations, a British observer characterized the American system of government as "all anchor, no sail." The President, this implied, was powerless to act effectively in the field of foreign affairs. Judging from the administrations of Harding, Coolidge, and Hoover, one might have said much the same of the Presidency in the field of domestic affairs. But in surveying the administrations of Franklin D. Roosevelt and of the Presidents who followed him, we get an altogether different picture. The Presidency has become a positive and dynamic institution. Almost every day's newspaper headlines reflect the fact that the Executive branch of our government has evolved into a political instrument of great power and prestige. So clear is this fact that our system, which has been described at times as "Congressional government" and in other periods as "government by the Judiciary," may now be characterized as "Presidential government."

The Presidency yesterday. It has been said that the delegates to the Constitutional Convention regarded George III of England as their model of what a President of the United States should *not* be. In other words, they took mental note of all the powers which this king had abused, and then made sure that history should not repeat itself in America. The result was a Chief Executive whose functions were to carry out the laws of Congress, to give Congress information with respect to domestic and foreign affairs, and to assist Congress in its deliberations by merely suggesting remedies for existing evils. Congress was in no way bound to accept the President's recommendations. Even the President's power to veto legislation was intended merely as a check on Congress—to restrain it from passing bad laws, rather than to guide or stimulate it to pass good laws.

The Presidency today. Under present-day practice, the President not only formulates legislative policies but also exercises a great deal of power to obtain favorable action upon them. He is, in truth, the "chief legislator." Furthermore, a rapidly expanding industrial civilization has imposed upon the President numerous duties and powers that his predecessors of earlier generations could not have dreamed of. His purely executive powers make him an extremely potent factor in the government of our country. This is largely a result of the popular demand that government concern itself *actively* with the welfare of the people. These statements apply to the powers of the President in *normal* times. In periods of *crisis*, such as war (cold or hot) or prolonged depression, the President can assume all but dictatorial powers. In the words of Edwin S. Corwin, an authority on the Presidency: "The history of the Presidency is a history of aggrandizement." "Kept within bounds," says another authority, "the power and prestige of the Presidency comprise the most valuable asset of the American people." What explains this changed conception of the Presidency?

Sources of the President's Growing Powers

The Constitution, a source of many powers. The Constitution gives the President, in explicit terms, some of his principal powers. They are the right to approve and to veto acts of Congress; to appoint officials and to make treaties, both of which require the advice and consent of the Senate; to pardon convicted violators of Federal laws; to serve as Commander-in-Chief of the armed forces; and to carry out the laws of Congress. These constitutional powers cannot be taken away. By themselves, they make the President a powerful executive—stronger than the executive heads of most other democratic governments today.

Powers derived from Congress and the courts. The disappearance of the frontier; the binding together of the country by a vast and complicated network of transportation and communication; the displacement of small independent concerns by giant industrial, distributive, and financial organizations; and the development of cities and urban life—all of these have produced a highly complex social order. If the various parts of this diverse struc-

Many Presidents, particularly those who exemplified the tradition of dynamic personal leadership, have been bitterly criticized in their own day as would-be "tyrants" and "dictators." Here we see a cartoon which leveled such charges at Theodore Roosevelt in the election of 1904.

ture are to function smoothly, leadership must be lodged in a single authority. Action (planning, engineering, controlling) must take the place of protracted debate. Responsive to this need, Congress has, from time to time, delegated greater authority to the President, and the Federal courts have made the power stick.

In 1933, for example, Congress passed an act giving the President enormous powers to inflate the currency. He was permitted to reduce the gold content of the dollar up to 50%; to issue $3,000,000,000 in paper money; and to purchase vast quantities of silver for coinage. As a result of this, the Congressional power "to coin money and regulate the value thereof" was now shared with the President. Numerous other instances of the same trend will be cited in this chapter.

The President, chief of the dominant party. There are approximately 26,000 Federal offices that the President fills by appointment with consent of the Senate. In recent years, the number has been constantly growing, largely because of the expansion of governmental activities in such areas as public works, the armed forces, social security measures, and the conduct of international affairs. This patronage gives the President a weapon against the party leaders in the Federal, state and city organizations that few care to disregard. After all, the primary urge that prompts many people to devote a good part of their lives to the service of a political party is the hope of getting a job, either for the income and security that it provides, or as a matter of prestige and self-fulfillment. People who succeed in obtaining such jobs want to hold on to them or get better ones. When we bear in mind, further, that a large number of party leaders hold seats in the Senate and in the House of Representatives, we can readily understand how the President uses his appointive power to exercise influence over legislation. The President's control of Federal patronage is considered one major reason that few Presidents of either party have failed of renomination for a second term.

Chief maker of public opinion. Having been chosen by the entire electorate, the President represents the whole country in a way that the individual members of Congress do not and cannot. This fact helps to explain why the American people, more and more, look to the President for the expression of their wishes, and for the use of his powers to put these wishes into effect. Also, it is this fact that explains why the President, more and more, appeals to the electorate, over the head of the Legislative branch.

President Woodrow Wilson addresses a joint session of Congress to ask for a declaration of war against Imperial Germany—April 2, 1917.

Through the powerful media of press, radio and television, the President is now able to reach actually the entire nation. Frequent conferences between the President and the press are held at which hundreds of reporters representing leading newspapers, the press associations, foreign newspapers, and magazines, as well as commentators from several radio-TV networks, meet to hear him expound the salient points of his policies. His utterances promptly become front-page news and are read by people all over the country. Thus, the President has his views translated into news before any criticism has been made of them. This is a tremendous advantage, which Presidents who have a gift for expression and a feel for public relations are quick to use to advance their policies and programs.

The role of personality. President Woodrow Wilson once said that when a man is placed in a position of unusual power and responsibility, one of two things may happen to him: either he grows, or he swells. A combination of the right personal qualities and of favorable political circumstances will enable a holder of the Presidency to "grow" and to use that great office to the fullest. Searching through the pages of political history, one comes across excellent examples of such combinations. The rugged Andrew Jackson was carried into office by a great surge of democratic sentiment. Here was a man who had an intuitive understanding of what was in the mind and heart of the rising "common man." Using this tremendously powerful public support, Jackson was able to ride roughshod over Congress, to defy the Supreme Court, and to employ his executive powers in all but regal fashion. For a time, at least, "Mr. President" gave way to "King Andrew the First." Presidents Lincoln, Theodore Roosevelt, Wilson, Franklin D. Roosevelt, Truman, and Johnson are other examples of the aggressive, dynamic, or "energizing" type of Chief Executive.

In contrast, our history provides many examples of the neutral or passive type of personality in the White House. This type tries to avoid excessive change or strong commitments. Fearful of being caught in cross-currents of change that may endanger his status, he tends to avoid controversial issues, or at least tries to develop formulas that will minimize the controversy. Presidents Buchanan, Taft, and Eisenhower (the last named particularly on domestic issues) may be classified among the Chief Executives who emphasized stability and continuity rather than dynamism.

"Eh ? What say?"

Every President eventually "has trouble with Congress," in the sense that he encounters more or less effective resistance to his legislative proposals. Here is a cartoon comment on President Lyndon B. Johnson's experience with Congress on one phase of the "Great Society" program.

Sanders in the *Kansas City Star*

Behind it all, the state of the nation. The most crucial single factor determining Presidential powers is undoubtedly the state of the nation as a whole. In its present status as a global power, the United States has learned that crisis is an ever-present part of the modern world. Thus, in spite of the built-in "machinery of deadlock" (remember the principles of *separation of powers* and of *checks and balances* underlying our Constitution), the nation's dynamism gathers its forces at the moment of crisis and asserts itself strongly. And the agency that most adequately reflects this capacity for change and mastery of circumstances is the symbol of national unity—the Presidency.

The Scope of the President's Powers

Classification of the President's powers. The powers which have been granted to the President may be classified under the following heads: (1) his purely *executive powers*, which are exercised in connection with the enforcement of Federal laws; (2) his *legislative powers*, which give him a share in the making of laws; (3) his *diplomatic powers*, which make him a vital factor in the regulation of foreign affairs; (4) his *military powers*, which devolve upon him by virtue of his position as Commander-in-Chief of the Armed Forces, including the militia of the several states when called into the service of the United States; and (5) his *judicial powers*—that is, powers by which he influences the courts and their processes.

This classification of powers is merely a convenient grouping for study purposes. In actual operation, a given act or policy by the President often cuts across the various areas of authority. Thus, when President Theodore Roosevelt signed the "Gentlemen's Agreement" with Japan in 1907, he exercised powers which were not only diplomatic in their character but also legislative. When President Eisenhower appointed Earl Warren Chief Justice of the United States, he performed a strictly executive act which nevertheless had a direct bearing on the judiciary.

A number of the President's powers, especially those which he derives from his leadership of the political party in power and which are, therefore, extra-constitutional, have not been included in this classification. They have been analyzed at the beginning of this chapter.

The President at work as an executive. The Constitution imposes on the President the duty to "take care that the laws be faithfully executed." The President performs this task through a vast multitude of "assistants," ranging from Secretaries of the Cabinet and bureau chiefs, to clerks, guards, and common laborers. Altogether the Executive branch employs more than 2,600,-000 persons (as of 1966) to "assist" the President.* Of this number, most positions have been filled, in recent years, by civil service competitive examinations. The President, with the consent of the Senate, as mentioned above, fills about 26,000 jobs by direct appointment. The remainder are appointed directly or indirectly by Cabinet officers and other agency heads. Of course, the President, through his appointment of high-ranking officials, can influence, if he wishes, many of these appointments.

Since the President is responsible for the execution of the laws, it is only proper that he be given the initiative in making important appointments. When he has selected anyone to serve as a member of his Cabinet, as a top official of an independent agency, as an ambassador, or as a Federal judge, he is required to send the name of his choice to the Senate for confirmation. A mere majority of the Senate is required for the confirmation of the appointment. Rarely does the Senate reject the President's choice of a Cabinet officer. The refusals of the Senate to confirm the appointments by President Coolidge of Charles B. Warren for Attorney General and by President Eisenhower of Lewis L. Strauss for Secretary of Commerce are almost unique. Presidential history records only eight occasions when the President was overruled in his Cabinet selections. In instances other than the Cabinet, the Senate's power is one to be reckoned with, as we shall see below.

Appointing as he does numerous officials, the President, of necessity, must depend largely on the advice of the Senators, Representatives, and political leaders in the states. In the matter of confirmation by the Senate, there has developed a custom called "Senatorial courtesy." According to this usage, no nomination of any officer, such as a postmaster, will be confirmed unless the nominee is satisfactory to the Senator or Senators of the President's party from the state in which the office is to be filled. In

---

* Federal and state labor relations statutes deny public employees the right to strike, but affirm their right to reasonable consideration of collective bargaining demands.

other words, a Democratic President is not supposed to nominate someone as postmaster of New York City without first consulting the Democratic Senator or Senators from New York State. Should the President overlook this requirement, the other Senators, out of "courtesy" to their colleague or colleagues from New York, may refuse to confirm the proposed appointee.

Removal of appointees from office. If the President's appointments need the confirmation of the Senate, do removals from office likewise require the Senate's consent? Time and again this question has been a pressing issue. Hamilton and Madison debated this matter in the pages of *The Federalist*. The latter maintained that the President could not fairly be held responsible for carrying out the laws unless he had the power to remove his subordinates at will. More than a century later, in 1926, the Supreme Court in a six-to-three decision upheld the President's power of removal in a test case brought by a postmaster in Portland, Oregon.

With the expansion of governmental services, administered by various agencies, such as commissions, bureaus and boards (see Chapter 6), this power has assumed tremendous importance. For example, a President might conceivably force the members of the Federal Communications Commission, which controls radio and television broadcasting, to surrender their independent judgment under the penalty of removal. This might mean political control of the air and ultimate suppression of criticism of the administration in power. The question came up again during the administrations of Coolidge and Hoover. Were these agencies mere instruments of the President, or were they set up by Congress in order to serve as bipartisan tribunals, exercising independent judgment? Finally, President F. D. Roosevelt posed the issue directly. After having sought unsuccessfully to bring about the resignation of William E. Humphrey—a member of the Federal Trade Commission—because their minds did not "go along together," he ordered his summary removal. In a decision rendered in 1935 in the now famous *Humphrey Case*, the Supreme Court ruled that the President did *not* have the power to remove officials, save on the statutory grounds provided by Congress in the act creating the FTC. This decision was a victory for all those who, believing that there is a limit to Executive domination, agree that the scope of the President's removal power should vary with the nature of the office.

The President in the role of legislator. Professor W. F. Willoughby has expressed the opinion that it is not going too far to say that the President now constitutes an organ of legislation scarcely second in power and influence to Congress itself. According to this conception, the President is not only Chief Executive but a powerful political leader as well. He not merely serves as an agent of Congress in carrying out its laws, but actually originates legislative measures and, with the help of administration leaders, directs their course through both houses of Congress. The promise of patronage and other Presidential favors given in the course of a conference or social function at the White House has influenced many a legislator.

By calling special sessions of Congress and by sending annual and special messages, the President is also able to exert considerable influence over legislation. At the beginning of every regular session, the President presents to Congress four messages of great importance. They are a message on *The State of the Union*, an *Economic Report, a Fiscal Report,* and a message on proposed taxation. Each such message is a broad picture of conditions, as the President interprets them, and each is accompanied by recommendations for action. The Economic Report is prepared by

President Franklin D. Roosevelt reports to Congress (and to the American people) on the State of the Union (January, 1938).

National Archives

the Council of Economic Advisers, whose members are appointed by the President, with the consent of the Senate. It is the duty of this Council (established by the Full Employment Act of 1946) to study economic conditions and trends and to recommend to the President courses of action which form the groundwork of economic legislation.

When the President's party controls a Congressional majority, he can be reasonably certain that his recommendations will be considered respectfully, unless he has antagonized his party leaders, or unless his views are sharply at variance with a powerful segment of legislative (and public) opinion. An outstanding example of Presidential direction of legislation occurred during the first term of the 89th Congress. President Johnson, a veritable "engineer at the throttle," was able to induce Congress to enact such significant laws as the anti-poverty program, Medicare, the Voting Rights Act, and several laws aiding public education on a far greater scale than ever before. No wonder journalists referred admiringly (if not always approvingly) to the "miracle" of President Johnson's "hundred days." It was really more than that, for Congress was kept at work until the late fall of 1965.

Blocking legislation: The veto power. In addition to his positive powers in lawmaking, the President has a negative power by which he may restrain Congress from doing certain things. This is his *veto power*. The Constitution specifies that every bill which has passed the two houses of Congress is to be submitted to the President for his approval. He is given ten days in which to consider it. If he favors the measure he may sign it; or, if Congress is still in session, he may, after ten days, allow it to become a law without his signature. If he disapproves of the measure he may *veto* it—that is, forbid it to become a law. In this case, he returns the bill to Congress with a statement of the reasons for his veto. Congress may pass it over his veto by a two-thirds majority of both houses. If Congress adjourns before the passage of the ten-day period, the President's failure to act on a bill "kills" it. This is the so-called *pocket veto*.

The free use of the President's veto power is a relatively recent development, which has accompanied the rise of Presidential leadership in the realm of legislation. Originally, the veto was intended to serve essentially as a weapon against encroachment by Congress upon Executive authority. Also, since the President is the representative of all the people, it was hoped that prudent use of the veto power would protect the nation against passage of bad legislation, through haste, poor judgment, or malicious intent. Early Presidents used the veto sparingly. It was not thought proper, except under very special conditions, for a President to set his judgment against the collective judgment of Congress.

Powers related to diplomacy. Another group of Presidential powers are those which deal with diplomacy, treaties and the handling of foreign affairs in general. As official spokesman for the nation, the President appoints ambassadors, ministers, and consuls to foreign countries with the approval of the Senate. Through these agents, together with the Secretary of State and other personnel of the State Department, he carries on the foreign affairs of the nation. He can recognize or ignore foreign governments by receiving or refusing to receive their ministers. The appearance of many new independent states during World War II and in the postwar years, and the revolutionary overthrow of many established governments during the same period, have made the exercise of this Presidential power far more than just a ceremonial function. And if a foreign ambassador or minister is deemed objectionable, as in the case of Genêt during the administration of President Washington, it is the President's duty to ask for his recall.

Although the President, through his subordinates, handles treaty negotiations with foreign governments, a treaty does not go into effect until it is approved by a two-thirds vote of the Senate. This prevents the President from engaging in the duplicity and intrigue associated with "secret diplomacy" in Europe and other parts of the world. True, the Senate has refused on occasion to ratify desirable treaties, and there may have been occasions when it was motivated in this by partisan political reasons. Some feel that this was the case in the Senate's refusal to assent to the Treaty of Versailles, which would have brought the United States into the League of Nations after World War I. Nevertheless, the Senate's check on Presidential treaty-making has, in the main, been regarded as beneficial to the nation.

Students of government are agreed that the treaty-making power assigned to the President and the Senate is no longer as significant in directing foreign affairs as it formerly was. The reason is that far greater emphasis is now given to enabling legislation *after* a treaty has been negotiated and ratified. It is such legislation (requiring approval by both houses of Congress) that lays down specific courses of action, provides the necessary funds, and in general makes a treaty a functioning reality. For example, the North Atlantic Treaty was negotiated and ratified by the Senate in 1949, but effective participation of the United States in NATO was made possible by the Mutual Defense Assistance Act later in 1949, and by much legislation since then. In this way, the House of Representatives, as well as the Senate, plays an essential part in implementing our foreign policy.

Expansion of the President's powers in foreign affairs. From his assigned diplomatic powers, the President has derived, through usage, three other powers. *First*, he may recognize a state of war resulting from the acts of some other nation or internal group and take measures accordingly. This was done by President Polk after an incident at the United States-Mexican border (1846); by President Lincoln in his proclamation blockading Southern ports (1861); by President Truman in the Korean crisis (1950); and by President Johnson in the South Vietnam situation (1964). *Second*, he may take steps which are technically acts of war in protecting American rights abroad. This was done during the Boxer Rebellion in 1900 and in the Dominican Republic in 1965. *Third*, he may take similar steps to protect our interests abroad, either because of a pending treaty or because of a general diplomatic policy. This was done by President Theodore Roosevelt in 1903 to prevent the invasion of the newly established state of Panama by Colombia; by President Wilson in 1919, when he sent troops to Siberia to cooperate with allied nations in opposing the expansion of the new Soviet government in Russia; and by President Eisenhower in the Lebanese crisis of 1958. The policy of sending forces to the Caribbean republics—begun by President Theodore Roosevelt, continued intermittently up to the administration of President Hoover, and revived by President Johnson—is illustrative of the same principle.

Probably the outstanding example of Presidential power in foreign affair is the note sent by President Franklin D. Roosevelt to Prime Minister Churchill in 1940, which transferred 50 "overage" United States destroyers to beleaguered Britain. This in effect irrevocably reversed two decades of American isolationism. According to Samuel F. Bemis, an authority on United States diplomacy, the executive agreement embodying this action "was another devastating encroachment upon the treaty-making power of the Senate, and far more important than most of the seven or eight hundred treaties the Senate had ratified."

The consequent erosion of the war-declaring power of Congress has been the subject of much discussion. Defenders of this expansion of Presidential authority usually emphasize the possibility of "all-out" or thermonuclear war. Few will deny that if the President learns that hostile atomic missiles have been launched against the United States, he has no time for consultation with Congress and no choice except to act in his unique capacity as Chief Executive and Commander-in-Chief. But it is guerrilla wars, undeclared wars, civil wars, and wars by subversion that now plague the world and are likely continue as the chief menace in the years ahead. It is in the area of foreign policy connected with such "little wars" that the people's representatives in Congress have seen a curtailment of constitutional responsibility. Of course, Congress in any event still controls the purse strings—but can it use this power independently when American soldiers, sailors, and airmen have already been committed to fighting on foreign shores?

The President's military powers. As Commander-in-Chief of the Armed Forces, and of the state militia when called into the

President Abraham Lincoln visits a group of Union generals at their headquarters, shortly before the battle of Antietam, September, 1862. No United States President has taken active command of the forces in the field, but his overall and ultimate responsibility as Commander-in-Chief of the Armed Forces is unchallenged, in war and in peace.

service of the United States, the President may in time of war exercise virtually dictatorial powers. Although he appoints officers to high command, with the advice and consent of the Senate, he may remove them at his own discretion during the progress of a war. A case in point occurred when President Truman relieved General MacArthur of his command in 1951 during the Korean crisis. The President orders mobilization, declares blockades, directs the movements of fleets and armies, regulates court-martial procedures, controls conquered territory, and arranges armistices. So vast were the powers of President Lincoln during the Civil War that his enemies called him a dictator. It is significant that Lincoln did not confine his special powers to the theater of war. In an effort to weaken and conquer the enemy, a function which inheres in the position of Commander-in-Chief, he suspended the privilege of the writ of *habeas corpus* in spite of the protest of Chief Justice Roger Taney. He emancipated the slaves in the rebellious states, an act which was tantamount to confiscation of private property.

Presidents Roosevelt and Truman demonstrated, during the years of World War II, that these Presidential powers have in no way diminished. Congress, in act after act, gave both Presidents all the authority they asked for to meet the emergency. Through the control of nearly all prices, transportation, foreign trade, production of munitions and all other commodities necessary for the conduct of the war, in addition to the exercise of military powers as such, the White House directed in effect, the whole industry, purpose, and life of the nation. There is indeed virtually no limit to the Presidential military powers in time of war. However, they are not without importance in any time of crisis, as has already been pointed out. In 1957, for example, President Eisenhower sent Federal troops to Little Rock, Arkansas, to prevent disorder resulting from compliance with the Supreme Court's desegregation ruling. President Johnson took similar action in 1965 in Alabama.

Quasi-judicial powers of the President. The President may pardon any person convicted of violating Federal laws, except in cases of impeachment. Furthermore, he may grant *reprieves* (that is, stay or postpone the enforcement of the penalty) and may *commute sentences* (reduce them in severity). He may grant an *amnesty* (a general pardon freeing a number of offenders at one time), as President Harding did when he granted amnesty in 1921 to a large number of individuals who had been convicted for obstructing enforcement of the draft laws during World War I. In the exercise of these quasi-judicial powers, the President relies upon the information, advice, and opinion of his Attorney General.

The President issues executive orders. We have noted how the President's powers involve functions that are not purely executive but of a quasi-legislative and quasi-judicial nature. The nature and scope of these multifarious activities are given only broad or generalized definition in the Constitution and in specific acts of Congress. It would be impossible for every law and treaty to be drawn up in such a way as to prescribe each step the President is to take in enforcing them. Consequently, Congress in framing laws usually outlines a general policy and leaves the details of administration and enforcement to be worked out by the President and his assistants. These details are implemented by means of directives and regulations known as *executive orders*. Such orders are regarded as having the full force of law and thus constitute still another power of the President—the *ordinance power*.

Executive orders can be issued on almost any governmental matter, and they have played an important part in our history since the earliest days. Prominent examples include President Polk's order sending United States troops across the Nueces River in 1846, an action that marked the beginning of the Mexican War;* President Lincoln's *Emancipation Proclamation* in 1863, so fraught with meaning for the course of the Civil War and for American society in general; President Wilson's extensive use of executive orders to utilize his immense powers during World War I; President Roosevelt's order changing the gold content of the dollar in 1934; orders by Presidents Truman and Eisenhower to give Negroes equal opportunities for employment on government projects (1948, 1953); President Kennedy's establishment of the Peace Corps in 1961; President Johnson's military initiatives in Vietnam and the Dominican Republic; and President Nixon's reorganization of the Executive Office of the President.

The authority to issue executive orders stems from (1) the President's powers inherent in the Constitution (*e.g.*, his role as

* Historians have identified about 130 separate instances in which the President took military action by means of executive orders without a declaration of war by Congress.

Commander-in-Chief of the armed forces); (2) statutory authority granted him by Congress (*e.g.*, the right to raise or lower tariff rates); and (3) powers implied by the provisions and the tone of laws and treaties to be executed. It is estimated that in the course of our history more than 11,000 executives orders have been issued.

Of course, the President must reckon with the system of checks and balances, so basic to our government. The Supreme Court has on many occasions nullified Congressional efforts to hand over some of its legislative authority to be exercised by the President and/or his administrative aids. A notable example of this is the Court's decisions in connection with the National Industrial Recovery Act and the Agricultural Adjustment Act in the 1930's. The Supreme Court held in these cases that the broad delegation of power which Congress had made to the Executive branch exceeded all justifiable constitutional bounds. In this way, the Court in effect short-circuited hundreds of potential executive orders. Frequently, Congress exercises a check on executive orders by means of its power to appropriate money.

A law passed in 1936 provides for an official *Federal Register,* issued daily, in which all significant executive orders are to be printed. The purpose of this is to make sure that the President's actions are given due publicity, and that no important actions are taken by executive authority, of which Congress and the nation as a whole are not aware.

Extraordinary Presidential powers are withdrawn. We have noted how, in times of military emergency, or economic depression, or internal strife, Presidents have been enabled to exercise unusually broad powers. This is certainly significant—but equally significant is the fact that these expanded powers have been withdrawn with the passing of the crisis. The nation, in the words of Blackstone, merely consents "to part with its liberty for a while in order to preserve it forever." It is this characteristic, among others, that differentiates our strong leaders from dictators, past and present. The acid test of any dictatorship is that it seeks self-perpetuation, and that the only way this can be prevented is by force of arms.

American history is replete with instances which show that no sooner is an emergency over than legislative or judicial opposition to what appear to be excessive Presidential powers sets in. This applied even to the very first President. Because of his magnificent services as commander of the Revolutionary armies, his accomplishments as President of the Constitutional Convention, and his unanimous election to the Presidency, George Washington appeared to have all the qualifications for the role of "man on horseback." But Washington as President encountered so much antagonism from Republicans in Congress and elsewhere that he welcomed retirement after serving two terms. The Senate's censure of Andrew Jackson in 1833 put him on the defensive; and, although his influence continued through the administration of his protegé, Martin Van Buren, it came to a close with the defeat of the latter in 1840. As the Civil War was approaching its close, and a Union victory seemed inevitable, President Lincoln was confronted with an attack from both houses of Congress that boded ill for his second term and for his successor. In fact, he was not sure of re-election in 1864, and won by a fairly narrow margin. Theodore Roosevelt's "big stick" methods and popularity with the voters were not sufficient to prevent Congress from turning down a host of Presidential recommendations. Toward the end of his second administration, he lost control of even his own party in Congress. The end of World War I left President Wilson all but powerless in Congress; in spite of his appeal to the country, he was defeated on the issue that was closest to his heart—the League of the Nations.

Presidential history and experience were much the same during the administration of Franklin D. Roosevelt. The same Supreme Court which, in 1934, had declared that "necessity confers many rights" in the following year delivered three decisions which reminded the President forcefully of his constitutional limitations. The general opinion was that these Supreme Court decrees, checking the New Deal, came as a result of an expected economic revival. The worst of the emergency was believed to be over. Even the 74th Congress (1935-36), in which the Democratic Party controlled about 75% of the membership, began to give the Democratic President trouble at the first signs of recovery and after most of the patronage had been distributed. The President's "honeymoon" with Congress was over. In the words of Frank R. Kent: "It is a genuinely frightened country, a real national crisis, a public in a panic, that gives the President real power and makes him irresistible."

To sum up, concentrated power in the hands of the President of the United States has proved to be neither lasting nor corrupting. Lord Acton's familiar epigram that "all power corrupts, and absolute power corrupts absolutely" has little application to the Presidency. Why? The reason, says the philosopher George Santayana, is to be found in the difference between *power* as a *generative* force and *domination* as a *frustrating* and *destructive* one. Furthermore, the American people have expanded and contracted Presidential power at will throughout their history. As Santayana again points out, only those unaccustomed to the expansion and contraction of power are corrupted by it.

The President can be impeached. Besides censure, the withholding of appropriations, and the activities of committees designed to expose misconduct in some Executive department or agency, there is another method by which Congress can "strike back" at the President. This is by impeachment. Under the provisions of the Constitution, the President, Vice President or any other high civil officer may have impeachment proceedings brought against him by the House. This leads to a trial, with the Senate acting as a jury. This procedure has been used only once in our history against a President. In 1868, a hostile and partisan House of Representatives impeached President Andrew Johnson, but the subsequent trial in the Senate fell one vote short of the two-thirds majority needed for conviction and removal from office.

The Vice President

"One heart beat from the White House." The first Vice President, John Adams, wrote to his wife that he had been chosen to the "most insignificant office that ever the invention of man contrived or his imagination conceived." Almost 150 years later, "Alexander Throttlebottom," a comic character in a popular musical comedy, *Of Thee I Sing*, was ashamed to tell his mother that he had been elected to so unimportant an office as the Vice Presidency. This satire brought gales of laughter from the American public.

Actually, however, history has demonstrated with grim finality that the Vice Presidency is not a joke. The Constitution provides: "In case of the removal of the President from his office, or of his death, resignation, or inability to discharge the duties of the said office, the same shall devolve on the Vice President. . . ." Thus, it may be said truly that the Vice President is "only one heart beat from the White House." Eight Presidents have died in office since Washington, four of them since 1900. In the years from 1789 to 1964, the Presidency has been filled more than 20% of the time (that is, more than one year out of every five) by men elected to the "insignificant" office of Vice President.

Growing importance of the Vice Presidency. Vital statistics do not wholly explain the growing importance of the Vice Presidential office. The office began to gain importance in Wilson's second term, when Vice President Marshall was given the responsibility of presiding over Cabinet meetings during the absence of the President in Europe. Vice President Coolidge sat regularly with Harding's Cabinet, thus starting a precedent. In 1949, the act setting up the important *National Security Council* (see page 139) made the Vice President a member. President Eisenhower further raised the prestige of the office when he asked Vice President Nixon to preside over the Council, and over meetings of the Cabinet, in his absence. As a result of these and other developments, the Vice President now has a far better opportunity than formerly to learn what is going on in the Executive branch. One of the first things President-elect Kennedy did immediately after his election was to send his Vice President-elect, Lyndon B. Johnson, to an important international conference in Paris. And Vice President Humphrey has been far more than a figurehead under President Johnson. The Vice President's preparation in this way is extremely important to the nation in the event that destiny stops that "one heart beat."

The growing prestige of the Vice President has tended to raise to a higher level his single constitutional assignment of serving as presiding officer of the Senate. On occasions, recent Vice Presidents have tried to further the administration's legislative program. Senate party leaders, regarding the Vice President as a responsible spokesman for the White House, are now inclined to treat him with more respect than they formerly gave to their presiding officer. President Kennedy found Vice President Johnson, formerly a powerful majority leader of the Senate, indispensable in his efforts to convert Democratic campaign promises into a successful legislative program. And President Nixon has used the oratorical skills of Vice President Agnew to criticize "militant" students, self-styled "intellectuals," and "radical liberals," and to win support for the administration among the more conservatively oriented segments of the electorate.

The Vice Presidency and the 25th Amendment. The 25th Amendment to the Constitution, adopted in 1967, gives further recognition to the importance of the Vice Presidency by making sure that this office will always be occupied. Thus far in the course of our national history, the government has been without a Vice President on sixteen different occasions. Eight of these Vice Presidents moved up to the Presidency; seven of them died in office; and one (John C. Calhoun in 1832) resigned after being elected to the Senate.

Under the 25th Amendment, the President is empowered to nominate a new Vice President whenever the office is vacant. This nominee becomes Vice President when confirmed by a majority vote of both houses of Congress.

A Pyramid of Power and Awful Responsibility

The decision is the President's alone, but knowledge and power are shared. No more poignant description of the President's "almost unbearable responsibility" (to use a phrase of Secretary of State Dean Rusk) was ever given than when President Lincoln announced to his Cabinet that he would issue a proclamation emancipating the slaves. On this occasion, President Lincoln said: "I have got you together to hear what I have written down. I do not wish your advice about the main matter, for that I have determined by myself . . . I know very well that many others might in this matter, as in others, do better than I can; and if I was satisfied that the public confidence was more fully possessed by any one of them than by me, and knew of any constitutional way in which he could be put in my place, he should have it. I would gladly yield it to him. But though I believe I have not so much of the confidence of the people as I had some time since, I do not know that, all things considered, any other person has more; and, however this may be, there is no way in which I can have any other man put where I am. I am here; I must do the best I can, and bear the responsibility of taking the course which I feel I ought to take."

The President's unique responsibility for making final decisions of great importance to the nation and the world cannot be shared, but he can and must share the vast burden of work that his duties entail. Merely to carry out his administrative task as head of the Executive branch of the government, he must fill thousands of major offices which are not under competitive examinations with able men and women who will be loyal to him. These appointees constitute the *Executive Office of the President* (including the White House Office) and the *Cabinet*—all of these "men around the President"—and the numerous officials who run layers upon layers of agencies and inter-agency commissions. The latter include dozens of boards, bureaus, commissions and administrations, which see to it that "the laws are faithfully executed." For example, advisers close to President Kennedy after his election in 1960 estimated that about 600 key posts had to be filled before there could be a "Kennedy administration" ready to go to work the day after inauguration. And before this administration could be fully in control of far-flung administrative activities of the Federal government, President Kennedy and his ranking associates were confronted with the problem of making more than 5000 appointments!

When Harry S. Truman was in the White House, he had a sign on his desk which read: "The Buck Stops Here." The President can and does delegate many important functions, but he cannot "pass the buck" when it comes to his responsibility for overall policies and key decisions in the national interest.

The baffling problem of responsibility. One of President Franklin D. Roosevelt's top aides, Jonathan Daniels, had this to say about the fix in which the President often finds himself: "Half of a President's suggestions which theoretically carry the weight of orders, can be safely forgotten by a Cabinet member. And, if the President asks about a suggestion a second time, he can be told that it is being investigated. If he asks a third time, a wise Cabinet officer will give him at least part of what he suggests. But only occasionally, except about the most important matters, do Presidents ever get around to asking three times." Does this suggest why a President, in selecting his aides, must put a premium on such qualities as dedication to the public service and personal loyalty to the President?

The Executive Office of the President

"The President needs help." In 1936, President F. D. Roosevelt appointed a committee of experts in government administration to undertake a study of the President's administrative functions and to determine what facilities he needed to perform these functions with maximum efficiency. The following year, this Committee on Administrative Management issued a report, often known as the *Brownlow Report,* which began with the frequently quoted statement: "The President needs help."

From the recommendations made in 1937, and from subsequent studies and developments, there has emerged a set of agencies designed to give the President the "help" he so sorely needs. These agencies are grouped under the general title of the *Executive Office of the President.*

The White House Office. This is the President's personal staff. Its organization and its exact functions will vary, naturally, in accordance with the President's personality, program, and method of operation. The top officials of the White House Office assist the President in such fields as personnel, press relations, appointments, relations with Congress, and speech-writing. There are also advisers to keep the President informed on various specialized areas, including foreign affairs, disarmament, atomic energy, and the arts and sciences. All clerical services, including correspondence and the handling of documents, are within the purview of the White House Office. The President's personal physician is also a member of the White House Office.

Other agencies in the Executive Office. Aside from the White House Office, the Executive Office of the President consists of a

Organization of the Executive branch of the Federal government.
(Only a few of the independent agencies are shown.)

number of agencies with specialized functions in advising, informing, and assisting the President.

1. *National Security Council.* Established in 1947, this body has been called "America's cold war general staff." The President is chairman, and the other members are the Vice President (who frequently serves as chairman), the Secretaries of State and of Defense, the Director of the Office of Emergency Preparedness, and other officers whom the President may wish to appoint. (The Vice President is a member of the National Security Council by statute.) In short, the NSC, made up of Cabinet and non-Cabinet members, was created to advise the President on the complex problems of foreign policy and defense. President Eisenhower, for example, referred most questions of "arms and diplomacy" to the NSC, rather than to the Cabinet. However, it must be borne in mind that, more often than not, such Cabinet members as State, Defense, and Treasury do sit in on NSC meetings.

2. *Council of Economic Advisers.* This group is composed of expert economists who advise the President on economic matters, report to him on the condition of the national economy, and assist him in the preparation of economic reports to Congress. They have been referred to as "human barometers," who take readings on the economic weather and send "storm signals" to their Chief regarding such matters as unemployment, inflationary trends, speculation, foreign trade balances, family income, etc. The CEA may recommend specific measures and policies to remedy unsatisfactory economic conditions or (more often) to prevent unfavorable trends from developing.

3. *Office of Emergency Preparedness.* This body is responsible for planning the emergency steps that must be taken in the event of war. It keeps tabs on the Selective Service Act and its implementation. It also has charge of the stockpiling of scarce strategic materials, and is always ready with a scheme for price-and-wage curbs in the event that such controls become necessary to the war effort. These powers indicate that the OEP belongs to the Executive Office only organizationally— not really in terms of function.

4. *Office of Management and Budget.* In addition to its responsibility for preparing the annual budget which the President submits to Congress, this agency helps the President in overall control and supervision of the entire administrative structure of the government. Set up in 1970 (as a successor to the Bureau of the Budget), this Office represents an attempt by the Nixon administration to bring greater efficiency and economy into government and to implement the program of administrative reform called the "New Federalism."

5. *Office of Economic Opportunity.* This office was set up in 1964 to assist the President in implementing the anti-poverty program. (See pages 272-273.)

6. *National Aeronautics and Space Council.* The purpose of this body is to keep the President informed regarding the policies, plans, and accomplishments of the agencies engaged in aeronautical and space activities. The Council also plays a part in determining future plans in this area.

7. *Central Intelligence Agency.* Under the direction of the National Security Council, the CIA engages in secret activity, both at home and abroad, in behalf of national security. Although supervision of the CIA nominally is vested in several Congressional subcommittees, experience has shown that Congress is able to exercise only the most cursory control. This is because of the need for secrecy in most CIA operations. Even special appropriations for the CIA are "hidden" in the Defense Department's multi-billion-dollar budget.

8. *Office of Science and Technology.* This body advises the President on the development of "programs to assure that science and technology are used most effectively in the interests of national security and the general welfare."

9. *Office of the Special Representative for Trade Negotiations.* This agency assists the President in carrying out the trade agreements program, whose general purpose is to lower tariff and non-tariff barriers to foreign trade, in a way that will be of maximum benefit to our economy and to our international relations. This Office carries out its functions under the Trade Expansion Act of 1962 and is intended to implement the policies of that act.

10. In addition to the Office of Management and Budget, the Nixon administration has made a number of other additions to the Executive Office of the President. (*a*) The *Domestic Council* advises the President on pressing domestic issues, such as race relations and civil rights. (*b*) The *Office of Intergovernmental Relations* serves as a clearing house for the handling of Federal-state-local problems. (*c*) The *Council on Environmental Quality* considers problems within the broad area of ecology or environment. (*d*) The *Office of Telecommunications Policy* and the *National Council on Marine Resources and Engineering Development* both advise and assist the President on matters that come within the scope of activities indicated by their names.

On an overall basis, it may be said that the Executive Office has had the effect of "institutionalizing" the Presidency. To a degree, the Presidency has become a staff operation, not so completely dependent as formerly on the direction, the talents, or the point of view of one individual. The extent to which the Presidency may "operate even without the President" depends on the personality and methods of individual Presidents.

THE PRESIDENCY AT A GLANCE

Nomination. Nominated by convention of national political party. Candidate is usually chosen from a pivotal state. Vice Presidential candidate, as a matter of practical politics, must not come from same geographical district as Presidential candidate.

Election. Elected by the voters, indirectly, through the Electoral College.

Term of Office. Four-year term; limited to two terms by 22nd Amendment.

Inauguration. Inaugurated on January 20th following election.

Compensation. $200,000 per year (fully taxable), plus use of White House, entertainment, travel, and clerical expenses.

Qualifications. Native-born; 35 years of age; must have lived in the United States for at least 14 years.

President's Powers (Article II, Sections 2 and 3 of Constitution).

1. Commander-in-Chief of Armed Forces, in peace and in war.

2. Heads Executive branch, made up of Executive Office, Cabinet, and independent agencies.

3. Legislative leader—requests and often formulates Federal laws.

4. Directs foreign relations—makes treaties with approval of two-thirds of Senate.

5. Makes appointments to top positions in Executive branch and Judiciary with Senate's consent.

6. "Chief tribune" of the people—has far-reaching influence on public opinion.

7. Leader of his party under the "unwritten Constitution."

8. Receives foreign diplomats and recognizes new governments.

9. Executes Federal laws in keeping with oath: "I do solemnly swear (or affirm) that I will faithfully execute the office of President of the United States."

Removal from Office. May be removed from office by impeachment (House) and conviction (Senate) for "treason, bribery, or other high crimes and misdemeanors." The President may also be removed for mental or physical disability. (For the procedure to be employed in determining whether or not the President is unable to carry out the duties of his office, see the provisions of the 25th Amendment.)

Terms You Should Know

Agency. Major administrative body, not of Cabinet rank.

Amnesty. General pardon for offenses, extended by the President or by Congress.

Cabinet. Body of top advisers and administrators chosen by a chief executive, such as the President or a governor.

Commutation. Reduction of penalties and punishments for a criminal act. This is one of the powers of a chief executive.

Congressional government. Government characterized by a relatively high degree of power lodged in Congress, rather than in the President.

Constitutionalist. Referring to a theory of government which emphasizes limitation of governmental authority in accordance with the letter of the basic law.

De facto. Actually in existence, regardless of legal right. A *de facto* government is one which holds power, even though its legal status may be questioned.

De jure. According to the law; sanctioned by legal authority. A *de jure* government is one which has a valid legal claim to power, although it may or may not hold power *de facto*.

Department. One of the twelve major divisions of the Executive branch of the United States government. Each department head is a member of the President's Cabinet.

Dictatorship. Concentration of unlimited governmental power in an individual, without regard to constitutional restrictions.

Executive order. A decision made by the President, without Congressional approval, that calls for some definite course of action.

Pardon. The power of the chief executive or some other governmental authority to absolve a person from the legal penalties for a crime.

Presidential government. Government characterized by a relatively high degree of power lodged in the President, rather than in Congress.

Reprieve. A delay in the carrying out of a punishment, such as imprisonment or execution, granted by the President or by a governor.

Senatorial courtesy. The custom prevailing in the United States Senate of withholding confirmation of a President's appointment to fill some office unless the Senator, or Senators, (of the President's party) from the state in which the office is to be filled approve the nomination.

Staff organization. A term used to describe the personal advisers and assistants to a chief executive.

Veto. Power of a President or a governor to reject bills passed by the legislature.

Questions and Problems Based on the Text

1. Indicate the powers which are vested in the President by the Constitution.

2. How have Congress and the courts served as sources of Presidential power?

3. What influence on government does the President exert by virtue of his position as head of his political party?

4. What advantages in the exercise of power and influence has the present-day President over his predecessors of fifty years ago?

5. How does the principle of checks and balances apply to the President?

6. (a) On what occasions may the President assume unusual powers? (b) Cite concrete examples from history, including the history of our own times.

7. To what extent is personality a factor in the exercise of Presidential power?

8. In what respect have modern military methods of containing Communist aggression increased Presidential powers at the expense of Congress?

9. How can the President be removed from office?

10. Trace the growing importance of the Vice Presidency.

11. Of what components is the White House staff made up? How does the staff function?

12. Draw a diagram showing the composition of the Executive Office of the President and the functions of each unit.

13. Skim through the pages of your favorite daily newspaper. How many articles have to do with the President of the United States? What is the significance of this?

14. Appraise this statement by Richard M. Nixon: "The office of Vice President of the United States is a hollow shell—the most ill-conceived, poorly defined position in the American political system."

15. To what extent does the 25th Amendment anticipate this complex situation: The status of the Vice Presidency reached its nadir in 1912 when some three million votes were cast for a dead man! Taft's running mate, James S. Sherman, died on the eve of election, too late to put another name on the ballot. Although the Taft ticket lost, the Sherman electoral vote had to be cast for somebody, and Nicholas Murray Butler, President of Columbia University, was asked if he objected having it cast for him. Butler agreed, "provided there is no chance of electing a Republican Vice President."

16. Adlai Stevenson once quipped: "Every American boy runs the risk of becoming President." (*a*) Does *every* American boy run the "risk"? (*b*) What did Mr. Stevenson mean?

17. The National Commission on Technology, Automation, and Economic Progress (a "blue ribbon" commission appointed by the President) presented the following recommendations, among many others, to the President in January, 1966: (1) that free public education for 14 years (through the second year of college) be provided for all qualified students from disadvantaged homes; (2) that a computerized job-man matching system (on national, regional, and local labor-market levels) be created in order to expedite job searches; and (3) that the Federal government provide a floor under family living standards by means of a guaranteed minimum income.

(*a*) Why do you suppose the President appointed such a commission?

(*b*) The President shelved this report. Why do you think he did this? (Bear in mind the domestic and foreign situation in 1966.)

Ideas to Think About and Discuss

1. "*Authority has been conferred upon the President sufficient to clothe with legality, should occasion arise, even the exercise of Caesar's prerogatives.*"

—CHARLES A. BEARD

2. "*Where the Strategic Air Command is, where U. S. Marines may quickly be brought into action, where U. S. paratroops stand on the alert, where the American fleets plow the seas or ride ready to strike, in their great bases, where the ultimate deterrent speaks its benign protection: There is peace—not certain, for only the foolish man looks for certainty—but at least more likely. If I sleep soundly in my bed at night, if I expect my children to be able to live peaceful and fruitful lives, it is because I count myself and them as citizens of the American empire.*"

—HENRY FAIRLEE

3. "I know no safe depository of the ultimate powers of society but the people themselves; and if we think them not enlightened enough to exercise their control with a wholesome discretion, the remedy is not take it from them, but to inform their discretion by education."

—THOMAS JEFFERSON

4. "We have given power to the President precisely in the area where his rash action might be uncheckable and irreversible—that is, in foreign and military policy—and we carefully fence him in those areas where Presidential errors could be limited and reversed—notably in domestic fiscal policy."

—JAMES M. BURNS

5. "I find the great thing in this world is not so much where we stand, as in what direction we are moving . . . We must sail sometimes with the wind and sometimes against it,—but we must sail, and not drift, nor lie at anchor."

—OLIVER WENDELL HOLMES

6. "There had never been such youthful euphoria in Washington since the early days of the New Deal. Kennedy's theory of the presidency was a dynamic leadership, like Roosevelt's rather than the "Laodicean drift" (as Allan Nevins calls it) of Eisenhower."

—SAMUEL E. MORISON

7. "The finest attribute of power is restraint."

—ARISTOTLE

8. "A Presidential system cannot easily adjust to an interregnum; a nation moving with such great mass and velocity needs the engineer at the throttle."

—DEAN RUSK

9. "The American Presidency is one of the few truly successful institutions created by men in their endless quest for the blessings of free government."

—CLINTON ROSSITER

10. "The guerrilla wins if he does not lose. The conventional army loses if it does not win.'

—HENRY KISSINGER

CHAPTER 6

Executive Departments
and Independent Agencies

The Cabinet

The importance of the Cabinet in our government fluctuates in accordance with the methods of operation of individual Presidents, as well as with changing external conditions. But the Cabinet has always, since its origin, provided some assistance to the Chief Executive, and has always shared its advisory functions with other individuals or groups.

Establishment of the Executive departments. The first department of the Executive branch of the United States government was the Department of Foreign Affairs, now the *State Department*. The *Treasury Department* was then created to manage the government's finances, and the *War Department* came next. In the Judiciary Act of 1789, Congress established the office of Attorney General, the legal adviser to the President, who is now head of the *Department of Justice*. Trouble with France, which threatened to erupt into a naval war, caused Congress to create a separate *Navy Department* in 1798. Although the office of Postmaster General was created as early as 1789, the Postmaster General did not become a Cabinet member until 1829; and there was not a full-fledged *Post Office Department* until 1872. Out of the vast annexation of territory resulting from the Mexican War grew the *Department of the Interior* (1849). Awareness of the distinctive problems of agriculture was responsible, in 1889, for the admission to Cabinet rank of the *Department of Agriculture*. The *Department of Commerce* and the *Department of Labor* were established in 1903 and 1913, respectively, in response to the growing demands of an industrial age. In 1947, Congress combined the various branches of the Armed Forces into the National Military Establishment, and two years later created the *Department of Defense*, headed by the Secretary of Defense, to direct all our military forces and policies. Under this Secretary of Cabinet rank are the three separate departments of the Army, the Navy, and the Air Force (each headed by a Secretary who is not of Cabinet rank), and various other agencies. In 1953 the *Department of Health, Education, and Welfare* was created to direct many activities whose scope is indicated by the name of the agency. Most recently, in 1965, came the *Department of Housing and Urban Development,* and in 1966, the *Department of Transportation.*

Functions of Cabinet members. Each member of the Cabinet has a variety of duties and responsibilities.

1. *He supervises the functioning of the various administrative agencies in his department.* In this capacity he is aided by under-secretaries, assistant secretaries, and specialized experts.

2. *He lends an ear to interested groups who seek to reach the President.* Sectional, socio-economic, and party interests are all in this category—for example, the Farm Bureau, the National Farmers Union, the United States Chamber of Commerce, the National Association of Manufacturers, the AFL-CIO, the National Education Association, and many others.

3. *A Cabinet officer advises the President, either individually or in the course of Cabinet meetings.* The frequency of such meetings and the significance of the "advice" offered depend on the President's attitude toward the individual official and toward the Cabinet as a whole. President Harding had great respect for his Cabinet, and Cabinet meetings were held regularly during his administration. Presidents Coolidge, Truman, and Eisenhower were particularly close to such individual department heads as Mellon, Marshall, and Humphrey, respectively. Presidents Jackson, Lincoln, and Wilson, in contrast, used their Cabinets basically as a sounding board, or as a means of confirming opinions already formed. The Cabinet, in the main, has probably influenced fewer substantive Presidential decisions than have informal "brain trusts," *ad hoc* committees, or personal confidants (for example, Colonel House under President Wilson, or Harry Hopkins under President Franklin D. Roosevelt). It should be noted that since Cabinet officers do not have constitutional status, the President may appoint, remove, or ignore them at will.

4. *A Cabinet officer plays a part in the lawmaking process.* Often, he or his department may prepare a bill which forms part

of the administration's legislative program. In seeking to get a bill through Congress, a Cabinet member may appear before the appropriate committee to testify, and his testimony may go far toward deciding the fate of the bill.

5. In the vast majority of cases, the President and his Cabinet members belong to the same political party. One Cabinet member who is particularly familiar with the party's internal affairs is usually named by the President to keep an eye on the political situation and to articulate the party's interests, at Cabinet meetings and elsewhere.

Having listed the functions of the Cabinet members, we must not lose sight of this important fact: that the Cabinet's main reason for existence is to administer and to give advice, not to make basic decisions. The Cabinet meeting is a place for informal give-and-take that leads toward determination of policies but recognizes always that the final decision must come from just one place—the President. In the last analysis, whether or not the President asks or takes advice from a Cabinet member depends upon that member's capabilities and on his personal relation with "the Chief." Usually, the advice the President will seek from a Cabinet secretary centers on the affairs of the department he heads. In purely departmental affairs, the President often gives the Secretary a wide range of authority to make decisions and take action "on his own."

The Department of State. The Secretary of State is usually a prominent political figure who is often chosen, in large part, for his influence in the party in power. His duties take on a dual character: he is in charge of foreign affairs, and he performs certain domestic functions. Among the latter, he publishes Federal laws and executive proclamations; proclaims the ratification of amendments to the Constitution; preserves original copies of treaties and all laws enacted by Congress; announces the admission of new states into the Union; and conducts all correspondence between the President and the governors of the states.

As the official in charge of foreign affairs, the Secretary of State is chief strategist and senior adviser on foreign policy. He is contact agent between our government and foreign states, of which there are now about 120 (some forty of which are tied to us in mutual defense treaties). Within the government, he is the "boss" of several dozen important international organizations (*e.g.*, the United States Mission to the UN, the Agency for International Development, the Development Loan Fund, etc.). He supervises ambassadors, ministers, and consuls sent to countries abroad. In addition to the traditional diplomatic functions, he now has charge of such activities as non-military foreign aid, surplus food disposal, a world-wide information service, secret intelligence, reciprocal trade treaties, and many others. One State Department agency with which many citizens have direct dealings is the Division of Passport Control, which issues visas, passports, and certificates of citizenship.

The growing importance of the Department of State is reflected in the vast increase in the size of its personnel; 210 in 1910; some 24,000 on a world-wide scale in 1965, not including personnel in the Agency for International Development and the Peace Corps. Worth noting, too, is the increase in the number of undersecretaries and assistant secretaries in charge of specific areas, such as Inter-American Affairs, Economic Affairs, African Affairs, Asian Affairs, Far Eastern Affairs, European Affairs, Near Eastern and South Asian Affairs, and Security and Consular Affairs.

The United States and the United Nations. Among the major responsibilities of the State Department is the *United States Mission to the United Nations,* which represents this country at the permanent headquarters of the UN in New York City. Headed by a Representative with ambassadorial rank, the Mission carries out the instructions of the President, as transmitted by the State Department, in conducting our operations at the UN. The Mission furnishes a base of operations for the delegations representing the United States at UN meetings and serves as the main channel between the State Department and various UN organs and agencies, as well as the missions and delegations of other member nations.

No administration since the UN was established has failed to support it both financially and morally. Secretary of State Dean Rusk was echoing the opinion of all his recent predecessors when he said that the UN will "eventually" became a vital factor in bringing about order into international relations—"the great central question of our day." "Eventually," said the Secretary. Why not now? The answer lies in the fact of a fragmented world, with aggressors or would-be aggressors threatening the peace in such places as Germany, Cuba, the Congo, Korea, and Vietnam. The United States, bypassing a helpless UN in these instances, was compelled to take action on its own, or in cooperation with allies. Our intervention checked aggression in these instances and may well have prevented aggression elsewhere. But the authority and prestige of the UN were scarcely enhanced. Persons not familiar with the accomplishments of the Specialized Agencies of the UN began to question the very existence of the international organization.

The Department of the Treasury. Next in order of seniority is the Secretary of the Treasury who handles the financial business of government. This Department supervises the collection, custody and disbursement of all the money in the possession of, or legally due, the United States government. The *Internal Revenue Service* and the *Bureau of Customs* assist in the collection of Federal taxes. The manner in which taxes are collected and money is borrowed against future income has a major impact on the national economy. This is referred to as the government's *fiscal policy*.

The Treasury Department includes two agencies which are responsible for maintaining our monetary supply: The *Bureau of the Mint*, which produces coins; and the *Bureau of Engraving and Printing*, which attends to the design, engraving, and printing of paper money, as well as Treasury bonds, bills, and notes, and postage stamps. The demands of a constantly expanding economy call for ever larger quantities of both coins and paper bills in the proper denominations, The Bureau of the Mint, in particular, has been hard put to keep pace with the tremendous need for coins, both to "make change" and to operate vast numbers of automatic dispensers. Shortages of silver and other metals have contributed to this problem.

Also within the Treasury Department is the *Comptroller of the Currency* * (appointed by the President for a 15-year term), who serves as the administrator of national banks and is responsible for the administration of all laws relating to national banks. Under the law, for example, his approval is required for the organization of new national banks, the conversion of state-chartered banks into national banks, and consolidations or mer-

---

* Not to be confused with the *Comptroller General of the United States,* who heads the General Accounting Office within the Legislative branch of the government (page 166).

gers of national banks with other banks. Each national bank is examined at least three times every two years by a staff headed by the Comptroller of the Currency.

The *Treasurer of the United States* (not the Secretary of the Treasury) is responsible for the receipt and custody of all government funds and for paying all of Uncle Sam's bills that have been properly authorized.

The Treasury Department includes a number of agencies which are not related directly to finances.

1. The *United States Coast Guard*, formerly under the supervision of the Treasury Department, was transferred to the recently created Department of Transportation in 1966. (In time of war, as formerly, the Coast Guard is controlled by the Navy.) Created originally to combat smuggling, the Coast Guard now has a broad variety of functions including rescue operations at sea, policing water traffic, and maintaining lighthouses and buoys.

2. The *Government Printing Office* produces and distributes a vast array of publications for all the departments and other agencies of the Federal government. The GPO has been called "the largest publishing organization in the world."

3. The *Bureau of Narcotics* is charged with the investigation, detection, and prevention of violations of Federal laws relating to narcotic drugs. It administers a system of licenses and quotas for legitimate use of these drugs and conducts a never-ending campaign against the criminal forces (many of them international in scope) which seek to profit from illegal sale of narcotics.

4. The *Secret Service* has the great responsibility of protecting the person of the President of the United States, as well as members of the President's immediate family, the Vice President, and former Presidents who may request such protection. It also detects and arrests any persons who commit offenses against laws relating to "coins, obligations, and securities of the United States." Essentially this means that it combats counterfeiting.

The Treasury Department has about 77,000 civilian employees, of whom more than 50,0000 are engaged in collecting taxes.

The Department of Defense. This Executive department, organized in 1947, is really a sort of "super-department," including separate departments for each of the three major military services, as well as other agencies. It is headed by the *Secretary of Defense*, who acts as the general director of policies and programs and seeks to avoid duplication of efforts among the services.

The *Department of the Army* (formerly the War Department) is headed by a Secretary of the Army. This Department is entrusted with organizing, training, and equipping our Army. Its overall responsibility is to defend the United States, to defeat enemy land forces, and to perform whatever other duties may be assigned to it by the Commander-in-Chief. Under the control of the Department of the Army are the Regular Army, the National Guard, and the several reserve corps. The Department performs other functions, too. It protects seacoast harbors and cities, supervises improvement of our waterways, undertakes flood control measures, maintains the United States Military Academy at West Point, and provides for the defense and administration of the Panama Canal Zone.

The *Department of the Navy* is headed by a Secretary of the Navy. It supervises and maintains (1) our various naval combat and service forces; (2) naval aviation; and (3) the Marine Corps, which specializes in amphibious military operations. The department also operates the United States Naval Academy at Annapolis, Maryland.

Three fighter-bomber pilots plan tactics before setting out on a mission.

U.S. Air Force Photo

The *Department of the Air Force* is headed by a Secretary of the Air Force. Its task is "prompt and sustained offensive and defensive combat operations in the air," especially operations to cripple an enemy by strategic bombing of essential resources and installations. Commissioned officers come mainly from the Air Force Academy at Colorado Springs, Colorado.

Thus we see that the Defense Department represents an attempt to bring about unified control of all agencies necessary for defending the nation and for waging modern warfare. Lack of harmony and coordination among the services, dramatized in the catastrophe at Pearl Harbor in 1941, made such action essential. Unfortunately, the "Pentagon" has grown so massive and so unwieldy that civilian control has become increasingly ineffective. There has been talk of restructuring the Defense Department under three civilian deputy administrators, to achieve better coordination, more effective testing of equipment, and lower costs.

The Department of Justice. The *Attorney General*, who is at the head of the Department of Justice, is essentially the administrator of a huge agency, rather than a practicing lawyer. Assisted by a Deputy Attorney General, and by a large and ever-growing staff, he performs the following duties: (1) He initiates and prosecutes all Federal criminal cases. (2) He administers the *Immigration and Naturalization Service*, which is in charge of all laws relating to the admission, exclusion, and deportation of aliens and of the naturalization of aliens living in this country. (3) He supervises the principal investigatory and crime-fighting agency of the national government—the famed *Federal Bureau of Investigation (FBI)*.* (4) He enforces governmental policies, as required by law, in non-criminal areas. For example, he may bring civil suits under the Civil Rights Act. (5) He advises the President on the scope of his powers under the law. For example, the President might ask the Attorney General for an opinion on whether or not he has the authority to forbid the use of Federal funds for public housing which is to be racially segregated. (6) He initiates antitrust cases, thus affecting the economic structure of the nation. (7) He brings suits for unpaid taxes. (8) He takes legal action to prevent persons from getting passports against the wishes of the State Department. (9) He seeks injunctions to prevent the calling of strikes which would be considered a menace

* Both the FBI and the Immigration and Naturalization Service are semi-autonomous within the Department of Justice.

to the "national health and safety," under the Taft-Hartley Act. (10) Finally, he supervises Federal prisons.

Somewhat obscured amidst the multiplicity of functions of the Justice Department that so often make the newspaper headlines is the important day-by-day work of the *Solicitor General*. He is the third ranking official of this department. In the legal profession, he has a reputation beyond his departmental status, for he is in charge of all United States government business in the Supreme Court. The Solicitor's office prepares all government briefs, and he or members of his staff argue cases before the Court.

The Department of the Interior. This has been called the "Department of Things in General" because its activities and responsibilities are so varied. Among other things, it carries on many conservation activities through such agencies as the Reclamation Service, the Fish and Wildlife Service, the United States Geological Survey, the Bureau of Mines; it administers about 750 million acres of public lands; it is in charge of Indian affairs; it runs the system of National Parks; it develops and manages hydroelectric power resources; it carries on experimental programs for converting salt water to fresh; and it is responsible for the welfare of the people inhabiting our island possessions.

The Post Office Department. This department, under the Postmaster-General, was responsible for the administration of the entire postal system of the United States. It employed more than 725,000 persons, and handled about 80 *billion* pieces of mail a year, with "sales" exceeding 6 billion dollars.

We use the past tense because a law enacted in 1970 abolished the Cabinet department and turned over the postal system to a newly established corporation, wholly owned by the government, to be called the *United States Postal Service*. The new scheme was to be fully operative within a year.

The U.S. Postal Service will be administered by an 11-man board of governors within the executive branch. This body will function much like the top management of a huge private corporation. It is empowered to raise capital by selling bonds, to negotiate and make contracts with the postal unions, to set postal rates, to modernize equipment and methods, and in general to do whatever is necessary to provide the nation with a fully satisfactory postal system.

Years ago, the Post Office System was the pride of the Federal service. There was general agreement, however, that it had become an unwieldy and inefficient giant. It had fallen far behind the times in use of automated equipment to process mail. The time-honored custom of using postmasterships as a means of political patronage was under increasing attack. Labor relations with the postal unions left much to be desired. Service deteriorated badly, and huge deficits were incurred each year.

Change was inevitable, but only actual experience can tell how successful the U.S. Postal Service will be.

The Department of Agriculture. Many years of study, experiment, and scientific development have been utilized to make the Department of Agriculture a major asset to the farmers of the United States and to the nation generally. Its services are applied in such fields as agricultural chemistry, animal husbandry erosion control, home economics, forestry, and entomology.

In addition to its scientific work, the Department now supervises a number of important bodies that extend credit to farmers and farmers' organizations, provide operating funds for agricultural borrowers, help to stabilize prices of farm commodities, and make loans for the electrification of rural areas.

The economic crisis of the 1930's led to several measures for crop control and for financial aid to the farmer. An *Agricultural Adjustment Act* passed under the New Deal program was invalidated by the Supreme Court in 1936. Thereupon, in the same year, a new act provided for benefit payments to farmers who were willing to cooperate in a program of soil conservation. This general policy, designed to avoid surpluses and stabilize prices, was continued in still another measure in 1938, the second Agricultural Adjustment Act. The government gave financial assistance to participating farmers to make up for any losses that might result from decreased production. The AAA of 1938 created the *Commodity Credit Corporation (CCC)*, an agency whose function was (and is) to make loans to farmers on the security of their crops. This has made it possible to carry over surpluses in government warehouses. Thus, farm incomes are protected, and a huge store of basic foodstuffs and other farm products has been created which can be released as needed, at home or abroad.

The advent of war in 1939, and our own entry into the conflict in 1941, changed conditions completely. The problem was no longer surpluses but the need for ever greater production. The law was changed to stimulate production and to regulate prices so that the average consumer would not suffer unduly.

After the war, the price support system was renewed and has continued with some modifications to the present day. The system has come under severe attack on these grounds: (1) Its benefits go mainly to large, wealthy farmers, including corporate combines. (2) It contributes to "squeezing out" the small farmer. (3) The heavy costs are borne by the taxpayer and the consumer (in the form of higher prices). (4) We should not spend huge sums to hold down food production at a time when world population is increasing rapidly and untold millions of persons (including many in this country) have an inadequate diet.

The Department of Commerce. This department performs a most useful service as a clearing house of information for business organizations all over the country. It supplies them with statistics and other types of factual data relating to all phases of domestic and foreign trade. The Department also contains the *Census Bureau,* whose function is to take a national census every ten years. The information gathered in this way throws light on such matters as population trends, family structure, employment, health, and distribution of national income. Another major agency of the Department of Commerce is the *Environmental Science Services Administration,* comprising the *Weather Bureau* and the *Coast and Geodetic Survey.* Also within this department are the *Patent Office,* the *Maritime Administration,* and the *National Bureau of Standards.*

The Department of Labor. Created "to foster, promote and develop the welfare of the wage earners of the United States," the department compiles information regarding wages, hours of work, child labor, and unemployment.

Two divisions (*Wage and Hour* and *Public Contracts*) carry out the provisions regarding minimum wages and maximum hours of employment in the Fair Labor Standards Act, originally passed in 1938 and amended many times since then. Various industries formerly not within the scope of this regulation now come under Federal control. In addition, these laws seek to prohibit "oppressive" child labor, to regulate child labor in exceptional circumstances, and to adjust claims for jobless benefits (*Bureau of Employment Security*). A *Women's Bureau* seeks to advance the interests of working women. Because of our paramount position in the United Nations and in the International Labor Organization, there have been added to the Department of Labor an *Office of International Labor Affairs.*

The Department of Health, Education and Welfare. This Department, often referred to as "HEW," was created by Congress in 1953. Under this authority, President Eisenhower transformed the Federal Security Agency (FSA) into the new Cabinet department. HEW administers most of the social welfare programs of the Federal government. Its principal agencies are: the *Office of Education*, the *Social Security Administration*, the *Public Health Service*, the *Food and Drug Administration*, the *Water Pollution Control Administration*, and the *Administration on Aging*. Under this last named agency (created in 1965) funds are made available to states, public bodies, and private non-profit agencies for the development of programs to help the aged.

In recent years, the emphasis in HEW has been increasingly on the "E." This was particularly true under the Johnson administration. In 1965, the Office of Education disbursed about 4 billion dollars in aid to state and local school systems, colleges (both public and private), research centers, and directly to students. The level of financial support in the future remains to be determined. In 1969, "Head Start," an important pre-school program for underprivileged children, was transferred to HEW from the Office of Economic Opportunity.

Referring to the White House Conference on the Aging (1971), U.S. Senator Winston Prouty of Vermont observed: "The most pressing need (in this area) is economic. When income is inadequate, the pursuit of happiness can become a hollow hope."

Department of Health, Education, and Welfare

The Department of Housing and Urban Development. This department of the Executive branch was created by Congress in 1965. The principal existing agency which it absorbed was the *Housing and Home Finance Agency*, responsible for a broad range of Federal housing activities, including those of the Home Loan Bank Board, the Federal National Mortgage Association, the Federal Housing Administration, and the Public Housing Administration. Other existing agencies which were absorbed by the new Department include the Urban Renewal Administration and the Community Facilities Administration. It is expected that the Department will assume new responsibilities, for example, in the field of urban and suburban transportation, which has become a problem of crisis proportions in most large cities. (These were *not* initially transferred to the new Department of Transportation—see below.)

The Department of Housing and Urban Development was created in response to the widespread belief that the problems of our great metropolitan areas have become so monumental and involve so large a proportion of the American people that they must be studied and analyzed, and remedial measures must be applied, on an integrated national scale at the highest level of government.

The Department of Transportation. Established in 1966, the Department of Transportation is the youngest department of the the Cabinet. It was created to consolidate the operations of about 35 previously scattered and uncoordinated agencies dealing with transportation. Some of the main agencies involved are the Federal Aviation Agency, the Bureau of Public Roads (formerly under the Commerce Department), the Coast Guard (formerly under the Treasury Department), and the St. Lawrence Seaway Development Corporation. The main purpose of this reorganization was to encourage the development of balanced, coordinated policies for the expansion and improvement of all types of transportation. It is also hoped that the new authority will establish procedures for executing these policies more quickly and more efficiently than has been the case in the past.

The jurisdiction of the new department, as originally set up, appears to be somewhat restricted. Among its responsibilities is the investigation of airplane safety, a function previously performed by the Civil Aeronautics Board. But, the CAB retains undiminished its powers to regulate the aviation industry. Similarly, the powers of the Interstate Commerce Commission and of the Federal Maritime Commission have remained unchanged.

In 1968, Congress accepted President Johnson's plan to transfer the Urban Mass Transit Program from the Department of Housing and Urban Development to the Department of Transportation. Since urban mass transit (including facilities for suburban "commuters") is undoubtedly the number-one transportation problem in the United States today, this move greatly increased the influence and prestige of the youngest department.

Proposals for Reform of the Cabinet

Many changes have been suggested to make the President's Cabinet and the Executive departments more efficient and creative instruments of government. Among those most worthy of consideration are the following:

♦ *Establish a "shadow Cabinet"* to provide strong leadership for the opposition to the administration in power. This idea is rooted in the British Parliamentary tradition. In the House of Commons, the opposition party (that is, the party out of power) contains members who follow closely the work of the Cabinet offices and are prepared to take charge of them as ministers whenever the government falls. Of course, in the American system, a "shadow Cabinet" would be a less cohesive group because there is no real parallel in our party system to a "loyal opposition."

♦ *Upgrade the Assistant Secretaries of State, who are responsible for relations with such important regions as Europe, Latin America, Africa, the Middle East and South Asia, and the Far East.* This would enable the Secretary of State to concentrate on his main function—overall policy determination and coordination in the field of foreign affairs. Of equal importance is the suggestion that there be created a cluster of roving "ambassadors-at-large," whose job it would be to handle major continuing negotiations as personal representatives of the President and the Secretary of State.

♦ *Create permanent undersecretaryships in each department of the Cabinet, to be filled permanently by career men.* In other words, they would continue in office regardless of changes in administration.

♦ *Set up a modernized training program to provide adequate manpower for diplomatic service overseas.* This would probably involve not so much the establishment of new training institutions as the utilization of colleges and universities to give intensive and integrated courses of the kind needed by our representatives abroad. Language and area studies would probably be stressed. Even secondary schools might have a part to play in this by providing preliminary training and motivation. The motivation is very important, for promising young people must be inspired to dedicate their working lives to the foreign service. Although this may seem like a "glamorous" career, the fact is that overseas assignments in many parts of the world involve real hardships and even dangers.

◆ *Let our ambassadors and other key diplomatic officials remain at their posts for at least four years, instead of the current average of less than three.* This would enable them to become more thoroughly familiar with their responsibilities and to work more productively. It is emphasized that serving as a top diplomatic representative of the United States has become an exceedingly complex task. For example, a recent report showed that 31 different United States agencies are represented at our embassy in Great Britain. Many foreign ambassadors in Washington have represented their governments for ten or more years.

◆ *Give the President authority to review periodically the salaries of employees in the Executive branch, and to make adjustments that seem justified, in order to keep pay scales in line with changes in the economy as a whole.* Such changes when recommended by the President would go into effect automatically, unless specifically disapproved by a resolution of either house of Congress.

◆ *Create a special "watchdog" commission composed of Congressmen and citizens appointed by the President, with broad powers to oversee the activities of Federal intelligence agencies.* This would be designed as a response to the criticism which has been made of the operations of such agencies as the CIA (page 140). The CIA, it is charged in some quarters, has been abusing its privilege of secrecy and has actually been attempting to make foreign policy and to commit the United States to ventures of which neither the government nor the people have approved.

◆ *Strip ROTC of its academic credits in colleges and universities, and make it an extracurricular activity. Or possibly sever its connection with educational institutions altogether.* (In 1969, ROTC supplied 50% of the Army's officers, 20% of the Navy's, and 35% of the Air Force's. In that year, 151,000 students were enrolled on 268 campuses.)

The Independent Executive Agencies

Why the independent agencies are treated separately. The Executive branch of the government includes the *Executive Office*, the *Cabinet*, and numerous other agencies known by such names as *boards, bureaus, commissions, authorities,* etc. All of the bodies in this last-named category are called collectively the "independent agencies." The term *independent* suggests that they are outside the structure of the twelve regular departments—not that they are free of Executive control. Like the Cabinet departments, the independent agencies help to administer Federal laws, programs, and treaties. They are numerous, and their work is so important that the *United States Government Organization Manual*, issued annually, devotes more space to the independent agencies than it does to the Legislative or the Judicial branch of the government. Some authorities have even referred to them as the "fourth branch of government." From our point of view, however, they form an integral part of the Executive branch.

History of the independent agencies. Unlike the Cabinet, which dates back to Washington's administration, the independent agencies are of comparatively recent origin. The first important body of this type was the *Civil Service Commission*, created in 1883. In spite of the fact that the Constitution makes no specific provision for the independent agencies, they have continued to multiply. Finding that it is "harder to run a constitution than it is to frame one," Congress throughout the 20th century has created many agencies to implement new laws and deal with new problems.

The independent agencies today are a far cry from their pygmy counterpart of 80 years ago. At that time, the Federal government was still in the "handicraft" era of office methods and administrative techniques. Without typewriters, telephones, or computers, the symbol of the bureaucracy was then the inkstained governmental copy clerk, scribbling away at his ledgers. He was an underpaid functionary, periodically shaken down for political contributions, and in constant fear of losing his job. His job was a part of the "spoils system" (patronage), and patronage was the very life of politics, the means of perverting government to personal and party purposes.

A recent study of the "fourth branch," lists about sixty independent agencies of the Federal government. These range from small and relatively unimportant bodies, such as the American Battle Monuments Commission, to such giant agencies as the General Services Administration, the Federal Reserve Board, the Veterans Administration, the Securities and Exchange Commission, the National Labor Relations Board, the Selective Service System, the United States Information Agency, and the Tennessee Valley Authority.

Staffing the independent agencies. The independent agencies today have about 380,000 employees. Except for the top officials, who are named by the President with the consent of the Senate, the vast majority of these employees obtain and hold their jobs under a *merit system*, based mainly on competitive examinations. This means that only a small percentage of the agency workers are replaced when there is a change of administration. (It should be noted that the merit system, with all its forms of protection, applies also to the vast majority of the more than 2.3 million employees of the twelve regular departments of the Executive branch.)

The Civil Service Commission maintains centers in all parts of the United States in an effort to recruit well-qualified young people to apply for jobs in the Federal government service.

Each agency is administered by a team of commissioners or directors, usually five or seven in number. One of them is designated to act as chairman, and he is the functioning head of the agency, comparable in many respects to the head of a regular department. The commissioners serve terms ranging from five to fourteen years—a fact which sometimes means that they may expect to outlast the President currently in office. Commissioners may be removed only on the basis of such specific charges as misconduct (for example, taking bribes). Mere disagreement with the President or Congress is not considered adequate grounds for removal from office.

Employees of the independent agencies (as well as of the regular departments) are protected by laws and regulations against political exploitation. For example, the *Hatch Act* of 1936 forbids "forced" contributions to political parties by Federal employees and by state and local employees engaged in Federally aided programs, such as the state unemployment insurance systems.

How "independent" are the independent agencies? In their day-to-day activities, the agencies are independent to a considerable degree. They function under Congressional standards which are so broad that the controlling officials have a good deal of latitude in setting policies and in determining their own methods of operation. For example, some agencies are directed by law "to prevent unfair methods of competition," or to regulate private business "in the public interest," or to "fix just and reasonable rates," or to issue licenses and franchises "as the public convenience may require." These provisions of the statutes, obviously, call for much personal interpretation by the responsible officials.

On the other hand, the independent agencies are by no means a law unto themselves. Congress creates them, and Congress can abolish them. The agencies are expected to operate in accordance with the broad policy lines laid down by Congress. The top agency officials are keenly aware of the fact that Congress must appropriate funds annually, and also that Congress can and does use its power to investigate. In short, the independent agencies, although they exercise tremendous powers, are ultimately subordinate to the elected officials of the government. As between the Legislative and Executive branches, it is Congress that usually exerts a greater measure of control.

However, it would be a mistake to discount the President's relationship to the agencies. The appointive power alone is a potent weapon. And even though an incumbent commissioner may not have been appointed by the President currently in office, and may not be thinking in terms of reappointment, there is usually a natural desire to please the head of the Executive branch. It is difficult indeed for a commissioner of an important agency to function effectively when he does not enjoy the confidence of the President.

INDEPENDENT EXECUTIVE AGENCIES

(A partial listing)

NAME	YEAR CREATED	NAME	YEAR CREATED
U.S. Civil Service Commission	1883	Federal Deposit Insurance Corporation	1935
Interstate Commerce Commission	1887	Civil Aeronautics Board	1940
Federal Reserve System	1913	Atomic Energy Commission	1946
Federal Trade Commission	1914	Federal Mediation and Conciliation Service	1947
Farm Credit Administration	1916	Housing and Home Finance Agency	1947-1965
U.S. Tariff Commission	1916	Selective Service System	1948
Veterans Administration	1930	General Service Administration	1949
Federal Power Commission	1930	Small Business Administration	1953
Tennessee Valley Authority	1933	U.S. Information Agency	1953
Export-Import Bank	1934	U.S. Civil Rights Commission	1957
Securities and Exchange Commission	1934	National Aeronautics and Space Administration	1958
Federal Communications Agency	1934	Agency for International Development	1947-1961
National Labor Relations Board	1935	U.S. Postal Service	1970

NOTE: From time to time, independent agencies may be "absorbed" into the regular Executive departments. For example, the Housing and Home Finance Agency became the nucleus of the Department of Housing and Urban Development. The Agency for International Development (previously known by other names) became part of the State Department. The Federal Aviation Agency and the Bureau of Public Roads became part of the Department of Transportation.

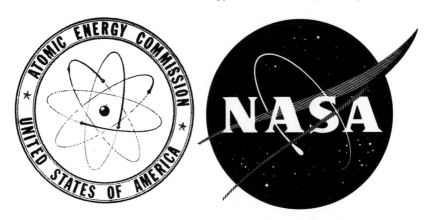

With our present-day civilization, resting on science and technology, it is not surprising that several of the most important independent agencies are concerned directly with the control and utilization of scientific knowledge. The AEC and NASA were established in 1946 and 1958, respectively.

Functions of typical Executive agencies. Following are summaries of the duties and responsibilities of a number of independent Executive agencies, more or less typical of all the governmental bodies in this category.

1. The *Civil Service Commission* holds competitive examinations for several hundred types of positions. By means of these tests, the Civil Service Commission recruits qualified personnel for Federal agencies. Announcements about examinations for civil service positions are placed in post offices and in other governmental buildings and public places.

2. The *Veterans Administration* is responsible for the construction and management of hospitals for disabled veterans. It also offers relief and aid to war veterans and their widows and orphans. The administration of pensions, war-risk insurance, compensation, and other financial benefits is also in the hands of the Veterans Administration. Among the independent administrative agencies, the VA has by far the largest number of employees.

3. The *National Labor Relations Board* enforces the laws that require employers to bargain collectively in order to settle wages, working hours, and general working conditions with organizations and representatives chosen by the workers. The NLRB also conducts secret elections to choose bargaining representatives.

4. The *Tax Court of the United States* holds hearings and decides cases that have been appealed by taxpayers on questions having to do with taxes on incomes, estates, excess profits and gifts.

5. The *Federal Deposit Insurance Corporation* insures deposits in most of the banks in the United States. Each depositor's account is protected to a maximum of $20,000.

6. The *United States Civil Rights Commission* was created in 1957 to investigate and, through the Attorney General, to bring action against local officials who obstruct the enforcement of civil rights laws. The Civil Rights Commission on occasion has recommended sending Federal officers to racial trouble areas and authorizing them to make on-the-spot arrests. The Commission has also recommended that Congress pass a broad law (under the interstate commerce clause and the 14th Amendment) that would make it a Federal crime to employ violence or threats of violence against persons engaged in civil rights activities.

7. The *General Accounting Office,* headed by the Comptroller General, has been called the "Watchdog of the Treasury." Its general function is to make sure that all public funds are properly deposited in the Treasury, and that all expenditures are made according to law. It prescribes principles and standards of accounting, and carries out regular audits of the accounts of all agencies—Executive, Legislative, and Judicial—to guard against misuse of public funds. A staff of about 10,000 employees is engaged in this work.

The GAO differs from the other agencies we have been discussing in that it is organized in the Legislative (rather than the Executive) branch of the government. It is responsible only to Congress for the proper performance of its duties. The thinking behind this distinctive status is that the GAO must be outside the regular Executive chain of command because it is, in a sense, "checking up" on the operations of the entire Executive branch. Although the Comptroller General is appointed by the President (with the consent of the Senate), his 15-year term of office tends to enhance his independence.

Classification of agencies. The "fourth branch" of the government may be divided into three categories: (1) the *independent administrative agencies;* (2) the *independent regulatory agencies;* and (3) *government corporations.* These three types are described briefly below in terms of their special functions.

The independent administrative agencies. A typical body of this type is the *Veterans Administration,* charged with the task of dispensing benefits to former servicemen, ranging from medical treatment to higher education. Another example is the *Atomic*

Energy Commission, entrusted with operating atomic installations, conducting research in this field, and licensing and supervising atomic installations owned and operated by private corporations. Still another example is the *Agency for International Development* (AID), set up to administer and coordinate our foreign-aid program. (Since AID is organized within the State Department, it is, strictly speaking, not an independent agency, but it has considerable autonomy and closely resembles the independent agencies in its methods of operation.)

The independent regulatory agencies. These are also the creations of Congress and are assigned to exercise certain powers and perform duties which Congress has delegated to them. Authorities on administrative law regard these regulatory agencies as powerful instruments of democratic government in a country with an economy as vast and as intricate as that of the United States. Unlike the group of agencies referred to in the previous section, which are purely administrative in their duties, the regulatory agencies perform quasi-executive, quasi-legislative, and quasi-judicial functions.

The first Federal agency of this type to be established, was the *Interstate Commerce Commission,* set up in 1887 to watch over the services and rates of railroads. In the years following, many other agencies were established to administer controls in new and burgeoning areas of interstate business, including finance, communications, and aviation. Among the most important of these are: the *Board of Governors of the Federal Reserve System,* the *United States Tariff Commission,* the *Federal Communications Commission,* the *Public Roads Administration,* the *Securities and Exchange Commission,* and the *Civil Aeronautics Board,* which now shares control of the commercial air lines with the more recently created *Federal Aviation Agency* (now part of the Department of Transportation).

These regulatory powers are not, of course, unlimited. For one thing, when an agency holds a hearing on a dispute falling within its jurisdiction and makes a ruling, the ruling can always be challenged in the Federal courts by any party which feels that its rights have been violated. Neither the independent agency nor the Executive branch as a whole can prevent such an appeal. Also, as we have noted, Congress has the power to take back what it has given an agency in authority and appropriations. Then, too, the President's Bureau of the Budget has some control over the amount of money any agency may ask of Congress. Thus, "independence" is a relative term, and "independent" agencies like any other part of our government, must operate within the framework of checks and balances.

Government corporations. This category includes such bodies as the *Tennessee Valley Authority*, the *Federal Deposit Insurance Corporation*, and the *Commodity Credit Corporation*. They are chartered and owned by the government, but they are run, to a large degree, in the same manner as a corporation. Each is managed by its own directors, appointed by the President.

The *Tennessee Valley Authority* (TVA), producer of cheap and abundant electric power and pioneer in creative community and regional planning, was for some years bitterly criticized as an example of "creeping socialism." However, its achievements have been so widely recognized by the people of the Tennessee Valley (which includes parts of seven states) that the controversy today is not whether TVA should continue but whether it should be allowed to expand.

The *Federal Deposit Insurance Corporation* (FDIC) insures deposits in all national banks and in most state banks. The insured institutions represent about 97% of all banks accepting deposits in the United States. The banks must insure each deposit up to a maximum of $20,000. The financial resources of this publicly owned insurance company are derived from the insurance premiums paid by insured banks.

The *Commodity Credit Corporation* (CCC) is in charge of the price support program for farm products. (This has been described on page 155.) Like the Agency for International Development, the CCC is organized within one of the regular departments (Agriculture), and is therefore not strictly speaking an independent agency. Its methods of operation, however, are much like those of other government corporations.

One advantage of the corporate type of organization for running a government enterprise is that it can operate with a high degree of independence of political interference. Experience has shown that when the directors are carefully selected, a government corporation can be run as efficiently as any private business. Some people have proposed that the Post Office Department be changed into a corporation since the corporate form seems to be well adapted to any agency which carries on functions somewhat like those of private business.

An Appraisal of the Independent Agencies

The case against government by commissions. Many observers see a danger of overcentralization in the growth of "government by commissions." They argue that the tendency is to remove government farther and farther from the people. If such a condition is permitted to exist, it is said, a bureaucratic government may develop in which the people will have little interest. When the people have lost interest and influence, tyranny is bound to set in.

The case for government by commissions. Under the conditions of modern life, in a society dominated by "big business," and "big labor," and (increasingly) "big agriculture," it is argued that we cannot avoid "big government" if we are to protect the public interest. If this involves what some critics call "bureaucracy" or "government by commissions," it is not a condition which we need fear, provided the proper safeguards are in effect. The following advantages are claimed for the American system of administration by independent agencies:

◆ *Freedom from political control.* The terms of commissioners are longer than that of the President (average, seven years). This makes them less sensitive to pressure from the White House. Moreover, as already pointed out, the President's power of removing commissioners has been limited.

◆ *Continuity of policy and personnel.* The vast majority of the employees of the independent agencies, including those in many posts calling for great ability and experience, are not affected by the shifting political scene. Thus, continuity of personnel and policies is assured.

◆ *More efficient and flexible procedures.* The size of Congress and the necessary restrictions of courts of law make it impossible for the Legislative and Judicial branches of the government to act with the speed and flexibility required by present-day conditions. The independent agencies have shown that they can supply these essential qualities in our governmental structure.

◆ *An experimental approach to government.* The commissions are in a position to experiment with new methods, procedures, and ideas. If these approaches work well, they can be continued. If they are not successful, they can be withdrawn before serious harm has been done. Thus, government becomes more progressive, dynamic, and responsive to changing needs and conditions.

♦ *Contacts with Congress.* Congress serves as a "watchdog" over the commissions, because investigating committees of either house can look into the affairs of any agency. Public hearings may be held at which commissioners are required to testify. This serves as a safeguard against abuses and helps to bring the Legislature in closer contact with the Executive branch.

Reform of the Independent Agencies

A step toward more effective control. For many years, efforts have been made to bring the administrative agencies under more effective and consistent control. Finally, in 1948, Congress passed the *Administrative Procedures Act.* This measure was designed to assure full publicity for the policies and acts of the various commissions, to afford legal redress for individuals and organizations who felt themselves harmed by commission rulings, to increase efficiency in methods of investigation, and to provide adequate judicial review of commission actions.

Report of the First Hoover Commission. One of the most ambitious programs of governmental reorganization was announced in 1949 by a commission of some 300 experts, headed by former President Herbert C. Hoover. This group, known as the Commission on the Organization of the Executive Branch of the Government (or more commonly as the "Hoover Commission"), had been set up by Congress in 1947 and given the mission of "streamlining" the administrative side of the Federal government, including the regular departments as well as the independent agencies.

The Hoover Commission found that basic principles of good administration were being flouted in many areas of the government. Among the weaknesses cited were: too many agencies, divided responsibility, overlapping functions, and conflicting interests. The President was handicapped by lack of adequate assistance, the heads of agencies by antiquated rules. The government was failing to attract the best administrative talent, and its methods of budgeting and accounting were old-fashioned and inadequate. To remedy these faults, the Hoover Commission made recommendations intended to achieve the following basic results: establishing clear lines of authority and responsibility; consolidation of closely related activities; abolition of unneeded activities and of superfluous agencies; and reduction of expenditures.

As a result of these recommendations, Congress passed the *Reorganization Act of 1949*, which authorized the President to propose reorganization plans involving nearly every agency within the Executive branch of the government. If within 60 days neither house of Congress has voted against such a proposal, the recommended change automatically goes into effect. There are a number of significant limitations on the President's authority. For example, the General Accounting Office (page 166) is specifically excepted from the operation of the law; a department cannot be abolished; the life of an expiring agency cannot be extended.

Many changes have been made under the authorization of the Reorganization Act. Moreover, other innovations recommended by the First Hoover Commission (such as the establishment of a new department to consolidate Federal health, education, and welfare activities) have become realities.

The Second Hoover Commission of 1953. The first Hoover Commission, as noted above, was concerned with the Executive branch, as a whole. The Second Hoover Commission, created in 1953, concerned itself mainly with the independent administrative agencies. Mr. Hoover and his fellow-commissioners expressed the opinion that in many of its activities the Federal government had invaded the field of private enterprise. They, therefore, recommended the return of a number of governmental activities to private interests. For example, it was suggested that the government quit the field of electric power production (a slap at the TVA), and drop the Postal Saving System altogether.

The response in this case was far less favorable than that to the earlier body. Indeed, the suggestions of the Second Hoover Commission were largely ignored.

President Kennedy revives the reform issue. In 1961, President John F. Kennedy sent a special message to Congress on the independent agencies. He pointed up the need for action in these words:

> The responsibilities with which they (the agencies) have been entrusted permeate every sphere and almost every activity of our national life. Whether it be transportation, communication, the development of our natural resources, the handling of labor-management relationships, the elimination of unfair trade practices—to take only a few examples—these agencies and their performance have a profound effect upon the direction and pace of

our economic growth. If it is in the public interest to maintain an industry, it is clearly not in the public interest by the impact of regulatory authority to destroy its otherwise viable way of life. Furthermore, the industries subject to their jurisdiction are intertwined with our national defense in such a degree that the health of these industries can well be regarded as an index of both our strength and our power to survive. Thus the capacity of these regulatory agencies to meet their responsibilities and the efficiency with which they dispatch their business become a subject of tremendous significance to the entire nation.

President Johnson in 1966 voiced similar sentiments when he declared, "Reorganization can mean a streamlined leadership, ready to do more in less time for the interest of all the people."

Scene at the Post Office Department in 1970, when President Nixon and Postmaster General Blount marked the transition from "Post Office Department" to "U.S. Postal Service." Mr. Blount is holding the seals of the Department and of the new Service, depicted on the wall. The other men in the picture are four of Mr. Blount's predecessors—both Democrats and Republicans—showing bipartisan support for this reform.

United Press International

Terms You Should Know

Arbitration. Settlement of disputes (*e.g.*, labor disputes) by an intermediary accepted by both parties. The arbitrator's decision may be binding on both parties (as previously agreed), or it may represent only a recommendation for settlement.

Bureau. An operating unit of governmental administration, usually a subdivision of a department or some other large agency.

Cabinet. Group of top officials chosen by a chief executive (such as the President or a governor) to advise him on policy and to assume administrative responsibilities.

Civil service. The entire body of employees of a government, exclusive of the military and elected officials.

Classified service. Those positions in the Federal civil service which, under the law, must be filled by a merit system of competitive examinations.

Commission. A name applied to an executive or administrative agency. Also, a warrant granting authority or conferring an office on an appointee.

Congressional Directory. Handbook issued annually which contains comprehensive information about the members of both houses of Congress.

Congressional Record. Official account of the proceedings of Congress, issued daily when Congress is in session.

Department. One of the major divisions of the Executive branch of the government. The heads of the departments form the President's Cabinet.

Foreign Service. Employees of the State Department who represent the United States in foreign countries, including ambassadors, ministers, staff officers and employees, local employees, and consular agents.

Government corporation. An administrative unit of the United States government which is given authority to operate with a considerable degree of independence, more or less like a private business. Examples are the Tennessee Valley Authority and the Commodity Credit Corporation.

Mediation. Use of a third party to settle a dispute (*e.g.*, a labor dispute) by suggesting formulas and compromises that may be acceptable to both parties. The mediator acts as a "go-between," without authority to make any binding decisions.

Merit system. Selection of government employees on the basis of demonstrated merit, usually (although not always) by competitive examinations.

Quasi. A prefix used to suggest a degree of resemblance, without actually partaking of the full character of the thing indicated. For example, the National Labor Relations Board has *quasi-judicial* powers —meaning that it functions somewhat like a court of law.

Regulatory agency. An administrative unit of the government having authority to regulate certain types of business or certain areas of activity within the nation or state. Examples are the Federal Communications Commission and the public service commissions of the various states.

Spoils system. The practice of regarding governmental jobs as so much plunder to be taken from members of the losing party and distributed to members of the winning party.

U.S. Government Organization Manual. A handbook issued annually that contains comprehensive data on the three branches of the United States government.

Questions and Problems Based on the Text

1. State three general functions of a member of the President's Cabinet.

2. Name the most recently established Cabinet office. Explain why it was established.

3. What is meant by the "fourth branch" of the government? Why is this name considered appropriate?

4. How do you account for the increase in the number of independent boards and commissions in the administrative branch of our government?

5. The administrative agencies may be divided according to the following functional classification: fact-finding, quasi-executive, quasi-legislative, quasi-judicial. Give two examples of each type of administrative agency.

6. Why do the terms of members of the independent agencies usually extend beyond the four-year term of the President? Why does the law require that the members of these bodies must represent both major political parties?

7. In what respects are the independent agencies not really "independent"?

8. Regulatory agencies are concerned largely with the economic segment of our economy. Give examples of this. Why is this type of activity considered necessary?

9. "What is needed is the protection of popular rights against the administrator's arbitrary whims and 'ideologies' in a system which makes the administrator the 'whole works'." What dangers does this statement suggest may be implicit in the Federal administrative machinery? What safeguards would you suggest against such dangers?

10. "The government not only *regulates* private business organizations but also fosters their growth." Show how the Federal government carries on activities to achieve both these ends.

11. President Truman accepted three of six recommendations for higher tariffs made by the United States Tariff Commission; President Eisenhower accepted six of fifteen.
(a) Show how this situation illustrates the principle of checks and balances in government. (b) How does it illustrate the quasi-legislative power of an independent agency? (c) How does it illustrate "government by bureaucracy"? .

12. (a) Distinguish between the *civil service* and the *merit system*.
(b) In what respects is the merit system superior to the spoils system?
(c) Some writers have referred to the "built-in weaknesses" of a civil service system in which the employees have virtually complete job security. Can you see what these weaknesses are? Can you make any suggestions to help overcome them?

13. (a) Research the *National Environmental Policy Act* (1969). What are the functions of the Atomic Energy Commission under this law? (b) Research the *National Air Quality Standards Act* (1970). What are the functions of HEW under this law? (c) What can you, as an individual citizen do to forward antipollution measures such as those represented by these two laws?

14. Summarize the recommendations made by the Hoover Commission on the Organization of the Executive Branch. To what extent have these recommendations been carried out? Do you think that the changes suggested by the Hoover Commission are still relevant to the situation facing the Federal government today? Explain.

15. "The United States Government is evolving from government by elected representatives of the people to government by reliance on specialists who are appointed to administer agencies, commissions and bureaus."

(a) Do you agree with this statement? (b) Under such conditions, how can government remain truly responsive to public opinion? (c) Will the traditional American system of checks and balances disappear in the "administrative state"?

Ideas to Think About and Discuss

1. *"If the transition to a new political order is to be accomplished by processes of **political evolution** rather than **social revolution**, the present democratic state must undergo such adaptations as are necessary to meet the changing situation, and to correct the defects which are becoming increasingly evident."*

    —W. J. Shepherd

2. *"The civil service system has its pros and cons. On the one hand, there is a good deal to be said for a system based on merit, that professionalizes the business of administering and assures continuity of administration regardless of changes in the party in power. But experience has shown that when employees are "set for life" their efficiency and zeal may decline with the years . . . . The case against the civil service is no argument for a return to the infamous spoils system. Nor does it mean that higher standards of morality and efficiency are found among private employees than among those who work for the government. It does mean that certain reforms are in order."*

    —From a report of the League of Women Voters of the United States

3. *"Like a lusty child, government with us has expanded in nature and grown great in stature, but has also become awkward in movement. The vigor and increase of its life has been altogether out of proportion to its skill in living. It has gained strength, but it has not acquired deportment."*

    —Woodrow Wilson

4. (In reference to Ralph Nader, a leader in the movement for consumer protection and higher safety standards.) *"If his many activities are successful, Nader over the coming years will alter significantly the balance between public and private power and, perhaps, the ways in which major corporations make their decisions. In short, he will bring about a kind of revolution . . . . Two differences stand out between Nader's approach to changing society and that of the noisier radicals. First is his commitment to lawful, orderly methods. Second are his skills as a trained lawyer and his mastery of facts."*

    —William V. Shannon

CHAPTER 7

The National Judicial Power

The Nature and Scope of the Federal Judicial Power

The need for a judicial power. The national judiciary, like so many other governmental institutions and practices, was an attempt on the part of the framers of the Constitution to correct the defects of the government under the Articles of Confederation. Under that system, Congress made the laws. These were interpreted, however, by the courts of the several states, each in its special way. The leading statesmen of the Constitutional Convention were keenly aware of the need for a remedy. Alexander Hamilton, for example, pointed out that "the want of a (national) judiciary power crowns the defects of the Confederation."

Accordingly, it was expected that a Federal system of courts would bring about uniformity. It would save the laws from the prejudices, and possibly from the obstruction, of different state authorities. To the average citizen these reforms would furnish a sense of convenience and security not hitherto realized. The Constitution, therefore, created a "judicial power of the United States." It vested that power in "one Supreme Court and in such inferior courts as Congress may from time to time ordain and establish." The Constitution also specified those circumstances to which "judicial power" was to extend.

The scope of the Federal judicial power. Chief Justice Marshall (1801-1835) classified under two heads the types of cases which, according to the Constitution, come within the authority or jurisdiction of the Federal courts.

The first class proceeds from *the nature of the case itself*. It includes matters which arise under the Constitution, laws, and treaties of the United States. It comprises, also, those cases which are related to maritime affairs, (seizures, claims, contracts, offenses, etc.) in time of war or peace.

The second class is based upon *the character of the parties involved in the litigation.* This includes the following categories:

1. Cases affecting ambassadors, other public ministers and consuls. (This presumably refers to representatives of foreign nations in the United States.)

2. Cases in which the United States is a party.

3. Cases between a state (or its citizens) and a foreign country (or its citizens or subjects).

Until the passage of the 11th Amendment in 1798, it was presumed and so expressed by the Supreme Court in the case of *Chisholm v. Georgia* (1793), that a state might, even without its consent, be sued by a citizen of another state in a Federal court. This was equivalent to the violation of the ancient principle that no sovereign state may be prosecuted by any of its citizens or subjects. The 11th Amendment closed the doors of the Federal courts to suits instituted by citizens of one state against another state, or by citizens (or subjects) of a foreign country against any of the states in the Union.

Limitations upon the Federal courts. The Federal judicial system is subject to a number of restraints, some of which are imposed by the Constitution, while others have resulted from statutes passed by Congress.

The Constitution prohibits Congress from abolishing the Supreme Court. It forbids the type of suit to which the 11th Amendment refers. It requires the consent of the Senate for the appointment of judges by the President. It prescribes that Federal judges may be removed by impeachment and conviction.

The Federal courts are also subject to limitations placed upon them by Congress. Congress has the power to increase or reduce the number of judges in the Supreme Court. It has decided what types of cases may be handled exclusively by the Federal courts. It has indicated what cases may originate either in a Federal court or in a state court, or may be appealed from state courts to the Federal judiciary. Congress has also declared that the United States government may not, without its consent, be sued by any of its citizens.

The Organization of the Federal Judiciary

The courts and the judges that compose them. The Constitution, as we have seen, provides for a Supreme Court and for such "inferior" courts as Congress chooses to establish. The organization of our judicial system, then, is based primarily upon the Constitution. It is based, secondarily, upon the Judiciary Act of 1789 and subsequent legislation enacted by Congress.

The Supreme Court crowns the entire system. The other courts are of two kinds. The first type includes courts which have general jurisdiction. These comprise the *District Courts* of the United States and its dependencies and the *Courts of Appeals*. The second type consists of courts which have special jurisdiction. Examples of these are the *Court of Claims*, the *Court of Customs and Patent Appeals*, and a separate system of courts which function solely for the District of Columbia.

To insure a judiciary that will be independent of political influence, the Constitution sets up a number of protective provisions for judges. We have already noted that Federal judges are appointed by the President with the consent of the Senate, and that they may be removed only by impeachment and conviction. They hold office "during good behavior." This practically implies life tenure. The salaries of judges may not be decreased by Congress during their term in office.

Whether the hopes of the founders of the Republic have been realized is a matter of question. There have been judges of undoubted integrity, and judges who have corrupted their high office. There have been judges possessed of broad social vision and judges whose outlook has been narrow, if not bigoted. No Constitution can foresee human virtues or human failings. If our judges are in any sense guardians of our social order, they are as good or as bad as the social order itself. The ideal toward which we might strive was well expressed in President Franklin D. Roosevelt's tribute to Justice Oliver Wendell Holmes, Jr.

> Imbued with a high sense of justice and right, he believed in the peaceful evolution of the new from the old. He had a fine perspective of history as a continuous and living thing, and, with courage and logic, believed in the shaping of government to changing conditions.

The jurisdiction of the Supreme Court. The most powerful tribunal in the world, the Supreme Court of the United States, now consists of nine men, a Chief Justice and eight Associate Justices. They hold court from October to May, but spend a large portion of the rest of the year in studying the vast number of cases submitted to them.

In cases "affecting ambassadors, other public ministers and consuls, and those in which a State shall be party," the Supreme Court has original jurisdiction. In other words such cases are tried for the first time in the Supreme Court.

But far more important is the power to hear *appeals* carried from the lower Federal courts and from state courts. This often occurs in cases presented to "test" the constitutionality of a particular statute. It is through the exercise of this power of *appellate jurisdiction* that the Court has become the interpreter of the

One of the constitutional duties of the Chief Justice of the United States is to preside over an impeachment trial of the President. This has occurred only once in our history, when President Andrew Johnson was impeached and tried in 1868. He escaped conviction by a single vote. This old print shows Chief Justice Salmon P. Chase presiding over the proceedings.

Library of Congress

Constitution, of Federal treaties and statutes, of the acts of public officials and, indeed, of the legal will and legal acts of the states and their subdivisions. Its decisions affect the destiny of millions of men and women and of billions of dollars of property. Its decisions carry authority. They are final, unless a later Court overrules the decision, and there is no appeal, unless it be by amendment of the Constitution, or, as in 1861, by resort to arms. Congress cannot abolish the Court. Only a constitutional amendment can do that.

Appeals may be carried from the lower Federal courts to the Supreme Court. Appeals may also be carried from the highest court of each state. This may be done if an action is involved which is alleged to be contrary to the Federal Constitution, or to a treaty, or to an act of Congress, and if the proper redress has not been assured through the medium of the state courts.

Appeal to the Supreme Court is, at best, an expensive procedure. The costs involved may be formidable even for large business organizations, and all but impossible for individuals. In some instances, where the cause of an obscure unfortunate involved a basic question of human rights, appeals have been financed by "defense funds" gathered from the contributions of sympathizers. This was true as far back as the Dred Scott case in 1857.

To sum up, the jurisdiction of the Supreme Court is both original and appellate. Cases of original jurisdiction make up only a small part of the Court's business. Most of the cases that reach the highest tribunal arrive there on appeal from the United States Courts of Appeals or directly from the District Courts.* In addition, there are cases appealed from the highest state courts.

This is not to say that the Supreme Court accepts all cases that litigants may wish to submit to it. More often than not, the Supreme Court finds itself in agreement with the decision of the lower court. Or it may decide that there is no basic constitutional question involved in the case that would warrant a review. It is estimated that only about 10% of applications for review by the Supreme Court are actually accepted. It should be noted that Congress is empowered by the Constitution to decide what kinds of cases may be appealed to the Supreme Court. In 1925, however, Congress enacted a law which authorized the Court to make its

---

* The Supreme Court sometimes directs a lower court to send up the entire record of a case for review. This is done by an order called a *writ of certiorari*. Such a writ may be issued in response to a petition by either of the litigants involved in a case.

own decisions as to which cases it will accept for review. This is essential to prevent the Court from being overburdened with work of secondary importance.

United States Courts of Appeals. Below the Supreme Court in the hierarchy of the Federal judicial system are the eleven *Courts of Appeals* (formerly called "Circuit Courts of Appeals"). The United States is divided into eleven judicial districts or *circuits*, in each of which there is a Court of Appeals. Each of these courts has from three to fifteen judgeships, with a total of 97 (as of 1970). Each circuit comprises from three to five states. (The District of Columbia is also considered a circuit.)

The Courts of Appeals were created chiefly to relieve the Supreme Court of a considerable part of its burden of work. The jurisdiction of these courts is *appellate* only. In other words, they hear cases only on appeal from the District Courts and from certain Federal regulatory agencies, such as the Securities and Exchange Commission and the National Labor Relations Board. In such instances, when there is no case of constitutionality involved, the decision of a Court of Appeals is final. In other cases, appeals may be taken to the Supreme Court.

Federal District Courts. There are at present 88 District Courts in the 50 states, plus one in the District of Columbia.* A district may include an entire state, but most of the states are divided into two or more districts. New York and Texas have four districts each. Each District Court has from one to 24 judges, depending on the amount of judicial work within its area.

The United States District Courts are exclusively *courts of first instance*, which means that they have only original jurisdiction. They have general jurisdiction in cases involving Federal laws and hold regular trials, with or without a jury. Cases decided by the District Courts may be appealed to the Courts of Appeals. There are, however, certain types of cases (injunction orders, decisions holding acts of Congress unconstitutional, and some criminal decisions) that may be appealed directly to the Supreme Court.

Actually, the calendars of all courts in the entire Federal judicial system are always crowded. It is, therefore, a task of no mean proportions constantly to adjust the organization, the business,

* In addition, the Commonwealth of Puerto Rico has a United States District Court with jurisdiction corresponding to that of the District Courts in the various states.

the processes of the courts to meet the challenges which are presented by the complexities and ramifications of modern civilization. The Omnibus Judgeship Act, passed by Congress in 1961, provided for an increase in the number of judges assigned to the various districts and circuits.

Lower courts of special jurisdiction. The *Court of Claims*, established in 1855, adjusts many types of claims against the United States. It carries out the principle that the government may not be "sued" without its consent. Accordingly there are no "suits" in the Court of Claims. Congress has determined what types of claims may be presented in this Court. If the Court makes an award, Congress, usually as a matter of routine, votes the necessary funds to order the payment.

The *Customs Court* examines complaints instituted by importers against the classification or the valuation of imported goods which is made by appraisers and used as a basis for duties collected at the various ports of entry. From this court, appeals may be carried to the *Court of Customs and Patent Appeals*. As the name implies, this tribunal is concerned not only with questions related to the classification of duties upon imports, but also with patents and trade marks.

Each of the incidents represented here might lead to proceedings in one of the special Federal courts. Identify the court in each case.

The *Tax Court* (organized as an independent Executive agency) hears and adjudicates controversies involving taxpayers and the Commissioner of Internal Revenue. Not only income taxes but also estate, gift, and excess-profits taxes may be involved.

The *United States Court of Military Appeals* is judicially independent, although it is administered as part of the Defense Department. It is the final court of appeal in court-martial proceedings in any branch of the Armed Forces.

The Processes of the Federal Courts

How cases reach the Federal judiciary. A case may appear in a Federal court for either one of the following reasons: First, because the Federal court has been given, either by the Constitution or by act of Congress, original jurisdiction in that case. Thus, a violation of Federal law, a case in bankruptcy, or a case involving two or more states would be tried in a Federal court. Second, because the case has been transferred from the trial jurisdiction of the state courts to the Federal courts. This happens whenever the Constitution of the United States, a Federal treaty, or a Federal statute is involved.

A Federal court does not consider an issue unless a specific case is brought before it through the regular channels. Federal courts do not "consider law in abstract or give advisory opinions." This policy was established very early in the history of the Republic. At that time the Supreme Court declined to answer a number of questions submitted to it by President Washington. It is important to keep this fact in mind since it has an important bearing on the entire problem of "modernizing our Federal courts."

The guardian of basic liberties. In carrying out their judicial duties, the courts are naturally concerned with matters which vitally affect the liberties of the individual citizens. Such "liberties" are understood in the familiar phrase, "the protection of life, liberty and property."

In the first place, the courts are required to protect the guarantees included in the Bill of Rights.* These refer to a number of

* The term *Bill of Rights* has come to include not only the first ten Amendments, but also the 13th, 14th, 15th, and 19th as well as the guarantees of individual freedom found in the body of the Constitution. All of these guarantees today are referred to as *human rights*.

historic civil rights. For example, in criminal cases the Bill of Rights lists a number of guarantees, related to such matters as trial by jury, the use of witnesses and counsel, the character of the penalties, and so on. In civil cases (those which pertain to private rights or claims), recent cases have focused on protection of voting rights, and other issues within the area of the Negro drive for full equality in American life.

THE FOUR GREAT WRITS

MANDAMUS — Order to administrative or executive officer of government to do his official duty.

HABEAS CORPUS — Order to officers of law to bring before court a person held in custody.

INJUNCTION — Order requiring or forbidding performance of a specified act.

CERTIORARI — Order by higher court to lower court to send up its record of a trial.

Second, the courts make use of three important decrees or writs which likewise affect the fundamental rights of citizens. Foremost is the *writ of habeas corpus* (literally, "you may have the body"), which a court may issue to prevent the unreasonable or illegal detention of an individual taken into custody by the police. In effect, the order makes it possible for a person who claims that he has been unlawfully detained by the police either to be released altogether, or to have the privilege of a preliminary hearing. The Constitution provides that "the privilege of the writ of habeas corpus shall not be suspended, unless when, in cases of rebellion or invasion, the public safety may require it."

Another is the *writ of mandamus* ("we order"). It may be applied to a private individual or to a corporation. But it is more commonly used to require a public official, or a lower court, to do something which the law prescribes.

Still another is the *writ of injunction*. This is applied by the courts in accordance with the legal requirements which deal with the issuance of injunctions. It is employed only when the facts at hand show that a given situation cannot be corrected by existing legal processes. The injunction may be used to compel the performance of a specific act—for example, fulfilling the terms of a contract. It may be used (and this is its more common application) to forbid the performance of something which has previously been declared to be illegal. It may have the effect of restraining people from doing certain things temporarily, until the subject of the dispute has been adjusted, or it may be a permanent restricting order. The frequent application of writs of injunction to labor disputes has provoked storms of protest. For this reason the use of injunctions has produced one of the most bitter chapters in the history of the American judicial system.

"Government by injunction." Injunctions have been used again and again by employers to prevent their workers from doing certain things, if these were likely to result in "irreparable damage" to the employer's interests. Labor unions have consistently opposed the injunction. Labor spokesmen maintain that injunctions have often been applied to persons not designated in the court's order. They have been used to break up or nullify the workers' weapons—the strike, picketing, orderly meetings and demonstrations. Another criticism is that in injunction proceedings, the judge is at the same time "legislator, judge, and executioner." He issues the injunction, holds "in contempt of court" those who violate his decree, and imposes the penalty.

Since the famous Pullman railroad strike of 1894, during which the Supreme Court upheld an injunction issued by a lower Federal court against Eugene V. Debs and other labor organizers, there have been vigorous efforts to curb the power of the Federal courts in their use of the injunction. In 1914, the *Clayton Antitrust Act* restricted the application of injunctions to industrial disputes. Since the courts continued to issue injunctions, free and sweeping in their prohibitions, the *Norris-LaGuardia Act* was passed in 1932. This allowed the use of injunctions only under certain specified conditions and in general provided labor with protective guarantees against misuse of such court orders.

After the close of World War II, as labor sought to make wage gains which had been held in check during the war years, there were many strikes. It was maintained in some quarters that this unrest was largely the result of the "one-sided" Wagner Act, and that a new overall labor law was needed to "restore the balance" between labor and management. In spite of the bitter opposition of the unions, a Republican-controlled Congress passed the *Taft-Hartley Act*, and this was finally enacted into law over President Truman's veto (1947). Although this law reaffirmed the right of labor to organize and to engage in collective bargaining, it contained a number of provisions clearly intended to curb the power of the unions. One of these was the outlawing of the *closed shop* agreement, under which the labor contract specifies that no worker can be hired unless he belongs to the union.* Moreover, in the case of strikes which were held to "imperil the national health or safety," the government was empowered to seek an injunction restraining the work stoppage for 80 days, while efforts were made at a settlement. Injunctions were applied in such major disputes as the railroad strike of 1948, the coal strike of 1950, and the steel strike of 1959. While union leaders have strongly opposed this provision of the Taft-Hartley Act, there is general agreement that it has not revived the abuses of the injunctive procedure which characterized labor relations before 1932. (The injunctive provisions of the Taft-Hartley Act were not modified to any significant degree by a later labor law—the *Landrum-Griffin Act* of 1959.) Labor controversies of a purely local nature, it should be noted, may still come within the range of injunctions issued by state courts.

The courts may curb the Executive in labor matters. The courts have not always gone along with the exercise of power by the Executive in labor relations disputes. For example, President Truman in 1952 moved to seize and operate the nation's major steel mills in an effort to avoid a nationwide strike. In a 6-to-3 decision, the Supreme Court declared the President's action to be illegal. Speaking for the majority, Justice Black emphasized the doctrine of separation of powers in our system of government and stated that only Congress has the power to take over private property in such cases. The fact that the President was seeking to prevent a crippling work stoppage did not justify his action.

* The law, however, permitted the *union shop*, under which employees may be required to join the union in question within a certain period *after* being hired by the employer.

The Power of Judicial Review

The importance of judicial review. One phase of the work of the Federal courts, and of the Supreme Court in particular, has been the subject of unending controversy ever since the founding of the Republic. This is the power of *judicial review*. The phrase refers to the power of the courts to pass upon the constitutionality of legislative acts by the Federal Congress, by state legislatures, and by local governmental bodies. This is a distinctive feature which pervades our entire system of government. Its scope extends from judgment upon the humble performance of some village council or local justice of the peace, to a statute of Congress, or a provision in the Constitution of the United States. Whenever a momentous decision has been rendered, the courts are sure to stir up conflicting reactions. They are defended as guardians of constitutional rights in some quarters. In others, they are bitterly attacked for "usurping" power or for holding up the wheels of progress. It is the Supreme Court which passes final judgment. Hence, the paeans of praise or the loud cries of denunciation center most often on that high tribunal.

Origins of the "judicial veto." The Constitution itself makes no positive, direct reference to the use of this power. The question had been considered in the Constitutional Convention. Hamilton argued that the right was inherent in the "courts of justice, whose duty it must be to declare all acts contrary to the manifest tenor of the Constitution void." His views were sustained by others. The Constitution did not specify that this power might be exercised. Yet it did not forbid it, nor did it place the power in any other branch of the government.

There appears to have been much sentiment in favor of the right of judicial review in the expression of the two leading parties and of public opinion in the early years of our history. In fact, a Connecticut law was declared unconstitutional by a Federal circuit court as early as 1791. The following year, another circuit court declared a Rhode Island law invalid. And, in the same year, still another circuit court nullified an act of Congress. The exercise of judicial review went unchallenged. But it was not until Chief Justice John Marshall's famous dictum in the case of *Marbury v. Madison* (1803) that the right of the courts to declare acts of the Federal government unconstitutional was formally asserted. The Constitution, Marshall argued, was "the superior paramount law" of the land, and therefore, any "legislative act contrary to the Constitution is not law." It is "the very essence of judicial duty," he maintained, for the courts to declare what is and what is not "repugnant to the Constitution." Thus, Marshall asserted the power of judicial review, not because it had been conferred upon the courts in so many words, but rather because, by "implication," its exercise was a necessary function belonging to the courts.

Supreme Court decisions on the constitutionality of laws may be overruled by two different methods—passage of a constitutional amendment, or a new decision by the Court itself. An important historical example of each method is represented above.

Since Marshall's day the power of the courts to review and to annul acts of the Federal and state governments has been asserted repeatedly. This assumption has provoked constant outcries that the power involves "judicial usurpation." It has been said that Congress, the President, and even the state legislatures are just as good judges of constitutionality as the Supreme Court.

How has the power of judicial review been used? Marshall during his 34 years as Chief Justice nullified only one statute of

Congress, although he also cut down a number of state acts. Indeed, for more than 50 years after the *Marbury v. Madison* decision in 1803, the Supreme Court did not annul a single act of Congress. In the many cases which the Supreme Court has considered throughout its history, it has upheld the constitutionality of the vast majority of the laws involved. Most of the annulments have occurred during the last half century. These have to do, for the most part, with conflicts involved in economic relationships. They have grown out of the "commerce clause" of the Constitution and the protection of civil rights expressed in the 14th Amendment. But always in the foreground there has been the question of the conservatism or the liberalism of the Court.

Seven Stages in the History of the Supreme Court as Reflected in Outstanding Cases

How has the nation fared under judicial review? Has the trend of Supreme Court decisions accurately reflected the political, economic and social views of each generation? We can answer these questions best by following the character of the Court's decisions in the important stages of its history.

The first stage—The nation and the states. Mention has already been made of *Marbury v. Madison* (1803), in which judicial review of Congressional acts was asserted. There were other decisions of the Marshall period (1801-1835) that clearly established judicial review. In *McCulloch v. Maryland* (1819), Marshall upheld the constitutionality of the United States Bank as an agency "necessary and proper" to the conduct of the Federal government. Since Congress had created the Bank on the basis of its implied powers in Article I, Section 8, Clause 18, the Supreme Court in effect sanctioned Congressional use of broad powers. In the same decision, the Court also voided an act of a state legislature (Maryland). Thus with one blow *McCulloch v. Maryland* opened the door to broader use of Congressional power at the expense of state power. A few years later, in *Gibbons v. Ogden* (1824), the Supreme Court was confronted with two questions: Did Federal authority over interstate commerce extend within the boundaries of a state? Did the Constitution imply a prohibition against state control of interstate commerce, thus giving the Federal government exclusive authority over such activities? Both questions were answered by the Court in the affirmative.

As noted, Marshall was attacked on all sides and for reasons which have a familiar ring in relation to the criticism leveled against the Supreme Court in our day. He was accused of stretching the powers of the national government beyond the constitutional warrant, and of reducing the states to a position of impotence. Time has demonstrated that these fears and criticisms were unwarranted. Marshall's great decisions have become part of our national heritage. In forcefulness, clarity, and farsightedness, they stand in the very front rank of judicial thought. The precedents they established have helped to shape the course of our history.

The second stage—The status of slavery. This period in the development of the Supreme Court parallels the great controversies over slavery. Most notable was the decision in the *Dred Scott Case* (1857). Dred Scott was a slave who had been taken by his master to free territory and then was returned to Missouri (a slave state). Scott sued in the Missouri courts for freedom for himself and his wife and children, on the grounds that their stay on free soil had made them all free. The case was brought into the Federal courts (on the ground of diversity of state citizenship) and ultimately reached the Supreme Court on appeal. The majority of the Court held that Scott could not bring suit in a Federal court because he was not a citizen of the United States. Chief Justice Roger Taney stated in his decision: "State citizenship does not enable him (Scott) to be a citizen of the United States, or of any other state for that matter." Thus was established the primacy of *national citizenship*. (Other aspects of the Dred Scott case, of great significance for the slavery controversy, are not considered here.)

The third stage—Civil rights during Reconstruction. The Supreme Court during this stage was concerned with matters which grew out of the Civil War, emancipation of the Negro slaves, and Reconstruction. The Court's chief task was to pass on questions arising from the interpretation and enforcement of the postwar constitutional amendments. Many of these questions affected the application of the civil rights which the states were required to observe under the first section of the 14th Amendment.

In the *Slaughterhouse Cases* (1873), for example, the Supreme Court ruled that the rights and privileges of national citizenship (defined by the 14th Amendment) did not include the protection of other rights. This interpretation meant that the great body of civil rights came under the protection or control of the states, rather than the national government.*

In the *Civil Rights Cases* (1883), the Supreme Court held that the Civil Rights Act passed by Congress in 1875 was unconstitutional. This law had made it a crime for any person to deny to any other person the right to full and equal use of public conveyances and of other public facilities, such as restaurants, theaters, and hotels. In effect, the Court ruled in these cases that the 14th Amendment did not forbid *private* discrimination—that the "equal protection of the laws" clause applied only to state governments and did not prevent the owner of a restaurant, for example, from barring his premises to certain groups. When such discrimination occurred, the aggrieved person would have to look to his state government for redress, not to the Federal government.

This period also saw the now repudiated *Plessy v. Ferguson* decision (1896). In this case, the Supreme Court upheld segregation under the "separate but equal" principle. According to this rule, state governments could require separation of whites and Negroes in schools, common carriers, hospitals, parks, and other public places, if the facilities provided to the two races were substantially equal. Thus the Supreme Court gave assent to the laws of Southern states designed to promote a dual environment—one that would effectively segregate the white and Negro races in all aspects of everyday life.

The fourth stage—Government and business. This stage of the Supreme Court's history accompanied the development of big business in the United States. There were insistent demands for reforms and controls, and the Supreme Court was called on to rule on many controversies in the area of labor relations, governmental regulation of business, and financial policies. There was much hostile criticism of the Court, provoked chiefly by two decisions in 1895. By a one-vote margin, the Court reversed an earlier decision and declared the basic features of the Federal income tax unconstitutional. Organized labor and the farmers of the

* Although the Slaughterhouse Cases were among the first involving an interpretation of the 14th Amendment, they did not actually deal with Negro rights. The cases grew out of the issue of whether or not a state government (the Reconstruction "carpetbag" government of Louisiana) had the right to grant a monopoly of the slaughterhouse business in New Orleans to a single firm, thus preventing hundreds of other citizens from engaging in that business. The Court affirmed the right of the Louisiana Legislature to grant such a monopoly.

South and West regarded this decision as favoring the moneyed classes. Organized labor likewise condemned the Court because it sustained the injunction against Debs and his associates in the Pullman Strike of 1894.

During the early part of the 20th century, the Court had to deal constantly with questions related to antitrust, labor, and social legislation. Its tendency in the earlier years was to sustain a number of efforts of the government to break up monopolies and other "combinations in restraint of trade." Thus, in 1904, the Court ordered the dissolution of the Northern Securities Company, a mammoth holding company for the Northern Pacific, the Great Northern, and the Chicago, Burlington and Quincy railroads. In 1911, it applied a similar policy toward the Standard Oil Company and the American Tobacco Company. However, after World War I, the Court pursued a less stringent course. Like the government itself, it was disposed to accept the inevitability of many types of large-scale industrial combinations.

It is hard for many of us today to realize that as late as the opening decades of the 20th century vast numbers of little children worked long hours in American industry. This "package boy" trudged the streets of New York City, carrying heavy loads of half-finished garments. The social evil of child labor has been eliminated not only by legislation and court decisions but also as a result of social and economic changes.

As regards labor and social regulation of the pre-New Deal era, the Supreme Court's record is a mixed one. Most of the laws in this area were enacted by the states. Many of them were upheld. Others, in spite of strong public support, were invalidated.

The fifth stage—Government and the welfare state. This period in the history of the Court involved the extent to which the government can determine the course of the economic and social life of the nation. The Court invalidated several of the New Deal measures in the 1930's, thus taking a conservative attitude toward the government's almost revolutionary program of reform legislation. Thereupon, President Roosevelt attacked the Court as having a "horse and buggy" mentality and proposed changes in the Court's organization, which many, in turn, attacked as an attempt to "pack" our highest tribunal. In this instance, however, time proved to be the great healer, for within a few years the Court, under the leadership of Chief Justice Charles E. Hughes, upheld such key New Deal measures as the modified Agricultural Adjustment Act, the Railway Labor Act, the Wagner (Labor Relations) Act, the Social Security Act, and the Fair Labor Standards Act. As the court manifested this change of attitude, and as vacancies gave President Roosevelt opportunities to appoint new Justices, the conflict between the Executive and the Judiciary receded into the background.

The sixth stage—Government and Communism. The period after World War II witnessed efforts on the part of the Federal and state governments to take action against persons who advocated overthrow of the government by force or subversion. The basis for action by the Federal government was, notably, the Smith Act of 1940 and the McCarran Act of 1950. In the states, measures were enacted requiring loyalty oaths of public employees and authorizing action against those found guilty of "subversive" activities. All such action was directed particularly against Communists, or persons suspected of Communist sympathies. The constitutionality of much of this legislation, the question of free speech and press, observance of due process of law and similar constitutional or legal aspects, were inevitably tested in the Supreme Court.

The Court, as we shall see by an examination of its various decisions in this area, has had difficulty in serving in the traditional role of the "calm in the midst of a storm." The decisions, which we present reveal, in their different phases, a Supreme Court that faced perplexing problems.

1. In the case of *Dennis v. United States* (1951), a majority of the Court upheld the conviction of leading officials of the Communist Party in the United States. The Court held that Communist leaders who had organized for the purpose of teaching and advocating the violent overthrow of the government could constitutionally be punished, even though their freedom to speak and publish their views was at stake. Did the Court, thereby, ignore the 1st Amendment? No, according to the Court's majority, because in the *Schenck Case* of 1919, limits had been put on free expression, if this expression presented a "clear and present danger" to the nation. In other words, the activities of the Communist leaders did constitute a "clear and present danger" to our national security. Congress, therefore, had the power to outlaw or restrict their activities. The Court thus seemed to reflect the great fear of Communism that prevailed during this period of the early 1950's.

2. In 1957, the Supreme Court all but invalidated the Smith Act. In three decisions that year (*Yates v. United States, Watkins v. United States,* and *Sweezy v. New Hampshire*), the Court ruled as follows: *(a)* That a distinction should be made between the advocacy of the forcible overthrow of government "as an abstract doctrine" and the advocacy of "action to that end." The former was declared permissible under the 1st Amendment. *(b)* That the House Un-American Activities Committee's demand that an accused person furnish names of former associates was unlawful. *(c)* That an investigating committee for the State of New Hampshire had also exceeded its authority when it demanded of an accused the names of past associates. Thus the Court seemed to back away from its position in the Dennis Case of 1951. Conservative-minded persons now began to attack the Court as being "soft on subversives."

3. In 1961, the Court, in several decisions, passed further judgments on Communism. In *Communist Party v. Subversive Activities Control Board*, the Court ruled that it is constitutional to require the Communist Party, which presents "a clear and present danger" to our national security, to register with the Department of Justice. In *Scales v. United States*, the Court upheld the clause in the Smith Act which declared active membership in the Communist Party to be illegal if the accused was aware of the Party's

objectives when he joined it. This seemed to herald still another change in the Court's position. But the tables were turned when, in 1965, the Court in a unanimous decision (with one Justice abstaining) voided a Federal law of 1962 which had restricted mail delivery of Communist propaganda. The Court declared that this particular clause in the law (the Postal Service and Federal Employees Salary Act) was an infringement of the 1st Amendment. Also, in 1965, the Supreme Court in a 5-to-4 decision ruled unconstitutional a Federal law making it a crime for a Communist to serve as an official of a labor union. Thus a section of the 1959 Labor Management Reporting and Disclosure Act (Landrum-Griffin Act) was nullified.

The conflicting viewpoints among members of the Court were well expressed by two of the Justices. The late Justice Felix Frankfurter had this to say:

> Against the impediments which particular governmental regulation causes to the entire freedom of individual action, there must be weighed the value to the public of the ends which the regulation may achieve.

Justice Hugo Black stated his position thus:

> My belief is that we must have freedom of speech, press and religion for all, or we may eventually have it for none.

4. In 1965, the Court in another unanimous decision (with one Justice abstaining) held that individual members of the Communist Party could not be forced to register with the Department of Justice under the Internal Security Act (McCarran Act) of 1950. Speaking for the Court, Justice William J. Brennan, Jr. ruled that an individual Communist required to register in the way could validly cite the 5th Amendment provision against self-incrimination, since "an admission of membership (in the Communist Party) may be used to prosecute the registrant under the membership clause of the Smith Act."

This seeming victory of the Communist Party was somewhat dampened when the Federal District Court imposed a fine of $230,000 for failure to register and submit a list of members. In 1967, however, a United States Court of Appeals overturned this decision, pointing out that subjecting the Party to "the combined sanction of compelling disclosure and criminal punishment (the fine) was hopelessly at odds with the 5th Amendment." It would be like "requiring thieves to register with the sheriff."

The seventh stage—Government and civil rights in general.
For almost six decades after the *Plessy v. Ferguson* decision of
1896, the Court had virtually nothing to say about the constitutionality of racially segregated public school systems on the basis
of "separate but equal" facilities. The sole exception to this was
a Supreme Court decision in 1938 concerned with equal rights
in higher education, but this was of limited application.

Then came the epoch-making *Brown v. Topeka Board of Education* decision in 1954. A unanimous Court declared that racially
segregated education can never be truly equal education, and that
therefore a public school system organized on these lines violated the "equal protection of the laws" clause of the 14th Amendment. Thus, the "separate but equal" doctrine which had held
sway for so long gave way in 1954 to "separate and therefore unequal." In 1955, the Supreme Court followed up with a desegregation decree which ordered local school boards throughout the
nation to make a "prompt and reasonable start" on a program of
integration, and to proceed toward this goal "with all deliberate
speed." The Federal District Courts were empowered to supervise the execution of this Supreme Court decree.

The following years saw supplementary judicial decisions that
struck at racial segregation in hotels, theaters, restaurants, stores,
parks, beaches, and other places of public assembly and on such
transportation facilities as buses, trains, boats, and airplanes, as
well as bus stations, railroad terminals, and airports.

Another important decision affecting education came in the
Schempp Case (1963), in which the Supreme Court by an 8-to-1
vote declared unconstitutional a Pennsylvania law requiring all
public schools to begin the school day with readings from the
Bible. Speaking for the majority, Justice Tom C. Clark declared:
"The place of religion in our society is an exalted one, achieved
through a long tradition of reliance on the home, the church, and
the inviolable citadel of the individual heart and mind. . . . We
have come to recognize through bitter experience that it is not
within the power of government to invade the citadel, whether
to aid or oppose, to advance or retard." Justice Potter Stewart,
the lone dissenter, stated: "The Constitution requires that such
efforts (the Pennsylvania law requiring the reading of the Bible)
be struck down *only* if they are proven to entail the use of secu-
lar authority of the government to coerce a preference among
religious beliefs."

In 1968, the court barred the color line in housing (rentals and sales), a decision based on the *Open Housing Act of 1968*. (For the Court's ruling on student picketing, see page 315, *Tinker v. Des Moines*, 1969.)

Decisions favoring academic freedom. The Supreme Court in recent years has issued a number of decisions that go far toward insuring full academic freedom for teachers in public schools and colleges. In 1957, the Court voided a contempt conviction of a New Hampshire professor who had refused to answer questions about views expressed in his lectures. In 1966, an Arizona law requiring all teachers to take a loyalty oath was found unconstitutional.

Then, in 1967 the Supreme Court issued an even more significant decision, declaring unconstitutional a "complicated and intricate scheme" of anti-subversive laws applying to teachers in New York State. The most important law at issue was the Feinberg Act, which required school and college teachers to sign statements that they were not Communists, and provided for the discharge of those who expressed "treasonable or seditious" ideas or endorsed writings that advocated the violent overthrow of the government. Speaking for the majority, Justice William J. Brennan, Jr. said: "Our nation is deeply committed to safeguarding academic freedom.... That freedom is a special concern of the First Amendment, which does not tolerate laws that cast a pall of orthodoxy over the classroom."

This sweeping decision appeared to doom similar "anti-subversive" laws in at least 26 other states.

Protection for persons accused of crimes. Another series of decisions that stirred up controversy during the 1960's dealt with the rights of persons accused of crimes. In two cases *(Escobedo v. Illinois*, 1964, and *Miranda v. Arizona*, 1966) the Supreme Court laid down the following guidelines for police interrogation of persons suspected of violations of the law:

1. The suspect must be informed of his right to remain silent before he may be interrogated by the police.

2. He must be warned beforehand that anything he says during interrogation may be used against him in a court of law.

3. He must be apprised of his legal right to the advice of counsel prior to interrogation.

4. He must be provided with a lawyer paid for by the state, if he desires legal advice but cannot afford it.

The Supreme Court based these sweeping decisions on the 5th Amendment, which provides that an individual "shall not be compelled in any criminal case to be a witness against himself." By providing protection against self-incrimination and insuring the right to counsel, the Court has moved vigorously to safeguard the rights of the individual. It has also reaffirmed the primacy of those rights even where they appear to run counter to long-established police methods of operation.

It is emphasized that the protection afforded by these Supreme Court rulings will apply particularly to suspects who are poor and friendless. Persons of means and influence who are accused of crimes have normally been able to engage able lawyers and secure full recognition of their rights by the police. It is the derelict, the unemployed stranger in town, the newcomer with limited command of English who is most in need of judicial protection. Significantly, the defendant in each of the cases mentioned above (and in a number of other similar cases decided by the Supreme Court) was poor and/or a member of a minority group.

Nonetheless, these decisions raise serious questions which have not yet been answered: Will the new requirements, however good their intentions, handicap police and contribute substantially to the ever-growing crime rate? Mindful of these problems, and encouraged by President Nixon, Congress in 1970 passed an *Organized Crime Control Act.* Among the provisions of this "tough" legislation are: the death penalty for fatal bombings; heavy prison sentences and fines for bombings that result in bodily injury and property damage; and severe penalties for disturbers of the peace on campuses.

The Enduring Nature of Supreme Court Decisions

Let us condsider the procedure which the Supreme Court follows in arriving at the decisions which have played, and continue to play, so important a part in our history.

The Court hears the case and renders its decision. When a case is presented to the Supreme Court on appeal, and the Court has agreed to hear it, the first step is to submit the complete record of the proceedings in the immediately lower court. This includes not only all the testimony and the exhibits offered but also the decision of the lower court. The lawyers for both sides supplement this material (often extremely voluminous) with written briefs and oral arguments. After these arguments have been heard and the members of the Court have perhaps directed questions to both lawyers, the Justices retire to consider the record.

In due time, a vote is taken, and the Court presents its decision. The decision is determined by a majority vote, with each member (including the Chief Justice) having a single vote. One or more Justices may fail to vote on a case for any one of a number of reasons, including voluntary abstention. Six Justices constitute a quorum. In case of a 4-to-4 vote, the decision of the lower court is regarded as upheld.

If the Chief Justice has voted with the majority, he will write the decision himself, or will appoint some other member of the majority to write it. If the Chief Justice has voted with the minority, the assignment to write the decision will usually be made by the senior member of the Justices in the majority. The decision not only indicates the legal disposition of the case being considered but also expresses the course of reasoning, constitutional and historical analysis, and supporting citations of precedents and authorities which the Court has utilized in reaching its conclusions. Many Supreme Court decisions, of course, have been documents of great intellectual scope and of outstanding literary quality.

A Justice who agrees with the decision of the majority, but who wishes to present a somewhat different line of reasoning or to emphasize other points, may write a *concurring opinion*. The minority Justices, in turn, may write one or more *dissenting opinions* to explain their point of view. It is not at all unusual for the Court in a given case to produce two, three, or even four opinions, in addition to the decision.

The decision becomes precedent. If the case is of some significance, the decision is more than a cut-and-dried legal document. It becomes an important contribution to legal and social thought. It reflects the vision and personality of its author. It may carry far-reaching influence. By the thought and language of the decisions which he wrote, Marshall established the supremacy of the Federal judiciary; Taney all but precipitated the Civil

War; Holmes and Brandeis echoed the hopes of millions of people that our democratic processes could be adapted to the social needs of an industrial age; Warren, speaking for a unanimous court in the 1954 desegregation cases, gave strength to a movement seeking to achieve a position of full equality for the Negro in American life.

All opinions are significant. It is the vote of the majority, of course, which constitutes the official and effective decision of the Court. Dissenting (minority) opinions have no immediate binding effect, but they may have deep significance for their day and for the future. The minority view in the Dred Scott Case expressed the belief of millions of Americans that the extension of slavery to the territories was an evil. The dissenting opinions of Holmes and Brandeis in many cases reflected a whole new social philosophy, based upon the primacy of human rights. Many other examples of this might be given. Moreover, minority opinions have been used by the Supreme Court itself as a basis for the reversal of earlier decisions. For example, in the case of *Plessy v. Ferguson* in 1896, Justice John Marshall Harlan dissented vigorously from the majority and expressed the belief that a system which prescribed by law the maintenance of "separate but equal" facilities for Negroes, in education and in other areas of everyday life, was unconstitutional. More than a half century later, this stand was vindicated when a unanimous Court outlawed public school systems segregated on the basis of race.

Decisions have national impact. When the Supreme Court nullifies an act of Congress in whole or in part, the law or that portion of it which the Court failed to sustain, is no longer enforced. Moreover, in such instances the Department of Justice drops its prosecutions for infractions of the law which the Supreme Court has declared unconstitutional. A decision of the Court sustaining or voiding an act of one state bears equally upon similar legislation in all the other states. Thus, the decision sustaining the right of New York to pass emergency housing laws upheld, in effect, the right of other states to do the same thing. On the other hand, the decision invalidating a Kansas statute which forbade employers to threaten with discharge workers who were affiliated with a trade union nullified laws of a similar type in other states. Decisions of the Federal courts may be criticized and protested, but they are nonetheless enforced.

Judicial Review—Arguments
Pro and Con Recapitulated

The argument for judicial review. Momentous decisions of the Supreme Court have often called forth staunch defenders of the power of "judicial review." What arguments have been offered in support of this institution?

It has been said that the Supreme Court is the only body in our government specifically equipped to protect and interpret the Constitution impartially. Its processes are not those of haste, but of mature deliberation. Membership on the Court seems to have a broadening and uplifting effect on many of its members. Thus, Justices who were portrayed as staunch conservatives, and even reactionaries, when appointed to the tribunal have often proved to be quite otherwise during their term of service. For example, Senator George Norris, in opposing the nomination of Charles E. Hughes in 1930, said, "No man in public office so exemplified the influence of powerful combinations in the political and financial world...." Yet Mr. Hughes as Chief Justice was repeatedly classed among the "liberals" in the Court. Unlike Congress, which makes our laws, the Court is not a continually changing group, subject to clashing emotions, to "sectional or class jealousies." The Court is, as Justice Holmes once called it, "the calm in the midst of the storm." It serves to restrain Congress, the Executive, the state legislatures, and even the lower courts from acting without constitutional sanction. Thus it is an essential factor in maintaining the principle of checks and balances in our Federal government.

It is likewise argued that even in relation to the states themselves, the Court has had a necessary function. The Court, it is said, has shielded the states against trespass upon their powers by the Federal government. It has protected individuals and corporations against attempts of the states to impair the obligation of contracts, to deprive them of life, liberty or property "without due process of law," to deny them "the equal protection of the laws."

The argument against judicial review. But what of the other side? From time to time, criticism has been made of the "nine old men," "of judge-made concepts and restrictions," of the "aristocracy of the robe" in a land of democratic traditions. The United States is the only large country in the world where the will of the national legislators can be rejected by judicial veto. In 5-to-4 decisions, which have occurred quite frequently, the fate of legislation has depended on the vote of a single judge. The constitutions of Canada and Australia provide for judicial review, but this power is far more limited than in the case of the United States. In Great Britain, in contrast, Parliament is the supreme judge of its own powers. During the early New Deal period, it was claimed, the judges of our Supreme Court had become, partly as a result of having served long terms in office, unresponsive to the great upheavals of their time. Critics charged that the Court tended to view social needs in terms of an outworn economic and social philosophy. Since World War II, there has emerged a Supreme Court that is considered too conservative by some and too liberal by others.

Proposals for Reform of the Supreme Court

Proposals for reform are about as old as the Supreme Court itself. You will recall from your study of American history the doctrine of nullification, which maintained that each state had the right to decide for itself whether an act of Congress is constitutional. This doctrine was set forth by the Virginia and Kentucky Resolutions, by the Hartford Convention, and by leading Southerners prior to the Civil War. Three of our most eminent Presidents (Jefferson, Jackson, Lincoln) were inclined to oppose what they termed "the patent usurpation of power" by the Supreme Court over legislative and executive action. More recently, the Court's decisions in cases involving desegregation and the rights of accused persons have brought forth a storm of protest. Over the years there have emerged many proposals for reform of the Court. They fall into three general categories: remedial measures of a limited nature; those favoring a Congressional curb on the Court's power; and those looking toward a constitutional amendment. The most familiar proposals may be summarized as follows:

◆ *Give Congress the power to override the Court's decisions, as it may now override the President's vetoes.* (This change was recommended by Senator Robert M. La Follette in 1924 when he was a Presidential candidate.)

♦ *Deny the power of judicial review over economic and social policies by limiting the Court's jurisdiction.* Note that under the Constitution, Congress has the right to define the Court's jurisdiction.

♦ *Require unanimous concurrence of the nine Justices, or at least of six or seven, to declare a law unconstitutional.* (Some feel that such a change would require a constitutional amendment, while others argue that it can be done by ordinary statute.)

♦ *Change the Court by appointing additional Justices who are believed to have a desired point of view.* Franklin D. Roosevelt's plan to increase the number of Justices in 1936, often attacked as a "court-packing" scheme, was the latest proposal of this type. Our history shows, however, that Presidents are often surprised by the independence shown by the Justices whom they appoint. The votes of these men turn out to be very different from the positions they were expected to take. The dissenting vote of Justice Holmes (appointed by President Theodore Roosevelt) in the Northern Securities Case is a notable example.

♦ *Let Congress enact, or the Supreme Court set up, a code of ethical conduct for the Federal judiciary.* Heated discussion of this proposal followed the disclosure that Supreme Court Associate Justice Abe Fortas had made financial arrangements with a financier to serve as his consultant. Justice Fortas resigned in 1969, under pressure in face of possible impeachment—a first in the history of the U.S. Supreme Court.

♦ Some authorities are of the opinion that a reduction in the work load of the Court, by limiting the number of cases brought to it for review, is long overdue. For example, Dean Edwin Griswold of the Harvard Law School has pointed out that the Court's "jurisdictional arrangements were established in 1925, when the nation's population was about two-thirds of its present size and was much less economically complex." As an example of what might be done, Dean Griswold has advocated the establishment of a separate Court of Tax Appeals to serve as a last resort in all tax cases, except those involving basic constitutional issues, which might still go to the Supreme Court.

The present arrangements of the Supreme Court are not sacrosanct,* and there is nothing at all improper in presenting suggestions for reform, exactly as with any other organ of government. But suggestions for reform are one thing, and intemperate attacks on the Court as an institution and on the individuals who compose it are another. Under our system of government, the Court

* The Court has undergone many changes in the past. For example, at various times, it has had six, seven, ten, and eight members.

THE FEDERAL COURTS AT A GLANCE

THE SUPREME COURT

Membership. Nine Justices appointed for life. (A Justice can retire on a full-salary pension at age 70, provided he has had 10 consecutive years of service.) Salary of Chief Justice is $62,500 a year; of Associate Justices, $60,000.

Original Jurisdiction. Supreme Court has original jurisdiction (meaning that it is the first court to hear a case) in cases affecting the higher diplomatic representatives of foreign countries, cases in which the United States is a party, and cases in which a state is a party.

Appellate Jurisdiction. Supreme Court has appellate jurisdiction in cases which are appealed to it after having been tried in lower Federal courts or in the highest state court.

OTHER FEDERAL COURTS

Courts of Appeals. Eleven courts throughout United States, with each court having three to fifteen judges, plus an assigned Supreme Court Judge. Chief task is to hear appeals from decisions made by the Federal District Courts and by certain executive agencies. (Formerly known as "Circuit Courts of Appeals.")

Federal District Courts: A total of 88 courts in the 50 states, with at least one in each state, plus one in the District of Columbia. Each District Court has from 1 to 24 judges, with a total of about 330. District Courts have original jurisdiction and may hold jury trials in cases involving violations of Federal laws.

SPECIAL COURTS

1. The *Court of Claims* (consisting of five judges) hears cases involving claims against the United States. If awards are made, Congress must appropriate funds. Small claims may be settled by the head of the government agency involved.

2. The *Customs Court* reviews decisions of customs officers regarding inspection of imports and appraisal of their value.

3. The *Court of Customs and Patent Appeals* reviews appeals from the Customs Court, the Patent Office and the Tariff Commission.

4. The *Tax Court* reviews appeals made by taxpayers regarding tax payments and liabilities.

5. The *U. S. Court of Military Appeals* reviews court martial proceedings in any branch of the Armed Forces.

6. The *Territorial Courts* function in territories of the United States (Virgin Islands, Puerto Rico, the Canal Zone, and Guam).

Appointment of Judges: All judges in Federal courts are appointed by the President with the consent of the Senate. They serve for life (or during good behavior), with same retirement rights as Supreme Court Justices (see above).

must consider many cases which not only are politically and economically important but have deep emotional overtones. As De Tocqueville wrote early in the 19th century: "Scarcely any question arises in the United States which does not become, sooner or later, a subject of judicial debate." It is inevitable that this "debate" at times will become heated, and that some citizens will feel that their rights have been ignored and that sound legal principles have been violated. But historic experience has shown that the Supreme Court (and the Federal judiciary in general) is an institution of great value in conserving the American political tradition and in preparing our society for necessary changes and leaps into the future. We may want to improve that institution in various ways, but there is no place for abusive criticism, for thoughtless demands for impeachment, or for irresponsible assaults on the very basis of our constitutional system.

Stampone in the *Army Times*

In this cartoon, a United States Army publication expresses its opinion of extremists who abusively criticize the Supreme Court and preach defiance of its decisions.

Terms You Should Know

Appellate jurisdiction. Power of a court to hear cases on appeal from lower courts.

Certiorari, writ of. An order by a higher court to a lower court to send up the record of a trial which the higher court may wish to review.

Concurring opinion. Opinion written by a judge which agrees with the majority decision of the court but offers a somewhat different legal basis for arriving at the decision.

Dissenting opinion. Opinion written by a judge which disagrees with the majority decision of the court.

Habeas corpus, writ of. A legal paper which directs police officers to bring before the court a person being held in custody so that the judge may decide whether or not his detention is justified under the law. This is considered a basic safeguard against unjust imprisonment.

Injunction, writ of. A court order which commands or prohibits the performance of a specified act on the grounds that the performance, or non-performance, of the act would cause "an irreparable injury" to a certain person or persons, or to the entire community.

Judicial review. Power of a court to consider acts of a legislative body or of an executive agency and to nullify or invalidate them if, in the court's opinion, they violate constitutional or statute law.

Majority opinion. Decision of a court supported by the majority of the judges.

Mandamus, writ of. An order of a superior court to a lower court (or to an executive official of the government) ordering the performance of some specific act required by law.

Obiter dictum. A part of a judicial opinion dealing with matters not essential to the decision.

Original jurisdiction. Power of a court to hear cases in the first instance—that is, before they have been heard by any other court.

Sociological jurisprudence. Extension of judicial power to matters that involve social problems and considerations, as opposed to purely judicial issues.

Subversive. Tending to overthrow or destroy, as a government or an established order of any kind.

Questions and Problems Based on the Text

1. Why did the Founding Fathers provide for a Federal judiciary in the Constitution?

2. To what types of cases does the Federal judicial power extend? What limitations have been placed upon that power?

3. Draw a diagram to summarize the organization of the Federal court system.

4. Distinguish between *original* jurisdiction and *appellate* jurisdiction. Give specific examples in the Federal court system.

5. Name the "special courts" of the Federal government and their functions.

6. How are cases carried to the Federal courts?

7. Describe each of the great writs issued by the courts.

8. Trace the rise of the doctrine of *judicial review.*

9. Prepare a chart on the "Seven Stages of the Supreme Court," indicating the significant decisions in each stage.

10. Define *due process of law* and *equal protection of the laws.* Show how each of these concepts is important in protecting the liberties of the American people.

11. In regard to the procedure of the Supreme Court, distinguish between a *decision,* a *concurring opinion,* and a *dissenting opinion.*

12. State briefly the part which each of the following has played in the evolution of the Supreme Court: John Marshall, Roger Taney, Oliver Wendell Holmes, Jr., Louis D. Brandeis, Charles E. Hughes, Felix Frankfurter, Hugo Black, Earl Warren.

13. Explain the statement that the national judiciary is "partly constitutional, partly statutory."

14. Write one of the following: (*a*) an imaginary account of "A Day in the Supreme Court," (*b*) an editorial supporting or opposing some important decision handed down recently by the Supreme Court, (*c*) a biography of a noted Supreme Court Justice stressing his attitude toward the great economic and social questions of his day.

15. In 1970, the United States Commission on Civil Rights reported a serious "gap" between the laws that guarantee protection of civil rights and their actual enforcement. While the report conceded progress in public accommodations, in voting, and in education, it found deficiencies in equal employment opportunities and in housing. Research the progress (or the lack of it) made in this area in your own community and your own state.

16. "Some lawyers feel that legal innovations should come from law-making bodies, and that the Supreme Court has gone too far in expanding its own powers." How does this statement throw light on the meaning of the phrase "legalistic vs. sociological jurisprudence"?

17. Each of the following describes briefly the ruling of the Supreme Court in a significant case. Give the name by which the case is usually known. The case may be known by the names of the plaintiff and defendant or just by the name of the plaintiff.

(a) The court outlawed restrictions upon voting by Negroes in primary elections in a Southern state.

(b) The Court forbade religious instruction during school hours in any public school building.

(c) The Court ruled that children who are members of Jehovah's Witnesses may not be compelled to salute the flag when attending public school.

(d) The Court ruled that segregation in public educational institutions and in public transportation is illegal.

(e) The Court has clarified and strengthened the traditional safeguards of a fair trial: that a man is to be considered innocent until proved guilty; that evidence obtained by use of the "third degree" is inadmissible; that the assistance of adequate counsel must be furnished the accused by the Federal government in all cases and by the states in certain cases; that no one can be subjected to double jeopardy; and that evidence obtained through wiretapping is inadmissible in a Federal court.

18. Here are two points of view on judicial procedure. To what extent are these statements in disagreement? Which do you consider more valid? Explain.

(a) "We have constructed a cordon of protection around defendants. This admirable solicitude for the accused assumes that they will honor and cherish the judicial procedure which protects them. They must not be allowed to defile that procedure and then complain that it is tainted." —Louis Nizer

(b) "The sound concept of law and order has come to conjure up visions of policemen clubbing students, Government authorizing electronic snooping, politicians seeking to stifle dissent. It is, therefore, nothing short of subversive of democracy to turn law and order into code words that stand for their antithesis—repression and acquiescence." —Peter Gay

19. President Eisenhower sent troops to Arkansas, and President Kennedy sent troops to Alabama to prevent violence there over desegregation issues, in spite of strenuous objection of the governors of those states. Was the Presidential action in both instances a violation of Article IV, Section 4 of the Federal Constitution? Explain.

20. In 1970, a Federal law was enacted which called for the reorganization of the District of Columbia courts, law enforcement methods, and the criminal justice system in general. Research the provisions of this law, and take a position as to whether or not it represents an improvement over existing practices. Bear in mind that this law has been widely suggested as a possible model for revamping state criminal procedures. (See page 248.)

Ideas to Think About and Discuss

1. *"Judicial review is the capstone feature of the American constitutional system. Hardly any aspect of our institutional life is wholly free from its shadow. Hardly any piece of important legislation escapes running its gauntlet. It is America's unique contribution to the science of politics. It is a subject of never-ending discussion and appraisal,—now laudatory, now condemnatory."*

—Howard L. McBain

2. *"This government is acknowledged by all to be one of enumerated powers. The principle that it can exercise only the powers granted to it is now universally admitted. But the question respecting the extent of the powers actually granted is perpetually arising and will probably continue to arise as long as our system shall exist."*

—Chief Justice John Marshall

3. *"We are under a constitution, but the constitution is what the judges say it is."*

—Chief Justice Charles E. Hughes

4. *"The present use of history by the Supreme Court is a perversion of the relation between truth and unity. It assumes that history can be written to serve the interests of libertarian idealism. . . . Thus, history is rejected in favor of sociology."*

—Alfred H. Kelly

5. "But because, inextricably, the Supreme Court is also an organ of statesmanship and the most powerful organ, it must have a seasoned understanding of affairs, the imagination to see the organic relations of society, above all, the humility not to set up its own judgment against the conscientious efforts of those whose primary duty is to govern."

—JUSTICE FELIX FRANKFURTER

6. "In recent decades, we have tended to rely almost exclusively on the Supreme Court—whose members, unlike Senators and Congressmen, are insulated by life tenure from the political pressure of the day. Yet it is becoming obvious that the contribution of the Court, although pre-eminent, is far from sufficient, and that the responsibility for guarding—and extending—our liberties needs to be more broadly shared."

"They (our basic freedoms) are meant to be used—and used vigorously. As we put them to use, we shall depend less upon courts of law and more upon the conscience of the community to make the exercise of freedom a living reality in our national life."

—JOSEPH L. RAUH, JR.

7. "The decisions of the courts on economic and social questions depend upon their economic and social philosophy; and for the peaceful progress of our people during the twentieth century we shall owe most to those judges who hold to a twentieth-century economic and social philosophy and not to a long outgrown philosophy, which was itself the product of primitive economic conditions."

—PRESIDENT THEODORE ROOSEVELT

8. "Citizenship is not lost every time a duty of citizenship is shirked. And the deprivation of citizenship is not a weapon that government may use to express its displeasure at a citizen's conduct, however reprehensible that conduct may be. As long as a person does not voluntarily renounce or abandon his citizenship . . . I believe his fundamental right of citizenship is secure."

—CHIEF JUSTICE EARL WARREN
(Trop v. Dulles, 1958).

9. "The seeming anxiety of judges to protect every accused person from every consequence of his voluntary utterances is giving rise to myriad rules, sub-rules, variations and exceptions which even the most alert and sophisticated judges and lawyers are taxed to follow." —CHIEF JUSTICE WARREN E. BURGER

CHAPTER 8

Our Fifty States

Growth of governmental powers and responsibilities on all levels. Today, the typical American citizen is reminded of the national government virtually every day of his life. Over the air and through the press, its activities make endless demands on his attention. The impression often conveyed is that all things of real significance in public affairs emanate from Washington, D.C., and that only secondary details are the concern of the governments in the state capitals.

While it is true that the powers and responsibilities of the national government have expanded tremendously in the 20th century, it is also true that the states have grown in importance. For instance, the 1965 budget of the national government, excluding the cost of national defense, amounted to 66 billion dollars. It may surprise you to learn that the annual budgets of our fifty states (including local governments) are approaching the 100-billion-dollar mark. Using these vast sums, the state governments and some 90,000 city, county, and other local units provide a myriad of services without which our modern society could not function.

State constitutions are long and intricate. The basis of each state government, the legal source of its many-sided activities, is the state constitution. Under our Federal system, the state exercises the vast field of "reserved" or "residual" powers (page 7). Accordingly, the state constitution is usually a long and intricate document. For example, the Constitution of Louisiana contains over 200,000 words, compared with the 7000 of the United States Constitution. New York's Constitution fills 189 pages of the State

Legislative Manual. Such matters as education, health, charities, police, crimes, property, marriage and divorce, corporations, banking, labor, the practices of political parties, and local government (city, town, county, village)—to note only a few—have been the subjects of state regulation. State constitutions often treat these functions not in broad outline but in minute detail. And as new social and economic problems arise, most states write into their constitutions provisions for dealing with them.

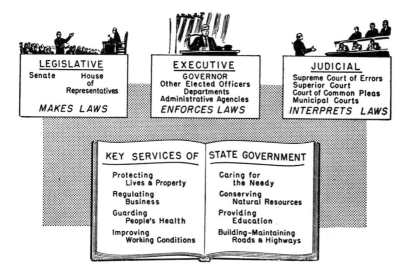

This chart summarizes the organization and the main services of the state government of Connecticut. The structure indicated is typical of most of the states.

Revising and amending state constitutions. Almost all the states make some provision for calling conventions to undertake a thorough revision and rewriting of their constitutions. Such recasting of the basic law is made necessary by far-reaching changes in social and economic conditions. In recent years a number of states (*e.g.*, Connecticut) have adopted new constitutions which are designed to meet the needs and problems of a largely urbanized population.

There are usually four steps in adopting a new state constitution: (1) a popular vote which authorizes the holding of a constitutional convention; (2) election of the delegates to such a convention; (3) the writing and approval of the constitution by the convention; and finally (4) the submission of the document to the people for ratification.

In addition, state constitutions are constantly being *amended*— far more frequently in most cases than the Federal Constitution. There are several general methods by which such amendments may be added.

An amendment may be proposed either by the legislature, or as in New Hampshire, by a popular convention. It is then submitted to the voters for approval. In some states, the proposal of an amendment requires a three-fifths or a two-thirds vote in the legislature. In others, a majority vote of the legislature at two successive sessions is necessary. And a few states require only a majority vote at a single session. In those states which have both the initiative and the referendum, an amendment may be both proposed and ratified by the voters. In some states, the governor's signature is needed on a proposal before the referendum may be submitted to the people.

The State Legislature

Organization of the legislature. In every state, with the single exception of Nebraska, the state legislature* is bicameral, or two-chambered, like the United States Congress. Members of both houses are elected by the people. In some cases, the election takes place in odd-numbered years to avoid the possibility of conflict with national issues.

The lower house in all cases is the larger body. In this house, representation is *supposed* to be based purely on population, with each legislative district containing an approximately equal number of people. In the upper house, or senate, representation in most states has traditionally been based on geographic areas or on units of local government, such as counties. The lawmaking powers of the two houses, with some minor exceptions in a few states, are coordinate.

Legislative sessions are held in most states every other year, but special sessions may be called by the governor. Partly because

* The lawmaking bodies of the states are known by a variety of names such as *Legislature, Legislative Assembly, General Assembly,* and *General Court.* In all states, the "upper house" is known as the *Senate*; the "lower house" is designated by such names as *Assembly, General Assembly, House of Representatives,* and *House of Delegates.*

many legislatures are limited both in the frequency and in the length of their regular sessions, and partly because current problems have created numerous emergencies, these special sessions have become more frequent in recent years.

Inequalities in representation in the legislature. The organization of the typical state legislature has met with difficulties that arise from inequalities in the basis of representation. Such inequalities have resulted not only from the practice of "gerrymandering" the state in the interest of the dominant political party but also because of the failure of state legislatures to draw new district lines according to population, especially for the lower house. Examples of flagrant inequality of representation resulting from this are shown in the table below. Each figure indicates the percentage of the state's total population living in the least populous districts from which a majority of legislators were chosen prior to the Supreme Court decisions of 1962-1964. The "ideal" figure would be slightly over 50%—which would indicate a majority of the people choosing a majority of the legislators. Thus, the deviation from 50% in each case is a measure of how far representation in that state legislature had deviated from fair apportionment on the basis of population. From this point of view, the situation in Alaska was relatively good; in Florida, extremely bad. (Virtually any one of the 50 states might have been chosen for this tabulation.)

STATE	SENATE	HOUSE
Alabama	25.1%	27.2%
Alaska	35.0%	48.9%
Arizona	12.8%	45.8%
Arkansas	43.8%	33.3%
California	10.7%	44.7%
Colorado	29.8%	32.1%
Connecticut	33.4%	12.0%
Delaware	22.0%	18.5%
Florida	12.3%	15.1%
Georgia	21.4%	22.5%

How did the inequalities come about? According to Census Bureau statistics, the last 75 years of our history have witnessed a shift in the nation's population from approximately two-thirds rural to two-thirds urban and suburban. Why did not the states adjust representation in the state legislatures accordingly?

First, provisions in some state constitutions had frozen the pattern of apportionment. For example, a provision in the Vermont Constitution (adopted in 1793!) gave one representative to each "organized" city or town, no matter how large or how small. Thus Stratton, a rural town in the Green Mountains of Vermont, was too small to have a post office, but when it came to deciding state legislation, the 38 constituents of this hamlet had as much to say as the more than 36,000 people of Burlington. Stratton and Burlington had one seat each in the Vermont House of Representatives.

Second, some states simply failed to redistrict in spite of major population shifts, and in spite of constitutional or statutory requirements. In the absence of an independent reapportioning agency, it was simply too much to expect legislators to initiate changes that might well result in putting them out of office.

Effects of failure to reapportion. The effects of unequal apportionment on state governments have been felt for a long time. The mushrooming problems of cities and suburbs (see Chapter 9) were either ignored or, at best, not fully appreciated in the state capitals. Fast-growing urban areas began to look to the Federal government in Washington for help, often without adequate response. Municipal governments, under which most Americans were living, were hard put to meet their constantly growing responsibilities in such fields as housing, education, transportation, water supply, and many others. Wholehearted, expert, and generous cooperation from the state government, which might have helped materially, was rarely forthcoming. The urban areas simply did not have the votes in the state legislature to "put through" the programs needed. One result of this was a marked loss of confidence in state government. President Eisenhower's Commission on Intergovernmental Relations, which had made a special study of the subject, concluded that the decline in the influence of the state governments was due in good part to their failure to "maintain an equitable system of representation."

The Supreme Court rules on legislative apportionment. On various occasions, the Supreme Court had refused to rule on cases involving the issue of legislative apportionment. The intention, clearly, was to give the states every opportunity to take remedial action on their own.

Finally, however, the Supreme Court agreed to hear a case brought by a group of Tennessee taxpayers. This resulted in the epoch-making *Baker v. Carr* decision in 1962. By a 6-to-2 vote, the Court held that under the "equal protection of the laws" clause of the 14th Amendment, citizens are entitled to certain forms of protection with regard to apportionment of representation in state legislatures. If these rights are ignored by the state government, then the Federal courts have power to enforce them. Although the case involved specific conditions in Tennessee, where legislative seats had not been reapportioned since 1901, the decision prompted public officials and courts in many other states to concern themselves with equitable representation. Unfortunately, the Supreme Court in *Baker v. Carr* failed to set up criteria for determining when a pattern of apportionment was unconstitutional; nor did it make clear what action District Courts might take to remedy conditions. Still another uncertain point was whether or not the decision applied to Congressional districts, which in many states are based closely on state legislative districts.

Two later Supreme Court decisions threw light on these undecided issues. In *Wesberry v. Sanders* (1964), the Court ruled in effect: as nearly as practicable, one man's vote in a Congressional election must be worth as much as another's.* Later in 1964 in a series of sweeping decisions involving legislative apportionment in six states, the Court ruled:

1. That the "equal protection of the laws" clause of the 14th Amendment "requires that the seats in *both* houses of a bicameral state legislature must be apportioned on a population basis."

2. That "mathematical exactness of precision" in carving out legislative districts may be impossible, but that apportionments must be "based substantially on population."

3. That "the so-called Federal analogy is inapplicable as a sustaining precedent for state legislative apportionments."

4. That these requirements are effective even if the people of a state, through referendum or initiative, have approved an apportionment based on any principle other than population. The Court reminded the state authorities that "a citizen's Constitutional rights can hardly be infringed upon because a majority of the people choose to do so."

* In this decision involving Congressional districts in Georgia, the Court pointed out that one Congressman from a rural district in Georgia served about 272,000 constituents, while another Congressman from Atlanta had over 800,000 constitutents.

Analysis of the decisions. The first two principles stated above may be summarized by the simple but essentially reasonable slogan, "One man, one vote." Few Americans will choose to quarrel with this idea.

On the other hand, there has been considerable uncertainty, and even misgivings, over the Court's rejection of the so-called "Federal analogy." In other words, if the United States Congress can have an upper house to which each state, regardless of population, sends two Senators, why cannot a state legislature have an upper house in which representation is based on counties (or on some other geographic unit), without concern for equality of population?

The analogy is false, said the Court, because the United States was created by thirteen sovereign states, and the Constitution embodies a theory of federalism which divides sovereign power between the nation and the states. Thus, the Senate was a condition of union which the Federal government, created by that union, has no power to destroy. In contrast, counties were never independent or sovereign. They are the creatures, not the creators, of the states. At any time, counties may be merged, subdivided, or abolished by the state government. Thus, there is no good reason to assign representation to counties in violation of the principles of fair apportionment based on population.

Another question has been raised: If representation in both houses of a state legislature is to be based primarily on population, what point is there in having a two-house legislature? The question, according to the Court's reasoning, rests on two false assumptions: (1) that the only function of bicameralism is to provide contrasting bases of representation in the two houses (that is, the bases of population and geographic areas); and (2) that if both houses are chosen on the basis of population, there can be no significant differences between them. The fact is that the essential function of the second house is to provide adequate checks and balances and to assure more mature and deliberate consideration before a bill becomes a law. It can do this even if the basis of representation is changed from counties to population. In any case, the two houses will not be identical; they will continue to differ in size of districts, term of office, and number of members. For example, in Massachusetts, Washington and Oregon, where both houses have been apportioned on the basis of population, experience has shown that each house is quite different in outlook and method of operation from the other.

The 40-member Senate of Massachusetts, for example, complements, rather than duplicates, the 24-member General Court.

Many of our states include minority groups living in certain areas. They may have special economic interests, as well as cultural traditions and patterns of their own. Will they be able to protect their interests in a state legislature in which both houses are dominated by the great population centers? This situation, it is said, is particularly marked in states such as New York and Illinois, where a very large part of the total population lives in a single metropolitan area. Will the people of the sparsely populated rural areas be able to make their voices heard at the state capital? The answer is that the United States Constitution and the state constitutions protect the essential rights of minorities as well as majorities. If representation is fairly distributed according to population, we can depend on the normal democratic processes to produce reasonably well-balanced legislation, adjusted to meet the needs of all the people of the state.

Changes resulting from the reapportionment decisions. As of mid-1967, all but a few of the 99 state legislative bodies had been reapportioned since 1962. These changes were intended to meet the "one man, one vote" standard set by the Supreme Court, but in some instances the highest state courts found the new districting unsatisfactory. Accordingly, some of the legislative houses were reapportioned several times.

Strong opposition to the Court's rulings appeared in Congress. Senator Everett Dirksen, minority leader in the Senate, led the forces seeking to enact a constitutional amendment that would authorize a state to choose one legislative house on a basis other than population. Senator Dirksen initiated a campaign to have Congress call a constitutional convention to modify the rea-portionment rulings. Under Article V of the Constitution, such a convention is to be called by Congress whenever the legislatures of two-thirds of the states request it. Thus far in our history such a convention has never taken place.

In summary, it can be said that while reapportionment of state legislatures is not a panacea, many authorities believe that it will bring a new stream of vitality to our state governments. Cities long under-represented will find a more adequate voice for their needs. The newer suburbs will gain more leverage at the state level. And it may be expected that in Congress under-representation of metropolitan areas will be rectified.

220 | OUR FIFTY STATES

The States and Qualifications for Voting. Under the U. S. Constitution, the states have the right to set qualifications for voting. The only limitations on this are that a state may not deny a citizen the right to vote on the basis of race, color, or previous condition of servitude (15th Amendment), or on account of sex (19th Amendment). Also, under the 24th Amendment, the right of a citizen to vote in Federal elections may not be denied "by reason of failure to pay any poll tax or other tax." (See pages 346, 347 and 350 for the text of these amendments.)

The *Voting Rights Act of 1965* further curtailed state power over fixing suffrage qualifications. It provided that literacy tests were to be suspended in any state or county where registered voters comprised less than 50% of all residents of voting age. This law had the effect of increasing substantially the number of black voters in some Southern states, where the evidence indicated that literacy tests had often been unfairly administered in order to keep black voters from the polls.

In 1970, the 1965 law was amended and extended for another five years. The new statute banned literacy tests in all states and set a uniform state residency requirement (not more than 30 days) for voting in Presidential elections. This gave further protection to minority group voters.

Extending the Vote to 18-Year-Olds. Another highly significant provision of the Voting Rights Act of 1970 lowered the voting age from 21 to 18 in all Federal, state, and local elections, beginning in 1971. It was estimated that this would extend the vote to about 11 million young people because (as of 1971) the minimum voting age was still set at 21 in 42 of the 50 states, including all of the larger ones.*

President Nixon signed this bill in approval of its purpose, but he expressed doubt of its constitutionality because he thought that a constitutional amendment might be needed to make such a change. The issue was promptly submitted to the courts. Late in 1970, the Supreme Court decided by a 5-to-4 vote that the law was valid in regard to Federal elections. In regard to state and local elections, however, the Court ruled (also by a 5-to-4 majority) that the states could not be required to set any particular minimum voting age.

* As of 1971, Alaska, Georgia, and Kentucky set the minimum voting age at 18; Montana and Massachusetts, at 19; and Hawaii, Maine and Nebraska, at 20.

With this decision, Congress moved promptly to introduce an amendment that would lower the voting age to 18 for all elections. The amendment was approved by both houses and submitted to the states for ratification. Here it made rapid progress, and it was ratified by the 38th state in June, 1971, in ample time for the elections later that year.

Meanwhile, many states moved to lower the voting age to 18 on their own. One purpose of this was to avoid the confusion that would result from having double sets of ballots—one for state and local elections (limited to persons over 21), and one for Federal elections (open to any qualified citizen over 18).

The legislature at work. The procedures of state legislatures are so similar to those of Congress that only a few outstanding exceptions and peculiarities need be noted here. Even more than the Speaker of the national House of Representatives, the presiding officer of the "lower house" of the average state legislature is a key official. He may shape the direction of legislation by his power to appoint committees, to refer bills to strategic committees, to rule on disputed points. Committee control over lawmaking is characterized by much the same advantages and possible abuses that we have noted in reference to Congress. It is generally agreed that the state legislatures, in general, have too many committees with overlapping functions. The influence of party machines and of lobbies and other pressure groups is as evident in the state legislatures as it is in Congress.

Limitations on the powers of the legislature. In the exercise of its powers, the legislature is subject to limitations placed upon the states by the United States Constitution, as well as limitations imposed by the state constitution itself. Conspicuous among the latter class of restrictions are those which refer to taxation, to the prevention of wasteful and extravagant expenditures, and to the passing of special and local legislation. Enactment of economic and social legislation has frequently produced a conflict between *property rights*, as guaranteed by the 14th Amendment and by the state constitution, and what is commonly known as the *police power* of the state (page 7). This is the power to legislate so as to protect the health, safety, morals, and general welfare of the people. Much of the work of both the Federal and state judiciaries has related to the clarification and adjustment of this conflict.

The initiative and the referendum. The *initiative* and the *referendum* constitute still another type of limitation upon the powers of the legislature in a number of states.

The *initiative* gives the voters an opportunity to introduce legislation by securing a required number of signatures to a petition. The process has two variations. In one form, known as the "indirect initiative," the petition containing a draft of the desired bill is offered to the legislature. If the legislature passes it, it becomes law. If the measure is rejected by the legislature, it is submitted to the voters for their approval. The "direct initiative" does not require consideration of the bill by the legislature. It is voted on directly by the electorate, which may accept or reject it.

The *referendum* gives the voters an opportunity to pass upon various matters, such as the calling of a constitutional convention, amendment of the state constitution, and approval of a bond issue or of another type of legislative act. By means of the "mandatory referendum," a required percentage of the voters may, by petition, order the legislature to submit a measure·to the people. The state constitution itself may specify that certain questions must have popular approval before they can become effective. Where the "optional referendum" exists, the legislature decides when a question is to be submitted to the people.

About twenty states now have both the initiative and the referendum. The use of the referendum alone is, however, more widespread. Opinion as to the accomplishments of these institutions is divided. They have undoubtedly acted both as a spur and as a deterrent to legislatures. On the other hand, largely because of the indifference of many voters, these lawmaking procedures have not been as effective as their advocates had hoped a generation or two ago.

Criticisms of state legislatures. Students of state government have been almost unanimous in their criticism of the functioning of state legislatures. The legislatures, according to many critics, have become "law mills." It is charged that they "grind out" many hastily and carelessly drawn bills and measures designed to favor all sorts of special interests. Such legislative acts often invite the governor's veto, clog the courts, and raise unending questions of constitutionality. Why is all this so? One reason is that the caliber of some of the men who seek and gain election to the legislature is not as high as it·should be, and the more able members, after serving for one or two terms, often leave for more prestigious posts. The processes of lawmaking are far too complicated, and lend themselves to manipulation by political machines. There is also the unfortunate fact that the legislature sometimes becomes a sort of arena in which a wide variety of pressure groups—political, economic, sectional, etc.—seek to assert their claims. In this atmosphere, any broad or disinterested concept of the public interest is not likely to receive too much attention.

Possible reforms of the state legislatures. Many suggestions have been advanced to reform our state legislatures. One proposal is to form a *legislative council* composed of the governor and selected members of the legislature to formulate a legislative program for each session. Many states, beginning with Kansas in 1933, have adopted the device of a legislative council.*

Another proposal advocates a sweeping reorganization of the committee system. It is felt that, in general, there are too many committees and that they are often too large. The committee system operative in Massachusetts has often been commended. In that state, bills are considered by joint committees representing both houses, and public hearings are held before the committees make their reports. Moreover, these reports must be made within a specified period of time, and no bills are "killed in committee." The use of the joint committee system appears to be increasing.

Another suggestion is to establish more effective control over lobbies. This has been tried with particular success in Wisconsin, where all lobbyists must register, and their activities receive extensive publicity.

Finally, it has been argued that much legislation could be easily and advantageously superseded by rules and regulations applied and enforced by the administrative officials of the state.

In search of ethical standards. Numerous regulations exist that guide the conduct of members of the executive and judicial branches of Federal and state governments. But rules dealing with the behavior of state legislative officials either are murky or tend

---

* The "model state constitution" sponsored by the National Municipal League provides for a legislative council of from seven to fifteen members, charged with the task of collecting information, consulting experts outside government, and reporting to the legislature on proposed legislation, as well as recommending legislation on its own initiative. Members of the legislative council would receive additional compensation for their services.

to be honored in the breach rather than in the observance. Left unsolved are moral questions that confront a legislator daily: Should he vote on issues in which he has a financial stake? How far should he go in presenting a constituent's case before a regulatory agency (e.g., the Public Service Commission or the State Liquor Authority)? Should he accept a large honorarium for speaking before an organization with a vested interest in pending legislation? Is he justified in putting relatives on his office payroll? Is he devoting too much time to his outside business? Should he accept a gift from a lobbyist?

These and other questions related to the ethical standards of state legislators have been raised with increasing frequency and insistence in recent years. In some states, attempts have been made to write into law more rigorous and enforceable codes regarding "conflicts of interests" and "full financial disclosures." Even more important than such laws, in all probability, is the development of a climate of public opinion that will condemn (and reject at the polls) any legislators or would-be legislators who are inclined to exploit the powers and privileges of their offices as a means of self-enrichment.

The State's Executive Officials

The position of the governor. The office of governor is "the highest public position in the gift of the people of the state." It is an office which has steadily grown in power, as popular confidence in the legislature has waned. It has become all the more important because of the prestige imparted to it by able and forceful chief executives in many of the states. The office is regarded as a logical step toward the United States Senate, and even toward the Presidency.

Every state chooses its governor by direct popular vote. The term of office is either two or four years, with about two-thirds of the states having a four-year term. In several states (e.g., Alabama), a governor cannot succeed himself; and in others (e.g., New Jersey) he is not eligible to serve a third consecutive term. As of 1965, the salary ranged from $10,000 to $50,000 per year. In spite of additional allowances (housing, transportation, entertainment expenses), a governor often finds that the expenses of his office exceed his official income.

The governor's power over lawmaking. The legislative powers of the governor of a state are similar in many ways to those of the President of the United States. There is, however, considerable variation from state to state. This is notably true of the veto power. All states, except North Carolina, give the governor power to veto bills. In some states, however, he must sign or veto a bill in its entirety, while in others he may veto certain specific items, such as appropriations, while approving the rest of the bill. The veto may be overridden in most states by a two-thirds vote of both houses of the state legislature; in some states either a simple majority or a three-fifths majority is required. In only about one-third of the states does the governor have the privilege of *pocket veto*—that is, the power to kill a bill by failing to act on it. In all the other states, if a governor fails to sign a bill or to veto it, it becomes law. Governors have, as a rule, exercised the veto power quite freely and have thus helped to check the enactment of much ill-considered legislation.

SEES THAT LAWS ARE PROPERLY EXECUTED.

APPOINTS AND REMOVES SEVERAL HUNDRED OFFICIALS.

SUPERVISES WORK OF ADMINISTRATIVE AGENCIES.

IS RESPONSIBLE FOR STATE BUDGET.

MAY INITIATE LEGISLATION.

MAY VETO BILLS.

This chart was prepared to summarize the main powers of the Governor of California. Does the Governor of your state have similar powers?

In about half of the states, in an effort to prevent extravagance on the part of the legislature, the budget is prepared under the direction of the governor (the so-called "executive budget"). The budget so prepared may be changed and, in some instances, even increased, by the legislature, but the governor's power of veto has often served as an effective check against this.

The governor's executive powers. The governor's executive powers are concerned largely with appointments, but his authority in this field is hardly comparable to the appointive function of the President of the United States. In the first place, many top state officials are still chosen by election.* The idea of the "short ballot" has by no means spread to all the states. Second, not all the states give the governor power over removal from office. Even where this power does exist, it is often hemmed in by constitutional or other legal restrictions. Such conditions explain, in large part, the lack of administrative harmony which so often characterizes the operation of state government.

Still another executive function of the governor is his command of the National Guard, the state militia, and the state police, where such a force exists.

The governor's judicial powers. "One of the governor's most difficult jobs," according to Alfred E. Smith, a distinguished Governor of New York State in the 1920's, "is to combine the legal responsibilities of executive position with the human responsibility of sympathy and compassion." This statement refers to the governor's power to grant pardons and reprieves, to commute sentences of imprisonment, and to parole offenders. In some states the governor shares this power with a special board. Despite the general condemnation of the "law's delays," there is much to be said for exhausting every reasonable possibility to prevent the punishment of an innocent man, or to mitigate a punishment which is unduly severe. "Let justice be done, though the heavens fall."

Other executive officials of the state government. In about three-quarters of the states, there is an elected *lieutenant-governor*, whose duties are comparable to those of the Vice President of the United States. He presides over the Senate, and usually he has a vote in this body in the event of a tie. In most cases, the lieutenant-governor succeeds to the governorship in the event of a vacancy, although some states provide for a special election to fill an unexpired term.

The *attorney-general*, usually an elective officer, is the chief legal adviser and prosecutor for the state government. His opinions often serve as valuable guides for the governor and the administrative departments.

* There are 37 states which still elect their lieutenant-governor; 38 which elect the secretary of state; 46 which elect the auditor or comptroller; 42 which elect the state treasurer; 46 which elect the attorney-general. Those officials not popularly elected are appointed by the governor in some states, by the legislature in others.

Almost all of our states have an *auditor* or *comptroller*, who examines the financial accounts of the state government and issues orders for payment of legal bills. The *treasurer* is custodian of the state's funds and makes payments upon due authorization.

The *secretary of state* is custodian of official state documents and usually performs such administrative tasks as issuing licenses and charters of incorporation.

The directing head of the state's educational system is known as the *superintendent of public instruction* or the *commissioner of education*. His powers vary from state to state.

In addition to these officials, there are in every state numerous administrative agencies directed (usually) by a single head or by a board of several members. The criticism has often been made that much of the decentralization and wastefulness of state governments has been the result of the existence of too many such agencies. In many cases, they are not directly responsible to the governor. Moreover, coordination among them is sometimes ineffective, and their powers and operations tend to overlap.

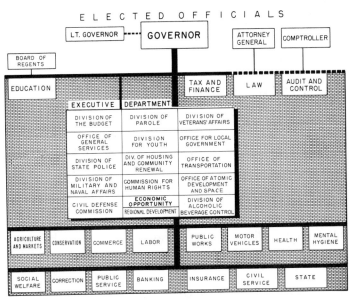

This chart represents the organization of the executive branch of the government of New York State. With modifications of terminology, it is quite typical of the setup in most states.

Impeachment and recall. Practically all of the states provide for the removal of executive officials by *impeachment.* The constitution of the state indicates the grounds for impeachment. The process used is quite similar to that specified by the United States Constitution. In practice, impeachment of executive state officials has been used only rarely. In addition to the constitutional restrictions, partisan political considerations make it extremely difficult to get the two-thirds majority vote needed to remove a governor or an agency head from office. A number of states, therefore, provide for the *recall* of public officials upon the more general grounds of unfitness.

The recall may be used for all state offices, or for only a few. A petition containing a statement of the charges against the official, if signed by the requisite number of voters, leads to a special election. At this election, the voters are asked to indicate whether or not they favor the removal of the official in question, and whom (if anyone) they prefer as his successor. The official whose recall is sought may, in an effort at vindication, have his name on the ballot. If he is re-elected, he naturally remains in office. The recall, in theory, is designed to enforce high standards of executive responsibility, especially in the case of officials who have broad powers and long terms of office. In practice, it has been used sparingly, for it has proved to be expensive to administer and not wholly free from partisan politics. Moreover, the threat of interference from the public, particularly in the case of judges, may unquestionably act as a handicap for a courageous and independent public servant.

The States as Promoters of Public Welfare

The effect of social changes upon state administration. One of the outstanding developments of state government has been an increase in the size and complexity of its administrative machinery. This is, to a large degree, the result of the industrialization of modern life, of vast economic and social changes, and more recently, of the problems created by rapid urbanization. These developments have placed a heavy burden upon state administration. Businesses have grown in size and number. The state has entered into new types of enterprises. New concepts of free educational opportunities have appeared. Scientific advances have revolutionized the regulation of health and sanitation. Conditions of farming and of farm life have changed. The concentration of population in large cities has brought about problems of transportation, water, crime, and public health. Armies of workers must be protected against the wastage of industrial life. Finally, there exists the ever-pressing question of revenues adequate to meet the increasing costs of state activities—costs that have increased sixfold during the period since the end of World War II.

It is our purpose in this section to explain the character of some of the leading state activities, and to show how they have complicated the machinery of state government.

Education: a state function of great importance. Education in the United States is distinctly a function of each state, and one of its most important. Each state controls a vast educational system which ranges from the kindergarten to the university, and which includes many specialized institutions.

Most states have an agency known as a *state board of education* which, acting under the direction of the state superintendent or commissioner, enforces the public education laws and distributes funds among the various localities. This agency supervises curricula, physical facilities and equipment, and vocational guidance. It regulates the training, employment, and discipline of teachers. It also exercises some degree of control over private and professional schools.

Education is a function which has entailed an increasing financial burden for the state. One of the most significant changes in local-state relations in recent years has been the growth of state aid to education. The extent of the aid still varies widely from

Our states take a fitting pride in their historic traditions and achievements. That is why we see roadside signs and markers such as the one shown here in all sections of the country.

state to state, but the general trend has been strongly upward, until today state contributions account for about 40% of all public education expenditures. This steady rise has been caused by the higher costs of construction, materials, and personnel, by the improvement in educational standards for all on both elementary and secondary levels, by the increasing demands for state-supported higher education, and by the rise in the number of children and young people of school age.

Fortunately, the Federal government has been granting increasing aid to the states for special educational programs. Besides earlier grants by the Federal government for the promotion of the teaching of agriculture and engineering (Morrill Act of 1862) and for vocational training (Smith-Hughes Act of 1917), there has been stepped-up aid for almost every phase of education under laws passed during the Eisenhower, Kennedy, and Johnson administrations.

Public health and sanitation. The support of public health services ranks among the leading efforts of the state in the furtherance of public welfare. "Public health is purchasable," says a noted health authority, "and within natural limitations any

The New Jersey State Hospital at Trenton is one of the oldest mental health facilities in the United States. It was founded in 1848, largely through the efforts of Dorothea Dix, a notable pioneer in the movement for better treatment of persons suffering from mental ailments.

New Jersey Dept. of Institutions and Agencies

community can determine its death rate." We need mention only a few of the state's activities to appreciate the magnitude of the problem. They include control over sanitation, sewage, water supply, inspection of foods, the care of the physically and mentally handicapped, and the maintenance of hospitals and sanitariums.

These and similar tasks are under the direction of a central board or department, and a large staff scattered throughout the state. The effective functioning of such agencies is hardly possible without the cooperation of local communities, of neighboring states, and often of the Federal government. The future will undoubtedly see an even greater expansion in the health program of the states, since the subjects of health insurance and of state-operated medical services have received serious consideration from the medical profession and the public. The extension of Social Security to include "Medicare" by the Federal government in 1965 may serve as an incentive to further action by the states.

The care of the needy. Every state maintains services to care for the poor and the helpless. It is no longer satisfied simply to leave the relief of the needy to local communities, even though it supplements their direct contributions with state funds. The states by no means show a uniform degree of progress in this respect. The lack of adequate programs in some cases may be due either to financial limitations or to the persistence of ideas of *laissez-faire* in regard to the care of the unfortunate. Nevertheless, throughout the nation, one finds such achievements as care, under state control, of homeless, neglected, or crippled children, various forms of maternity aid, mothers' and widows' pensions, relief for the unemployed and their families, institutions and pensions for the aged, and old-age insurance. Many of these activities are carried out as a joint Federal-state program under the Social Security Act. (See chart on page 232.)

One significant change in recent years has been the tendency wherever feasible, to provide outright cash relief to the needy, in preference to committing them to institutional life. Another notable development is the subsidizing, under various degrees of Federal control, of the state's welfare projects by the Federal government.

Labor legislation. Because of the increasing size of the labor force, and the complexities and hazards of industrial life, the improvement of labor conditions has likewise become an important

HOW SOCIAL SECURITY WORKS

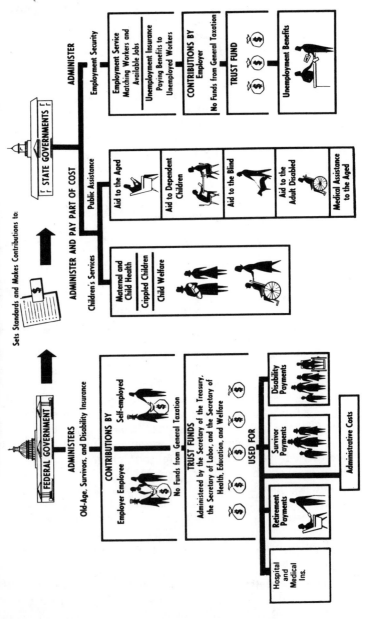

FEDERAL GOVERNMENT

ADMINISTERS
Old-Age, Survivors, and Disability Insurance

Sets Standards and Makes Contributions to:

STATE GOVERNMENTS

CONTRIBUTIONS BY
Employer Employee   Self-employed
No Funds from General Taxation

TRUST FUNDS
Administered by the Secretary of the Treasury,
the Secretary of Labor, and the Secretary of
Health, Education, and Welfare

USED FOR

Retirement Payments   Survivor Payments   Disability Payments

Hospital and Medical Ins.

Administrative Costs

ADMINISTER AND PAY PART OF COST

Children's Services
Maternal and Child Health
Crippled Children
Child Welfare

Public Assistance
Aid to the Aged
Aid to Dependent Children
Aid to the Blind
Aid to the Adult Disabled
Medical Assistance to the Aged

ADMINISTER
Employment Security
Employment Service Matching Workers and Available Jobs
Unemployment Insurance Paying Benefits to Unemployed Workers

CONTRIBUTIONS BY
Employer
No Funds from General Taxation

TRUST FUND

Unemployment Benefits

field of state legislation. There is no uniformity of programs, but most states have adopted a complex pattern of protective legislation. Every state has a *department of labor*, which is charged with the enforcement of measures relating to safety, health, and hours of work in industrial and commercial establishments. Child labor laws aim to restrict the employment of minors in hazardous or unsuitable occupations, prohibit night work, regulate hours of labor, and prescribe the conditions of attendance at school. Other laws limit the employment of women.

All states have *workmen's compensation laws.* Such laws provide that the employers must insure their employees (or the dependents of employees) against losses due to injuries, disease, or death incurred while at work. A number of states prescribe the minimum wages which must be paid in certain industries—usually local industries (such as laundries) not covered by the Federal Fair Labor Standards Act. Some states regulate the practices of private fee-charging employment agencies. Machinery for the peaceful settlement of industrial disputes exists in all the states. Some states have outlawed the "yellow dog contract" (an agreement by which a worker pledges himself not to join a union while in the employ of a particular employer). Some states have provided for jury trials in injunction proceedings in labor disputes.

Unemployment insurance became effective in some states even prior to the advent of the national Social Security System in 1935. (Wisconsin was a notable pioneer in this field.) Today, all the states have unemployment insurance systems which meet the standards set up by the Social Security Act and subsequent Federal regulations.

Many states and municipalities have laws which forbid discrimination in employment because of race, creed, color, or national origin.*

State control over business. Every state exercises some supervision over various phases of corporate activity. The states issue charters to corporations, examine the issue of securities, and license their sale. Through public service commissions, they regulate the charges made by public utilities companies and the stand-

---

* In 1966, fair employment acts were in effect in Alaska, California, Colorado, Connecticut, Delaware, Hawaii, Idaho, Illinois, Indiana, Iowa, Kansas, Massachusetts, Michigan, Minnesota, Missouri, New Jersey, New Mexico, New York, Ohio, Oregon, Pennsylvania, Rhode Island, Vermont, Washington, and Wisconsin.

ards of the services they provide. Banking and insurance also come under state control. The state inspects the books, accounts, reserves, and investments of these companies. Extensive as all these forms of state control have become, they are, nevertheless, a subject of constant dispute. For example, it is maintained that some states have issued charters without proper safeguards, and that the regulation of holding companies and of their securities has been inadequate.

Natural resources and public works. The development of natural resources and the protection and the promotion of industries which involve these resources are likewise functions of the states. Through numerous special administrative bodies the states, with increasing assistance from the Federal government, control the product of farm, plantation, orchard, forest, and stream. They supervise the dairy and livestock industries. They also regulate those industries which relate to mineral wealth and to other subsoil deposits. They maintain or subsidize agricultural colleges and experimental stations. They provide machinery for the encouragement of cooperative marketing. In recent years the states have passed much legislation to protect farm lands and homesteads against foreclosures.

Every state has one or more conservation and public works agencies which are concerned with the protection and development of parks, forest preserves, camp sites, water resources and water works, power plants, and irrigation projects. Billions of dollars, for example, have in recent years been borrowed through state bond issues for the improvement of area-wide water systems so that they will serve more effectively for such purposes as water supply, sewage, transportation, and recreation. The construction and maintenance of good roads, which the vast increase in motor vehicle traffic has made necessary, and which has been aided by Federal grants, constitutes a very important state function. Some of the states have lately encouraged and subsidized low-income and middle-income model housing projects. And some 25 states have even constructed factories to lease to privately owned companies. This is a method of keeping or attracting new industries.

The interlocking of state and Federal activities. Obviously many of the state activities surveyed above—regulation of business, protection of labor, help for the needy, conservation of natural resources, etc.—are also performed by the Federal government. Does this suggest duplication of services or competition between the two levels of government? Theoretically, no. Within the framework of our Federal system, the national government concentrates on activities and problems which are *interstate* in character; the state governments (and the localities) limit themselves to matters which are *intrastate*—within the borders of a single state.

Thus, as we have noted, the Federal Fair Labor Standards Act sets minimum wage rates for workers who are involved (directly and indirectly) in interstate commerce. The coverage of this law has been extended several times since it was enacted in 1938. (For details of the most recent revision of the law, see page 272.) Despite such extensions, there are still millions of workers employed by enterprises whose operations are considered essentially local and which therefore do not come under the Federal standards. Laundries, theaters, and restaurants are examples. Such workers may be protected by means of state minimum wage laws. Also, the state regulation may extend to working conditions (safety, sanitation, employment of women, etc.) even in factories and other establishments whose operations are interstate in character. The state government has jurisdiction here because the workers involved perform their functions entirely within the state's boundaries.

To take another example, the Federal government regulates such transportation facilities as railroads, airlines, and trucking companies which cross state lines. But local bus lines are subject to the authority of the states and their subdivisions. There are, of course, borderline cases of businesses and occupations whose character (*interstate* or *intrastate*) must be decided by the administrative authorities or by the courts.

In the 20th century, with the new problems brought on by an increasingly complex and interdependent society, there has been a strong tendency for the Federal government to "invade" areas formerly under state authority. This has been done largely by use of the Federal government's massive financial powers. For example, Federal grants-in-aid are available to the states to provide help to various types of unfortunates (the blind, dependent children, elderly persons not under OASDI). To become eligible for these grants, the states must provide matching funds under a formula set by Federal law. Thus, the states are in effect following a directive of the Federal government. More recently, Congress has enacted programs to aid education, to help solve the urban transportation mess, to protect our air against pollution, and to combat poverty, especially in our great urban centers. In these and other cases, the Federal government has sought to emphasize local initiative and direction, but so long as Washington supplies the financial "muscle," it is bound to play a big role.

This is why so many observers view with alarm what they consider the continuing erosion of the independence and authority of the state governments. Speaking to the Forty-ninth Annual Governors' Conference in 1957, President Eisenhower said: "Unless we preserve the traditional power and responsibilities of State government, with revenues necessary to exercise that power and discharge those responsibilities, then we will not preserve the kind of America we have known; eventually, we will have instead another form of government and, therefore, quite another kind of America."

The picture, however, is not all black. In recent years, under able and vigorous governors, some states have initiated significant new legislative programs that are a reminder of the days when the state governments were veritable social laboratories.

Problems Raised by the Growth of State Activities

The problem of reorganizing state governments. The expansion of the state's interests, especially in economic and social fields, has raised numerous problems. One of these is the question of more centralized and economical administration. The many official studies of state government, which have been made with a view to possible reorganization, have revealed glaring defects. There appear to be too many administrative agencies. The duties of these agencies duplicate and overlap. This adds heavily to the costs of government. Moreover, the sharing of tax revenues between the state and its subdivisions, and huge subsidies given by the state to the local communities, produce endless conflicts over state and local control.

Achievements in reorganization. A number of states have either planned, or have already put into operation, schemes for more effective government. One reform has been the consolidation of independent departments, bureaus, etc., into a relatively few units. They are headed by individuals who are appointed and removed by the governor, and whose term of office is the same as that of the governor. New York and Virginia have been outstanding examples of states which have instituted departmental reorganization, combined with the short ballot.

Some states have gone even further in the direction of making the governor truly the responsible directing head of the government. One of the most important of these reforms has been the "executive budget," a system found in thirty-seven states. Under this arrangement, the governor may be directly responsible for formulating the program of state expenditures, or the budget may be prepared by the comptroller, the budget director, and a budget bureau under the governor's supervision. In either case, the governor has both the power and the responsibility to plan for the wise use of the state's financial resources. In states that do not have executive budgets, there are laws providing for budgetary boards or commissions, consisting usually of the governor, one or two of his executive officers and a committee of the legislature.

The state civil service. Structural changes in government, to have any significance, must be accompanied by a method of screening and selection that fills thousands of subordinate positions with able and honest men and women. As William Penn remarked centuries ago: "Governments, like clocks, go from the motion men give them, so by them they are ruined, too."

A governmental unit which sets up machinery to select the great majority of its public (civil service) employees impartially, on the basis of demonstrated qualifications, is said to have a *merit system* in effect. The usual method employed for this purpose is competitive examinations. Candidates who pass the examinations are placed on an eligible list, from which appointments are made, in accordance with some established procedure. Employees who do their work satisfactorily are protected against dismissal for personal or political reasons, thus avoiding one of the worst evils of the "spoils system." Moreover, promotions to better jobs are also based on merit, as demonstrated by examinations or by satisfactory service and other qualifications.*

It should be noted, in passing, that a merit system does not in all cases imply competitive examinations. For example, doctors

---

* The terms "merit system" and "civil service" are often used more or less interchangeably. Properly speaking, however, the *civil service* refers to the entire body of governmental employees, exclusive of (1) elected officials and (2) the military forces. The aim of the civil service reform movement has been to base the selection of the great mass of civil service employees on demonstrated *merit*, usually (although not always) by a system of competitive examinations.

and dentists may be selected for public employ if they can demonstrate the proper professional preparation and experience. This would certainly be considered selection on the basis of "merit," even though no special examinations are involved. At the other extreme, it would hardly be feasible to set up competitive examinations for jobs involving common labor or other forms of routine or unskilled work.

It is acknowledged by students of government that many top administrative posts are properly appointive and that such appointments should be subject to termination by the responsible elected official. This would not be considered a violation of the merit system.

More than half of the states (with New York and Massachusetts pioneering in the 1880's) have set up civil service merit systems of general application. These systems for the most part are modeled after the Pendleton Civil Service Act adopted by Congress for the Federal government in 1883. As we have noted above, a state to be eligible for Federal grants-in-aid (for example under the Social Security system or the road-building program) must set up a merit system meeting minimum standards for all employees working in those areas. All fifty states have done so.

In general, however, our cities have made greater strides in applying merit principles to the civil service than have the states. Teachers, firemen, policemen, health workers, engineers, and many other categories of municipal employees in most large cities now work under a merit system that is a far cry from the corruption that attended the spoils system of earlier days.

The problem of senior citizens. On page 157 we called attention to the problem of the care and well-being of the aged in our society. It cannot be denied that this has become one of the major economic and social concerns of American society. There are now about 20 million persons over 65 in the United States. Their numbers will increase, thanks largely to the progress of medical science. At 65, or perhaps a few years later, most people retire from their jobs and depend in the future on savings, pensions, and other forms of fixed income. In the face of the persistent increase in the price level, many retirees often experience a steady dwindling of their real income. Compounding this situation are the rising bills for medical treatment and hospitalization that so often accompany the later years of the life span. So important have the problems of our older citizens become that several states have already established a permanent agency to deal with them.

The most important type of pension scheme for the aged now in effect in the United States is the system of *Old Age, Survivors, and Disability Insurance* (OASDI), set up by the Social Security Act. In 1971, about 25 million retired or disabled workers (or their families or survivors) were receiving pensions ranging from $70 to $482 a month. A worker may retire at age 65 (or at age 62 with reduced benefits). The system is financed by a payroll tax paid by both employers and employees. Thus, the retired worker receives his pension as a matter of statutory right, not of charity, and without regard to need. The program today provides for coverage of almost all persons engaged in regular gainful employment, including the military. Recent amendments (1969-71) have extended coverage to domestic workers, agricultural workers, and self-employed persons. Benefits have been raised to cover cost-of-living increases. Beginning in 1972, the maximum creditable earnings for Social Security purposes are $9,000.

In addition, there are many private pension plans in operation in the United States. Some are run by employers; some by labor unions. The most common arrangement today, however, especially in strongly unionized industries, is a pension plan jointly financed, and administered by employers and the union. Such plans have become an important feature of collective bargaining agreements. The pensions paid are usually supplementary to OASDI benefits.

Of course, there are also millions of retired persons who supplement their pensions with income derived from their savings and investments.

Finally, there are still considerable numbers of persons too old to work who are not covered by OASDI pensions or other pension schemes, or whose income from these sources is too small to support them. These may receive help from local welfare agencies or from private philanthropic organizations. Under the Social Security Act, the Federal government aids the state in giving assistance to needy aged persons not covered by OASDI.

Problems of interstate cooperation. "State lines," it has been said, "are boundaries of political demarcation." This means simply that the state is a self-governing political unit within the limits of its own territory. There are, however, innumerable problems which go beyond state lines. They may be common to a group of states. Such matters as water supply, prevention of air and water pollution, navigation, irrigation, labor, crime control, and regulation of public utilities often necessitate cooperative action among several states. What is more, common economic interests often compel states to work together closely with neighboring states, or with states which have a similar economic base, in agriculture, mining, industry, etc.

In order to solve problems of common regional interest, the states have resorted to various devices. By far the most common of these are *interstate compacts* or agreements, made (as the Constitution provides) with the consent of Congress. The custom of settling boundary disputes by compacts is a very old one in the experience of the states. However, more recently, the scope of these compacts has been expanded to include a wide variety of matters. For example, Kansas and Missouri used this method to adjust problems related to water supply. New York and New Jersey created the Port of New York Authority in this way. Compacts have often been made among several states. Thus, an agreement concerning the use of the Delaware River, or the promotion

The great George Washington Bridge across the Hudson River between New York and New Jersey was built and is maintained by the Port of New York Authority, an agency set up by the two states.

of irrigation projects in the West, or the adoption of minimum-wage standards and flood control in New England has involved a group of states in each instance. More than twenty states have now established permanent standing commissions for the study and promotion of interstate compacts. Recently, for example, New York, New Jersey, and Connecticut inaugurated a joint program to help solve urgent transportation problems centering on the metropolitan area of New York City.

Interstate cooperation has been sought in still other ways. The annual conference of state governors (initiated by President Theodore Roosevelt in 1908) and the Council of State Governments (established in 1933) have been used to discuss problems and to recommend desirable legislation. Other state officials have held similar conferences for the adoption of uniform legislation on particular subjects. In many instances two or more states, without resorting to the formal expedient of a compact, have agreed to extend mutual benefits to one another in such matters as providing for exemptions from income and inheritance taxes, or for the licensing of professions. Competitive business and labor conditions in certain regions of the country have led whole groups of states in those areas to consider uniform legislation in order to prevent efforts to attract industry by offering "inducements" (such as tax exemptions) that may in the long run harm all of the states involved.

Interstate comity under the Constitution. The United States Constitution says (Article IV, Section 1): "Full faith and credit shall be given in each state to the public acts, records, and judicial proceedings of every other state." This is the basis for what has been referred to as *interstate comity*. Without this provision, which serves as a binding force, we should probably have had a situation approaching anarchy. This provision is supplemented by the sections which declare that citizens of one state are citizens of another and that, in the punishment of crime, the several states must cooperate with one another. As a result of these constitutional provisions, the fifty states function as a unit. To illustrate, these sections mean that a marriage, if valid in New Jersey, where it was contracted, is valid in Florida or California; that a native-born or naturalized citizen coming from Maine is entitled to all the privileges and immunities of a citizen of Oklahoma, should he happen to be in Oklahoma; that the Governor of Oregon is under moral obligation to surrender a person who is charged with having committed a crime in Ohio to the Ohio police.

The Organization of State Courts

The judicial systems of the fifty states present so great a variety of organization and jurisdiction that it is all but impossible to classify them exactly with a uniform terminology. For purposes of simplification we may use the following common and convenient designations (1) lower courts; (2) intermediate courts; (3) courts of appeals.

The lower courts. At the very base of the state judicial system are the *justice of the peace courts*. These have jurisdiction in minor criminal and civil matters. They also conduct hearings which are preliminary to a trial by a higher court, if the case warrants a trial. Nearly all cities have so-called *municipal courts*. In the larger cities there are special municipal courts for criminal and for civil cases. Since the legal problems of cities are so numerous and varied, provision is very often made for courts of special types. Thus, one finds *domestic relations* (or "family") *courts*, and *juvenile courts* to handle cases involving young delinquents. In a few states there are also courts which adjust small claims and settle minor disputes by the use of simple and informal procedures. In many counties there is a special *probate court* (sometimes called *orphans'* or *surrogate court*). It probates or proves wills, manages the property of persons who died without leaving a will, directs the administration of trust funds, and designates guardians for minors.

The intermediate courts. Above the courts that we have just described are various types of intermediate courts, usually organized on a county basis. They are known by different names, such as *district, county, superior*, and *civil courts* and *courts of common pleas*. They have original jurisdiction in important criminal and civil cases. In contrast to the simple and direct procedure of most inferior courts, they employ the machinery of trial by jury. They also have appellate jurisdiction, for appeals may be carried to them from the lower courts.

Courts of appeals. In a number of states there are various high courts of appeals. These have final jurisdiction in certain types of cases defined by law, and they exist chiefly to relieve the pressure upon the highest appellate court of the state. However, if a question arises which involves a provision of the state or Federal constitution, appeal may be made to the state's highest court.

In most states this top judicial body is called the *supreme court*. In others it is known as the *court of appeals*, or the *court of errors and appeals*. Its position with reference to the judicial system of the state is comparable to that of the Supreme Court in the Federal system. In a few states the highest court is required to render advisory opinions on questions of law, when requested to do so by the governor or by the legislature. The United States Supreme Court has consistently refused to do this.

The state court of claims. In accordance with the ancient principle that a sovereign state may not be sued without its consent, some of the states have established a special *court of claims*. Here, claims may be brought against the state. However, the legislature must make the necessary appropriation before the claim awarded by the court can be paid.

State judges: Their selection and term of office. The judges of state courts are selected in one of three ways: by popular election; by appointment by the governor, with or without the consent of the state senate; and (in South Carolina, Vermont, and Virginia) by the state legislature. Experience with all of these methods of election seems to indicate that good and bad judges may be chosen no matter which method is used. The trend seems to be toward appointment, with longer terms on the bench. The governor is usually expected (or required) to get the advice of bar associations and of other citizen groups, and to make his choices without regard for party affiliation.

The terms of judges vary in length from state to state. In general, it may be said that the higher the office, the longer the tenure. Judges are removable by impeachment (a process resorted to on only rare occasions). In some states, they may be removed by the governor or legislature, and in a few states by popular recall.

The Business of State Courts

The work of the state judiciary. The jurisdiction of the courts is defined by the constitution and the laws of the state. The courts handle civil and criminal matters which come under the state constitution and laws. Whenever a case arises which involves the Federal Constitution or a Federal statute or treaty, the state courts must observe the Federal act in question. The higher courts of the state have the power of judicial review over the acts of legislative bodies and of administrative officials. They may annul acts which they consider to be in violation of the state constitution. Where a national or interstate matter is involved, however, appeal may be taken to the Federal judiciary. The exercise of the judicial veto by the state courts, especially over economic and social legislation, has been as much a subject of controversy as has the corresponding action in the Federal system.

Sources of law applied by the courts. Cases in state courts arise under the state constitution and statutes, and under one other important source, the *common law*. Common law refers to the body of laws inherited from England. It is based largely on judicial precedents. It is applied in our states, though it has been expanded and modified to suit new and distinctive conditions. *Equity* is part of the common law, and is also an inheritance from England. This is a branch of law which aims to protect rights, or to prevent possible damage, or to secure redress in cases in which the ordinary processes of common law are inadequate. Equity is associated with the issuance of injunctions, which, as we noted in an earlier chapter, are generally used by the courts to prevent irreparable damage to property rights.

Types of cases before the courts. The cases which the courts handle are of two types: *civil* and *criminal*.

Civil cases refer to private wrongs or injuries. They include such matters as a breach of contract, or a question of property rights, or some personal wrong for which money damages may be claimed by the aggrieved party. The individual, not the state, is the complainant.

Criminal cases involve the commission of an act which is an offense against the state. The state, then, is the accuser, the prosecutor, and the plaintiff. Examples of criminal offenses are acts of treason, felonies, and misdemeanors. Treason against a state is an attempt to overthrow the government, or to aid its enemies in war. A felony is a crime of a serious nature, such as murder, burglary, arson, or kidnaping. It may be punishable by imprisonment and in some states even by death. A misdemeanor is an offense of a less serious character, such as the violation of parking regulations, a Sunday-closing ordinance, or a minor health regulation. It may be punished by a fine or by a relatively short jail term.

Procedure in a civil suit. Nearly all states provide for a jury in civil suits. In some states, however, the jury may be smaller than the traditional number of twelve, and a unanimous verdict is not required. The jury is expected to pass upon questions of fact. The judge instructs it as to the law. Upon the basis of this instruction, the jury makes its decision.

Procedure in a criminal case. The procedure in a criminal case is decidedly more elaborate. If there is enough evidence against the accused, the magistrate holds him for further proceedings. Release on bail may or may not be allowed; this depends upon the gravity of the offense and on the reputation of the accused party. The next step is formal accusation or indictment, either by the grand jury or by the prosecutor, as the state law may provide. If the individual is indicted, he receives a trial before a judge and a jury in an open court. He may, if he wishes, waive his right to a jury trial. He has the right to be represented by counsel. In fact, the court will assign counsel if the defendant cannot afford to engage one. The accused (or his counsel) has the right to examine and to cross-examine witnesses. Indeed, many rights and privileges are accorded to an accused party by the bill of rights of the state constitution.

Austin (Texas) Police Department

The United States today is a "society on wheels," and it is not surprising that a high proportion of all court cases deal with traffic offenses. Here we see a typical scene in a traffic court.

After all the evidence has been introduced by both sides, the lawyers present their cases to the jury, and the judge "charges" the jury upon points of law. One of three things may then happen. The jury may deliver a verdict of acquittal. It may disagree, in which event a new trial must be held. It may declare the defendant guilty as charged, perhaps with a recommendation for leniency or mercy. If the accused is convicted by the jury in accordance with the law, he has the privilege of appeal to higher courts. Since appeals are very costly, the state often defrays the expenses of those who plead poverty.

The grand jury and the process of indictment. One of the most important aspects of criminal procedure is the machinery for investigating charges of commission of crimes. In about half the states this function is performed by the *grand jury*, a body which is selected by lot from a specially prepared list or panel. The size of the grand jury varies from state to state. Its membership may contain as few as seven or as many as twenty-three. Its action usually does not require a unanimous vote. The grand jury investigates charges of crime that are presented to it by a court or by the prosecutor. It may even launch an investigation of its own. Sometimes an "extraordinary" or "special" grand jury is summoned to inquire into some unusually alarming condition, such as flagrant crime or corruption. Such an investigation may, by its disclosures and recommendations, render a genuine public service. The proceedings before a grand jury are said to be *ex parte;* that is, the jury listens only to evidence presented against the accused. The grand jury has the power to call witnesses. In the light of the evidence before it, it may dismiss the charge, which results in the release of the accused person. Or, finding that there is "probable cause" for further action, it may issue a "true bill of indictment," thus clearing the way for a trial. Also it may issue a "presentment" against anyone it believes to have committed an offense. This sort of charge or accusation does not have the legal force of an indictment, but it may influence further action.

About half the states now rely on indictment by "information." This means that the accusation against the party suspected of wrong-doing is drawn up solely by the prosecuting attorney.

The place of the trial jury. Reduced to their simplest terms, the facts about jury trials are these. In criminal cases the jury is usually composed of twelve citizens. Some states provide for a thirteenth juror in order to guard against an unforeseen occurrence to one of the twelve. In civil suits the number may be smaller. Some states permit the accused individual to waive—that is, to dispense with—the right to a jury trial. In cases in which the penalty may be death, and generally in cases involving felonies, a unanimous verdict is required. However, in other types of criminal and civil cases, state laws vary in their requirements.

Much has been written for and against the place of the trial or petty (petit) jury in the administration of justice. The right to a trial by a "jury of one's peers" is sanctioned by long tradition and by constitutional guarantees. Nevertheless, students of judicial procedure have questioned the value of much of the system as it operates today. For example, they point out that assembling a jury is often a costly procedure. Since both sides have the right to "challenge" prospective jurors, the process of selection may be long and tiresome. Busy people with personal responsibilities frequently seek to escape service, with the result that the most capable and intelligent citizens are less likely to be selected for jury duty.

The problem of judicial reform. In order to make the overall administration of justice more honest, prompt, and efficient, a number of reforms have been proposed. Many of the experts who have studied the problem of judicial reform believe that the number of courts in each state ought to be reduced, but that they should be more adequately staffed. The power of appointing and removing judges, they say, should be vested in some central authority—perhaps the governor, with the advice and guidance of a special group chosen from the legal profession. Most authorities agree that the election of judges, although it appears to be "democratic," means in practice that judges are selected by the dominant leaders of the major political parties.

Some states have established a "judicial council," composed of leading members of the bench and bar, as well as public officials, whose task it is to plan for improvemnts in the state judiciary.

Improvement of criminal justice. In particular, the administration of criminal justice has been an object of much investigation and criticism. Criminal trials sometimes degenerate into public shows, catering (as a report of the American Bar Association recently put it) "to the morbid desires of sensation seekers." It is charged that wealthy defendants who can afford high-priced lawyers and can take full advantage of the law's technicalities have an undue advantage over the prosecution. On the other hand, impoverished defendants are often at an unfair disadvantage because they must depend on court-appointed attorneys (usually young lawyers of limited experience) and because they lack funds for various purposes, such as bringing in friendly witnesses from distant points. In short, it is said, the administration of criminal justice often favors the well-to-do.

One way to remedy this situation, at least in part, is to appoint public defenders—that is, lawyers attached to the court and paid from public funds whose function it is to defend accused parties, just as it is the district attorney's function to prosecute them. Many communities already have such a system.

There are those who believe that much of the red tape which has made the "law's delays" notorious in this country should be ruthlessly cut. Supporters of a "tough" approach to this problem have advocated measures such as those embodied in a District of Columbia Crime Act passed in 1970. These include: *preventive detention* that would allow judges to jail for two months defendants considered a danger to society if released pending trial; authorizing the police to enter premises under certain conditions without announcement—the so-called *"no-knock" entry clause;* expansion of the power of the police to carry on wiretapping; lowering from 18 to 16 the minimum age at which juveniles can be tried as adults; and stiffer mandatory sentence provisions.

Recent Supreme Court decisions have emphasized that every defendant in a criminal proceeding is entitled to be represented by an attorney, and that a conviction obtained without the participation of a defense attorney, even if based on a confession, may not be valid. Also, a person accused of a crime has the right to see a lawyer as soon as he is taken into custody and questioned by the police. If this right is not respected, the entire subsequent proceeding may be invalidated. (See the discussion of the *Escobedo* and *Miranda* cases on page 198.)

Detection and Punishment of Crime as State Functions

State agencies for law enforcement. Related to the proper administration of justice is an efficient system of law enforcement. Every state has a department of justice, but, as a rule, it is not unified and centralized. In fact, there is much dispute over control between state authority and local enforcement officers.

The organization of a distinct department of law enforcement would help to improve the machinery for crime detection and prevention. The establishment of law-enforcing agencies organized along semi-military lines, such as the militia, highway patrols, and the state police, has done much to make up for lack of centralization.

A typical state agency is the citizens' militia, or the *National Guard*. It may be called out during emergencies, upon the initiative of the governor. The militia cannot be employed effectively as a permanent police force, for it is made up of private volunteers, most of whom have regular full-time occupations. In wartime emergencies, however, the National Guard may be inducted into Federal service, in which case a "State Guard" may be organized to perform local service.

The state also depends on large numbers of local police officers, such as policemen, constables, sheriffs, and prosecutors. In the more populous centers, there are large police forces, highly organized and making use of the most modern crime-fighting equipment. The police force of New York City, for example, consists of 28,000 men, possibly the largest in the world. At the other extreme, sparsely populated regions usually have very small police organizations, and may depend heavily on volunteer or part-time assistants. In normal times, these limited forces are likely to be quite adequate, but in times of emergencies or serious disturbances, outside help may be imperative.

This is one reason most of the states have organized state police forces. Such a force is usually headed by a board or superintendent appointed by the governor. The men on a typical state police force are carefully selected, often by competitive examinations, and receive intensive training. They render highly competent services wherever they are needed, usually outside the area of incorporated cities. In most states, they specialize in highway patrol and enforcement of motor vehicle laws. "State troopers," as they are commonly known, often perform various duties outside the usual police functions, such as fighting forest fires, enforcing health regulations, and providing aid during catastrophes. Some states have supplemental police forces for special functions, such as enforcement of game laws or liquor laws.

Penal reform. The treatment of persons who are found guilty of crimes and are sentenced to serve terms in prison is one of the major problems that face the states today. In many ways, this

An example of enlightened modern penology is this conservation camp, set up by the California Department of Correction. It is used for the rehabilitation of juvenile lawbreakers, usually first offenders. They are trained to do conservation work in forests and other state-owned areas.

problem is even weightier for the states than it is for the Federal government, since the definition and punishment of crime are, under our system of government, left largely to state authority.

Enlightened, modern criminology is concerned with far more than taking "revenge" on the criminal. It is interested in the prevention of crime, and also in "punishment" as a way of protecting society, reforming the offender, and deterring him and others from committing crimes. The intelligent and humane administration of state prisons, reformatories, and penal farms, schools, and hospitals is one aspect of the problem. Another is the long-debated question of the efficacy of capital punishment. Is the electric chair, the noose, or the lethal gas chamber cruel and futile? Is it really a deterrent to crime? Thirteen states have already answered these questions by abolishing capital punishment.

Still another problem that confronts judges and penal administrators is the adjustment of prison sentences to individual conditions. In virtually all states today, the sentence imposed on a convicted lawbreaker is set between rather wide limits—for example, from four to ten years. This means that after serving the minimum sentence of four years, the prisoner is eligible for *parole*. Usually, he must appear before a parole board and convince the members that he represents a good risk for conditional release. The board will take into consideration the nature of the crime committed, the prisoner's overall background, and his behavior while in prison. Accordingly, the report and recommendations of the prison authorities carry great weight. When the prisoner is released on parole, he must report at regular intervals to parole authorities to prove that he is leading a law-abiding life and obeying all regulations. If he violates such regulations, or gets into any trouble, he may be returned to prison. It should be noted that the function of a parole officer is not only to check up on the parolee but also to help him adjust to life "on the outside," including finding employment.

A judge may also release a convicted lawbreaker without sending him to jail at all. In such cases, the released man will probably be on *probation* for a specified period of time. This means that he is subject to certain restrictions and must report regularly to a probation officer. Violation of the rules may mean that the suspended jail sentence will go into effect. Probation is employed particularly with first offenders and with juvenile offenders.

State Finances

Standards for taxation. Revenue to government is what oxygen is to living things. And taxes, if we are to live in an organized society enjoying services which can be furnished only by government, must be considered as essential as respiration by a plant or animal. But though the principle is clear, there are practical questions which are the subject of endless debate: How much should be paid in taxes? How should the money be collected? How should the burden be distributed among the population?

Almost 200 years ago, the great British economist Adam Smith laid down principles of taxation still generally accepted.

1. Taxes should be based on *ability to pay*. Or, as one observer put it, "Lay the heaviest burden on the broadest back." Under this principle, a millionaire should not only contribute more in taxes than a person with a modest income but he should also pay a higher *rate* of taxation.

2. A tax should be *certain*. The taxpayer should know exactly what his liability is, and the government should have a clear understanding of what it is authorized to collect and a reasonably accurate idea of how much the tax will yield.

3. The way in which the tax is levied and the time at which it is collected should be as *convenient* as possible for the taxpayer.

4. The tax should be *economical to collect*. As little as possible of the money contributed by the taxpayers should be used for administering the tax itself.

To bring Adam Smith's principles up-to-date, we might add these additional characteristics of a good tax system. The taxes should produce sufficient revenues to meet the expenses of government. There should be adequate safeguards to prevent evasion and to punish violators. The taxes should not be so high, or imposed in such a way, that they tend to depress or discourage productive business activity.

Taxing power of the state legislature. Aside from a few constitutional provisions, each state has the legal power to levy any taxes it considers suitable. It is the state legislature which decides what taxes are to be used. Moreover, the legislature authorizes

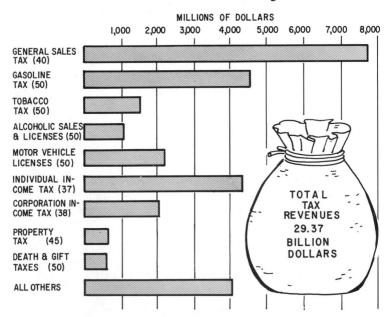

Leading sources of tax revenues collected by all states in 1965. The number in parentheses next to each type of tax indicates the number of states using that tax. (Data from Tax Foundation.)

the taxes may be imposed by local governments. In the case of "home rule" cities and counties, the state legislature may spell out in broad terms in the charter what the taxing powers of the locality are and leave the details to the local authorities. Even in such instances, however, the city or county must ask permission from the legislature if it wishes to make an important change in its taxing system. This was true, for example, when the government of New York City imposed a city income tax (1966) and a tax on off-track betting (1970).

Taxes used by the states. The graph on page 252 indicates the principal taxes levied by the states in a recent year. The most important single source of revenue, it will be noted, is the sales tax. Most states also rely to a considerable extent on a personal and corporate income tax. (This is apart from the Federal income tax, which involves much higher rates.) Other major sources of state revenues are taxes on motor fuels, alcoholic beverages and tobacco products, license fees, and highway and bridge tolls. The general property tax, which used to raise large sums for the states, has been given over largely to local governments.

One noteworthy development in recent years has been the introduction of a state-run lottery in two states — New York and

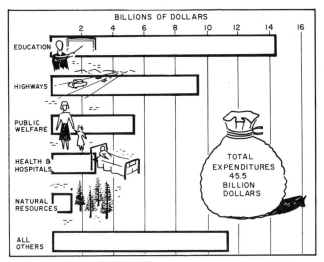

Principal expenditures of all states in 1965, including payments to local governments. (Data from Tax Foundation.)

New Hampshire. This in effect represents a sort of "voluntary tax" on. the people who buy lottery tickets and do not win a prize. Many authorities question whether a lottery can be defended as a sound and desirable way of raising state revenues, even when the money is earmarked for admittedly good purposes, such as education.

The figures in the graph represent the nationwide picture, but there is a great deal of variation from state to state. This applies not only to the kinds of taxes used but also to the size of the tax burden. In 1964, for example, the national average of per capita state tax collections was about $150, but in New Jersey the figure was only $75. At the time New Jersey was the only state which had neither a general sales tax nor a personal income tax. This may appear to be a happy state of affairs for the taxpayers of New Jersey, but the fact is that the state found itself unable to provide the services needed and demanded by the people. A sales tax was introduced in 1966, and many advocated a state income tax.

> NOTE: Proposed reforms of state government have been treated throughout the body of this chapter.

Terms You Should Know

Capital punishment. The death penalty for a crime.

Civil case. A judicial proceeding that involves claims for private wrongs or injuries.

Common law. The general and ordinary law based on an established custom and on judicial decisions accepted as precedents. The common law is subject to alteration both by legislative enactment and by new judicial interpretations. The common law is largely a development of England and of countries, such as the United States, which have inherited English legal traditions.

Criminal case. A judicial proceeding that involves the commission or the omission of an act which is an offense against the state. The state, then, is the accuser, the prosecutor, and the plaintiff.

Ex parte. Judicial proceedings in the course of which a grand jury listens only to evidence presented *against* the accused.

Felony. A serious criminal offense, such as murder, burglary, etc.

Grand jury. A body that considers charges of criminal acts presented to it by a court or prosecutor (district attorney). In some cases the grand jury may launch an investigation on its own initiative. In the light of evidence presented to it, the grand jury may dismiss the charges; or finding that there is "probable cause" for further action, it may issue an *indictment,* thus clearing the way for a trial.

Grant-in-aid. Contribution of the Federal government to a state, or of a state to a local government, in accordance with certain requirements set by the granting authority.

Indictment. A formal accusation of criminal wrong-doing presented by a grand jury. An indictment is usually required if a person is to be tried for a felony.

Initiative. A form of direct legislation according to which voters propose a law by petition.

Misdemeanor. A criminal offense less serious than a felony, such as most traffic violations.

Nullification. Process of rendering a law legally void or inoperative. For example, the Supreme Court may nullify laws which it considers unconstitutional. At one time states claimed the right to *nullify* national laws within their own boundaries.

Petit jury. A body that sits in judgment during a trial and renders a verdict of conviction or acquittal (Also a *trial jury.*) A petit jury may also sit in civil cases to decide whether or not there has been a violation of private rights and to determine the damages to be paid.

Presentment. A charge or accusation made by a grand jury against anyone it believes to have committed an offense. It does not have the force of an indictment, but it may influence further action.

Recall. A form of direct legislation according to which voters may remove a public official by petition, with a resulting new election to that office. The *recalled* official may run again to test whether or not he has the support of the general body of voters.

Redistricting. Process of rearranging the legislative districts within a state (or some other political division) usually with the purpose of obtaining a more equitable distribution of representation on the basis of population. Also called *reapportionment.*

Referendum. A form of direct legislation according to which legislative acts require popular approval before they become laws. Also, a draft of a new state constitution or a proposed amendment to the constitution may require a referendum before acceptance.

Short ballot. A ballot which calls on the voters to choose a relatively small number of key officials. The assumption is that other officials will then be appointed by these responsible elected officers.

States' rights. Doctrine that opposes expansion of the powers of the Federal government at the expense of state powers.

Questions and Problems Based on the Text

1. How do you explain the fact that most state constitutions are much longer and more detailed than the United States Constitution?

2. How are state constitutions revised and amended?

3. (a) Why has there been a tendency in many states to increase the powers of the governor? (b) Compare the lawmaking, executive and judicial powers of a typical governor with those of the President.

4. Discuss this statement: "Generally speaking, the 'one man, one vote' decisions have been bad news for the Republican Party. In many states, Republicans had been profiting for years because the rural areas, under their control, had been electing more state legislators than they were entitled to on a strict population basis."

5. (a) Define *initiative, referendum, recall.* (b) Give the pros and cons for each.

6. What suggestions have been made for improving the procedures of state legislatures?

7. (a) Define *gerrymandering.* (b) Show how gerrymandering differs from unequal apportionment of representation on the basis of population. (c) How have recent Supreme Court decisions affected such practices? (d) What progress has been made thus far in the correction of inequities in representation in the state legislatures and in Congress?

8. Name five chief executive officers of your state other than the Governor.

9. Describe the operations of your state civil service system.

10. Give examples of legislation enacted by the states in the following fields: education; public health; care of the needy; labor; control of air and water pollution; housing; conservation; control of corporations; welfare of the aged.

11. (a) Define the "short ballot." (b) What advantages are claimed for it? Can you see any disadvantages? (c) What progress has been made toward the "short ballot" in Federal, state, and local elections?

12. (a) Give examples of Federal subsidies to the states. (b) What advantages are there in the rapid growth of such Federal subsidies? Can you see any disadvantages?

13. Illustrate ways in which states have sought closer cooperation with one another.

14. (a) Describe the organization of a typical state judiciary. (b) What arguments are presented in favor of selecting judges by appointment, rather than election?

15. (a) What is the jurisdiction of the state judiciary? (b) What sources of law do state courts use? (c) Distinguish between civil suits and criminal suits.

16. Distinguish between the work of a *petit* (trial) *jury* and that of a *grand jury*.

17. What suggestions have been offered for reforming the administration of justice in state courts?

18. (a) Discuss the various resources which the states employ for law enforcement. (b) How effective is each of these as an agency for preserving law and order? (c) State the pros and cons of capital punishment.

19. Present arguments for or against each of the following:

(a) The unicameral legislature is preferable to the bicameral legislature.

(b) The Federal Constitution should be amended to permit states to have one legislative body based on population and another based on geographical areas.

(c) Wide powers of appointment should be vested in the governor in each state.

(d) The problem of Social Security, including medical insurance, can be handled more effectively by private means than it can by the existing Federal-state arrangement.

(e) Expansion of Federal subsidies should be discouraged since they endanger the sovereignty of the states.

(f) Capital punishment should be completely abolished.

20. Many state constitutions contain a provision which prohibits the use of any public funds, directly or indirectly, to aid schools that are wholly or in part under the control of any religious denomination, or in which any denominational tenet or doctrine is taught.

Do you favor the repeal or retention of such a provision? Why?

Ideas to Think About and Discuss

1. *Only within the framework of the law can anyone's liberties be preserved. Violence must be stopped wherever it occurs. But the solution is not unselective, overly aggressive enforcement. Harsh, repressive laws directed toward either racial minorities or students serve to grind the hostilities deeper and to increase the danger of violence. Hitler maintained order. So when we talk about order in society, let's be clear what we are talking about."*

—U.S. Senator Harold Hughes

2. *"Poverty demoralizes."*

—RALPH WALDO EMERSON

3. *"If anything about this proposed amendment (prohibiting dis-crimination on the basis of sex) is clear, it is that it would trans-form every provision of law concerning women into a constitutional issue to be ultimately resolved by the Supreme Court."*

—PROFESSOR PAUL FREUND

4. *"If we progressively deprive the community of those usufructs of liberty and civilization which contribute to the vitality of the ethos of caring to rise from poverty and knowing how to do so, if we deprive the people of self-government on a local level, if we deprive them of private property by steeper and steeper taxation, if we integrate at the expense of educating, isn't it likely that something will happen worth worrying about?"*

—WILLIAM F. BUCKLEY, JR.

5. *"The great thing in this world is not so much what we are, but what we are becoming."*

—HORACE KALLEN

6. *"Hinging freedom on wealth, as bail does, denies the equal pro-tection of the law as guaranteed by the Fifth and Fourteenth Amendments."*

—LOUIS NIZER

7. *"The life of man is made up of two parts. He lives as a social animal in the larger world and as an individual within his own internal world. The movement for civil rights must grapple with both. It must ask of Negro citizens to strive for excellence just as it demands of white citizens that they strive for equality."*

—WHITNEY M. YOUNG, JR.

8. *"Mister, they're beating those Jews!"*
"Please, I don't want to get involved."

"Sir, they're attacking those Negroes!"
"Please, I don't want to get involved."

"Sir, look—he's stabbing that woman!"
"Please . . ."

"Madam, they're killing your son!"
"No, thank God, I just looked. He's not mine."

—ALICE MOOLTEN SILVER

CHAPTER 9

Local Government— Grassroots Democracy

American Cities and Their Governments

Growth of the city. The rapid growth of our cities in the 20th century, with the resulting urbanization of American life, has presented many new challenges to local governments. The census of 1940 showed that about 48% of the nation's population, or roughly 63 million people, lived in 1077 cities of more than 10,000 population. By 1965, over 79% of all Americans, or nearly 155 million persons, were living in urban areas. And according to Robert C. Weaver, first Secretary of the Department of Housing and Urban Development: "In the United States, we are faced with 120 million more persons in cities by the end of the century. . . . With the arrival of the 21st century, more than four out of five Americans will live in urban areas."

Multiplication of city problems. The great population movement to the cities has confronted municipal government with major problems in such areas as education, health, recreation, crime, traffic, housing, the care of the needy, water supply, air and water pollution, traffic within the city, and transportation throughout the metropolitan area. These problems call imperatively for both immediate action and long-range planning. No wonder the city has been called the "great challenge to American civilization in the second half of the 20th century"!

The city's legal relation to the state. The American city is, in the legal sense, a creature of the state in which it is located. The state defines the city's territorial limits and its type of government. It determines what state functions are to be administered by the city, and also what purely local functions the city

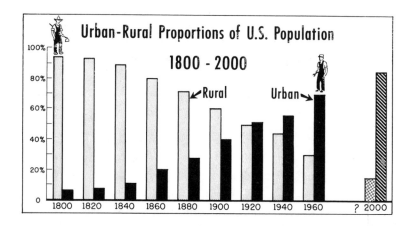

In the course of its history, the United States has changed from a predominantly rural to a predominantly urban nation. And, as the graph above suggests, this trend is still continuing.

may carry on. The relationship between the state and the city (and for that matter between the state and all local governments) is, therefore, quite different from that which exists between the Federal government and the state. The state, remember, has a legal existence quite aside from that of the national government, and within the area of its own powers it is considered to be sovereign.

There are many ways in which the state controls city government. For one thing, the state exercises administrative controls of various types. For example, the governor of the state appoints and may remove some city officials. The state sets standards for many city services and activities, and supervises the way in which they are carried out. This applies, for example, to education, health, public relief and other social services, public utilities, and finance. The state also exercises judicial control. The courts functioning within the city are authorized by the state government. State courts may have jurisdiction in cases which involve obligations and liabilities incurred by the city.

The city charter. The most important instrument of overall control, however, arises from the fact that the state, acting through the legislature and in accordance with its constitution, grants *charters* to cities. The charter is, in effect, the "city constitution." It sets up the city as a corporation, with power to act as an entity, a single person. In this capacity, the city may sue or be sued, just like a private corporation. It may impose taxes. It may exercise the right of eminent domain—that is, the right to take away private property for a necessary public purpose, upon payment of fair compensation. The charter also places a number of limitations upon the city. These include such matters as debts, taxes, the granting of franchises, and the extent to which the city and those in its employ are liable for acts of wrong-doing or for negligence.

Abuses in city government brought to light. Just before the beginning of the 20th century, city governments in the United States were, on the whole, so badly administered that an outstanding British observer* summed up an intensive study of the American governmental structure with this statement: "The faults of the state governments are insignificant compared with the extravagance, corruption and mismanagement which have marked the administration of most of the great cities." Early in the present century, this evaluation was confirmed by top journalists, such as Lincoln Steffens, and by prominent educators and statesmen, notably Andrew D. White, President of Cornell University.

Efforts at periodic "housecleanings" were generally ineffective because of the persistent power of well-intrenched political machines. "Good government crusades" produced considerable excitement, but the attendant reforms almost always proved to be short-lived. In time, reformers came to the conclusion that the basic mechanism of city government would have to be revamped. This was the origin of the movement for charter reform, emphasizing new plans of city government.

We turn, accordingly, to a consideration of the forms of city government used in the United States today.

Mayor-council form of city government. In spite of the emphasis on charter reform and on developing new mechanisms of municipal government, the fact remains that the traditional mayor-council form of government has maintained its ascendancy until the present day. In the mid-1960's, more than half of all cities over 5000 population were governed in this way. Even more sig-

* James Bryce in *The American Commonwealth*.

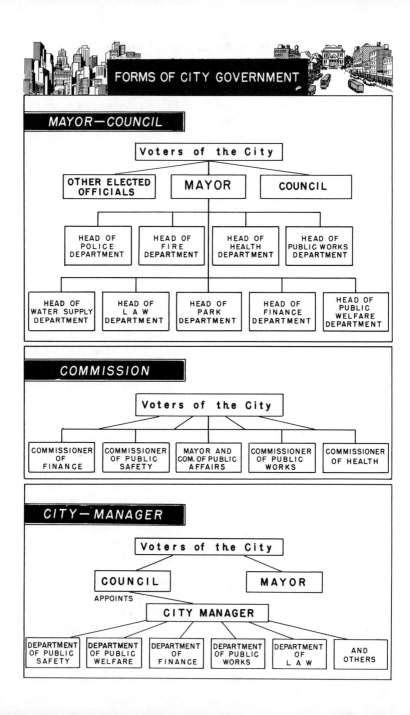

FORMS OF CITY GOVERNMENT

MAYOR—COUNCIL

Voters of the City

OTHER ELECTED OFFICIALS | MAYOR | COUNCIL

HEAD OF POLICE DEPARTMENT | HEAD OF FIRE DEPARTMENT | HEAD OF HEALTH DEPARTMENT | HEAD OF PUBLIC WORKS DEPARTMENT

HEAD OF WATER SUPPLY DEPARTMENT | HEAD OF LAW DEPARTMENT | HEAD OF PARK DEPARTMENT | HEAD OF FINANCE DEPARTMENT | HEAD OF PUBLIC WELFARE DEPARTMENT

COMMISSION

Voters of the City

COMMISSIONER OF FINANCE | COMMISSIONER OF PUBLIC SAFETY | MAYOR AND COM. OF PUBLIC AFFAIRS | COMMISSIONER OF PUBLIC WORKS | COMMISSIONER OF HEALTH

CITY—MANAGER

Voters of the City

COUNCIL | MAYOR

APPOINTS

CITY MANAGER

DEPARTMENT OF PUBLIC SAFETY | DEPARTMENT OF PUBLIC WELFARE | DEPARTMENT OF FINANCE | DEPARTMENT OF PUBLIC WORKS | DEPARTMENT OF LAW | AND OTHERS nificant, of all cities over 500,000 population, Cincinnati was the only one which did not have the mayor-council form of government.

The mayor-council plan reflects the system of separation of legislative and executive powers and the emphasis on checks and balances which characterize both the Federal government and the various state governments. The executive head of the government is the mayor, who is elected directly by the people. He has the power to approve, and generally to veto, measures passed by the city council. In many cities, there are provisions for overriding the mayor's veto, usually by a two-thirds vote of the council. The extent of the mayor's authority to appoint and to remove the heads of city departments varies from city to city. In general, however, there has been a tendency to vest greater appointive powers in the mayor, and thus to bring about a greater degree of centralized control. This is in line with the generally accepted *"strong-mayor"* form of government, under which the mayor prepares the budget, has overall responsibility for administration, and is expected to formulate a legislative program for action by the council. Such concentration of power and leadership in the mayor is characteristic of most large American cities today. It reflects the tendency toward strong executives evident on every level of government.

Many smaller cities, however, retain the *"weak-mayor"* plan, under which most governmental authority is centered in the council. The mayor in this case may be little more than a ceremonial officer.

The legislative body of the city is usually known as the *council*, but it may have other names, such as *board of aldermen*. In practically all cases, this body is now single-chambered. The number of members varies widely—from five or nine to as many as fifty. The councilmen are almost always popularly elected, usually on a ward or district basis, although in some cases election at-large is employed. Such elections may be partisan or non-partisan—that is, with or without designation of political parties on the ballot. Councilmen are usually paid a salary, but in some smaller places they may serve without compensation or for only a nominal sum.

The council has the power to pass local ordinances, to fix tax rates, and to vote expenditures. In such matters, it is subject to limitations imposed by the state constitution and by state laws. It is also subject to the leadership and initiative exercised by the mayor under the "strong-mayor" plan of government.

Commission plan of city government. The commission plan of city government was pioneered in Galveston, Texas, in 1901, in the wake of a natural catastrophe that had all but "knocked out" the normal life of the city. It represented a reaction against what had been widely criticized as the excessive power concentrated in the mayor under the mayor-council system—a power that at times seemed to result in corruption, mismanagement, and general inadequacy in the face of major problems.

The essential feature of the commission plan is the combination of legislative and executive powers in a small group of commissioners (usually five), who are elected by the people and are, in one way or another, responsible to them. The commissioners have the power to pass ordinances, to appoint the heads and assistant heads of municipal departments, and to grant franchises. The commissioners divide among themselves the general supervision of the various departments, such as public safety, public works, and finance. One of the commissioners is designated as mayor, but this office is essentially ceremonial; the mayor has no more real power than do his fellow-commissioners.

In the first few decades of the 20th century, the commission plan gained considerable popularity, and even today it is found in about 250 American cities, mostly with populations of from 5000 to 25,000. The fact is, however, that this form of government is fast declining. A number of larger cities (*e.g.*, Des Moines and New Orleans) have dropped it. Dissension among the commissioners, the difficulty of fixing responsibility for maladministration, and the lack of checks and balances may explain its weaknesses.

Council-manager plan of city government. This represents a step in the direction of centralization and efficiency, qualities that have often been found wanting in the commission plan. The city manager may be compared with the general manager or top executive of a large business corporation. He is, in effect, the "efficiency expert" of the city. The manager is hired by the popularly elected council. The length of his service and the other terms of his employment are usually based on a contract with the city. He carries out the city's ordinances, has considerable powers of appointment and removal, and is expected to furnish advice and guidance on matters of finance, sanitation, traffic control, public safety, and a host of other specialized problems that confront the city today. The manager is frequently "imported" from outside the city, on the theory that a qualified "outsider" is less likely to be hindered by local political ties. A city manager with a good background of experience and accomplishment usually commands a sizable salary. For example, the city manager of Cincinnati (the largest city which has this form of government) receives $35,000 a year (1966).

Almost half the cities in the United States with populations of 25,000 or more now have the council-manager plan of government. It seems to be favored, however, by medium-sized cities below 500,000. The criticism most often made of the plan is that it tends to reduce municipal government to the level of a mere technical or business operation, without giving adequate scope to imagination, idealism, and creative leadership in striving to solve the city's problems.

Problems Confronting Large Cities Today

Urban renewal. President Johnson defined this problem succinctly when he declared: "The old, the poor, the discriminated against are increasingly concentrated in the central city ghettoes; while others move to the suburbs leaving the central city to battle against immense odds." This picture drawn by the President applies accurately, according to the Advisory Commission on Intergovernmental Relations, to 190 of the 212 "standard metropolitan areas" of the nation. The Commission defined the urban renewal problem as "the basic central city-suburban dichotomy of social and economic characteristics." What this means, in effect, is that the older "downtown" areas of many of our great cities are rapidly becoming slums, inhabited by the unfortunate and the disadvantaged, while the exodus of the middle class to the suburbs continues unabated.

The problem of urban renewal was in the public eye before President Johnson presented it as a major point in his Great Society program. Congress recognized its importance as far back as 1937, when it authorized the construction of public housing for low-income groups. Twelve years later, Congress launched a huge slum-clearance program under the Housing Act of 1949. This law was later amended to embrace not only public housing and financially assisted private housing but also rehabilitation of downtown shopping areas, construction of community facilities for recreation and other purposes, restoration of historical sites, and the improvement of metropolitan transportation facilities. The

Two aspects of urban renewal in New York City. Above, a middle-income housing project, providing housing for 209 families. Below, Philharmonic Hall, a part of Lincoln Center, a great cultural complex built on a former slum site.

New York State Division of Housing and Community Renewal

program of urban renewal became so comprehensive and so costly that President Kennedy in 1961 and 1962 called for the creation of a new Cabinet post to coordinate and direct the various activities. No action was taken at that time, but in 1965 Congress did create the *Department of Housing and Urban Development*. This absorbed such existing agencies as the Housing and Home Finance Agency and the Urban Renewal Administration.

What has been accomplished thus far by the urban renewal program? It is estimated that from 1949 to 1966, the Federal government spent over 5 billion dollars on renewal projects in cities, large and small, throughout the nation. To this must be added the smaller sums provided under the law by municipal governments and private interests. These expenditures have made possible impressive accomplishments in such cities as New York, Philadelphia, Chicago, Pittsburgh, Miami, etc. Some of the worst slums have been torn down and have been replaced by good housing and other needed facilities. Undoubtedly, many thousands of families have been enabled to lead a better life.

On the other hand, it is only too obvious that in relation to the vast dimensions of the problem of "urban blight," the remedial measures have been on a minute scale. The Secretary of the Department of Housing and Urban Development has estimated that an annual expenditure of 10 billion dollars would be needed to make substantial progress in transforming our cities! And this would have to be continued for many years.

Inadequate financing is not the only weakness that has appeared in the urban renewal program. It is acknowledged that there has been faulty planning, resulting at times in the clearance of slums before replacement housing is available. Thus, low-income families, including many elderly people, have lost their apartments (admittedly substandard) without being able to find anything better. The new housing built on the former slum sites is sometimes priced beyond what the old tenants can afford. In the opinion of some critics, there has been too much emphasis on "luxury" or at least middle-income housing, and on non-residential construction. On the other hand, some of the large housing projects occupied almost exclusively by low-income families have deteriorated rapidly and have manifested severe social problems.

Experienced students of the urban-renewal program have suggested these principles or guidelines for the future: (1) Careful planning is essential, so that slum clearance and construction of new housing are coordinated with transportation improvement

This prize-winning aerial photograph shows New York City "swimming in a sea of smog" (Thanksgiving Day, 1966). Control of air pollution has become one of the most urgent problems facing larger cities (and many smaller communities) in all parts of the United States.

and provision of schools, parks, and other needed services, as well as commercial facilities. The proportion of the land to be used for these various purposes must be expertly controlled. (2) Massive Federal aid is needed. The cities simply do not have the resources to do the job. They are faced with demands for ever more costly services, and they rely primarily on a tax on real estate which represents a constantly dwindling proportion of the national wealth. (3) The program must be planned on a long-term basis and must be sustained for as long as is necessary. Spasmodic efforts, which begin a project one year, and discontinue it or contract it the next, may actually do more harm than good. (4) Strong local leadership is needed to make sure that the money is spent as effectively as possible. The job cannot be done "from Washington." Only people with an intimate knowledge of local conditions can plan realistically to rebuild whole communities. Only local governments can enact and enforce wise zoning laws, update building codes, provide adequate police and fire protection, and in general do all the things that are needed for better neighborhoods. (5) Finally, we must do much more to enlist the active participation of the average citizen in his neighborhood affairs. To arrest urban blight and make our cities truly livable we need not only new construction on a vast scale but also vast numbers of people who care about their housing, their street, their community. This is the only safeguard against the creation of new slums after the construction projects have been completed.

Unemployment and poverty. The problem of slums and poverty is closely related to the problem of chronic unemployment. The social cost of a persistent shortage of jobs can be observed in the demoralization of those groups (composed largely of Negroes and teenagers) who usually find employment only when everyone else is already employed.

This condition is reflected in the swollen relief budgets of our cities and in many signs of social breakdown—crime, broken homes, juvenile delinquency, narcotic addiction, mental illness, etc. The problem is extremely complex, and all authorities agree that no single type of remedial action is likely to be effective. A many-sided approach is necessary, including such programs as the following .

1. *Our educational system must be adapted and improved to meet present-day conditions.* In particular, better occupational training and employment guidance programs are urgently needed. This should include counseling services, not only to develop motivation and self-respect but also to help the unemployed (particularly young people) with concrete problems related to getting and holding a job. For older displaced workers, large-scale *retraining* programs are required.

2. *We must maintain a healthy economy, with a vigorous growth rate.* This means that we must not merely avoid major economic collapses, on the style of 1929, but must provide for sustained expansion. Vast numbers of new jobs will be needed to absorb additions to the work force, and also to replace jobs which are eliminated by automation and other technological advances. This, in turn, implies an expanding standard of living for the great masses of our citizens. Some writers, attempting to peer into the future, have suggested that in the years to come, there may be less emphasis on multiplication of "gadgets" and "hardware" and correspondingly more on providing a clean, healthful, and pleasant environment, with opportunities for better health services, travel, enjoying nature, continued education, and participation in arts, sports, and other rewarding activities. To make this possible, a larger share of the total national income

would have to go to the "public sector"—that is, to the services provided by government on all its levels. But there would also be broadened opportunities for private enterprise to contribute to a richer life for all Americans. It is pointed out that as relatively fewer people work on production of goods, and more on providing services, there will be less occasion for automated equipment to replace workers.

The steadily expanding economy which we need and want calls for cooperative action by all sectors of our economy—government, private business, and labor. Government can help immeasurably by prudent use of two great weapons—*fiscal policy* and *monetary policy*. *Fiscal policy* refers to all the activities of government in raising money (through taxation and borrowing) and in spending it. *Monetary policy* refers to the controls which government exercises over the supply of money and the availability and cost of credit, largely through its central banking facilities (that is, the Federal Reserve System). We need also dynamic, farsighted, and socially minded businessmen; and enlightened labor leaders, thinking in terms of increased levels of production, which will make possible more jobs, greater security, and higher real wages for all workers, organized and unorganized.

When families live in poverty, it is the children who are most cruelly victimized. At a crucial time in their lives, they are forced to bear a burden of disadvantages that may stunt their development and prevent their ever escaping from the "vicious cycle of poverty breeding poverty."

3. *We must eliminate discrimination in employment.* This is one way of helping directly the minority groups (mainly Negroes) who suffer from a much higher rate of unemployment than the population as a whole. A number of cities, following the lead of their respective states, have passed fair employment practices acts. The purpose of such legislation (as explained on page 233) is to make sure that race, religion, and nationality do not become factors in employment. Local and state anti-discrimination laws are supplemented by the Federal government's efforts, through the President's Committee on Equal Employment, to eliminate discrimination in the employment policies of Federal agencies, as well as of private employers holding Federal contracts. In this connection, it is essential that labor unions eliminate all remaining restrictions (official and unofficial) on admitting members of minority groups to membership, including apprenticeship programs.

4. *We must plan to provide retired workers with more adequate pensions from Social Security and other sources.* One writer has spoken of the "silent poor"—large numbers of elderly people barely getting by on fixed incomes which were inadequate to begin with and have been constantly eroded by rising prices. This is one case where poverty is not the result of unemployment. There has been talk of automatic increases in Social Security benefits keyed to changes in the Consumer Price Index.

As time goes on, we may also want to encourage people to retire at an earlier age, thus "opening up" more jobs for younger workers. One step in this direction was a recent change in the Social Security Act to permit retirement at age 62, rather than 65. However, the generally low level of the benefits paid, further reduced by inflation, offered only limited inducement to workers to retire at the lower age. To meet this need, President Johnson and Congress took steps to increase benefits. Coupled with Medicare, this was progress, indeed, for our "senior citizens."

5. *Some good can be done by enforcing standards of minimum wages and maximum hours and by improving these standards as the productivity of labor increases.* It should be noted that not only government (Federal and state) but also labor unions play a part in bringing about advances in this area. The Federal Fair Labor Standards Act, as amended in 1966, set a minimum

rate of $1.40 an hour effective in 1967, and $1.60 effective in 1968. Moreover, about 7 million additional workers were brought under the protection of the laws (in small retail establishments, hospitals and related institutions, large farms, etc.). In these cases, the maximum is set at $1.00 an hour with provisions for later increases.

Unfortunately, inflation has eroded some of the gains represented by the minimum wage standards. Moreover, in some industries and occupations, the minimum tends to become the maximum (or very close to it). Thus, in every large city today, there are heads of families working at full-time jobs who make so little that they must receive supplementary welfare payments.

It is evident from all that has been said above that the causes of poverty, and the cure for it, go far beyond the city as such. Indeed, the problem of poverty reaches deep into our economic institutions and the overall structure of our society. It should be remembered, too, that there are sizable "pockets of poverty" in the United States outside our urban centers—for example, the displaced miners and other workers of Appalachia; the rural Negroes and "poor whites" of the Deep South; the marginal farmers and migratory farm workers in many sections of the country.

Nonetheless, it is true that most of the poor people today are to be found in the teeming populations of our great cities. It is also true that in the cities, poverty exacts its greatest costs in terms of social disorganization and personal tragedy. Accordingly, most observers agree that it is in the cities, above all, that the campaign against poverty must be planned, fought, and won. But it appears clear that the hard-pressed cities cannot hope to carry out such a campaign without massive Federal aid.

The Economic Opportunities Act. It was in response to the continued existence of unemployment and poverty in the United States that Congress passed the *Economic Opportunities Act* in 1964. Under the provisions of this legislation, the Federal government provides funds to communities that submit satisfactory anti-poverty programs to the newly established Office of Economic Opportunity. The plans laid down by local communities have emphasized work-training programs to employ young people locally; a "domestic peace corps" (Volunteers in Service to America, VISTA), to provide badly needed educational and social services in underprivileged neighborhoods; and a Job Corps, to provide training and work experience in fields where there is a lively demand for labor. Thus, a young man who has no marketable skill may be trained as an air-conditioning technician; an older worker who has been "automated" out of his factory job may take a course in drafting or in dental mechanics. In many instances, the men and women who are retrained in this way must first receive instruction in reading, writing, and other basic educational skills.

The Economic Opportunities Act was given a three-year life span, (extended later) and Congress made annual appropriations for the program. Communities throughout the nation hastened to take advantage of the Federal law, although there was some criticism to the effect that the anti-poverty program was a "political gimmick," and might degenerate into a "pork-barrel."

In 1969, President Nixon, eager to curtail government expenditures and streamline "barren and duplicating agencies," transferred the Job Corps to the Labor Department, and Head Start (the pre-school program) to HEW from the OEO.

The lag in education. Just as our ideas about political democracy have undergone a change, so the American city of today has been challenged to revise its ideas about democracy in education. The traditional type of school, traditional courses of study, and traditional methods of instruction can no longer meet the needs of many of the young people who attend our public schools today. Compounding this problem is the movement for desegregation of education in the United States (page 197). But, as Dr. Kenneth B. Clark* has said: "There is encouraging evidence that children can learn what they are expected to learn . . . that meaningful desegregation of public schools can occur only if all schools in a given system are raised to the highest standards so that the quality of education does not vary according to either the income or the social status of the neighborhood." In other words, the goals of school integration and of quality education for all must be achieved simultaneously; they are interdependent, in the sense that neither is possible without the other. It is primarily in the public school systems of our great cities that this struggle for educational equality and upgrading must be won.

Relations between cities and suburbs. The people who live in the suburbs but work in the city enjoy many of the city's services. To them, the city is a source of employment, recreation,

* Kenneth B. Clark, *Dark Ghetto* (Harper and Row, 1965)

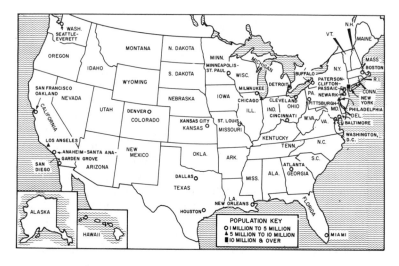

This map shows all the metropolitan areas in the United States above
1 million population.

shopping, transportation, and other activities. But since the sub-
urb is typically outside the city's limits, the "commuters" pay
fewer direct taxes to the city government than do the regular
residents. And this at a time when the cities desperately need
additional revenues.

To deal with this situation, local governments have tried the
following experiments: (1) Voluntary arrangements between the
center city (or county) and the suburbs, under which the city
sells to the suburban communities such services as water supply,
sewage disposal, fire protection, and even certain educational
facilities. The suburbs may, in turn, extend to the city the use of
parks and recreational facilities. This type of cooperation recognizes the fact that the city and its suburbs form a *metropolitan
area*, and that the need for many vital public services often cuts
across political boundaries. (2) Creation of *special districts* to
perform area-wide functions, such as water supply, sewage disposal, transportation, etc. *Special districts* are governmental units
set up to perform a particular function or functions. (3) Extending the city's authority and functions by annexing suburban territory. In 1963, for example, Kansas City annexed 187 square miles
of adjoining areas, thus doubling its area. Los Angeles County

has grown steadily in the 20th century by annexation of territory. (4) Consolidating city and county governments into a single unified structure to serve a metropolitan area. Successful consolidations of this type have been made in Los Angeles County and in Dade County (Miami), Florida. In 1962, Davidson County in Tennessee voted to merge with the city of Nashville under a common governmental authority called the "Metropolitan Government of Nashville and Davidson County."

In Chapter 6 (page 168), we noted the use of public corporations by the Federal government to run special enterprises analogous to private business operations. The Tennessee Valley Authority and the Federal Deposit Insurance Corporation are examples of this type of agency. In recent years, local government has also made use of governmental corporations that are run more or less like private businesses, but with the purpose of advancing

As our metropolitan areas grow in size and in population, the transportation problem becomes ever more pressing. Here is a scene on one of the Los Angeles "freeways," probably the most advanced system of limited-access roads to be found in any city in the world. But the question remains whether we can best hope to meet the transport needs of our great cities by providing more and better *roads for private automobiles,* or rather by emphasizing more and better *public transportation facilities.*

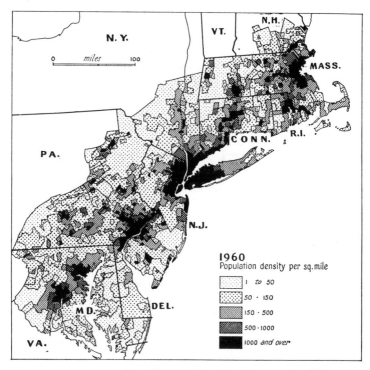

From *Megalopolis* by Jean Gottman (the M.I.T. Press—
A Twentieth Century Fund Study)

In several regions of the United States, the expanding urban communities have grown so close together that they actually "run into each other." This creates a continuous zone or strip of high population density, extending perhaps for hundreds of miles. The outstanding example of such a "Megalopolis" is the area along the Atlantic coast, from Boston in the north to Washington, D.C. in the south, as shown in the map above.

the public interest, rather than of earning profits. For example, New York State in 1965 established the Metropolitan Commuter Transportation Authority. This body was granted power to maintain and operate commuter transportation facilities in New York City and seven densely populated adjacent counties. The authority of the MCTA extends to land, marine, and air transport facilities. Responsible only to the Governor of New York, the agency is free of supervision by all local and state agencies. It will raise capital funds, as older governmental corporations have done, by selling tax-exempt revenue bonds.

This is an example of how new governmental forms are developed to meet the ever-increasing problems of our great urban population centers. It will be noted that, in most cases, the authority and programs of these newer agencies extend not just to the central city, as legally defined, but rather to the entire *metropolitan area*. Regardless of where boundaries may be drawn by law, the central city and its suburbs form an organic social unit, interdependent in many ways. Programs designed realistically to grapple with urban problems must take this into account.

Money, Money, Money! The most pressing single problem facing the nation's cities today is setting up and maintaining a revenue system adequate to support the services that Americans have come to expect of their local governments. This problem is made more difficult by the fact that cities possess only those taxing powers which are granted to them by the states. What are the chief sources of revenues under this system?

1. The *property tax*—primarily a tax on real estate—is the chief source of income for almost all municipal governments. It accounts for almost 90% of all local tax revenues in the United States. It is determined in the following way: Each piece of

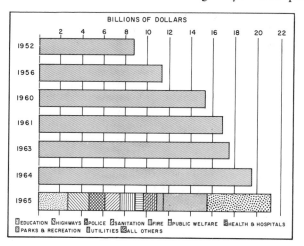

Expenditures by all cities in the United States in selected years from 1952 to 1965. (Data from Tax Foundation.)

real estate is examined by officials called *assessors* who place a *valuation* upon it. After the assessed valuation of all the property in the locality has been determined, the responsible officials decide how much must be raised by the property tax to meet the city's needs. The ratio between the amount to be raised and the total assessed valuation determines the *tax rate*, which is then applied to all taxable property. The arithmetic is simple; the practical difficulties of administering the tax are often far less simple.

The property tax has certain advantages. First, since real estate cannot be hidden, it is a relatively easy tax to administer. Second, the rates may be easily adjusted (at least in theory) to meet the needs of government. Third, the tax reaches all citizens of the city, either directly, or indirectly as a part of rentals. On the other hand, objections to the dependence on the property tax have frequently been voiced. A city resident may be very wealthy while owning little or no real estate. In this event, the property tax does not reach him, except as a small part of his rent. Conversely, the owner of a small piece of property, such as a modest home, may be taxed heavily. In short, the weakness of the property tax applied primarily to real estate, is that it is not based on *ability to pay* (page 251).

2. The *sales tax* was first used in the United States in West Virginia in 1921, and since then has been adopted by most states and by many cities and other local governments. It is a direct tax which is added to each purchase at a set rate, usually ranging from 1% to 5%. As a rule it applies only to retail sales, although in some states wholesale transactions may also be taxed. In either case, it is the consumer who foots the bill.

In the past the sales tax has been severely criticized as being *regressive*. In other words, the charge is made that this tax is not based on ability to pay and therefore weighs most heavily on the lower-income groups. More recently, however, many economists have come to favor the sales tax as an important element in an overall tax program. The arguments offered in its favor are that it can raise large amounts of revenue; that it is relatively easy to administer; that it requires some contribution for public services from practically everyone in the community; and that (unlike ever higher income taxes) it does not tend to blunt individual initiative. The regressive feature of the tax can be minimized by exempting purchases of food, drugs, children's clothing, and other necessities which represent a large part of the purchases of the typical lower-income family.

Other important sources of local revenues are licenses, and fees and (increasingly) grants from the state and Federal governments. Some cities, desperate for additional revenues, have considered a tax on personal and business income. It is argued that this would broaden the city tax base and would permit taxation closely adapted to ability to pay. But it is scarcely surprising that city residents, already paying income taxes to the Federal government and, in many cases, to the state government as well, show little enthusiasm for a third withholding from their pay checks. Nevertheless, New York City adopted an income tax in 1966, after receiving special authorization from the state government.

Borrowing by cities. Besides the usual sources of revenue, cities are usually empowered to borrow money by issuing bonds for the purpose of building new capital facilities, such as schools, hospitals, etc. Many localities are barred by law from borrowing for other purposes, such as current expenses. These restrictions have often been assailed by mayors of large cities, who contend that cities must have more financial freedom if they are to meet their pressing obligations at a time of rapid growth and truly massive problems. The advocates of economy answer that bond issues (or any other form of borrowing) create a burden of debt which, in effect, mortgages the city's future income. In many cities, the debt-service charges are already one of the largest items in the budget. Most authorities agree that it makes sense to borrow to build a capital facility which will be used for perhaps 50 years, and which therefore should not be charged entirely against any one year's income. But borrowing to meet current expenses, such as the city payroll, is much harder to justify.

State and Federal assistance. Cities and other local units have long depended on financial aid from the state government to help maintain essential services. In New York State, for example, the state government in recent years has spent about 59 cents of every dollar to help the localities with schools, health, social welfare, housing, and other public services. At the receiving end, New York City depends on state aid to furnish about 20% of all its revenues. The picture is much the same in other states and cities.

As the responsibilities and problems of the cities have grown, and as the city governments have approached the limits of their taxing and borrowing capacity, there have been more pressing demands for an expansion of state aid. To some extent the state governments have responded to this, but as is usual in such situations, there is often a sharp difference of opinion between state and city officials as to how much is "adequate" and how the state's contributions should be divided. In the big cities, it has long been argued that although the state raises most of its revenues from city residents and business (for example, through the income tax and sales-tax), a disproportionate share of the aid goes to rural and small-town areas. Reapportionment of state legislatures to give cities more adequate representation may enable them to obtain increased state aid—provided the rapidly growing suburban areas do not provide a counterforce to the political influence of the inner cities.

The Federal government has also become an important factor in the financial picture for local government. Billions of dollars have been flowing to the cities for education, urban renewal, anti-poverty programs, and many other purposes. Moreover, by its contributions to the states for such purposes as social security and highways, the Federal government has greatly aided city governments in meeting their responsibilities to their residents.

'A Couple Hundred Billion Would Help'

The ever-increasing dependence of the nation's big cities on financial help from the Federal government called forth this cartoon comment in a New York City newspaper. What are some of the main "problems" for which help is being asked? Do you think that contributions made by Uncle Sam for this purpose can justly be characterized as a "handout"?

Don Hesse in the New York *World Journal Tribune*

County Government—A Form
of Government in Transition

Number and size. One of the most important types of local government found throughout the United States is the county. There are about 3000 of them, varying in size from San Bernardino County, California, which is bigger than the states of Vermont, Delaware, and Rhode Island .combined, to New York County (Manhattan), which contains 22 square miles. The divergencies in population are even greater; at one end of the scale we have Los Angeles County, California, with about 7 million residents, and at the other end, small rural counties with a few hundred residents widely scattered.

Every state is divided into counties, although in Louisiana they are known as *parishes,* and in Alaska as *boroughs.*

Varying characteristics. County government varies in importance. In the New England states, for example, counties are subordinated to the cities and towns. For the most part, the counties survive there as mere historical carry-overs, with minimal functions, or in some cases with no functions at all. In contrast, in the South and in many of the Western states, the county is the dominant form of local government outside the cities. Even in densely populated areas, such as the suburbs surrounding the great cities of the East, we find counties performing many vital services for residents and undertaking costly development programs.

There has been a well-defined trend, however, for the counties to give up some of their functions to the state. Thus, in 1931, North Carolina took over the building and maintenance of county roads, and in 1933, the county school systems. In 1938, Illinois took over the selection of the employees of the county welfare departments. In 1959, Connecticut abolished counties as functional governmental units; they remained merely as geographic subdivisions of the state and as judicial areas in the state court system. The state took over all county property and assumed all debts and all the governmental powers and duties of its counties. In Rhode Island, also, the counties no longer exist as functioning units of government.

In still other states, city and county governments are concurrent; that is, their responsibilities are so closely related that they are run by the same government unit. For example, Denver, Colorado, is both a city and a county; similarly, the city and county of San Francisco cover the same area. New York City comprises five different counties.

Plans of county government. There is no uniform plan of county government in the United States. However, in the great majority of the states, each county has a *county board* to run its affairs. Members of these boards are called by various names, such as "supervisors," "county commissioners," "freeholders," and "justices of the peace." The board members are elected. One of the largest county boards (more than 140 members) is that of Wayne County, Michigan, which contains the city of Detroit.

The county board has only those powers which are given to it by the state constitution and the legislature. These powers vary from state to state, but in general a county board sets the county tax rate, looks after the county roads, cares for the poor, fixes the salaries of some county officials, and conducts elections.

Besides the members of the county board, there are a number of lesser county officials.

The *sheriff* is the peace officer of the county and carries out orders of the local (county) court. He enforces state laws within the limits of the county and has charge of the local jail. He is

In many sections of the United States, the county sheriff is still the basic law-enforcement official. Here we see a group of Texas sheriffs attending a special school maintained by the State Department of Public Safety. They are receiving instruction in the use of the polygraph ("lie detector").

Texas Dept. of Public Safety

often assisted by the state police. In emergencies, he may call on the aid of any able-bodied citizen of the county to help him maintain the peace. For special purposes, such as capturing a fugitive from justice, he may form a *posse*. In extreme cases of large-scale crime or disorder, the sheriff may ask the governor to call out the militia. The sheriff is usually elected.

The *prosecuting attorney* serves as legal adviser to county officials and appears in court as state prosecutor. It is very important that he be honest, fair, industrious and equipped with a good knowledge of the law. If he does not act promptly against law-breakers operating within the county, there is no one else to do so, and the county may become the refuge of antisocial forces. This has actually happened in more than one county in the United States. Like the sheriff, the prosecuting attorney is usually elected.

Other county officials include the *coroner*, who inquires into deaths from what appear to be unnatural causes; the *assessor*, who sets the valuation of taxable property; the *auditor*, whose responsibility it is to check the county's financial accounts; the *recorder*, or *registrar of deeds*, who keeps records of deeds and other documents pertaining to the ownership of real property; the *county clerk;* and the *treasurer*. There may also be a *county superintendent of schools*. These officials may be either elected or appointed, depending on local laws.

The future of the county. As we have indicated, the county has declined sharply in importance in many densely populated urban areas, where strong city governments are in operation. Thus, the five counties of New York City retain only a few vestigial functions. Philadelphia, St. Louis, San Francisco, and Nashville are among the cities that have merged city and county governments. In New England, the cities and the towns have so contracted the activities of county governments that they have disappeared completely as functional units in two states and seem to be on the way out in others.

It may be expected that this trend will continue where county services are clearly no longer needed or can be performed more efficiently and economically by other units. In some cases, county governments may be replaced by *special districts* that will concentrate on particular services, such as education, public health, or recreation. Such districts may cut across the area of several former counties. There have already been significant developments along these lines in various sections of the country.

On the other hand, there are still areas where the county "makes sense" as a unit of local government. In such cases, the county will undoubtedly survive, but as with virtually all units of local government, there is a pressing need for reform and modernization. One promising development is reorganization of the county government to give it a strong executive head, known as the *county manager* or *county executive*. (Lack of executive leadership has long been the most characteristic weakness of county government.) It has been demonstrated in the densely populated suburban counties around our great cities that popularly elected county executives, vested with adequate powers, can do much to improve the performance of local government. Nassau County, outside New York City, is an example. Some observers believe that the office of county executive in large counties may become a high-prestige post, and thus may attract able and ambitious young men, eager to gain public attention and to move upward in their political careers. This represents a marked change from the old image of county government as a "political graveyard."

As a unit of government, the county still, in many parts of our country, gives the citizens a chance to get together and come to grips with local problems. What Alexis de Tocqueville said over 125 years ago is still true: "I believe that provincial institutions are useful to all nations, but nowhere do they appear to me to be more necessary than among a democratic people. How can a populace unaccustomed to freedom in small concerns learn to use it temperately in great affairs?"

The New England Town

Historical development. Interest in fishing and in trade, the need for protection against Indians, and devotion to the church caused the people in colonial New England to form compact communities called *towns*. These consisted typically of one or more centers of population, together with the surrounding rural area.

The town still serves the people of New England as an important form of local government. There are about 1400 of them in the six New England states. Their boundaries in most cases are natural ones, dating back to the days of the early settlers. The usual size is 25 to 35 square miles. This small size originally made it possible for all voters to attend *town meetings* and to discuss and vote directly on questions concerning local government. This was a classic example of *direct*, as opposed to representative, democracy.

> NOTE: The centers of population within the towns are unincorporated communities. If such a community grows to a substantial size, it will usually become an *incorporated municipality* or *city*. It will then obtain a charter from the state authorizing it to set up and run its own city government.

Survival of the town meeting. Today, especially in the larger towns, the great majority of the voters do not customarily attend town meetings. Indeed, it would usually be impossible to find a meeting place large enough to accommodate all the citizens if they wished to attend.

In practice, then, the town meeting is made up of a relatively small group of the more interested and conscientious citizens— or perhaps of those with much free time on their hands. This group, in effect, makes up the town's legislative body. Meetings continue to be held annually, usually in March or October. The

A typical town meeting in progress. A citizen has risen to express his opinion on an issue under discussion. The officials at the table include the *moderator* (presiding officer), the *town clerk,* and the *selectmen.*

Connecticut Development Commission

town meeting hears reports and passes ordinances relating to traffic control, sanitation, zoning, road maintenance, and other local matters. The most important overall function of the town meeting is usually financial because this body allocates funds to meet the expenses of the town government.

At a typical town meeting in a recent year, the voters considered a list of fourteen articles. Here are some of them:

Article II: To select four town officials.

Article VI: To appropriate $2800 for a new ambulance.

Article IX: To appropriate $100 for a caretaker for the town park.

Article X: To appropriate $400 for the installation of streets lights on a road.

Article XI: To appropriate $500 for the salary of a part-time traffic officer.

Article XII: To enlarge the town water supply system. (This item was defeated.)

Bear in mind that all of these very practical decisions were made by the people themselves—not by a council or by an executive official.

Town officials. The town officials are selected by secret ballot at the town meeting. They include typically a *board of selectmen* (usually three in number), a *treasurer*, a *clerk*, and a *moderator*. The last-named presides at the town meeting. The selectmen are in charge of day-to-day administration of town affairs between the annual town meetings. As the town meetings receive limited popular interest and participation, there has been a tendency for the board of selectmen to assume greater responsibilities.

Other town officials include several *tax assessors*, one or more *constables*, and one or more *justices of the peace*.

Some towns have experimented with a salaried *town manager*, usually appointed by the selectmen. He is the chief administrative officer and is in charge of all town expenditures, except usually those for education.

Towns and the state legislature. In New England, towns have been traditionally used as a basis of apportionment for the lower house of the state legislature. Each town was entitled to at least one representative in that house, although the larger towns might have several. This is one reason the legislatures in the New England states have been unusually large. The Supreme Court's "one man, one vote" ruling is expected to bring about sweeping changes in this method of apportionment.

The Township

Historical development. The township as a unit of local government was introduced into many of the states in the Middle West as New Englanders made their way westward in search of new homes. The states in which the township developed extended all the way from New York, New Jersey, and Pennsylvania to the Dakotas.

The township, although closely related to the town, shows some significant differences. The township was designed for areas much larger than the typical New England town. Moreover, these areas at first were predominantly rural and sparsely populated, without the population center that served as the core of the New England town. In the Western areas where the township was introduced, the county was the established form of local government, and this tended to minimize the importance of the township.

Township government. Townships to this day function essentially as subdivisions of the county to carry out county functions. For this purpose, there is usually some form of *township board* to fix the tax rate and to decide what amounts of money are to be spent for various township purposes. Other officials include justices of the peace, constables, assessors, tax collectors, town clerks, and highway supervisors. These names suggest the main services provided by the township government.

Recent trends in townships. There are many observers today who feel that the township has become superfluous as a form of local government and should be abolished. Townships have never existed in about half of the states, and some states have taken steps to get rid of them. It is said that with modern means of transportation and communication, each county government could readily take over the duties of its various constituent townships, with no loss to anyone except perhaps a number of public job holders. It is pointed out that in the large Southern states, the county governments manage to operate without townships.

Many rural townships, as well as villages, have in recent years become bustling suburbs. A generation ago, these areas were composed of crossroads hamlets, farmlands, woods, and meadows. Today although still green in spots, they boast of sprawling split-level developments, garden apartments, shopping centers, industrial complexes—and overcrowded schools. Under such conditions, some township governments have assumed new functions and have shown considerable vitality. On the other hand, the very growth of these township areas makes them candidates for incorporation into larger urban units of government.

This densely populated suburban housing development in New Jersey stands on land which only a few years ago was used for farming. Similar communities may be found in all parts of the United States.

Village Government

Development. There are many communities known popularly as "villages" which have no formal governmental machinery of their own. After reaching a certain population, however, some communities of this type may apply to the state for a charter or other legal authorization to form a so-called *incorporated village*. The incorporated village is then able to organize a municipal government and carry on many of the functions of a self-governing community.

Village officials. The nature of the government set up in this way depends on the size of the village. The government of a small village is likely to be very simple, with much direct participation by the citizens themselves. A large village usually has a local *council* or *board of trustees*, with power to levy and collect taxes, to make assessments, and to attend to local services. The members of this body often serve without pay, on a part-time basis.

As a village becomes larger, it may develop into a city. In fact, many of our present-day cities once had the status of villages. However, the people of a large village may not wish to assume a city-type government, with its more elaborate and more costly structure. Also they may not care to become subject to certain state laws affecting cities. This is why we find villages today which, on the basis of population, would ordinarily be regarded as cities. Thus, Oak Park, Illinois, with a population of over 60,000, chooses to retain the status of an incorporated village. In New York State, such villages as Freeport, Hempstead, Port Chester, and Kenmore are larger than many cities in the state.

NOTE: The term *village* is used commonly throughout the Northeast and the Middle West, but in other sections of the country communities of this type may be known by such names as *towns* or *boroughs*. Note that a "town," in this sense, is not the same as the New England town or the township. The village form of government is adapted for an urban or semi-urban community, not for the surrounding rural area, as in the case of the New England town or township.

Proposals for Reform of Local Government

In the course of this chapter, we have already mentioned a number of reforms in the structure of local government, either proposed or actually in operation. A few other programs of this type are set forth below.

♦ *Proportional representation.* We have already mentioned proportional representation in connection with the allocation of a state's vote in the Electoral College. As applied to a local legislative body, proportional representation (or P. R.) refers to a scheme of voting which is designed to divide membership among the various parties in proportion to their popular support, as reflected in voting strength. Under the usual method of voting by wards or districts, a party which wins, say, 70% of the popular vote in a city or county will probably win all, or almost all, of the seats in the law-making body. Under P. R., it would get roughly 70% of the seats, and the various minority parties would gain seats in proportion to their votes.

A reform movement in the 1930's led to the adoption of P. R. in New York City. Under an extremely elaborate voting formula, a large number of political groups participated in the elections to the city council, and many of them succeeded in winning seats. There was widespread criticism that the method of voting was so complicated that most citizens did not understand it, and also that the council elected was made up of discordant splinter groups, without a strong and responsible majority. After two members of the Communist Party succeeded in winning election to the council, P. R. was voted down by a popular referendum in 1948.

There appears to be little likelihood that P.R., as such, will be revived in New York City or in any other large American city. There remains, however, the problem of obtaining reasonable representation for minority parties which control a large part of the total vote but, under present arrangements, are able to elect few, if any, members to the local lawmaking body.

♦ *Weighted voting.* Under the traditional system of county government, each member of the board of supervisors casts one vote, regardless of the size of the population that he represents. Thus, a community within the county with a population of about 2000 will have as much to say in determining the annual county budget as a community with a population of perhaps 70,000. Under such circumstances, a scheme of *weighted voting* would continue the one vote of the supervisor from the smaller community but would give the supervisor from the large community 35 votes. The voting strength of the other members of the board would be weighted accordingly.

Naturally, the principle of weighted voting could be applied to other bodies besides a county board of supervisors. Supporters of this device feel that it would be in accord with the spirit of the Supreme Court's "one man, one vote" decision. Opponents, who defend the present system, claim that a scheme of weighted voting would fail to take into consideration the historical and social factors which have developed over long periods of time. Many township and village lines, they say, go back to pre-Revolutionary times, and they reflect special needs and conditions which cannot be weighted arithmetically on the basis of relative population.

◆ *Improving the selection of judges.* Some authorities are of the opinion that the quality of the judges serving on municipal and other local courts could be greatly improved by better methods of selection. For the most part, these authorities favor ending the popular election of such judges and vesting the power of appointment in the mayor or another local executive official. The mayor, however, would have to choose from a list of candidates recommended by a judicial nominating commission. The members of this commission would be public-spirited citizens familiar with legal affairs but not holding any other public or political office. Some members might be named by the mayor, others by the presiding justices of the highest courts of the state. Obviously, many variations are possible in specific arrangements, but the purpose would be to take judgeships out of the area of partisan politics, in which they are unfortunately involved in many cases today.

◆ *Demonstration Cities Act.* In 1966, Congress passed the *Demonstration Cities Act,* which authorized the distribution of about 1.2 billion dollars among selected cities to help them upgrade blighted neighborhoods and, in the process, to develop new techniques of urban rehabilitation. The Nixon administration, departing from the original concept of the Act (building examples of urban renaissance), gave mayors the option to extend the Model Neighborhoods to all poverty areas in their jurisdiction. This means that the local governments will simply use Federal grants for general improvement of blighted areas.

Terms You Should Know

Central city. The older "downtown" area of a city as distinguished from outlying sections and the suburbs.

City charter. The basic legal authorization ("constitution") for establishment as a corporate entity. The city may sue and be sued; it may impose taxes; and may exercise the right of eminent domain. Charters also place certain limitations—for example, in regard to debts, taxes, and granting of franchises.

City-manager plan. A form of city government under which executive powers are vested in a professional manager hired by the elected city officials. The mayor under this setup has little authority.

Commission plan. A form of city government under which an elected commission exercises both executive and legislative powers.

County. A unit of local government found in most parts of the United States. A typical county includes both rural and urban areas, although some may be predominantly rural and some may be located entirely within the limits of cities.

Eminent domain. The right of a governmental body to take over private property for a necessary public purpose upon payment of fair compensation.

Franchise. A special privilege which a governmental authority grants to a private business organization—*e.g.*, the right to use city streets for a bus line. In another sense, *franchise* refers to the citizen's right to vote.

"Gray area." The parts of a city that lie between the urban center and the suburbs.

Home rule. The right of a local government, usually a city, to exercise a considerable measure of authority in controlling its own affairs, without interference of the state government.

Justice of the peace. A local magistrate whose judicial power extends to minor civil and criminal cases.

Mayor-council government. A form of city government under which an elected council serves as the legislature and the mayor as the executive authority. Depending on the degree of power exercised by the mayor, this form may be of the "strong-mayor" or "weak-mayor" variety.

Metropolitan area. An urbanized area including and surrounding a large central city. A metropolitan area is usually confronted with problems common to the entire area but often lacks a coordinated governmental authority and program for solving them.

Special district. A unit of government with authority to carry out a particular function (*e.g.*, water supply, transportation) within a designated area.

Town. A unit of local government in New England, comprising typically a center (or centers) of population and the surrounding rural area. The traditional source of governmental authority in the town is the *town meeting,* which all qualified citizens may attend to discuss and vote on local affairs (direct democracy).

Township. An administrative unit or subdivision of a county.

Urbanization. Expansion of city life and city institutions as opposed to rural aspects.

Urban renewal. A program to clear away slums and in general create better living conditions in our urban population centers. Although based primarily on Federal legislation, urban renewal involves cooperation among the Federal, state and local governments, as well as private business and other organizations.

Village. A type of local government, usually employed by smaller communities. An *incorporated village* may have many of the characteristics of a city.

Weighted voting. A scheme of voting in an administrative or lawmaking body where each official has voting power roughly in proportion to the number of people he represents.

Questions and Problems Based on the Text

1. (*a*) In what way does the state control municipal government? (*b*) What is the nature of the city charter? (*c*) How has the "home rule movement" affected city charters?

2. Discuss the strengths and weaknesses of city government in the United States today.

3. Describe briefly each of the following types of local government: (*a*) mayor-council, "weak" and "strong," (*b*) commission, (*c*) city-manager.

4. (*a*) List five problems or fields of activity encompassed by the urban renewal movement. (*b*) Show how the various levels of government, as well as private organizations, cooperate in this program. (*c*) Summarize the provisions of the *Demonstration Cities Act* of 1966.

5. (*a*) What are the basic provisions of the Economic Opportunity Act of 1964, and of later laws in the "war on poverty" program? (*b*) To what extent has your community taken advantage of this program? (*c*) What have been the accomplishments of this program thus far? What shortcomings have been revealed?

6. Discuss the leading educational problems in your community. What steps are being taken to meet these problems?

7. (*a*) What is meant by a *metropolitan area?* (*b*) Explain how the key problems of American local government today center on the metropolitan area. (*c*) What types of action are being taken to meet these problems?

8. (*a*) List three main sources of city revenues. (*b*) Why are American cities so badly in need of additional revenues? (*c*) How do the state governments and the Federal government aid local governments financially?

9. What are the main types of local government for rural areas in the United States? How do the problems of these areas differ from those of urban areas?

10. (*a*) What are the typical functions performed by the county? (*b*) What county officials carry out these functions?

11. Mention the leading defects of county government. What measures have been proposed or tried in recent years to overcome these defects?

12. Distinguish between the New England town and the township elsewhere in the United States.

13. (*a*) What are the boundaries of the county or township in which you reside? (*b*) What are the duties of its chief officials? (*c*) Can you name the individuals who hold these offices?

14. (*a*) What is an incorporated village? (*b*) What advantages are there in such incorporation?

15. Make a study of the extent to which outside funds have made it possible for your city (or for a city close to your home) to carry out important public improvements. In your opinion, has the money been spent wisely?

16. Make an analysis of the methods used in your city (or in some other city) to develop civic consciousness and to promote greater participation by citizens in city affairs.

17. If you live in or near a rural community, make a study of how conditions in this community have been improved by Federal and state funds.

18. "So, in the township, as in the nation, those who take thought about government are confronted with the problem of reconciling democracy and efficiency." Discuss this statement from Charles A. Beard's *American Government and Politics,* and illustrate its application to rural government.

19. Set up class committees to organize in-depth studies relating to the following questions on your local government:

(a) What special local problems are currently being debated within the community—for example, traffic improvement, air pollution control, water supply, slum clearance, unemployment, illiteracy, and poverty? What different points of view are emerging?

(b) What suggestions have been made recently to improve the functioning of local departments such as police, sanitation, health, education?

(c) What suggestions have been made for changing the form of your local government? What possibilities are there for better distribution and control of the powers and responsibilities of local officials?

(d) The 1970 Census has showed a marked growth of the population of suburban areas, while the population of central (inner) cities has remained relatively constant. What problems may result from this?

Ideas to Think About and Discuss

1. *"The flight of middle class leadership to the suburbs has destroyed the physical tightness of cities, taking with it all sense of community, of common responsibility."*

—DR. YORK WILBERN

2. *"We are the stewards for posterity. We should be true conservatives, abreast of our times, aware of the future, but discarding none of the hard-earned lessons of the past until something definitely better has been found."*

—ROBERT MOSES

3. *"What is novel in it (Federal aid for church-affiliated elementary and secondary schools) and highly significant is the recognition by Congress that religious schools are American schools. That they are an essential part of the American school system. Inasmuch as the religious schools instruct in religion, they cannot be given Federal aid without contravening the First Amendment. But insofar as they provide education which is non-religious, they are entitled to receive Federal aid."*

—WALTER LIPPMANN

4. *"Remorse goes to sleep during a prosperous period and wakes up in adversity."*

—JEAN JACQUES ROUSSEAU

5. *"Our capacity to maintain and develop vital institutions of local self-government may well decide the fate of grass-roots democracy. In so doing, it may ultimately determine the fate of constitutional democracy nationally."* —NORTON E. LONG

6. *"At a time when there are probably more slum dwellers than farmers, it is estimated that we allocate to our cities only one-thirteenth the amount of Federal aid that is allocated to save farms. . . . We spend as much in developing a single space shot as we do in Federal assistance to urban renewal. Yet in many cases we have not found a way to get a man from his home to his place of work in less time than it takes him to orbit the earth. . . . The cities are the dustbowls of the 1960's."* —MAYOR HENRY W. MAIER of Milwaukee

7. *"If ye put a beggar on horseback, ye'll walk yersilf."* FINLEY PETER DUNNE ("Mr. Dooley")

8. *"Let's say you're a mayor who wants a slum-area park and a councilman says, 'I'll vote for it if you'll give my brother a job.' What do you do, stay pure and throw him out of your office, or make a deal to accomplish your purpose?"* —HUEY LONG

9. *We must move toward Federal assumption of the responsibility for income maintenance. It is unfair that taxpayers in New York City paid 12 times as much to support welfare activities as taxpayers in Mississippi."* —JOHN V. LINDSAY

10. *"A major problem confronting our city schools is revenue. This problem cannot be solved without Federal aid."* —JAMES B. CONANT

11. *"Washington made extraordinary efforts to resettle Hungarian refugees in the 1950's and Cuban refugees in the 1960's, but has done almost nothing for Americans driven from their homes by forces no less imperious."* —DANIEL P. MOYNIHAN

12. *"Money should be given to the poor for them to spend as they see fit. Food stamps are degrading."* —ROBERT H. FINCH

CHAPTER 10

What's to Come Is Yours

Toward a Better Society

Achievements on the national level. Despite troubles at home and abroad, our social and governmental system has in recent years chalked up a remarkable record in developing a "more perfect union" and a more viable civilization. Differences between North and South, labor and management, black and white, city and country, rich and poor remain. But through the instrumentality of government—national, state, local—tensions have eased among all these contending groups. If at times our complaints seem to be overwhelmingly loud and intense, it is also at these times that one can see the emergence of an enormous reservoir of energies and good will to protect and project our democratic heritage.

Specifically, what have been the achievements? No basic problem has been fully solved, but there have been significant improvements in many areas. Progress has been made in the battle against poverty in the city and rural slums by means of anti-poverty and housing legislation. The elderly and the sick, long neglected by a predominantly young society, are now to receive more adequate attention under recent amendments to the Social Security laws. The long disenfranchised Negroes in some states have already shown that the new voting rights legislation gives them political power that may be translated into major gains in other areas. The state-church issue, long a barrier to effective Federal aid to elementary and high school education, has been circumvented, thus extending the effective aid to higher education started several years back. Nor should we overlook the various measures adopted to streamline the machinery of government: reapportionment; the 24th and 25th Amendments, the creation of two new Cabinet-rank departments (Housing and Urban Development, and Transportation); the efforts to raise technical and ethical standards of Congressional procedures.

State and local achievements. Meanwhile the states have made substantial progress toward a more equitable distribution of voting power under the Supreme Court's order to redistrict the state legislatures, and as a result of the Voting Rights Acts of 1965 and 1970. Also, they have advanced the Court's desegregation decisions in the broad area of racial equality and civil rights.

Our great cities have also moved to tackle the difficulties created by the massive growth and redistribution of population. They have shown an increasing awareness of the fact that the crucial problem of our vast urban agglomerations is neither crime control, nor traffic unsnarling, nor industrial development, nor fiscal reform (important as these and other individual items may be) but rather, in the broadest sense, the creation of a more livable environment for tens of millions of American families.

Good government, a blessing and a responsibility. It must be clear from all that we have said about the evolution of our democracy, that as government assumes additional obligations and provides new services, it must demand more from its citizens. Accordingly, it imposes a great variety of taxes to meet the constantly mounting costs of the innumerable activities. It prescribes conditions for the exercise of business, trade, and the professions. It expects obedience and loyalty from the individual in peace and in war.

But the individual must not fail to assert his rights firmly to the same degree that he assumes his obligations willingly. Democratic society needs citizens who crusade for causes. It needs citizens who will make themselves heard—who will assemble, talk, and petition for redress of grievances. Each citizen must be willing to serve as a self-appointed watchdog against abuse, corruption, or inefficiency—whether they occur in government or in the many aspects of our associational life, which often give direction to government.

Civil rights and self-interest. Important as it is to assert our individual or collective rights, it is equally important to be concerned about the rights of others. Too often the Bill of Rights is defended actively only by those who have a direct, personal stake in one or more of its provisions. For example, those who make a living out of the communications media are keenly interested in the 1st Amendment. Do they devote as much attention to other traditional American freedoms? Persons likely to be investigated by a governmental agency seem dedicated to the 5th Amendment. Are they also dedicated to the other amendments that make up the Bill of Rights? Extreme "states-righters" insist on the sanctity of the 10th Amendment. Are they as concerned about other parts of the Constitution that safeguard individual rights? The "spirit of liberty," declared the great jurist Learned Hand, "is the spirit which seeks to understand the minds of *other* men and women. The spirit of liberty remembers that not even a sparrow falls to earth unheeded."

" PROCLAIM LIBERTY THROUGHOUT ALL THE LAND AND TO ALL THE INHABITANTS THEREOF."
— LEV. XXV, 10

But there is more unity than meets the eye. We Americans often seem to be more impressed by our problems than by our assets. We talk of the voters' prejudice, apathy, conformity, greed, lack of courage, and so forth. All of these liabilities are very real, but they must be seen in a realistic overall context. If we view the past in perspective, we find images of ingenuity, intelligence, idealism, courage, as these qualities were reflected in events symbolized by such years as 1776, 1789, 1861, 1917, 1941—or in such movements (to confine ourselves to the 20th century) as the Square Deal, the New Freedom, the New Deal, and the New Frontier as it advances under the direction of the Great Society. And, today, there seems to be a growing realization in the nation that no one class, or region, or race can achieve its objectives in isolation from the rest, and that modern science, technology and education are challenging both citizens and institutions to cultivate, in their own interests, a new spirit of cooperation. Neither the Republicans nor the Democrats, for example, now think that they can win the support of a majority of the nation by appealing to sectionalism or factionalism. On a local level, we see the state governors, long the symbol of states' rights and state pride, now forming regional compacts and working together on regional problems that transcend state boundaries.

The trend toward compromise and cooperation on the home front, in spite of occasional and dramatic conflict, has been blurred and sometimes overwhelmed by a contrary trend toward contention, division, and violence in international relations. But this is all the more reason to recognize the progress where it exists.

We still have a private-enterprise economy. All too often, good government (one that attempts to pay attention to the future as well as the present) provokes shrill warnings that "anti-business" or "socialistic" forces have usurped power in Washington or in the state capital. The fact is, except for the special controls necessitated by total war effort, the permanent controls established as an integral part of our economic system leave ample opportunity for individual initiative and growth. The following figures throw light on this point: The number of private businesses operating in the United States at the beginning of 1966 was

The "inevitable collapse of capitalism" as a result of internal weaknesses and "contradictions" is one of the basic dogmas of Marxism. But even orthodox Marxists have come to realize that capitalism, as it operates in the United States and other advanced democratic nations, shows impressive evidence of vigor, growth, and adaptability. A healthy economy that operates in the interests of the great mass of the people is still our best answer to Communist propaganda.

Justus in the *Minneapolis Star*

over 5 million—the highest in our history. Despite the inexorable march toward mergers and absorptions, and despite the increased number of bankruptcies and failures resulting from the economic decline that began late in 1968, the total number of new businesses set up each year exceeds the number that disappear. This seems to reflect faith in the long-term prospects of our economy.

Disagreement is inevitable in a democracy. Frequently, the foreign policies of our government evoke sharp clashes of opinion. Why large-scale foreign aid year after year? Why military intervention into what seem to be the internal affairs of other countries? The spokesmen of our government reply: "The world has shrunk. Whether we like it or not, we are deeply involved in the affairs of other nations all over the world. 'Brushfire wars' may be local today, but they must be extinguished before they spread. We must act out of regard for the long-range interests of our nation." And dissenters retort: "Such policies undermine American values. Excessive preoccupation with foreign problems over a long period of time diverts a nation from the basic sources of its strength, which lie in its domestic life."

We commit mistakes in domestic as well as foreign affairs, but as long as there is free discussion of them, there is a good chance to make corrections before too much damage has been done. The greatest enemy of any society is the enemy *within*—the forces that cause apathy, inertia, and silent despair. This enemy, up to now, we have held at bay, a condition that justifies us in referring proudly to our "open society." We will continue to hold it at bay unless we lapse into the vicious habit of name-calling, such as "You're a John Bircher!" or "You're a Communist!" Let us debate, and let us debate freely, but when we do let us focus on the substance of the issues, without calling personal motives into question.

Both houses of a state legislature based on population? Reorganization of local government to give it the vitality needed to deal with problems of an increasingly urbanized and suburbanized society? Changes in our foreign policy? The status of big business and big labor? All of these issues, and many, many others, must be discussed and decided by Americans in the years ahead. Let us hope that this can be done without undue bitterness and without splitting the population into factions and weakening the underlying basis of national unity.

Political Parties in a Democracy

The origin of political parties in America. In his Farewell Address, President George Washington advised against the formation of political parties. According to him, political parties "enfeeble the public administration ... agitate the community with ill-founded jealousies and false alarms; kindle the animosity of one part against another; foment occasionally riot and insurrection.... They open the door to foreign influence and corruption...." In spite of Washington's condemnation, statesmen like Hamilton and Jefferson set about forming the first parties in our history—the Federalists and the Republicans. They built their parties so well that the Federalist Party has served as the spiritual ancestor of the present-day Republican Party, and the Jeffersonian Republican Party as the direct forerunner of the Democratic Party as we know it today.

Why did these great men differ so diametrically about the role of parties in a democracy? George Washington felt that the young Republic was economically too insecure and militarily too vulnerable to assume the risks of internal disagreement and conflict. Patriotism, he thought, should prompt people to rise above politics and thus create a functioning national unity. But Hamilton and Jefferson were more realistic. They understood better than did the first President that the personal and property interests of some individuals will inevitably clash with those of others, and that in a free society, citizens will organize into groups or parties to safeguard and further their special interests. The individual by himself is all but powerless. Accordingly, he joins with others whose interests he identifies with his own to create an effective political force. In condemning the "factionalism" of parties, Washington did not foresee that in a period of overriding crisis, either internal or external, opposing parties would be able to submerge their differences and work together to promote the national interest.

The "split" between the Federalists and the Republicans shows clearly how different groups in a free society come to espouse different principles and form parties to implement these principles by gaining control of the government. These differences, as they developed in the early years of our national history, are summarized in the tabulation on page 303.

FEDERALISTS	REPUBLICANS
(followers of Hamilton)	*(followers of Jefferson)*
1. Active encouragement by the government of finance, industry, commerce and shipping.	1. A broad diffusion of wealth by favoring the interests of the small farmers, tradesmen and mechanics.
2. Policies favorable to creditor interests.	2. Policies favorable to debtor interests.
3. Advocacy of a strong national government under executive leadership. Hence loose construction of Constitution.	3. Distrust of centralized government. Hence states' rights and strict construction of the Constitution.
4. An inclination to aristocracy, represented by the educated, propertied, "well-born" classes.	4. Faith in the perfectibility of man. Hence vigorous interest in free public education.
5. Distrust of the people's capacity to govern.	5. Confidence in the view that the people, acting through representative institutions, could be left to govern themselves.

Does this political alignment mean that one group was more "virtuous" or "patriotic" than the other? Not at all. It indicates simply an honest disagreement over the kind of society that was best for mankind and over the type of government needed to realize the objectives of such a society. Associated with this were different ideas of the methods and techniques to be used in dealing with social problems—for example, the speed with which changes should be made.

The political party's pyramid of influence. As we have already indicated, political parties are neither recognized nor provided for by the Constitution. Like many other institutions, American political parties have evolved with the times. They are regarded as part of the "unwritten constitution." Nonetheless, parties have become an essential part of the American governmental system.

Just what is a political party? Charles A. Beard aptly described it as "a state within a state." Like a state, a party is equipped with a mechanism of government or control, with a hierarchy of officers, and with a system of rewards and punishments for the faithful and the disloyal.

Each political party is a highly organized pyramid. At the very base of the pyramid is the precinct or district organization. At its head is the precinct or district executive, called the leader or captain. His job is to win a loyal following and "deliver the vote." Above the district leader is the ward chief or executive. His domain comprises several precincts or districts. His club is a popular and powerful center for political and social affairs. His voice is of great influence in the selection of minor candidates. He has important contacts with city or county officials in the dispensation of jobs.

Still higher in the party hierarchy are the city and county committees. Their chairmen and other top executives are powers to reckon with. They are sometimes known by the rather unflattering name of "bosses," but this in itself should not suggest any moral condemnation. They are simply men whose business is politics, and like all successful businessmen, they work at it intensively and even single-mindedly. They have power over the policies and the discipline of the city or county organization or "machine." They control much patronage. They are highly influential in deciding who will sit in the city council and the state

TWO UNREALISTIC VIEWS OF POLITICAL PARTIES

As They Portray Themselves | As The Cynics See Them

PUBLIC SERVICE
IDEALS
PRINCIPLES
"HONESTY IS THE BEST POLICY"

INTERESTS OF PEOPLE
PUBLIC FUNDS
BILL OF RIGHTS
INEFFICIENCY AND WASTE

legislature, and what measures and policies will emerge in those bodies. Under their direction, the "machine" nominates the party's candidates in the primaries. If it succeeds in electing them, the power of the "boss" is immense.

One step higher is the state committee which controls the activities of the party in statewide elections and represents the party in national contests.*

The services performed by political parties. Political parties perform valuable services.

1. By molding vague desires into definite issues and focusing the attention of the voter on them, they serve as an educational force.

2. By uniting discordant factions and sections, thus compelling compromise, they make possible a functioning democratic government.

3. By nurturing men and women of talent within the party organization, they bring to the fore competent candidates for public office.

4. By serving as a critic and gadfly, the opposition party stimulates the party in power to do a better job of administering the government.

5. By keeping an eye on the party in power, the opposition party often discloses to the public unwise measures, wastefulness, inept administration, and on occasion outright dishonesty.

6. Even when the major parties are in agreement on fundamental principles (for example, acceptance of the institutions of a capitalist democracy), they may differ in their conception of what modifications are necessary and at what rate of speed changes should be introduced. One political party may say that we are now going as fast as public opinion, financial capacity, and administrative skill warrant. The other may say, "We're not moving fast enough to meet pressing needs. Full speed ahead!" Thus, the voting public is presented with the basis for a significant choice.

In short, our two-party system provides the opportunity for direct competition between differing points of view. Freedom to make choices is the heart of the democratic process.

* For the role of political parties in national conventions, see pages 90-96.

Political organizations—good or bad? We have enumerated the services performed by political parties. We have pointed to the powers that party functionaries exercise. Whether such services and powers are influences for good or for evil depends in the last analysis on the great mass of citizens. In *The Great Game of Politics*, the late Frank R. Kent put it this way: "Political organizations run politics because of the lack of active interest and clear understanding on the part of the ordinary citizen. This general political inertia, these hazy and confused political ideas, this tendency to think of politics as something low and slimy which ought to be left to the politicians—particularly the primaries—these are things that make the machines possible and powerful. In proportion as the voter becomes interested and informed, the bulk and power of the machine decreases."

Even under the most ideal conditions, the political machine will not simply wither away. There must always be *some* kind of political organization to run the party's affairs throughout the year, to attend to the mechanics of elections, to help to arouse and channel public interest. The question is whether this organization is to be manipulated cynically by a small group of "in-

EXPERT AT RIDING THEM OUT

Carmack in the *Cleveland Plain Dealer*

Political campaigns in the United States are often spirited and even bitter. As the campaign progresses, voices become shriller, and charges and counter-charges are flung about freely. The rival candidates and opposing parties may give the impression of deep distrust and antipathy. But the typical voter, as this cartoon suggests, usually remains quite calm. He knows by experience that the "whirlwind" of partisan talk will subside quickly after the election, and that the victory of either party will not be as disastrous as the opposition usually maintains.

siders," or controlled democratically by active and alert citizens representing the community at large.

Attempts to control campaign expenditures. For many years Congress has attempted to limit contributions and expenditures in political campaigns and to require public disclosure of where the money comes from and how it is spent. Under so-called "corrupt practices acts," the national committee of each major party is now limited to overall expenditures of 3 million dollars in a Presidential campaign. Limitations are also placed on candidates for the Senate and the House, depending on the size of the state or the district. National banks, corporations engaged in interstate commerce, and labor unions may not make contributions to political campaigns. Of course, individuals connected with these organizations may contribute, but there is a ceiling of $5000 for such individual contributions. Public statements of election finances must be made by the national committees of the various parties, by state and local committees when campaigning for national office, and by the candidates. The Hatch Act, as we have noted (page 163), forbids undue pressure in obtaining contributions from Federal job holders. Most of the states have somewhat similar corrupt practices legislation applying to state and local elections. (The Supreme Court has ruled that such controls may also apply to primary elections.)

On the face of it, this may seem to be a rather impressive set of legislative safeguards to prevent abuses in campaign finances. The fact is, however, that knowledgeable observers agree that the statutes now on the books are "more loopholes than law," and organizations and candidates are spending vast sums of money which do not figure in their public reports. This is done without technically violating the law through organization of "independent" campaign committees, over which the candidates and parties nominally have no control. There are other devices such as "testimonial dinners" to candidates or office-holders. On these occasions supporters (lobbyists, big businessmen, and party faithful) may pay as much as $1000 a plate to attend, and the funds raised become available for campaign "war chests."

Experts on political spending report that the total bill for Presidential, state and local compaigns in 1968 came to about $300 million, $100 million more than the previous high in 1964. Nowhere was the high cost of "politicking" more in evidence than in the race for the Presidency. Large sums were spent by would-be nominees in pre-convention phase of the campaign. After the conventions came the campaign itself, waged on a national scale with extensive use of television and other media of mass communication.

In 1970, both houses of Congress passed a bill which would have limited a candidate's spending on radio-TV in Federal elections to 7 cents for each vote in the last comparable election. President Nixon vetoed the bill because he considered it the "wrong answer," although its goals were "widely supported."

Checking machine politics through primary elections. A device by which the individual's vote may be given greater significance is the direct primary. Its original purpose, as we have indicated in Chapter 4, was to put an end to the old political system under which conventions and other party meetings confronted the voter with machine-picked candidates. Voting in regular elections amounted to little more than confirming a slate of hand-picked candidates. Thus one of the most important steps in the election process—the selection of candidates—was in the hands of professional politicians. In 1903, Wisconsin adopted the direct primary on a state-wide scale, and in the next year Oregon followed suit. By 1915, more than two-thirds of the states had adopted it. Today, almost every state has the direct primary. It is used for some or all offices.

Under the direct primary system, the voters nominate by ballot the candidates of their party. Any party member, provided he gets the required number of signatures on his petition and meets other legal requirements, can aspire to a nomination for public office. Each party represented at the primary election has a separate ballot, prepared and administered at public expense. In most states, this privilege is operative only in the case of parties which showed a certain minimum voting strength at the last general election. In most states, also, the arrangement in effect is the *closed primary*—that is, the voter must have previously established a party preference, and he receives at the election only the ballot of that party (or has access only to the voting machine set up for that party). In the *open primary*, the voter can decide at the polls in which party he will vote.

There was a time when it was widely hoped that primary elections would "revitalize" and "purify" American political life. It has not worked out this way in practice, basically perhaps because in most cases voters have failed to turn out in great numbers at the primaries. Thus, the political "professionals" often make the decisions anyway. There have, however, been some notable exceptions in which primary elections have aroused keen interest, motivated much discussion, and brought out heavy votes. Even the unsuccessful aspirants to nomination have an opportunity to present their views to the rank-and-file party members. All of this, certainly, must be considered a "plus" for the democratic process.

Another criticism of the primary is that it involves a would-be candidate in heavy expenses, even before he has begun the regular election campaign. Indeed, the primary may be more costly to the individual than the regular election because, after the nomination has been won, the party organization may be expected to "take over" and, in one way or another, assume most of the costs of conducting the campaign. But in the primary, an aspirant may have to depend on his own resources, or on the generosity of personal friends. Obviously, this gives a considerable advantage to men of wealth. Indeed, it may be said, without undue cynicism, that personal wealth is a distinct asset in launching any kind of political career. It may also be said, without undue naiveté, that men of extremely modest means can be and have been highly successful in political competition.

Primary elections in "one-party states." In sections of the country where one party is clearly dominant, the primary election often becomes much more of a political contest than the regular election. This applies particularly to the Democratic Party in the South. The South, to be sure, is not so "solid" as it once was. The Republican Party is improving its organization there, has carried some states repeatedly in recent Presidential elections, and has succeeded in electing Congressmen from Alabama, Georgia, Virginia, Texas, and other states. The fact remains that in the vast majority of local and statewide elections, the Democratic nomination is practically equivalent to election.

Under such conditions, obviously, political power depends on effective participation in primary elections. Prior to the 1940's, efforts were made in some states to bar Negroes from the Democratic primaries on the grounds that a political party is a "private" organization. This kind of discrimination, however, has been struck down by Supreme Court decisions and civil rights laws. Although the problem is not yet entirely solved, Negroes have been voting in Democratic primary elections throughout the

South in increasing numbers. They have even won nomination and election to such offices as county sheriff—offices which have not been held by Negroes since the Reconstruction.

Meanwhile, it can be said that virtually all qualified observers agree that the South will be far better off politically when it has a functioning two-party system, and when primary elections are normally followed by genuine electoral contests between the candidates of the rival parties.

Single-party systems are not parties at all. In spite of all the imperfections of our multi-party system, the American voter does have a range of significant choices to make. He can join either party of the two major parties. If he wishes, he may give his support to a reform element or a dissident group within the party. Such a group, if it is ably and vigorously directed, may be able to take over control of the party machinery and attempt to put its ideas into effect. A citizen who becomes affiliated with a party is not "bound" to it. He can vote for the opposition party in a particular election, or go over to it entirely whenever he feels that this is desirable. Moreover, if the citizen finds neither

In 1966, Lucius D. Amerson, shown here, was elected Sheriff of Macon County, Alabama—the first black sheriff in that state since Reconstruction. Sheriff Amerson gained this office by entering the primary election of the Democratic Party—and winning it. Since then blacks have won many more important governmental posts (Federal, state, and local) in all parts of the country. In 1970, there were about 400 black elected officials in the states of the Deep South, as compared with 70 in 1965.

of the major parties to his liking, he has the right to join with, or even to help form, a minor party. Every student of American history knows that minor parties have played an important, and on the whole an honorable, part in our national development.

What can the disgruntled citizen do in the Soviet Union, or in Red China, or in the smaller countries under personal dictatorship —countries where only one party is legal? Only one of three things: He can resign himself to his fate. He can lie to his own conscience and convince himself that he is living in the best of all possible worlds. He can try to escape to the outside world, as so many have done.

A glimpse into the one-party system in Red China will make clear why the average citizen there is restricted to the given alternatives noted above. The Communist Party, the official party, serving as the "eyes and ears" of the government, constitutes a tiny fraction of the population. In reality, this single party, whose membership is limited by the acid test of obedience to the rulers in power, is not a political party at all. It is essentially a tool serving the interests of the power élite.

In countries under personal dictatorships (such as the military dictatorships in the Middle East, Africa, the Far East, and Latin America, as well as Yugoslavia, Portugal and Spain), there is also a single party in control. If other parties are tolerated at all, they have been rendered impotent by the dictator and his party in control of the government. This is effected by imprisonment or execution of opposition leaders and by the denial of such civil liberties as free speech and free press—or perhaps simply by the threat to "crack down" ruthlessly if a meaningful opposition develops. The dictators in these countries often describe their rule by such euphemisms as "guided democracy" or "controlled democracy." They begin usually by railing against the weaknesses and delays of "parliamentary squabbling." They end by converting the nation into a huge prison camp.

Conclusion. What are our choices? A multi-party system supported by informed and active citizens to advance progress? A multi-party system under the thumbs of "machine" politicians who, in the long run, may produce corruption and chaos? A single-party system that converts a nation into a huge prison camp?

Most Americans have chosen the first alternative, although there are too many who, inadvertently, subscribe to the second.

As for the third alternative, the single-party system, many nations have succumbed to it and no remaining free nation is immune to it. Walt Whitman made this point clear when he wrote: "There is no week nor day nor hour when tyranny may not enter this country if the people lose their confidence in themselves.... Tyranny may always enter, there is no charm, no bar against it. The only bar against it is a large resolute breed of men."

Public Opinion, Spark Plug in the Democratic Motor

Public opinion defined. Truly democratic government gets its direction from the views, attitudes, and demands of the general public on economic, political, and social questions. This force, called *public opinion*, exerts its pressure in various ways: it directs the citizen's vote; it influences the officials of all branches of government; it brings the great mass of people in touch with the day-to-day functioning of government.

A variety of public opinions. The public is composed of a large number of individuals, grouped according to occupation, income, religion, politics, and other interests. Opinion on public questions naturally varies from one group to another, so that there is seldom a fully united public opinion. There is disagreement even among individuals within the same group.

The "pyramid" of public opinion. In trying to analyze the structure and influence of the various public opinions in our society, some writers have used the metaphor of a pyramid. At the base of the pyramid is the mass public. These people, for the most part, are quiet and passive. They make their voices heard mainly at election time. (Indeed, as we have noted, many of them do not express themselves even then.) A much smaller middle area of the pyramid consists of the so-called "attentive public." This is made up of people who read widely, who belong to political and civic groups, who discuss public affairs with friends and neighbors, and who in general make themselves heard and exert influence on others. Finally, at the apex of the pyramid is the comparatively small group of those who shape public opinion. These include government officials, dominating figures in political parties, newspaper and magazine publishers and well-known writers on these publications, owners of radio and television stations and their newscasters, prominent educators, and leaders of business and labor.

Rebellious youth expresses its opinion. Unfortunately a large segment of young people in America seem to feel that there is no place for them in the "pyramid" of public opinion. According to these youthful "rebels," those at the apex are smug and reluctant to change; those in the middle are hamstrung by inner contradictions and "rationalizing hypocrisy"; those at the base are paralyzed by ignorance and apathy. Viewing the pyramid" as a blind alley leading nowhere, many young Americans had turned to "the street"—that is, to militant action so as to awaken the adult world to its responsibilities. The immediate causes of this action, aside from the deeper ones that have always characterized the "younger generation," have been ascribed to the corrosive social and moral climate engendered by the war in Vietnam; the continuing racial injustice; and the depersonalization resulting from our massive, computerized society.

One thing is certain: Seldom before in recorded history has the younger generation been so concerned, so committed, so active, as this one, in the social issues of the times. From grade school to graduate level, groups of students have been demonstrating their ability to disrupt and even shut down institutions of learning. They have adopted the slogan: "It is very important in your life to do your own thing." As a group, they believe, adult social values are tarnished by inhumanity and injustice.

Rebellious youth can be divided into three groups: the militants; the "hippies" and "flower children"; and the emotionally sick.

The militants are inclined to over-react to a variety of issues. The whites among them, rejecting conventional values and ways, often look upon their schools and colleges as veritable "Bastilles." In their furious hostility, they forget that the seats of learning, in spite of their admitted imperfections, are the last stronghold of the domain of reason in a society that is admittedly in crisis. But their hostility goes beyond the campus. Conscious of their present lack of political power, theirs is essentially a rebellion against adult values. (The same patterns of rebellion have appeared in other countries all over the world.) The blacks among the militants have more specific targets. They want open enrollment in the colleges, special courses, special staffs, special dormitories and other facilities. Although some of their demands have been deemed valid and have been met, a number of prominent Negro leaders (such as Roy Wilkins and Bayard Rustin) question the wisdom of an ethnic nationalism that might isolate the Negro from the mainstream of American life. If *self-assurance* displaces *social insurance*, are not the Negroes in the long run reducing their opportunities to be ready for the real world that will confront them beyond the campus?

The second group is made up of the "hippies and the flower children." They are the quiescent ones whose rebellion takes many forms—drugs, love, gentleness, general passivity. Were it not for their frequent self-debasement, their behavior might be characterized in Emersonian terms as "insolent serenity." Their beards, bangles, and beads more often provoke pity than anger. In somewhat hyperbolic language, one might call the militants the "terrorists" and the hippies and flower children the "nihilists," of the current "revolution." Both these groups, however, are far from "revolutionists" in the classic sense of this term. They are without ideology, without specific programs, without political apparatus. But, unfortunately, their dissents and disruptions have created enough of a stir to open wide the door to countervailing forces that are only too ready to impair democracy in the name of "law and order." Perhaps the granting of suffrage to 18-year-olds, made mandatory by the Voting Act of 1970, may lessen the sense of frustration among the young and, thereby, prevent the growth of militant reaction.

The third group of young people have always been with us, and will continue to be with us as long as mortal flesh is heir to ills and outrage. They are the fragile, the troubled, the anguished, under deep psychological strains. They express their inner problems by taking on the worst characteristics of the adult society against which they are rebelling. They are included here as a safeguard against those of us who are inclined to make quick generalizations.

Response of adult society. Adult opinion in response to youth's rebellion has also varied. There are those who would "crack down," unmindful of the fact that the demands of the rebels are not always unjust; and that, if only from a practical viewpoint, we must consider the fact that they represent a large section of the population. While the vast majority of youth have not joined the ranks of the rebels, sophisticated politicians are mindful of the fact that, by 1973, 55 per cent of all Americans will be under 25 years of age!

Then there are idealists among the adults who forgive, if not admire, the concerns and the commitments of the younger generation. They are likely to recall the lessons parents and teachers gave children a generation ago: that war is terrible; that people are much the same the world over; that civilization cannot be based merely on materialism; that a person should not be judged by his bank account and conformance to "respectable" standards. They are reluctant to blame the young, even though the concepts taught are acted out with terrifying literalness. They contend that rebellious young people, in spite of occasional lapses into violence, are constructively arousing the adult world from its Rip Van Winkle sleep.

The position of the middle-of-the-road adult on the issue of rebellious youth was well expressed by the U.S. Supreme Court in its decision in the case of *Tinker v. Des Moines* (1969). The court upheld the right of students to picket outside their school while wearing black armbands in protest against the Vietnam War. Justice Hugo Black, staunch supporter of civil rights, dissented in a 7-to-2 decision in these words: "This decision is untimely because groups of students all over the land are already running loose, conducting break-ins, sit-ins, lie-ins, and smash-ins." The majority of the Court emphasized that the Constitution does not protect demonstrations when they are disorderly and disruptive, and made it plain that it was approving only demonstrations that do not sabotage normal school life.

"Ask What You Can Do for Your Country!"

The individual citizen is not helpless nor does he have to resort to violence—provided he takes advantage of the opportunities that a democracy puts at his disposal. He can best perform his functions as a political person in the following ways: broadening his education, discussing public affairs with friends, becoming active in a political or civic organization; keeping in touch through letters or telegrams wth government officials; writing letters to the press or to radio-television stations; reading newspapers and magazines (the latter serving as a check on the former); voting, if of age, in every election, including primaries; and running for public office when a suitable opportunity occurs.

Finally, it should be noted that, although we have been using the pronoun "he," all of these duties and opportunities apply to women fully as much as to men. Women more and more are moving into the forefront of American political life, not only as active and intelligent citizens but also as top party officials, as candidates for elective office, and as appointees to administrative and judicial posts on the local, state and Federal levels.

The essence of this thought was expressed in the late President Kennedy's Inaugural Address. We can do no better than to end this book with his memorable words:

> Now the trumpet summons us again—not as a call to bear arms, though arms we need—nor as a call to battle, though embattled we are—but as a call to bear the burden of a long twilight struggle year in and year out, "rejoicing in hope, patient in tribulation"—a struggle against the common enemies of man: tyranny, poverty, disease and war itself. . . . And so, my fellow Americans, ask not what your country can do for you—ask what you can do for your country.

Terms You Should Know

Bipartisan. Involving or representative of both major parties.

Capitalist economy. An economic system based on private enterprise and on the profit motive; distinguished from a *socialist economy.*

Disfranchise. To deprive of the privileges of citizenship, especially of the right to vote.

Extra-constitutional. Outside the Constitution, or not provided for by the Constitution.

Great Society. The program of reform goals set up by President Lyndon B. Johnson; comparable to Kennedy's New Frontier, Truman's Fair Deal, F. D. Roosevelt's New Deal, Wilson's New Freedom, and T. Roosevelt's Square Deal.

Hierarchy. A body of officials or authorities arranged in order of rank. This term, derived from church organization, is now applied to any governmental or quasi-governmental setup.

Machine (political). A term usually applied in a derogatory sense to any highly disciplined political organization headed by a "boss."

Multi-party system. A political system characterized by the existence of more than two strong political parties competing for power.

Ombudsman. An official who is authorized to represent individual citizens with grievances against public officials or agencies. (Swedish in origin.)

Public opinion. The attitude or belief which most people, or any considerable group of people, accept in regard to any particular issue or toward public issues in general.

Socialism. An economic-political system characterized by state (public) ownership of the means of production and distribution.

Socialistic. Similar to or smacking of socialism; a term usually employed in a derogatory sense.

Stereotype. An image or preconceived idea fixed in the mind of a person or of a large number of persons. A common example is stereotypes relating to persons who belong to various racial and national groups. (Also called a *cliché*.)

Totalitarian. Said of a highly centralized government which seeks to control all important aspects of life and refuses to grant recognition or representation to any opposing political forces.

Voluntary associational life. Organizational activities conducted on a non-compulsory, non-governmental level. Includes churches, labor unions, professional societies, chambers of commerce, fraternal orders, clubs, etc.

Questions and Problems Based on the Text

1. (*a*) List what you consider the outstanding achievements of the Federal government within the past three years. (*b*) Do the same for your state and local governments. (*c*) In what respects, if any, did each of these levels of government fail to measure up to its responsibilities and opportunities?

2. "Good government is both a blessing and a responsibility." What is meant by this?

3. In your own words, explain the quotation on page 299 from Judge Learned Hand.

4. How does our society represent the ideal of "unity in diversity"?

5. Trace the origin of political parties in the United States.

6. Describe the structure of a major political party today.

7. Discuss the services performed by a political party.

8. What is meant by *party machines*? What evils may result from excessive domination by such machines? What can individual citizens do to prevent this?

9. "Under a so-called single-party system, there are really no political parties at all!" Comment on this statement.

10. (*a*) Define *public opinion.* (*b*) How is it controlled or influenced? (c) How is it measured?

11. Cite examples of the influence of "special interests" in your community.

12. How can the individual citizen make his influence felt?

13. Describe three types of citizens whom you have recognized in your community. Which of these types do you consider most valuable or constructive? Which do you consider least valuable? Explain.

14. Write to the Friends Committee on National Legislation, 104 "C" Street, N.E., Washington 2, D.C. for their informative pamphlet *Beliefs Into Action.* Also write to the nearest office of the League of Women Voters for their publications.

15. Discuss the statement: "American political life as we know it owes its origins to the profound differences which developed inside George Washington's cabinet between Thomas Jefferson and Alexander Hamilton. The Federalist party grew out of Hamiltonian financial and economic concepts. Thomas Jefferson deliberately built what was then called the Republican party for the purpose of thwarting 'Hamiltonianism'."

16. Can you give examples of new governmental policies which have arisen as the result of activity on the part of public interest groups?

17. Title VI of the Civil Rights Act of 1964 bans racial discrimination in any Federally assisted enterprises, such as housing projects. Do you know of any projects in your community that have been affected by application of Title VI? Explain.

18. In many recent cases the Supreme Court has tried to defend the rights of persons accused of crimes. It has been concerned particularly to make sure that even poor and friendless persons enjoy the full protection of the law. The charge has been made that the Court, however good its intention in these cases, has been giving an undue advantage to criminals and "tying the hands" of law-enforcement officials.

Comment on this dispute. Do you think that the ever-growing crime rate may give some effective ammunition to critics of the Court? On the other hand bear in mind Benjamin Franklin's dictum to the effect that "those who would give up essential liberty to purchase a little temporary safety deserve neither liberty nor safety."

19. There has been growing discussion lately of the need for machinery to handle complaints lodged by the public against the police.

(*a*) Do you favor establishing a non-judicial civilian "review board" independent of police authority?

(*b*) Do you favor establishing a review board which would ultimately be subject to police control? In such an arrangement, a board composed of 4 civilians and 3 policemen could only investigate complaints and make recommendations to the police commissioner, who might or might not accept them at his discretion.

(*c*) Do you favor the Swedish system of *ombudsman*, in which a citizen with a complaint can bring his grievance to the attention of an official (the ombudsman) empowered to investigate the matter and make recommendations?

(*d*) Do you favor using such review boards or ombudsmen in handling complaints voiced against other public servants, such as prison authorities, welfare officers, public housing officials, and public school teachers? Why?

Ideas to Think About and Discuss

1. *"Governments, like clocks, go from the motion men give them, so by them they are ruined, too."*

—WILLIAM PENN

2. *"... for I say at the core of democracy, finally, is the religious element. All religions, old and new, are there."*

—WALT WHITMAN

3. *"Life is not a having and a getting; but a being and becoming."*

—MATTHEW ARNOLD

4. *"The concept of the neighborhood school is dead. The new concept is excellence for all schools."*

—KENNETH B. CLARK

5. *"The two-party system is a reflection of the competitive system in American business and industry. A one-party state is a political monopoly."*

—JOSEPH C. HARSCH

6. *"A poor guy can come along and have great qualifications and you put him in against a rich guy who doesn't know the time and it's no contest. What are we going to do—have only rich guys running our lives?"*

—KENNETH O'DONNELL

7. "Not the violent conflict between parts of the truth, but the quiet suppression of half of it, is the formidable evil; there is always hope when people are forced to listen to both sides; it is when they attend only to one that errors harden into prejudices, and truth itself ceases to have the effect of truth, by being exaggerated into falsehood."

—JOHN STUART MILL

8. "Those who encourage minority groups to believe that the United States Constitution and Federal laws give them a right to patrol and picket in the streets whenever they choose, in order to advance what they think to be a just and noble end, do no service to those minority groups, their cause, or their country."

— SUPREME COURT JUSTICE HUGO L. BLACK

9. "The pseudo-conservative is a man who, in the name of upholding traditional American values and institutions and defending them against more or less fictitious dangers, consciously or unconsciously aims at their abolition."

—T. W. ADORNO

10. "The tragedy of our day is the climate of fear in which we live, and fear always breeds repression. Too often sinister threats to the Bill of Rights are concealed under the patriotic cloak of anti-communism. Patriotism is not the fear of something, it is the love of something. It is the love of the ideals of liberty of man and of mind in which this Republic was born and to which it is dedicated."

—ADLAI STEVENSON

11. "Our two-party system works when there is a consensus majority in the center. Now (1970) our majority is at both ends. We are, therefore, in trouble."

—JAMES A. MICHENER

12. "It is only when society acknowledges it (the Bill of Rights) as a right and backs it by the power of the state and the respect of the majority of its responsible citizens that the right exists."

—VICE PRESIDENT SPIRO T. AGNEW

SUMMARY TEST ON AMERICAN GOVERNMENT

Select the item that best completes each of the following statements or answers the question:

1. The United States Senate differs from the House of Representatives in that (a) the Senate is continuously in session (b) a two-thirds vote is required to pass bills in the Senate (c) one-third of the Senate is elected every two years (d) Senators must be native-born

2. The process of amending the Constitution is (a) part of our unwritten law (b) patterned after English practice (c) based on a decision of the United States Supreme Court (d) provided for in the Constitution itself

3. Which of these quotations is from the Declaration of Independence? (a) "Nor shall any person ... be deprived of life, liberty, or property without due process of law." (b) "Frame such just and equal laws ... as shall be thought most meet and convenient for the general good." (c) "They are endowed by their Creator with certain unalienable rights." (d) "To form a more perfect union."

4. After a bill has been introduced into either house of Congress, usually it is first (a) signed by the presiding officer of that house (b) debated by members of that house (c) referred to a committee of that house (d) considered by a joint committee representing both houses

5. Which of the following is basic to the idea of a federal system of government? (a) division of powers between national and state governments (b) creation of a strong Executive branch (c) distribution of powers between the Senate and the House of Representatives (d) establishment of an independent Supreme Court

6. Who checks the President's treaty-making power? (a) the House of Representatives (b) the United States Supreme Court (c) the Senate (d) the state legislatures

7. Members of the President's Cabinet remain in office (a) for a term of four years (b) for a term fixed by the House of Representatives (c) at the pleasure of the Senate (d) at the pleasure of the President

8. By consulting the Federal Constitution, one can find out (a) how a political party may get its name on the ballot (b) whether treaties must be ratified by a power outside the Executive branch (c) how many members are in the President's Cabinet (d) all about the qualifications for voting

9. According to the Constitution, Congress is required to meet (a) twice a year (b) annually (c) once every two years (d) only when called into session by the President

10. Freedom of the press is guaranteed by the (a) Preamble to the Constitution (b) Declaration of Independence (c) 1st Amendment (d) Zenger case decision

11. The Bill of Rights provides that (a) "the accused shall enjoy the right to a ... trial by an impartial jury" (b) the Constitution shall "secure the blessings of liberty to ourselves and our posterity" (c) "all men are created equal" (d) "all persons born or naturalized in the United States ... are citizens of the United States"

12. According to the Constitution of the United States, new states may be admitted into the Union by (a) Congress (b) the President (c) the legislature of the territory concerned (d) a vote of the state legislatures in convention

13. The Constitution provided long terms for Federal judges in order to (a) make the job attractive to persons who seek economic security (b) make it easier to render decisions without political influence (c) lessen the burdens of the President (d) enable judges to gain a great deal of experience

14. What was the chief reason for adoption of a bicameral system by the Constitutional Convention of 1787? It (a) created more jobs for officeholders (b) satisfied both the small and the large states (c) was a common practice among the colonial governments (d) was practised by the former mother country

15. The Bill of Rights refers to (a) the 1st Amendment (b) the first ten amendments (c) all the amendments (d) the Declaration of Independence

16. The "supreme law of the land" is embodied in the (a) checks-and-balances system (b) Declaration of Independence (c) Constitution and laws of the United States (d) state constitutions and laws passed by state legislatures

17. Officials appointed by the President must be approved by the (a) Supreme Court (b) House of Representatives (c) local governments (d) Senate

18. An example of powers exercised concurrently is the power to (a) levy income taxes (b) coin money (c) pass marriage and divorce laws (d) regulate interstate commerce

19. Which best describes the government of the United States? (a) centralized republic (b) bureaucracy (c) confederation (d) federal republic

20. Powers specifically granted to Congress are often called (a) concurrent (b) reserved (c) implied (d) expressed

21. The report, *Smoking and Health,* made by the Advisory Committee to the Surgeon General of the United States, (a) was approved by the Tobacco Institute (b) indicted cigarette smoking as a "health hazard" (c) recommended smoking of pipes and cigars (d) empowered the Federal Trade Commission to fix prices

22. Which Supreme Court decision justified the use of the implied powers clause by Congress? (a) *McCulloch vs. Maryland* (b) *Dartmouth College vs. Woodward* (c) *Marbury vs. Madison* (d) *Brown vs. Topeka Board of Education*

23. Which is the implied powers clause? (*a*) "To lay and collect taxes, duties, imposts and excises." (*b*) "To promote the progress of science and the useful arts." (*c*) "To make all laws which shall be necessary and proper for carrying into execution the foregoing powers." (*d*) "To regulate commerce."

24. What was the importance of the Dartmouth College Case? (*a*) John Marshall wrote the opinion for the majority. (*b*) It declared an act of a state legislature unconstitutional because it was contrary to the Federal Constitution. (*c*) Daniel Webster was one of the lawyers in this case. (*d*) Institutions of higher learning were thereafter free of supervision by the states.

25. "All persons born or naturalized in the United States, and subject to the jurisdiction thereof, are citizens of the United States and of the state wherein they reside" is a quotation from the (*a*) 24th Amendment (*b*) 14th Amendment (*c*) 15th Amendment (*d*) 25th Amendment

26. What are a Congressman's "constituents"? (*a*) the people he appoints to office (*b*) the people he represents (*c*) his official papers (*d*) his constitutional rights

27. Which is an example of the use of an "implied" power of Congress? (*a*) establishing a postal service (*b*) providing for an army, navy, and air force (*c*) granting copyrights and patents (*d*) setting up a Federal Reserve System

28. Which of these is levied only by the state (or local) governments? (*a*) inheritance tax (*b*) gasoline tax (*c*) general property tax (*d*) income tax

29. What proportion of the votes of the Justices is required for a decision by the United States Supreme Court? (*a*) majority (*b*) unanimity (*c*) three-fourths (*d*) two-thirds

30. Progressive efforts to improve municipal government included all of the following *except* (*a*) the adoption of the commission form of government (*b*) the adoption of the city-manager form of government (*c*) a revival of the town meeting on a city-wide level (*d*) reforms in the mayor-council type of government

31. All of the following represent a democratic trend *except* (*a*) the "one man, one-vote" rule (*b*) the President's frequent press interviews (*c*) the *Brown vs. Topeka Board of Education* decision (*d*) the lengthening of terms of office of state legislatures

32. What significant contribution to the law-making process is made by the committee system in Congress? (*a*) It reduces lobbying to a minimum. (*b*) It eliminates the filibuster. (*c*) It makes possible more careful consideration of bills. (*d*) It reduces the amount of time consumed by debates.

33. The place designated in each election district for registering and voting is called a (*a*) caucus (*b*) ward (*c*) party machine (*d*) polling place

34. Which is *not* true of the Packaging and Labeling Act of 1966? (*a*) The Secretary of Commerce is authorized to fix prices of standard brands. (*b*) It provides for clear and uniform labeling, giving contents in ounces, pounds or liquid measures. (*c*) It permits Federal officials to regulate size and descriptions, such as "giant," "economy size." (*d*) Such promotional devices as "save" and "cents off" are not permitted on labels.

35. A person who votes illegally in more than one election district, or in an election district not his own, is known commonly in American politics as a (*a*) preferential voter (*b*) floater (*c*) write-in voter (*d*) dark horse

36. The right to keep a position in governmental employ as long as duties are carried out satisfactorily and the position is needed is called (*a*) unclassified service (*b*) tenure (*c*) provisional appointment (*d*) probationary period

37. All of the following statements about the various levels of government are true *except:* (*a*) The role of the Cabinet under our system of government is significantly different from its role under the British parliamentary system. (*b*) A metropolitan area includes only the area of a single incorporated city. (*c*) Although the powers and responsibilities of the Federal government have grown, the states are still important. (*d*) "Due process of law" must apply to the lowest as well as the highest courts.

38. Who determines whether a person elected to the lower house of Congress is qualified to take his seat? (*a*) the Senate (*b*) the United States Supreme Court (*c*) the House of Representatives (*d*) the legislature of his home state

39. Which of the following has the authority to grant a passport for travel in a foreign country? (*a*) the Secretary of Defense (*b*) the United States Secretary of State (*c*) the United States Secretary of Commerce (*d*) the Secretary of State of the state in which the applicant resides

40. Which is most essential to a democracy? (*a*) a one-house legislature (*b*) a cabinet system of government (*c*) free elections (*d*) an unwritten constitution

41. By what means does Congress *most effectively* control the activities of the Executive departments of the Federal government? (*a*) by Senate and House committees (*b*) by creating agencies under administrative heads (*c*) by challenging the heads of departments when they appear before committees (*d*) by controlling appropriations

42. Which of the following best describes the most important function of our diplomatic officials abroad? (*a*) to act as guides to American tourists (*b*) to discover business opportunities for American investors (*c*) to keep the the Secretary of State informed about conditions in other countries (*d*) to approve the passports of aliens planning to migrate to the United States

43. Which of the following is the greatest hindrance to the development of sound public opinion? (*a*) Political problems are beyond the intelligence of the average citizen. (*b*) The average person has no time to inform himself on governmental issues. (*c*) The mass of people form their opinions on the basis of emotion, not fact. (*d*) Officials have shown a growing disregard for public opinion.

44. The major purpose of the Bill of Rights in the Constitution of the United States is to (*a*) protect the states against encroachment by the Federal government (*b*) protect the liberties of the individual against undue interference by the Federal government (*c*) protect local governments against state governments (*d*) protect the small states

45. The chief purpose of the committee system in Congress is to (*a*) make possible consideration of the merits of a bill by experts (*b*) reward the majority party (*c*) effectuate closer cooperation between Congress and the Executive branch (*d*) reduce expenses of government

46. Which of these statements best describes recent trends in the office of state governor? (*a*) He is gradually losing power. (*b*) His power to grant pardons and parole has been shifted to the state courts. (*c*) His term of office is being shortened. (*d*) Like the President, his powers are growing at the expense of the legislature.

47. What is the primary function of the "conference committee" employed in the Federal government? (*a*) to settle differences between the President and Congress (*b*) to hold weekly conferences with the Speaker and the presiding officer of the Senate (*c*) to resolve differences between the major parties in Congress (*d*) to eliminate differences between the Senate and the House on the provisions of a bill

48. How did the amendment ratified between 1950 and 1960 alter the Federal Constitution? It (*a*) extended voting rights in the District of Columbia (*b*) fixed the terms of the President, Vice President and Congress (*c*) created presidential electors for the District of Columbia (*d*) provided that no person shall be elected to the office of President more than twice

49. The principal effect of the 13th and 14th Amendments to the Federal Constitution has been to (*a*) streamline the office of President (*b*) limit the powers of the Supreme Court (*c*) widen the participation of people in their government (*d*) preserve states' rights

50. Which statement applies to the governments of both Great Britain and the United States? (*a*) Members of the lower house of the legislature are elected directly by the voters. (*b*) Cabinet members may introduce bills in the legislature. (*c*) The Chief Executive may be removed from office by impeachment. (*d*) The courts decide on the constitutionality of any law passed by the legislature.

51. The Constitution of the United States prohibits the passage of a bill of attainder. The effect of this prohibition is that a citizen is guaranteed (*a*) a trial (*b*) the right to vote (*c*) the right to bear arms (*d*) freedom of religion

52. The idea that the Constitution of the United States provides for a central government of limited sovereign power is supported by the (a) exercise of residual powers by the states (b) use of implied powers by Congress (c) grant of military power to the President of the United States (d) right of judicial review of lower court decisions by the United States Supreme Court

53. The ideal of *direct* democracy is best exemplified by (a) manhood suffrage (b) the initiative and referendum (c) the city manager form of government (d) the commission form of government

54. Patents and copyrights give individuals and corporations who receive them (a) unlimited control of a product (b) control of the product for a limited length of time (c) public grants to make manufacturing profitable (d) immunity from antitrust laws

55. Before a Federal income tax could be levied, which clause in the United States Constitution had to be changed? (a) "... a tax or duty may be imposed on such importation, not exceeding ten dollars for each person." (b) "No capitation or other direct tax shall be laid, unless in proportion to the census...." (c) "... all duties, imposts and excises shall be uniform throughout the United States...." (d) "No state shall, without the consent of the Congress, lay any imposts or duties on imports or exports...."

56. The decision to embark on a space program is an example of Congress' use of (a) implied powers (b) police powers (c) concurrent powers (d) reserved powers

57. Which action required a two-thirds vote of the United States Senate to become effective? (a) declaration of war against Japan in 1941 (b) appointment of Earl Warren as Chief Justice of the United States Supreme Court (c) ratification of the Nuclear Test Ban Treaty in 1963 (d) President Truman's removal of General Douglas MacArthur from his Far Eastern command

58. The President may exercise all of the following powers during a war *except* (a) suspend the writ of *habeas corpus* (b) establish a blockade (c) declare war against another enemy nation (d) issue executive orders that fix wages and prices

59. The power of the United States Supreme Court to nullify acts of Congress and of state legislatures was (a) enacted by Congress (b) provided for by an amendment to the Constitution (c) established by early decisions of the Supreme Court (d) specifically granted in the original Constitution

60. All of the following tend to provide for more direct participation of the people in political affairs, *except* (a) home rule (b) a multi-party system (c) initiative (d) filibuster

61. Which Federal agency is not concerned with solving problems of the nation's economic welfare? (a) Federal Deposit Insurance Corporation (b) U. S. Tariff Commission (c) Federal Bureau of the Budget (d) Civil Service Commission

62. Which is the *weakest* reason for strengthening state and local governments? (*a*) Decentralized government permits a variety of values, thus protecting legitimate minority and regional interests. (*b*) Healthy state and local government increases citizen participation. (*c*) Historically, the Federal government is the creature of the states. (*d*) State and local governments provide a source of strength for the party out of power at the national level and thus contribute to meaningful two-party politics.

63. "We have reached the point as a nation when we must take action to save the Constitution from the Court and the Court from itself. We want a Supreme Court which will do justice *under* the Constitution, not *over* it." It is a reasonable assumption that the speaker wanted to (*a*) abolish the Court (*b*) abolish judicial review (*c*) curb some of the Court's powers (*d*) enhance the powers of the Court

64. The "one man, one vote" rule of the Supreme Court (*a*) increased the representation of rural areas (*b*) voided state laws on voting qualifications (*c*) strengthened urban representation (*d*) applied only to reapportionment of Congressional districts

65. What Federal agency was *not* absorbed by the Department of Transportation? (*a*) Federal Aviation Agency (*b*) Federal Maritime Administration (*c*) U. S. Coast Guard (*d*) Civilian Aviation Board

66. Which of the following is *not* a proposed reform which has had considerable effect in recent years: (*a*) a four-year term for Representatives (*b*) home rule for the District of Columbia (*c*) restrictions on the power and prestige of the U. S. Senate (*d*) appointment of judges by the governor or mayor, utilizing the advice of a judicial council or bar association

67. Which statement about lobbying is *wrong*? (*a*) The Federal Regulation of Lobbying Act (1946) requires lobbyists to register and file financial reports with both houses of Congress. (*b*) Lobbies are legitimate expressions of organized citizens exercising their constitutional right of petition. (*c*) The compensation of lobbyists is limited by law. (*d*) In a pluralistic society, such as that of the United States, it is inevitable that various groups will attempt to influence legislation.

68. The term "Watchdog of the Treasury" is applied to the (*a*) FBI (*b*) Bureau of the Budget (*c*) White House Office (*d*) General Accounting Office

69. At an impeachment trial of the President of the United States, the presiding officer is the (*a*) Chief Justice of the United States (*b*) majority leader of the Senate (*c*) Vice President of the United States (*d*) Speaker of the House

70. What is *not* true of the National Labor Relations Board? (*a*) It supervises collective bargaining in labor disputes. (*b*) It upholds the right of the worker to join unions. (*c*) It encourages "right to work" laws. (*d*) It believes in the open shop.

71. Which of the following methods of financing political campaigns would probably be favored by most students of government? (*a*) large contributions by corporations and labor unions (*b*) a special tax placed on all voters (*c*) allotments made to the parties from public funds (*d*) relatively small contributions made by large numbers of citizens on a voluntary basis

72. Which statement would be most *difficult* to prove, using objective or factual data? (*a*) Franklin D. Roosevelt was elected four times. (*b*) The seniority rule in the operation of Congressional committees subverts their democratic functioning. (*c*) The Senate of the United States is composed of more persons of political experience than those in the House. (*d*) The Supreme Court of the United States is the highest judicial tribunal in the country.

73. Which is more characteristic of a dictatorship than of a democratic society? (*a*) respecting the rights of the individual (*b*) indoctrinating the youth of the nation with unquestioned loyalty to those in power (*c*) free elections (*d*) insuring a legal succession to office

74. Which is more characteristic of a democratic society than of a dictatorship? (*a*) single political party system (*b*) establishment of a system of nation-wide espionage (*c*) respecting the guarantees of personal liberty (*d*) glorification of those in power

75. According to the Federal Constitution, the House of Representatives has the sole power to (*a*) approve appointments (*b*) impeach Federal officials (*c*) override presidential vetoes (*d*) make laws

76. According to the Federal Constitution, the United States Senate has the sole power to (*a*) ratify treaties (*b*) vote on tariff bills (*c*) conduct investigations (*d*) declare war

77. According to a law of Congress, the person next to the President and the Vice President in line of succession is the (*a*) Secretary of State (*b*) Speaker of the House (*c*) Secretary of the Treasury (*d*) President pro tempore of the Senate

78. The persons who usually exercise greatest control over the making of Federal laws are (*a*) members of the President's Cabinet (*b*) members of Federal boards and commissions (*c*) Congressional committee members (*d*) lobbies

79. What two amendments to the Federal Constitution have the segregationists and the anti-segregationists invoked respectively? (*a*) 1st and 5th (*b*) 13th and 14th (*c*) 14th and 15th (*d*) 10th and 14th

80. Which of the following powers does the President *not* have? (*a*) He speaks for the whole nation on matters of foreign policy. (*b*) He has responsibility for "full employment." (*c*) He is the head of his political party. (*d*) He renders decisions when the Supreme Court is deadlocked.

81. How are amendments to the Federal Constitution ratified? (*a*) by a two-thirds majority of the voters (*b*) by a majority of Congress (*c*) by three-fourths of the states (*d*) by Executive ordinances

82. Which of the following is a power granted to Congress? (a) to regulate all labor problems (b) to legislate on divorce (c) to control interstate commerce (d) to legislate the curricula of the public schools and colleges of the nation

83. Which is an example of the "unwritten Constitution"? (a) Presidential electors vote, usually, for their party candidate. (b) Each state has two Senators. (c) The Senate has the power to confirm appointments of the President. (d) All revenue bills originate in the House of Representatives.

84. What vote is necessary for a bill to become a law over the veto of the President? (a) two-thirds vote of Congress (b) a majority vote of the Supreme Court (c) three-fourths of Congress (d) three-fourths of the Senate

85. Which of the following statements best describes a federal system of government? (a) All the powers are concentrated in the central or national government. (b) The states are supreme. (c) There is a system of cabinet or ministerial responsibility. (d) Powers are divided, however unequally, between the national or central government and the state governments.

86. According to the 10th Amendment to the Federal Constitution, the powers not delegated to the United States by the Constitution, nor prohibited by it to the states, are reserved to (a) Congress (b) the Supreme Court (c) the President with the advice and consent of the Senate (d) the states

87. Where, besides the 5th Amendment, does the clause "nor shall be deprived of life, liberty, or property, without due process of law" occur? (a) Article I (b) the 14th Amendment (c) the 1st Amendment (d) Article III

88. The Constitutional Convention of 1787 created a government in which (a) powers are shared among separate coordinate branches (b) each separate branch has unrestricted authority in its own field (c) the Executive branch is dominant over the other two (d) the states exist only as creatures of the Federal government

89. When is the President Commander-in-Chief of the Army, Navy and Air Force? (a) at all times (b) only during a war (c) only when the Chief of Staff is abroad (d) only by special act of Congress

90. What do we mean when we speak of the "dual system" of the United States government? (a) Both the United States Senate and the House of Representatives have independent powers. (b) The President appoints Cabinet officers with the consent of the Senate. (c) Treaties made by the President must be ratified by the United States Senate. (d) Each of the fifty states has powers independent of the powers exercised by the Federal government.

91. Which is the *least* valuable service of political parties in a democracy? (a) It selects candidates for public office. (b) The party out of power keeps an eye on the party in power. (c) It distributes patronage. (d) It helps get out the vote.

92. Which of these statements about the writ of *habeas corpus* is *not* true? (*a*) Its chief purpose is to insure that no person shall be kept in prison without a trial. (*b*) It may be suspended when, in cases of rebellion or invasion, the public safety may require it. (*c*) The danger of its suspension is that innocent persons may be kept in prison. (*d*) When served, it at once releases a person from custody.

93. Which of these statements is true about the 15th Amendment? (*a*) It gives the right to vote to all citizens. (*b*) It says that all male citizens have the right to vote. (*c*) It says that no person shall be deprived of the right to vote on account of race, color, or previous condition of servitude. (*d*) It says that no person shall be deprived of the right to vote on account of race, color, creed, or previous condition of servitude.

94. Which of the following best describes an injunction? (*a*) a stoppage of work in violation of a contract (*b*) the refusal of a group of people, such as a union or consumers' organization, to make public its membership rolls (*c*) a court order commanding an individual, an employer, or a union to refrain from performing certain acts which the court considers harmful to the property rights of the employer, the union, or other parties. (*d*) the same as writ of *certiorari*

95. What is meant by a "graduated" income tax? (*a*) Income taxes are adjusted to the cost of living. (*b*) The larger a man's income, the greater the percentage he must pay in taxes. (*c*) Income taxes are withheld by the employer. (*d*) It is a regressive tax.

96. What is the chief source of Federal revenue today? (*a*) individual and corporate income taxes (*b*) excise taxes (*c*) sale of bonds (*d*) inheritance taxes

97. To whom did Supreme Court Justice Oliver Wendell Holmes, Jr. believe free speech should be denied? (*a*) to no one at any time (*b*) to aliens (*c*) to radicals of the right and left (*d*) to anyone, if what he said or wrote presented a clear and present danger to the nation

98. Which department of the Cabinet is most concerned with slum clearance? The (*a*) Department of Transportation (*b*) Department of Housing and Urban Development (*c*) Department of the Interior (*d*) Department of Labor

99. Why have Congressional investigating committees been the object of considerable criticism? (*a*) They investigated Communist infiltration in Federal employment, entertainment, and education. (*b*) Congress has no business investigating anybody for any reason. (*c*) Some committees have been accused of ignoring the standards of due process of law. (*d*) They found racketeering in labor unions.

100. The Supreme Court in *Brown vs. Topeka Board of Education* ruled that (*a*) segregated educational systems can never be truly equal (*b*) a system of separate but equal educational facilities is possible (*c*) education is not the concern of the Federal government (*d*) the students in the public schools of the nation were being poorly taught

CONSTITUTION OF THE UNITED STATES OF AMERICA

The literal text of the United States Constitution is given below. The brief phrases which introduce the various articles and sections are not part of the original document and are included here only for convenience.

All material included in brackets, [ ], is no longer in effect. In most cases, footnotes indicate how these provisions have been superseded.

PREAMBLE

We, the people of the United States, in order to form a more perfect union, establish justice, insure domestic tranquillity, provide for the common defence, promote the general welfare, and secure the blessings of liberty to ourselves and our posterity, do ordain and establish this CONSTITUTION for the United States of America.

ARTICLE I—THE LEGISLATIVE BRANCH

Section 1—Makeup of Congress

All legislative powers herein granted shall be vested in a Congress of the United States, which shall consist of a Senate and House of Representatives.

Section 2—The House of Representatives

1. The House of Representatives shall be composed of members chosen every second year by the people of the several States, and the electors in each State shall have the qualifications requisite for electors of the most numerous branch of the State Legislature.

2. No person shall be a Representative who shall not have attained to the age of twenty-five years, and been seven years a citizen of the United States, and who shall not, when elected, be an inhabitant of that State in which he shall be chosen.

3. Representatives and direct taxes shall be apportioned among the several States which may be included within this Union, according to their respective numbers, [which shall be determined by adding to the whole number of free persons, including those bound to service for a term of years, and excluding Indians not taxed, three-fifths of all other persons.][1] The actual enumeration shall be made within three years after the first meeting of the Congress of the United States, and within every subsequent term of ten years, in such manner as they shall by law direct. The number of Representatives shall not exceed one for every thirty thousand, but each State shall have at least one Representative; [and until such enumeration shall be made, the State of New

[1] Superseded by the 13th and 14th Amendments.

Hampshire shall be entitled to choose three, Massachusetts eight, Rhode Island and Providence Plantations one, Connecticut five, New York six, New Jersey four, Pennsylvania eight, Delaware one, Maryland six, Virginia ten, North Carolina five, South Carolina five, and Georgia three.]

4. When vacancies happen in the representation from any State, the Executive authority thereof shall issue writs of election to fill such vacancies.

5. The House of Representatives shall choose their Speaker and other officers; and shall have the sole power of impeachment.

Section 3—The Senate

1. The Senate of the United States shall be composed of two Senators from each state, [chosen by the legislature thereof],[2] for six years, and each Senator shall have one vote.

2. Immediately after they shall be assembled in consequence of the first election, they shall be divided as equally as may be into three classes. The seats of the Senators of the first class shall be vacated at the expiration of the second year, of the second class at the expiration of the fourth year, of the third class at the expiration of the sixth year, so that one-third may be chosen every second year; [and if vacancies happen by resignation or otherwise, during the recess of the legislature of any State, the Executive thereof may make temporary appointments until the next meeting of the legislature, which shall then fill such vacancies.][3]

3. No person shall be a Senator who shall not have attained to the age of thirty years, and been nine years a citizen of the United States, and who shall not, when elected, be an inhabitant of that State for which he shall be chosen.

4. The Vice-President of the United States shall be President of the Senate, but shall have no vote, unless they be equally divided.

5. The Senate shall choose their other officers, and also a President *pro tempore*, in the absence of the Vice-President, or when he shall exercise the office of President of the United States.

6. The Senate shall have the sole power to try all impeachments. When sitting for that purpose, they shall be on oath or affirmation. When the President of the United States is tried, the Chief Justice shall preside: and no person shall be convicted without the concurrence of two-thirds of the members present.

[2] Superseded by the 17th Amendment.

[3] Superseded by the 17th Amendment.

7. Judgment in cases of impeachment shall not extend further than to removal from office, and disqualification to hold and enjoy any office of honor, trust or profit under the United States: but the party convicted shall nevertheless be liable and subject to indictment, trial, judgment and punishment, according to law.

Section 4—Elections and Meetings of Congress

1. The times, places and manner of holding elections for Senators and Representatives shall be prescribed in each State by the legislature thereof; but the Congress may at any time by law make or alter such regulations, except as to the places of choosing Senators.

2. The Congress shall assemble at least once in every year, [and such meeting shall be on the first Monday in December, unless they shall by law appoint a different day.]⁴

Section 5—Powers and Duties of Congress

1. Each house shall be the judge of the elections, returns and qualifications of its own members, and a majority of each shall constitute a quorum to do business; but a smaller number may adjourn from day to day, and may be authorized to compel the attendance of absent members, in such manner, and under such penalties, as each house may provide.

2. Each house may determine the rules of its proceedings, punish its members for disorderly behavior, and with the concurrence of two-thirds, expel a member.

3. Each house shall keep a journal of its proceedings, and from time to time publish the same, excepting such parts as may in their judgment require secrecy; and the yeas and nays of the members of either house on any question shall, at the desire of one-fifth of those present, be entered on the journal.

4. Neither house, during the session of Congress, shall, without the consent of the other, adjourn for more than three days, nor to any other place than that in which the two houses shall be sitting.

Section 6—Members of Congress: Privileges and Prohibitions

1. The Senators and Representatives shall receive a compensation for their services, to be ascertained by law and paid out of the treasury of the United States. They shall in all cases, except treason, felony and breach of the peace, be privileged from arrest during their attendance at the session of their respective houses, and in going to and returning

⁴ Superseded by the 20th Amendment.

from the same; and for any speech or debate in either house, they shall not be questioned in any other place.

2. No Senator or Representative shall, during the time for which he was elected, be appointed to any civil office under the authority of the United States, which shall have been created, or the emoluments whereof shall have been increased, during such time; and no person holding any office under the United States shall be a member of either house during his continuance in office.

Section 7—The Process of Making Laws

1. All bills for raising revenue shall originate in the House of Representatives; but the Senate may propose or concur with amendments as on other bills.

2. Every bill which shall have passed the House of Representatives and the Senate, shall, before it becomes a law, be presented to the President of the United States; if he approves he shall sign it, but if not, he shall return it with his objections to that house in which it shall have originated, who shall enter the objections at large on their journal, and proceed to reconsider it. If after such reconsideration two-thirds of that house shall agree to pass the bill, it shall be sent, together with the objections, to the other house, by which it shall likewise be reconsidered, and, if approved by two-thirds of that house, it shall become a law. But in all such cases the votes of both houses shall be determined by yeas and nays, and the names of the persons voting for and against the bill shall be entered on the journal of each house respectively. If any bill shall not be returned by the President within ten days (Sundays excepted) after it shall have been presented to him, the same shall be a law, in like manner as if he had signed it, unless the Congress by their adjournment prevent its return, in which case it shall not be a law.

3. Every order, resolution, or vote to which the concurrence of the Senate and House of Representatives may be necessary (except on a question of adjournment) shall be presented to the President of the United States; and before the same shall take effect, shall be approved by him, or being disapproved by him, shall be repassed by two-thirds of the Senate and House of Representatives, according to the rules and limitations prescribed in the case of a bill.

Section 8—The Powers of Congress

The Congress shall have power:

1. To lay and collect taxes, duties, imposts, and excises, to pay the debts and provide for the common defence and general welfare of the United States; but all duties, imposts and excises shall be uniform throughout the United States;

2. To borrow money on the credit of the United States;

3. To regulate commerce with foreign nations, and among the several States, and with the Indian tribes;

4. To establish a uniform rule of naturalization, and uniform laws on the subject of bankruptcies throughout the United States;

5. To coin money, regulate the value thereof, and of foreign coin, and fix the standard of weights and measures;

6. To provide for the punishment of counterfeiting the securities and current coin of the United States;

7. To establish post offices and post roads;

8. To promote the progress of science and useful arts by securing for limited times to authors and inventors the exclusive right to their respective writings and discoveries;

9. To constitute tribunals inferior to the Supreme Court;

10. To define and punish piracies and felonies committed on the high seas and offences against the law of nations;

11. To declare war, grant letters of marque and reprisal, and make rules concerning captures on land and water;

12. To raise and support armies, but no appropriation of money to that use shall be for a longer term than two years;

13. To provide and maintain a navy;

14. To make rules for the government and regulation of the land and naval forces;

15. To provide for calling forth the militia to execute the laws of the Union, suppress insurrections, and repel invasions;

16. To provide for organizing, arming and disciplining the militia, and for governing such part of them as may be employed in the service of the United States, reserving to the States respectively the appointment of the officers, and the authority of training the militia according to the discipline prescribed by Congress;

17. To exercise exclusive legislation in all cases whatsoever, over such district (not exceeding ten miles square) as may, by cession of particular States, and the acceptance of Congress, become the seat of government of the United States, and to exercise like authority over all places purchased by the consent of the legislature of the State, in which the same shall be, for the erection of forts, magazines, arsenals, dock-yards, and other needful buildings;—and

18. To make all laws which shall be necessary and proper for carrying into execution the foregoing powers, and all other powers vested by this Constitution in the government of the United States, or in any department or officer thereof.

Section 9—Powers Denied to the Federal Government

[**1.** The migration or importation of such persons as any of the States now existing shall think proper to admit shall not be prohibited by the Congress prior to the year 1808; but a tax or duty may be imposed on such importation, not exceeding $10 for each person.][5]

2. The privilege of the writ of *habeas corpus* shall not be suspended, unless when in cases of rebellion or invasion the public safety may require it.

3. No bill of attainder or *ex post facto* law shall be passed.

4. No capitation, or other direct, tax shall be laid, unless in proportion to the census or enumeration hereinbefore directed to be taken.

5. No tax or duty shall be laid on articles exported from any State.

6. No preference shall be given by any regulation of commerce or revenue to the ports of one State over those of another; nor shall vessels bound to, or from, one State, be obliged to enter, clear, or pay duties in another.

7. No money shall be drawn from the treasury, but in consequence of appropriations made by law; and a regular statement and account of the receipts and expenditures of all public money shall be published from time to time.

8. No title of nobility shall be granted by the United States: and no person holding any office of profit or trust under them, shall, without the consent of the Congress, accept of any present, emolument, office, or title, of any kind whatever, from any king, prince, or foreign state.

Section 10—Powers Denied to the States

1. No State shall enter into any treaty, alliance, or confederation; grant letters of marque and reprisal; coin money; emit bills of credit; make anything but gold and silver coin a tender in payment of debts; pass any bill of attainder, *ex post facto* law, or law impairing the obligation of contracts, or grant any title of nobility.

---

[5] This clause referred to the slave trade.

2. No State shall, without the consent of the Congress, lay any imposts or duties on imports or exports, except what may be absolutely necessary for executing its inspection laws; and the net produce of all duties and imposts, laid by any State on imports or exports, shall be for the use of the treasury of the United States; and all such laws shall be subject to the revision and control of the Congress.

3. No State shall, without the consent of Congress, lay any duty of tonnage, keep troops, or ships of war in time of peace, enter into any agreement or compact with another State, or with a foreign power, or engage in war, unless actually invaded, or in such imminent danger as will not admit of delay.

ARTICLE II—THE EXECUTIVE BRANCH

Section 1—The President and Vice-President

1. The executive power shall be vested in a President of the United States of America. He shall hold his office during the term of four years, and, together with the Vice-President, chosen for the same term, be elected as follows:

2. Each State shall appoint, in such manner as the legislature thereof may direct, a number of electors, equal to the whole number of Senators and Representatives to which the State may be entitled in the Congress; but no Senator or Representative, or person holding an office of trust or profit under the United States, shall be appointed an elector.

3. [The electors shall meet in their respective States, and vote by ballot for two persons, of whom one at least shall not be an inhabitant of the same State with themselves. And they shall make a list of all the persons voted for, and of the number of votes for each; which list they shall sign and certify, and transmit sealed to the seat of the government of the United States, directed to the President of the Senate. The President of the Senate shall, in the presence of the Senate and House of Representatives, open all the certificates, and the votes shall then be counted. The person having the greatest number of votes shall be the President, if such number be a majority of the whole number of electors appointed; and if there be more than one who have such majority, and have an equal number of votes, then the House of Representatives shall immediately choose by ballot one of them for President; and if no person have a majority, then from the five highest on the list the said house shall in like manner choose the President. But in choosing the President the votes shall be taken by States, the representation from each State having one vote; a quorum for this purpose shall consist of a member or members from two-thirds of the States, and a majority of the States shall be necessary to a choice. In every case, after the choice of the

President, the person having the greatest number of votes of the electors shall be the Vice-President. But if there should remain two or more who have equal votes, the Senate shall choose from them by ballot the Vice-President.][6]

4. The Congress may determine the time of choosing the electors, and the day on which they shall give their votes; which day shall be the same throughout the United States.

5. No person except a natural born citizen, or a citizen of the United States, at the time of the adoption of this Constitution, shall be eligible to the office of President; neither shall any person be eligible to that office who shall not have attained to the age of thirty-five years, and been fourteen years a resident within the United States.

6. In case of the removal of the President from office or on his death, resignation, or inability to discharge the powers and duties of the said office, the same shall devolve on the Vice-President, and the Congress may by law provide for the case of removal, death, resignation, or inability, both of the President and Vice-President, declaring what officer shall then act as President, and such officer shall act accordingly, until the disability be removed, or a President shall be elected.

7. The President shall, at stated times, receive for his services a compensation, which shall neither be increased nor diminished during the period for which he shall have been elected, and he shall not receive within that period any other emolument from the United States, or any of them.

8. Before he enter on the execution of his office, he shall take the following oath or affirmation:—"I do solemnly swear (or affirm) that I will faithfully execute the office of President of the United States, and will, to the best of my ability, preserve, protect and defend the Constitution of the United States."

Section 2—The President's Powers

1. The President shall be commander-in-chief of the army and navy of the United States, and of the militia of the several States, when called into the actual service of the United States; he may require the opinion, in writing, of the principal officer in each of the executive departments, upon any subject relating to the duties of their respective offices; and he shall have power to grant reprieves and pardons for offences against the United States, except in cases of impeachment.

2. He shall have power, by and with the advice and consent of the Senate, to make treaties, provided two-thirds of the Senators present

[6] Superseded by the 12th Amendment.

concur; and he shall nominate, and by and with the advice and consent of the Senate, shall appoint ambassadors, other public ministers and consuls, judges of the Supreme Court, and all other officers of the United States, whose appointments are not herein otherwise provided for, and which shall be established by law: but the Congress may by law vest the appointment of such inferior officers, as they think proper, in the President alone, in the courts of law, or in the heads of departments.

3. The President shall have power to fill up all vacancies that may happen during the recess of the Senate, by granting commissions which shall expire at the end of their next session.

Section 3—The President's Powers (continued)

He shall from time to time give to the Congress information of the state of the Union, and recommend to their consideration such measures as he shall judge necessary and expedient; he may, on extraordinary occasions, convene both houses, or either of them, and in case of disagreement between them, with respect to the time of adjournment, he may adjourn them to such time as he shall think proper; he shall receive ambassadors and other public ministers; he shall take care that the laws be faithfully executed, and shall commission all the officers of the United States.

Section 4—Impeachment of the President

The President, Vice-President and all civil officers of the United States, shall be removed from office on impeachment for, and conviction of, treason, bribery, or other high crimes and misdemeanors.

ARTICLE III—THE JUDICIAL BRANCH

Section 1—The Federal Courts

The judicial power of the United States shall be vested in one Supreme Court, and in such inferior courts as the Congress may from time to time ordain and establish. The judges, both of the Supreme and inferior courts, shall hold their offices during good behavior, and shall, at stated times, receive for their services, a compensation, which shall not be diminished during their continuance in office.

Section 2—Jurisdiction of the Federal Courts

1. The judicial power shall extend to all cases, in law and equity, arising under this Constitution, the laws of the United States, and treaties made, or which shall be made, under their authority;—to all cases affecting ambassadors, other public ministers and consuls;—to all cases of admiralty and maritime jurisdiction;—to controversies to which the United States shall be a party;—to controversies between two or more States;—between a State and citizens of another State;[7]—between citizens of different States;—between citizens of the same State claiming lands under grants of different States, and between a State, or the citizens thereof, and foreign states, citizens or subjects.

2. In all cases affecting ambassadors, other public ministers and consuls, and those in which a State shall be party, the Supreme Court shall have original jurisdiction. In all the other cases before mentioned, the Supreme Court shall have appellate jurisdiction, both as to law and fact, with such exceptions, and under such regulations as the Congress shall make.

3. The trial of all crimes, except in cases of impeachment, shall be by jury; and such trial shall be held in the State where the said crimes shall have been committed; but when not committed within any State, the trial shall be at such place or places as the Congress may by law have directed.

Section 3—Treason Defined

1. Treason against the United States shall consist only in levying war against them, or in adhering to their enemies, giving them aid and comfort. No person shall be convicted of treason unless on the testimony of two witnesses to the same overt act, or on confession in open court.

2. The Congress shall have power to declare the punishment of treason, but no attainder of treason shall work corruption of blood, or forfeiture except during the life of the person attainted.

ARTICLE IV—THE STATES AND THE FEDERAL GOVERNMENT

Section 1—Recognition of State Acts and Records

Full faith and credit shall be given in each State to the public acts, records, and judicial proceedings of every other State. And the Congress may by general laws prescribe the manner in which such acts, records, and proceedings shall be proved, and the effect thereof.

Section 2—Interstate Relations

1. The citizens of each State shall be entitled to all privileges and immunities of citizens in the several States.

2. A person charged in any State with treason, felony, or other crime, who shall flee from justice, and be found in another State, shall on demand of the executive authority of the State from which he fled, be delivered up, to be removed to the State having jurisdiction of the crime.

[7] This clause was modified by the 11th Amendment.

3. [No person held to service or labor in one State, under the laws thereof, escaping into another, shall, in consequence of any law or regulation therein, be discharged from such service or labor, but shall be delivered up on claim of the party to whom such service or labor may be due.][8]

Section 3—New States, Territories

1. New States may be admitted by the Congress into this Union; but no new State shall be formed or erected within the jurisdiction of any other State; nor any State be formed by the junction of two or more States, or parts of States, without the consent of the legislatures of the States concerned as well as of the Congress.

2. The Congress shall have power to dispose of and make all needful rules and regulations respecting the territory or other property belonging to the United States; and nothing in this Constitution shall be so construed as to prejudice any claims of the United States, or of any particular State.

Section 4—The Federal Government's Protection of the States

The United States shall guarantee to every State in this Union a republican form of government, and shall protect each of them against invasion; and on application of the legislature, or of the executive (when the legislature cannot be convened) against domestic violence.

ARTICLE V—METHODS OF AMENDING THE CONSTITUTION

The Congress, whenever two-thirds of both houses shall deem it necessary, shall propose amendments to this Constitution, or, on the application of the legislatures of two-thirds of the several States, shall call a convention for proposing amendments, which, in either case, shall be valid to all intents and purposes, as part of this Constitution, when ratified by the legislatures of three-fourth of the several States, or by conventions in three-fourths thereof, as the one or the other mode of ratification may be proposed by the Congress; provided [that no amendments which may be made prior to the year one thousand eight hundred and eight shall in any manner affect the first and fourth clauses in the ninth section of the first article; and][9] that no State, without its consent, shall be deprived of its equal suffrage in the Senate.

[8] This statement referred to fugitive slaves. It was invalidated by the 13th Amendment.

[9] A temporary measure.

ARTICLE VI—NATIONAL DEBTS; SUPREMACY OF NATIONAL LAW; OATHS

1. All debts contracted and engagements entered into, before the adoption of this Constitution, shall be as valid against the United States under this Constitution, as under the Confederation.

2. This Constitution, and the laws of the United States which shall be made in pursuance thereof; and all treaties made, or which shall be made, under the authority of the United States, shall be the supreme law of the land; and judges in every State shall be bound thereby, anything in the Constitution or laws of any State to the contrary notwithstanding.

3. The Senators and Representatives before mentioned, and the members of the several State legislatures, and all executive and judicial officers, both of the United States and of the several States, shall be bound by oath or affirmation, to support this Constitution; but no religious test shall ever be required as a qualification to any office or public trust under the United States.

ARTICLE VII—RATIFICATION OF THE CONSTITUTION

The ratification of the conventions of nine States shall be sufficient for the establishment of this Constitution between the States so ratifying the same.

AMENDMENTS TO THE CONSTITUTION

Article I—Guarantees of Religious and Political Freedom[10]

Congress shall make no law respecting an establishment of religion, or prohibiting the free exercise thereof; or abridging the freedom of speech, or of the press; or the right of the people peaceably to assemble, and to petition the government for a redress of grievances.

Article II—Guarantee of Right to Bear Arms

A well-regulated militia, being necessary to the security of a free State, the right of the people to keep and bear arms shall not be infringed.

Article III—Restrictions on Quartering of Troops

No soldier shall, in time of peace, be quartered in any house, without the consent of the owner, nor in time of war, but in a manner to be prescribed by law.

Article IV—Protection Against Unreasonable Searches and Seizures

The right of the people to be secure in their persons, houses, papers, and effects, against unreasonable searches and seizures, shall not be violated, and no warrants shall issue but upon probable cause, supported by oath or affirmation, and particularly describing the place to be searched, and the persons or things to be seized.

Article V—Protection for the Individual in Criminal Proceedings

No person shall be held to answer for a capital, or otherwise infamous crime, unless on a presentment or indictment of a grand jury, except in cases arising in the land or naval forces, or in the militia, when in actual service in time of war or public danger; nor shall any person be subject for the same offence to be twice put in jeopardy of life or limb; nor shall be compelled in any criminal case to be a witness against himself, nor be deprived of life, liberty, or property, without due process of law; nor shall private property be taken for public use without just compensation.

Article VI—Fair Procedure in Criminal Cases

In all criminal prosecutions, the accused shall enjoy the right to a speedy and public trial, by an impartial jury of the State and district wherein the crime shall have been committed, which district shall have been previously ascertained by law, and to be informed of the nature and cause of the accusation; to be confronted with the witnesses against him; to have compulsory process for obtaining witnesses in his favor, and to have the assistance of counsel for his defence.

[10] The first ten Amendments were adopted as a group in 1791. They constitute our original *Bill of Rights*. In general, they protect the individual against the exercise of undue power by the national government—*not* by the states. However, the Supreme Court has extended some of the provisions of the Bill of Rights to the states. Each of the various state constitutions also contains a bill of rights.

Article VII—Fair Procedure in Civil Cases

In suits at common law, where the value in controversy shall exceed twenty dollars, the right of trial by jury shall be preserved, and no fact tried by a jury shall be otherwise re-examined in any court of the United States than according to the rules of the common law.

Article VIII—Protection Against Excessive Bail and Cruel Punishment

Excessive bail shall not be required, nor excessive fines imposed, nor cruel and unusual punishments inflicted.

Article IX—Rights and Powers Reserved to the People

The enumeration in the Constitution of certain rights shall not be construed to deny or disparage others retained by the people.

Article X—Powers Reserved to the States or the People

The powers not delegated to the United States by the Constitution, nor prohibited by it to the States, are reserved to the States respectively, or to the people.

Article XI—Powers of the Federal Courts Limited[11]

The judicial power of the United States shall not be construed to extend to any suit in law or equity, commenced or prosecuted against one of the United States by citizens of another State, or by citizens or subjects of any foreign state.

Article XII—Election of President and Vice-President[12]

The electors shall meet in their respective States, and vote by ballot for President and Vice-President, one of whom, at least, shall not be an inhabitant of the same State with themselves; they shall name in their ballots the person voted for as President, and in distinct ballots the person voted for as Vice-President, and they shall make distinct lists of all persons voted for as President, and of all persons voted for as Vice-President, and of the number of votes for each, which lists they shall sign and certify, and transmit sealed to the seat of the government of the United States, directed to the President of the Senate;—the President of the Senate shall, in the presence of the Senate and House of Representatives, open all the certificates and the votes shall then be counted;—the person having the greatest number of votes for President shall be the President, if such number be a majority of the whole number of electors appointed; and if no person have such majority, then from the persons having the highest numbers not exceeding three on the list of those

11 Adopted in 1798, superseding a provision in Article II, Section 2, Clause 1.

12 Adopted in 1804, superseding Article II, Section 1, Clause 3.

voted for as President, the House of Representatives shall choose immediately, by ballot, the President. But in choosing the President, the votes shall be taken by States, the representation from each State having one vote; a quorum for this purpose shall consist of a member or members from two-thirds of the States, and a majority of all the States shall be necessary to a choice. And if the House of Representatives shall not choose a President whenever the right of choice shall devolve upon them, [before the fourth day of March next following],[13] then the Vice-President shall act as President, as in the case of the death or other constitutional disability of the President. The person having the greatest number of votes as Vice-President, shall be the Vice-President, if such number be a majority of the whole number of electors appointed; and if no person have a majority, then from the two highest numbers on the list, the Senate shall choose the Vice-President; a quorum for the purpose shall consist of two-thirds of the whole number of Senators, and a majority of the whole number shall be necessary to a choice. But no person constitutionally ineligible to the office of President shall be eligible to that of Vice-President of the United States.

Article XIII—Abolition of Slavery[14]

SECTION 1. Neither slavery nor involuntary servitude, except as a punishment for crime whereof the party shall have been duly convicted, shall exist within the United States, or any place subject to their jurisdiction.

SECTION 2. Congress shall have power to enforce this article by appropriate legislation.

Article XIV—Citizenship Defined and Civil Rights Guaranteed[15]

SECTION 1. All persons born or naturalized in the United States, and subject to the jurisdiction thereof, are citizens of the United States and of the State wherein they reside. No State shall make or enforce any law which shall abridge the privileges or immunities of citizens of the United States; nor shall any State deprive any person of life, liberty, or property, without due process of law, nor deny to any person within its jurisdiction the equal protection of the laws.

SECTION 2. Representatives shall be apportioned among the several States according to their respective numbers, counting the whole number of persons in each State, excluding Indians not taxed. But when

[13] Changed by the 20th Amendment.

[14] Adopted in 1865. This Amendment and the 14th Amendment supersede Article I, Section 2, Clause 3.

[15] Adopted in 1868.

the right to vote at any election for the choice of electors for President and Vice-President of the United States, Representatives in Congress, the executive and judicial officers of a State, or the members of the legislature thereof, is denied to any of the male inhabitants of such State, being twenty-one years of age and citizens of the United States, or in any way abridged, except for participation in rebellion or other crime, the basis of representation therein shall be reduced in the proportion which the number of such male citizens shall bear to the whole number of male citizens twenty-one years of age in such State.

SECTION 3. No person shall be a Senator or Representative in Congress, or elector of President and Vice-President, or hold any office, civil or military, under the United States, or under any State, who, having previously taken an oath as a member of Congress, or as an officer of the United States, or as a member of any State legislature, or as an executive or judicial officer of any State, to support the Constitution of the United States, shall have engaged in insurrection or rebellion against the same, or given aid or comfort to the enemies thereof. But Congress may, by a vote of two-thirds of each house, remove such disability.

SECTION 4. The validity of the public debt of the United States, authorized by law, including debts incurred for payment of pensions and bounties for services in suppressing insurrection or rebellion, shall not be questioned. But neither the United States nor any State shall assume or pay any debt or obligation incurred in aid of insurrection or rebellion against the United States, or any claim for the loss or emancipation of any slave; but all such debts, obligations, and claims shall be held illegal and void.

SECTION 5. The Congress shall have power to enforce by appropriate legislation the provisions of this article.

Article XV—Right of Suffrage[16]

SECTION 1. The right of citizens of the United States to vote shall not be denied or abridged by the United States or any State on account of race, color, or previous condition of servitude.

SECTION 2. The Congress shall have power to enforce this article by appropriate legislation.

Article XVI—Federal Income Tax[17]

The Congress shall have power to lay and collect taxes on incomes, from whatever source derived, without apportionment among the several States, and without regard to any census or enumeration.

[16] Adopted in 1870.

[17] Adopted in 1913, modifying Article I, Section 2, Clause 3.

Article XVII—Popular Election of Senators[18]

SECTION 1. The Senate of the United States shall be composed of two Senators from each State, elected by the people thereof,[19] for six years; and each Senator shall have one vote. The electors in each State shall have the qualifications requisite for electors of the most numerous branch of the State Legislatures.

SECTION 2. When vacancies happen in the representation of any State in the Senate, the executive authority of such State shall issue writs of election to fill such vacancies: Provided that the Legislature of any State may empower the executive thereof to make temporary appointments until the people fill the vacancies by election as the Legislature may direct.

SECTION 3. This amendment shall not be so construed as to affect the election or term of any Senator chosen before it becomes valid as part of the Constitution.

Article XVIII—National Prohibition[20]

[SECTION 1. After one year from the ratification of this article the manufacture, sale, or transportation of intoxicating liquors within, the importation thereof into, or the exportation thereof from the United States and all territory subject to the jurisdiction thereof for beverage purposes is hereby prohibited.

SECTION 2. The Congress and the several States shall have concurrent power to enforce this article by appropriate legislation.

SECTION 3. This article shall be inoperative unless it shall have been ratified as an amendment to the Constitution by the legislatures of the several States, as provided in the Constitution, within seven years from the date of the submission hereof to the States by the Congress.]

Article XIX—Woman Suffrage[21]

SECTION 1. The right of citizens of the United States to vote shall not be denied or abridged by the United States or by any State on account of sex.

SECTION 2. The Congress shall have power to enforce this article by appropriate legislation.

[18] Adopted in 1913.

[19] Supersedes Article I, Section 3, Clause 1.

[20] Adopted in 1919; repealed by the 21st Amendment.

[21] Adopted in 1920.

Article XX—The "Lame Duck" Amendment[22]

SECTION 1. The terms of the President and Vice-President shall end at noon on the 20th day of January, and the terms of Senators and Representatives at noon on the 3d day of January, of the years in which such terms would have ended if this article had not been ratified; and the terms of their successors shall then begin.[23]

SECTION 2. The Congress shall assemble at least once in every year, and such meeting shall begin at noon on the 3d day of January unless they shall by law appoint a different day.[24]

SECTION 3. If, at the time fixed for the beginning of the term of the President, the President elect shall have died, the Vice-President elect shall become President. If a President shall not have been chosen before the time fixed for the beginning of his term, or if the President elect shall have failed to qualify, then the Vice-President elect shall act as President until a President shall have qualified; and the Congress may by law provide for the case wherein neither a President elect nor a Vice-President elect shall have qualified, declaring who shall then act as President, or the manner in which one who is to act shall be selected, and such person shall act accordingly until a President or Vice-President shall have qualified.[25]

SECTION 4. The Congress may by law provide for the case of the death of any of the persons from whom the House of Representatives may choose a President whenever the right of choice shall have devolved upon them, and for the case of the death of any of the persons from whom the Senate may choose a Vice-President whenever the right of choice shall have devolved upon them.[26]

SECTION 5. Sections 1 and 2 shall take effect on the 15th day of October following the ratification of this article.

SECTION 6. This article shall be inoperative unless it shall have been ratified as an amendment to the Constitution by the legislatures of three-fourths of the several States within seven years from the date of its submission.

[22] Adopted in 1933.

[23] Supersedes a provision of the 12th Amendment.

[24] Supersedes Article I, Section 4, Clause 2.

[25] Covers matters not defined by the 12th Amendment.

[26] Covers matters not defined by the 12th Amendment.

Article XXI—Prohibition Repealed[27]

Section 1. The eighteenth article of amendment to the Constitution of the United States is hereby repealed.

Section 2. The transportation or importation into any State, territory, or possession of the United States for delivery or use therein of intoxicating liquors, in violation of the laws thereof, is hereby prohibited.

Section 3. This article shall be inoperative unless it shall have been ratified as an amendment to the Constitution by conventions in the several States, as provided in the Constitution, within seven years from the date of the submission hereof to the States by the Congress.

Article XXII—President Limited to Two Terms[28]

Section 1. No person shall be elected to the office of the President more than twice, and no person who has held the office of President, or acted as President, for more than two years of a term to which some other person was elected President shall be elected to the office of the President more than once.

But this article shall not apply to any person holding the office of President when this Article was proposed by the Congress, and shall not prevent any person who may be holding the office of President, or acting as President, during the term within which this Article becomes operative from holding the office of President or acting as President during the remainder of such term.

Section 2. This Article shall be inoperative unless it shall have been ratified as an amendment to the Constitution by the legislatures of three-fourths of the several States within seven years of the date of its submission to the States by the Congress.

Article XXIII—Voting for President in District of Columbia[29]

Section 1. The District constituting the seat of Government of the United States shall appoint in such manner as the Congress may direct:

A number of electors of President and Vice-President equal to the whole number of Senators and Representatives in Congress to which the District would be entitled if it were a State, but in no event more than the least populous State; they shall be in addition to those appointed by the States, but they shall be considered, for the purposes of the election of President and Vice-President, to be electors appointed by a State; and they shall meet in the District and perform such duties as provided by the twelfth article of amendment.

27 Adopted in 1933, superseding the 18th Amendment.

28 Adopted in 1951.

29 Adopted in 1961.

SECTION 2. The Congress shall have power to enforce this article by appropriate legislation.

Article XXIV—Poll Tax Prohibited as Voting Requirement[30]

SECTION 1. The right of citizens of the United States to vote in any primary or other election for President or Vice-President, for electors for President or Vice-President, or for Senator or Representative in Congress, shall not be denied or abridged by the United States or any state by reason of failure to pay any poll tax or other tax.

SECTION 2. The Congress shall have power to enforce this article by appropriate legislation.

Article XXV—Presidential Succession[31]

SECTION 1. In case of the removal of the President from office or his death or resignation, the Vice-President shall become President.

SECTION 2. Whenever there is a vacancy in the office of the Vice-President, the President shall nominate a Vice-President who shall take the office upon confirmation by a majority vote of both houses of Congress.

SECTION 3. Whenever the President transmits to the President pro tempore of the Senate and the Speaker of the House of Representatives his written declaration that he is unable to discharge the powers and duties of his office, and until he transmits to them a written declaration to the contrary, such powers and duties shall be discharged by the Vice-President as Acting President.

SECTION 4. Whenever the Vice-President and a majority of either the principal officers of the executive departments, or of such other body as Congress may by law provide, transmit to the President pro tempore of the Senate and the Speaker of the House of Representatives their written declaration that the President is unable to discharge the powers and duties of his office, the Vice-President shall immediately assume the powers and duties of the office as Acting President.

Thereafter, when the President transmits to the President pro tempore of the Senate and the Speaker of the House of Representatives his written declaration that no inability exists, he shall resume the powers and duties of his office unless the Vice-President and a majority of either the principal officers of the executive department, or of such

[30] Adopted in 1964.

[31] Adopted in 1967.

other body as Congress may by law provide, transmit within four days to the President pro tempore of the Senate and the Speaker of the House of Representatives their written declaration that the President is unable to discharge the powers and duties of his office. Thereupon Congress shall decide the issue, assembling within 48 hours for that purpose if not in session. If the Congress within 21 days after receipt of the latter written declaration, or, if Congress, is not in session, within 21 days after Congress is required to assemble, determines by two-thirds vote of both houses that the President is unable to discharge the powers and duties of his office, the Vice-President shall continue to discharge the same as Acting President; otherwise, the President shall resume the powers and duties of his office.

Article XXVI—Voting Rights for 18-Year-Olds [32]

SECTION 1. The right of citizens of the United States, who are eighteen years of age or older, to vote shall not be denied or abridged by the United States or any state on account of age.

SECTION 2. The Congress shall have the power to enforce this article by appropriate legislation.

[32] Adopted in 1971.

DECLARATION OF INDEPENDENCE

In Congress, July 4, 1776

THE UNANIMOUS DECLARATION OF THE THIRTEEN UNITED STATES OF AMERICA

When, in the course of human events, it becomes necessary for one people to dissolve the political bands which have connected them with another, and to assume, among the powers of the earth, the separate and equal station to which the laws of nature and of nature's God entitle them, a decent respect to the opinions of mankind requires that they should declare the causes which impel them to the separation.

We hold these truths to be self-evident:—That all men are created equal; that they are endowed by their Creator with certain unalienable rights; that among these are life, liberty, and the pursuit of happiness. That, to secure these rights, governments are instituted among men, deriving their just powers from the consent of the governed; that, whenever any form of government becomes destructive of these ends, it is the right of the people to alter or to abolish it, and to institute new government, laying its foundation on such principles, and organizing its powers in such form, as to them shall seem most likely to effect their safety and happiness. Prudence, indeed, will dictate, that governments long established should not be changed for light and transient causes; and accordingly all experience hath shown that mankind are more disposed to suffer while evils are sufferable, than to right themselves by abolishing the forms to which they are accustomed. But when a long train of abuses and usurpations, pursuing invariably the same object, evinces a design to reduce them under absolute despotism, it is their right, it is their duty, to throw off such government, and to provide new guards for their future security. Such has been the patient sufferance of these colonies; and such is now the necessity which constrains them to alter their former systems of government. The history of the present King of Great Britain is a history of repeated injuries and usurpations, all having in direct object the establishment of an absolute tyranny over these states. To prove this, let facts be submitted to a candid world.

He has refused his assent to laws the most wholesome and necessary for the public good.

He has forbidden his governors to pass laws of immediate and pressing importance, unless suspended in their operation till his assent should be obtained; and when so suspended, he has utterly neglected to attend to them.

He has refused to pass other laws for the accommodation of large districts of people, unless those people would relinquish the right of representation in the legislature—a right inestimable to them, and formidable to tyrants only.

He has called together legislative bodies at places unusual, uncomfortable, and distant from the depository of their public records, for the sole purpose of fatiguing them into compliance with his measures.

He has dissolved representative houses repeatedly, for opposing, with manly firmness, his invasions on the rights of the people.

He has refused, for a long time after such dissolutions, to cause others to be elected, whereby the legislative powers, incapable of annihilation, have returned to the people at large for their exercise; the State remaining, in the mean time, exposed to all the dangers of invasions from without, and convulsions within.

He has endeavored to prevent the population of these States; for that purpose obstructing the laws for the naturalization of foreigners; refusing to pass others to encourage their migration hither, and raising the conditions of new appropriations of lands.

He has obstructed the administration of justice, by refusing his assent to laws for establishing judiciary powers.

He has made judges dependent on his will alone for the tenure of their offices, and the amount and payment of their salaries.

He has erected a multitude of new offices, and sent hither swarms of officers to harass our people and eat out their substance.

He has kept among us in times of peace, standing armies, without the consent of our legislatures.

He has affected to render the military independent of, and superior to, the civil power.

He has combined with others to subject us to a jurisdiction foreign to our constitutions, and unacknowledged by our laws; giving his assent to their acts of pretended legislation:

For quartering large bodies of armed troops among us;

For protecting them, by a mock trial, from punishment for any murders which they should commit on the inhabitants of these States;

For cutting off our trade with all parts of the world;

For imposing taxes on us without our consent;

For depriving us, in many cases, of the benefits of trial by jury;

For transporting us beyond seas, to be tried for pretended offences;

For abolishing the free system of English laws in a neighboring province, establishing therein an arbitrary government, and enlarging its boundaries, so as to render it at once an example and fit instrument for introducing the same absolute rule into these colonies;

For taking away our charters, abolishing our most valuable laws, and altering, fundamentally, the forms of our governments;

For suspending our own legislatures, and declaring themselves invested with power to legislate for us in all cases whatsoever.

He has abdicated government here, by declaring us out of his protection, and waging war against us.

He has plundered our seas, ravaged our coasts, burned our towns, and destroyed the lives of our people.

He is at this time transporting large armies of foreign mercenaries to complete the works of death, desolation and tyranny, already begun with circumstances of cruelty and perfidy scarcely paralleled in the most barbarous ages, and totally unworthy the head of a civilized nation.

He has constrained our fellow-citizens, taken captive on the high seas, to bear arms against their country, to become the executioners of their friends and brethren, or to fall themselves by their hands.

He has excited domestic insurrection among us, and has endeavored to bring on the inhabitants of our frontiers the merciless Indian savages, whose known rule of warfare is an undistinguished destruction of all ages, sexes, and conditions.

In every stage of these oppressions we have petitioned for redress in the most humble terms; our repeated petitions have been answered only by repeated injury. A prince whose character is thus marked by every act which may define a tyrant, is unfit to be the ruler of a free people.

Nor have we been wanting in our attentions to our British brethren. We have warned them, from time to time, of attempts by their legislature to extend an unwarrantable jurisdiction over us. We have reminded them of the circumstances of our emigration and settlement here. We have appealed to their native justice and magnanimity; and we have conjured them, by the ties of our common kindred, to disavow these usurpations, which would inevitably interrupt our connections and correspondence. They, too, have been deaf to the voice of justice and consanguinity. We must, therefore, acquiesce in the necessity which denounces our separation, and hold them, as we hold the rest of mankind, enemies in war, in peace friends.

We, therefore, the Representatives of the United States of America, in General Congress assembled, appealing to the Supreme Judge of the world for the rectitude of our intentions, do, in the name and by authority of the good people of these colonies, solemnly publish and declare, That these united Colonies are, and of right ought to be, free and independent states; that they are absolved from all allegiance to the British crown, and that all political connection between them and the state of Great Britain is, and ought to be, totally dissolved; and that, as free and independent states, they have full power to levy war, conclude peace, contract alliances, establish commerce, and to do all other acts and things which independent states may of right do. And, for the support of this declaration, with a firm reliance on the protection of Divine Providence, we mutually pledge to each other our lives, our fortunes, and our sacred honor.

JOHN HANCOCK

[*Signatures of representatives of the thirteen states added on August 2, 1776.*]

Resolved, That copies of the Declaration be sent to the several assemblies, conventions, and committees, or councils of safety, and to the several commanding officers of the continental troops; that it be proclaimed in each of the United States, and at the head of the army.

BOOKS ABOUT AMERICAN GOVERNMENT AND ITS PROBLEMS

(Many of the titles listed are available in paperback.)

BAILEY, S. K., and SAMUEL, H. D.—*Congress at Work,* 1952

BAILEY, T. A.—*Presidential Greatness,* 1966

BARTH, A.—*Government by Investigation,* 1955

BLUM, J. M.—*The Promise of America,* 1966

BOWEN, C. D.—*Miracle at Philadelphia,* 1966

BOWEN, C. D.—*Yankee from Olympus,* 1944

BRANT, I.—*The Bill of Rights: Its Origin and Meaning,* 1965

BRUCE, H. R.—*American National Government,* 1964

BURNS, J. M.—*Congress on Trial,* 1949

CLARK, KENNETH B.—*Dark Ghetto,* 1965

CLAYTON, J. E.—*The Making of Justice,* 1964

Congressional Quarterly, 1735 K Street, N.W., Washington, D.C. 20006

CORWIN, E. S.—*The President: Office and Powers,* 1958

CURTIS, C. P.—*Lions Under the Throne,* 1947

DOUGLAS, W. O.—*The Rights of the People,* 1958

EVANS, R., and NOVAK, R.—*Lyndon B. Johnson: The Executive Power,* 1966

FORTUNE MAGAZINE—*The Exploding Metropolis,* 1955

GREEN, C. M.—*The Rise of Urban America,* 1965

GRUEN, V.—*The Heart of Our Cities,* 1964

HADLEY, A. T.—*Power's Human Face,* 1965

HAND, LEARNED—*The Bill of Rights,* 1958

HARRINGTON, M.—*The Accidental Century,* 1965

HARSCH, JOSEPH C.—*The Role of Political Parties, U.S.A.,* (pamphlet), 1955

HERRING, P.—*Politics of Democracy: American Parties in Action,* 1966

HYMAN, S.—*The American President,* 1954

INTERNATIONAL CITY MANAGERS ASSOCIATION—*Tomorrow's Government Today* (guide to films)

JONES, H. W.—*The Courts, the Public and the Law Explosion,* 1965

KELLY, A. H., and HARBISON, W. A.—*The American Constitution,* 1963

KENNEDY, J. F.—*Profiles in Courage,* 1955

KENT, F. R.—*The Great Game of Politics,* 1959

LEISERSON, A.—*Parties and Politics,* 1958

LENS, S.—*Radicalism in America,* 1966

LEWIS, A.—*Gideon's Trumpet,* 1964

LEWIS, A.—*The Supreme Court and How It Works,* 1966

LISTON, R. A.—*Tides of Justice: The Supreme Court and the Constitution in Our Time,* 1966

MASON, A. T.—*Brandeis: A Full Man's Life,* 1956

MASON, A. T.—*William H. Taft: Chief Justice,* 1965

NATIONAL GEOGRAPHIC SOCIETY—*Equal Justice Under Law*, 1965

NORRIS, GEORGE W.—*Fighting Liberal,*1945

PADOVER, S. K.—*The Living United States Constitution*, 1954

PERRY, G. S.—*Cities of America*, 1965

PHILLIPS, C.—*The Truman Presidency*, 1966

RESTON, J.—*The Artillery of the Press: Its Influence on American Foreign Policy*, 1967

RIENOW, R., and L. T.—*The Lonely Quest: The Evolution of Presidential Leadership*, 1966

ROSSITER, C.—*The American Presidency*, 1956

SAGARIN, M.—*Equal Justice Under Law*, 1966

SCHLESINGER, A. M., JR.—*A Thousand Days*, 1965, (Chapters 1 to 6)

SCOTT, A. M. and HUNT, M. A.—*Congress and Lobbies*, 1966

SEVERN, B.—*Adlai Stevenson: Citizen of the World*, 1966

STEINBERG, S.—*Contemporary Governments in a Changing World*, 1965

SWISHER, C. B.—*Historic Decisions of the Supreme Court*, 1958

TENNESSEE VALLEY AUTHORITY—*TVA Today*, 1965-1966

TUFTS CIVIC EDUCATION CENTER—*It Has Been Done*

TUGWELL, R. G.—*How They Became President*, 1965

WEAVER, R. C.—*Urban Complex*, 1964

WHITE, L. D.—*The Republican Era, 1869-1901: A Study in Administrative History*, 1958

WHITE, T. H.—*The Making of the President—1964*, 1965

WIT, D.—*Comparative Political Institutions*, 1960

WRIGHT, J.—*You and Your Congressman*, 1965

YOUNG, D.—*American Roulette: The History of the Vice Presidency*, 1965

INDEX